KENTUCKY'S NATURAL HERITAGE

THE KENTUCKY STATE NATURE PRESERVES COMMISSION

The Kentucky State Nature Preserves Commission (KSNPC) is a small agency with a big task. Our mission is to protect Kentucky's natural heritage by:

1. identifying, acquiring, and managing natural areas that represent the best known occurrences of rare native species, natural communities, and significant natural features in a statewide nature preserve system;
2. working with others to protect biological diversity; and
3. educating Kentuckians as to the value and purpose of nature preserves and biodiversity conservation.

KSNPC was created by legislative enactment in 1976; its initial staff of four has since increased to around 20. A state nature preserve system of 59 preserves and more than 24,000 acres has been established, approximately 60% of the state has been systematically inventoried for natural areas, and more than 11,000 records have been entered into our biological database.

The Natural Heritage Branch of the KSNPC is responsible for finding and monitoring rare species and natural communities. For some groups, like fungi and some invertebrates, there is little or no information about their diversity in Kentucky. As the Natural Heritage Branch continues to expand and to evaluate Kentucky's biodiversity, we hope to add new information about these lesser-known organisms and advance the story of Kentucky's natural heritage.

We collect biological information during field surveys, from literature reviews, and by visiting existing collections, both those that are privately held and those found in museums. Other biologists throughout the state contribute their data as well. KSNPC is also the state's official "cooperator" with the U.S. Fish and Wildlife Service in working on the recovery of federally listed and candidate plant species in Kentucky.

After information on the locations and conditions of rare species and natural communities is compiled, its accuracy is verified, and then it is recorded in the state's natural heritage database. KSNPC's database contains the most complete and accurate set of information on rare species and natural communities in Kentucky. The database is maintained in partnership with Nature-Serve, an international, nonprofit conservation organization that specializes in management of biological data. KSNPC has been a partner with NatureServe and its predecessor organization, which was operated under the auspices of the Nature Conservancy, since 1977. Our natural heritage data are used for many purposes, such as environmental review and planning of private and government activity, development of species and habitat conservation strategies, and scientific research. The database contains a geographic information system component that enables users to analyze and display biological data.

The goal of the Nature Preserves and Natural Areas Branch at KSNPC is to provide a *perpetual* safe harbor for rare species and the natural communities in which they live. The Nature Preserves Branch is engaged in protecting and restoring some of the most biologically diverse and significant natural areas in Kentucky. Conserving at-risk species and natural communities while giving the public access for observation and enjoyment is a daunting challenge and a never-ending task. One of the commission's long-term goals is to protect a representative of each of the major natural communities found in Kentucky within the nature preserve system.

KSNPC also administers a Natural Areas Registry program to offer education and guidance to property owners with lands that sustain significant natural elements. This voluntary, nonbinding program encourages conservation by both private and public landowners to protect sites of biological value. About 93% of Kentucky's landscape is under private ownership, making it critical to work with private landowners for biodiversity conservation.

KSNPC could not do its vital work alone, and we are fortunate to have many partners among other state agencies, federal agencies, nongovernmental organizations, and individual citizens.

—DONALD S. DOTT JR., Director,
Kentucky State Nature Preserves Commission

Kentucky's Natural Heritage

AN ILLUSTRATED GUIDE TO BIODIVERSITY

EDITED BY Greg Abernathy, Deborah White,
Ellis L. Laudermilk, and Marc Evans

FOREWORD BY Wendell Berry

THE UNIVERSITY PRESS OF KENTUCKY

A portion of the proceeds from the sale of this book goes to the Kentucky State Nature Preserves Commission and is used for biodiversity protection.

Scholarly publisher for the Commonwealth,
serving Bellarmine University, Berea College, Centre
College of Kentucky, Eastern Kentucky University,
The Filson Historical Society, Georgetown College,
Kentucky Historical Society, Kentucky State University,
Morehead State University, Murray State University,
Northern Kentucky University, Transylvania University,
University of Kentucky, University of Louisville,
and Western Kentucky University.

Editorial and Sales Offices:
The University Press of Kentucky
663 South Limestone Street,
Lexington, Kentucky 40508-4008
www.kentuckypress.com

14 13 12 11 10   5 4 3 2 1

Library of Congress Cataloging-in-Publication Data
Kentucky's natural heritage : an illustrated guide to
biodiversity / edited by Greg Abernathy . . . [et al.].
   p. cm.
Includes bibliographical references and index.
ISBN 978-0-8131-2575-6 (hardcover : alk. paper)
1. Kentucky—Guidebooks. 2. Natural history—
Kentucky—Guidebooks. 3. Biodiversity—Kentucky—
Guidebooks. 4. Natural areas—Kentucky—Guidebooks.
I. Abernathy, Greg.
F449.3.K48 2010
508.769—dc22   2009044728

 This book is printed on 100% recycled acid-free paper meeting the requirements of the American National Standard for Permanence in Paper for Printed Library Materials.

Design and composition by BW&A Books, Inc.
Manufactured in China

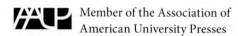 Member of the Association of American University Presses

The support of the following contributors is gratefully acknowledged:

Kentucky Waterways Alliance
U.S. Fish & Wildlife Service

THE CARE OF THE EARTH is our most ancient and most worthy and, after all, our most pleasing responsibility. To cherish what remains of it, and to foster its renewal, is our only legitimate hope.

—WENDELL BERRY[1]

THIS BOOK IS DEDICATED to all the biologists, naturalists, and nature lovers, past and present, who have contributed to our knowledge of Kentucky's flora, fauna, and natural communities. We further dedicate it to all citizens of the Commonwealth of Kentucky with the hope that it will instill in each one a deep appreciation for—and desire to preserve— the plants and animals of our state and the habitats upon which they depend.

CONTENTS

WHEN WE CONSIDER all that we have lost, ruined, or squandered since our European forebears came to live in this place only 235 years ago, we have to conclude that, as a people, we Kentuckians have had only a vague and feckless sense of where we are. Though we have had sufficient time and opportunities, we have failed to develop an effective culture of land stewardship. Efforts and lineages of stewardship have persisted among us from the time of our arrival until now, but any form of land conservation has been a minor theme almost conventionally overpowered by some form of land exploitation. There are reasons for this, and we should take care to understand them.

To begin at the beginning, our ancestors came here necessarily as strangers. They may have known, more or less, where they had come from, but they didn't know where they were when they got here. They had heard of a rich and abounding land to the west, understandably an attraction to people in need of land or of a new start. Some came hoping, predictably, for a lot of something for a little expense or effort; some came looking, like some of their descendants, for something indefinably "better"; some came because land they had ruined in the east would no longer support them; some came for adventure or to escape. Some, more honorably, came for a place to settle in and stay. But all came, almost inevitably, to impose on this place some preconceived wish or demand formed in the place they had left.

In the best of circumstances, authentic settlement of this "new" country would have been diffi-cult. To know a place and to use it well takes a long time and a lengthy practice of observation, forbearance, temperance, caution, and affection. Opposed to the motive of settlement would always be the motives of the speculator, the swindler, and the exploiter. It was, at the beginning, a country that looked vast in its abundance—limitlessly so. How could so much ever be used up? Inevitably accompanying the wish to live within bounds and take care of what you had was that other wish, still predominantly with us: to take from the land as much as you can get of whatever you want, charge it to nature or your neighbor or the future, and move on.

Like the rest of our country, moreover, our state was "settled" by a people historically unsettled. The first would-be settlers came here *because* they were unsettled, unwilling or unable for a variety of reasons to stay put. And what we would now call "social mobility" has continued and worsened. Kentucky's settlers came in the process of moving on with the frontier, and for that reason many settled here only temporarily. And by the time these newcomers were arriving in Kentucky on foot or horseback or by drifting down the Ohio River, the Industrial Revolution was already beginning. The steam engine was patented in 1769, six years before the settlements at Harrodsburg and Boonesborough. By 1811 steamboats were navigating the Ohio River.

Increasingly until the Civil War, and ever more rapidly after that, industrialism provided a second option for the unsettled. They could move laterally westward, or they could "move up" to a city job, better wages, or a salary and a white shirt. For Kentuckians, moving up has often required moving out, and the state's education system has in general subserved and encouraged the impulse of movement. Kentucky schools have functioned somewhat as factories, processing young people for export from country to city and from Kentucky to other states.

Our educational system has educated least of all for settlement, or for what Wes Jackson has called homecoming. Often explicitly, almost always by implication, the theme of education in Kentucky has been "You don't want to be just a farmer" or "You can't amount to anything by staying here." There has never been much likelihood that a student in Kentucky schools, from grade one through college, would learn anything of local history or local geography or local biology and ecology. The idea of growing up to a life's work on a family farm, or in a family profession or trade in a hometown, might come from your family or a friend; you were not likely to learn it at school. Because we have seen no virtue in education for settlement, we have drifted easily into job training in service to the industrial corporations, most of which have been by principle dislocated and without loyalty to any place.

So displacing an idea of education with its cult of science and technology did not come about by chance. Its way was prepared by the displacing religion that we brought with us—a religion already long divorced from even the biblical concerns with economy and economic behavior, the daily "housekeeping" by which we make our livings and our lives. The history of religion in Kentucky is impossible to make sense of. Along with our eagerness to secure earthly places for ourselves—deeded boundaries that would belong to us, our heirs, and assigns forever—we brought along this juiceless and desiccating Protestantism (mostly) that deferred all sanctity and worth to Heaven. It was a strictly "spiritual" religion that made a rule of despising the earth and earthly life. The odd result of this religion was to make our earthly life and economy strictly materialistic. The materialist force of the industrial economy has thus been able to exploit a territory in effect abandoned by religion. The history of materialism in Kentucky, as elsewhere, is also impossible to make sense of. For how could this modern materialism, resting upon its supposedly enlightened sciences and ascribing ultimate value to matter, have become so utterly destructive of the material world?

Given our histories of settlement and unsettlement, of a displacing education subordinating everything to upward mobility and a disembodying religion aspiring only to Heaven, it would be surprising indeed if we had developed a state politics and government encouraging to good stewardship of the land. On the contrary, our politicians have aligned state government with a national government increasingly dominated by the great corporations, and subserving a land-destroying economy that has become so conventional that government officers and university intellectuals scarcely have thought even to question it. If our state government in Frankfort is different, it is so only by exaggeration—in, for example, its virtual enslavement to the coal industry.

The history of the coal economy in Kentucky is the extreme instance that bespeaks our general failure to acquire any effective knowledge of where we live, or any effective sense of the good care we owe to the land we once were so fortunate to come to in our need. This history proves that industrial corporations will stop at nothing, will do anything, to achieve the highest possible income at the least possible cost. It proves at the same time the unwillingness of our people and our politicians to set limits and impose restraints upon any gigantic economic power. In the official political and academic view, the economy of Kentucky has no connection with the land of Kentucky. This is the definition of an economic ignorance that is conventional, criminal, and suicidal.

To live we depend unconditionally on our membership in the community of creatures, living and unliving, that we call the ecosphere. Every life in the terrestrial ecosphere depends unconditionally, in turn, on a thin layer of fertile topsoil which in most places is a few inches or a few feet deep and which accumulates slowly. In a climate such as ours it deepens by perhaps one inch in a thousand years. This layer of topsoil is made by the decay of rock, by sunlight and rain, and by the life and death of all the creatures, but mainly of the plants—mainly perennial plants—that grow from it, die into it, and by covering it year-round protect it from erosion and hold it in place.

About the topsoil, the creatures that inhabit it, from the microorganisms to the tallest trees, and their complex interdependences, we humans know very little, and we are unlikely ever to know very much. We do know, we seem always to have known, that upon this great gift, this great mystery, we and all our generations absolutely depend. The Bible, as some have begun again to understand, requires our gratitude for this gift, as well as our care and caution in the use of it. To forget this, so as to destroy the topsoil and the plant cover that protects it, surely is a desecration, if desecration means anything at all. And yet our present economy is based upon this forgetfulness and this desecration, which are formalized in all our industries of land use, and which culminate in mountaintop removal mining in the Appalachian coal fields.

In *A Darkness at Dawn,* published forty years ago, Harry M. Caudill wrote, "No one in government complained that . . . whole communities of people and entire mountain ranges with their infinitely complex ecology had been sacrificed." This is mostly still true—though the damage by now is inconceivably worse. Mountaintop removal, which destroys entirely the original biotic community and replaces it with a flimsy scrim of exotic plants, is the perfect antithesis of the native abundance of the land that lay before those uprooted strangers who came purportedly to "settle" in 1775. It took us only a little more than two hundred years to pass from intentions sometimes approximately good to this horrible result, in which our education, our religion, our politics, and our daily lives all are implicated. This is original sin, round two.

It is necessary to say further that the same economy of production-by-exhaustion is at work, only more slowly, in our landscapes that are forested or farmed. The state and national, and now global, economies pay only for production from these landscapes, not for the best work, not for maintenance. The land still produces, but it does so at an ever-increasing, unlimited, and unrestrained cost in soil erosion, chemical pollution, community destruction, degradation of the cultures of husbandry, and by now in reduction of the land-using population almost to disappearance.

Perhaps the most tragic irony of our history was in the industrialization of agriculture after World War II. By the mid-1940s an ecological standard for land use had been made available by the work of ecologists such as Aldo Leopold and agriculturists such as Sir Albert Howard and J. Russell Smith. The work of these men and their colleagues was widely recognized, and their writings were published in books and reputable journals.

But at the same time industries that had grown rich and powerful in support of the war effort were faced with disemployment. The solution to this problem was to industrialize agriculture. The machines and chemicals developed to defeat foreign enemies were turned against the farmland and the farmers on the "home front." The aim of industrialization then as always was to replace, and to displace, human workers with "more efficient" technologies. This project was abetted and justified by the

Committee for Economic Development, whose experts (university presidents and corporation executives) decreed that there were "too many farmers." The surplus farmers, supposedly not needed for land maintenance and stewardship, and as mere producers readily replaceable by machines and chemicals, were needed instead as new members of the industrial workforce (to keep wages "under control") and as consumers (to increase the market for food and other industrial products). Any possibility that agriculture could be structured according to ecological models adapted to specific localities was abandoned and forgotten.

Imposing everywhere the same methods, technologies, varieties, and breeds without respect to place, industrial agriculture acquired with astonishing speed the stature and force of a national (by now a global) orthodoxy, solidly supported by government departments of agriculture, land-grant colleges of agriculture, agricultural journalism, and large grants of money and extensive advertising by the agri-industrial corporations. And so it was just tough luck for small farmers, small farms, small fields, fences, shrubby fencerows, grassed waterways, wetlands, farm woodlands, clean streams, native communities of plants and animals, and incalculable tonnages of eroded topsoil. Tough luck, in short, for the natural heritage and the ecological underpinning of the economic landscapes of Kentucky, as of the whole nation.

Though it was granted the justification of a hireling "science" and the standard of a purely financial and mechanical "efficiency," there was in fact no excuse, scientific or political or moral, for this all-out industrial transformation of agriculture. But there was a lot of money in it for corporations, for research and development, for universities—a lot of money, that is, for everybody but farmers. For a brief interlude after about 1940, the agricultural economy was favorable to farmers, who enjoyed even a bit of prestige and appreciation during the war years. But in 1952 the Eisenhower administration came in,

issuing to farmers maybe the cruelest, most undemocratic proclamation ever made to American citizens: "Get big or get out." Farmers were then abandoned to the mercy of the industrial economy and the "free" market, which in only forty or so years squeezed most of them out of farming and into the "labor pool." Their places were taken to some extent by migrant workers, predictably disesteemed and exploited, but mostly by mechanical and chemical technologies and fossil fuels that greatly increased costs for the remaining farmers—costs that invariably increased faster than farm income. The idea that farmers should be conservationists has been fairly commonplace since at least the 1930s, and it is a fact, to some extent acknowledged, that the survival of agriculture depends upon the conservation of nature. But too few experts and officials have realized that conservation in agriculture requires an adequate number of farmers adequately paid. You can't expect a minimal farm population, minimally paid and struggling for survival, to be devoted conservationists.

The power and wealth of agriculture have accrued more and more to corporations, less and less to the primary producers. Meanwhile, because of the growth of urban populations and increasing specialization in production, the geographic basis of the food economy has grown more and more extensive. For a long time now the economies of agriculture and food have been dependent on long-distance transportation. One of the significant unaccounted costs of long-distance transportation has been the rapid, accidental but inevitable, spread of exotic organisms. Our present version of industrial agriculture, then, has "incidentally" produced two dire ecological results: it has destroyed or damaged local communities of native species, and it has supplanted or corrupted them with introduced diseases, weeds, and pests. When the accounting is finally done, these results will be shown to be too expensive both ecologically and economically, initially damaging and difficult or impossible to put right.

And so the history of our state, inseparable in most ways from the history of our nation, has brought us in a remarkably short time to an economy that is increasingly tremulous and questionable, resting (though most economists evidently are unaware) upon ecosystems that are increasingly impaired and threatened.

That is the history and those are the circumstances in which The University Press of Kentucky and a staff of committed authors and editors have given us *Kentucky's Natural Heritage,* a publication and an event of inestimable significance. This volume could hardly be more needed, or more welcome to Kentuckians who have at heart the health and the real wealth of their state.

No other book that I have read has helped me so much to think about the *land* of Kentucky, of the reciprocity of influence and the sharing of fate between the land and ourselves. This book is at once an appraisal, within acknowledged limits an inventory, and inescapably a history. It gives us a competent sense of the state's native health and abundance before European settlement, of what and how much we have lost or wasted or used up, and of what is left—differences heartbreaking to think about. And so this book also is inescapably a lamentation.

It is an ambitious book, for it does what has never been attempted before. It is also properly modest; the authors acknowledge on the first page of the first chapter that their work "provides only a glimpse." They return again and again to one of the book's most telling themes: how much is not yet known, how much we need to know that we must endeavor to learn. We must see this book, then, as a monument, marking the starting point of a great and fascinating task. It is an excellent beginning for it sets the agenda for further work, and tells us how to carry it on. If we live up to what this book does for us and asks of us, we eventually will gather such knowledge of every region of our state, every county, every natural and human neighborhood, every least watershed, every farm, woodland, and field. We will do the work and the study that this requires because we will know—the time is rapidly approaching when we will *have* to know—that our lives depend upon such an effort. Upon such knowledge rests the work of local adaptation, of fitting our economy to the demands of ecological health, without which no species can survive for long.

Obtaining this knowledge obviously calls for a system of education oriented to localities—to preparing people to live and to make their livings in places naturally distinct, and in ways that will enhance the natural and human health of those places. To reorient education in this way does not mean that we will cease to teach the sciences, the liberal arts, and the enduring works of human culture. But we will add to those the arts and sciences of ecological restoration, land stewardship, and husbandry. We will teach the whole curriculum with the understanding that the most reliable and the ultimate standard of success is the health and beauty of the land.

The most fundamental and necessary change will be in the teaching of biology. There will need to be a new emphasis on what used to be known as natural history. Colleges and universities will need to staff the elementary and high schools with competent field biologists, practical naturalists, who will lead their students outdoors, teaching them to "read" the history and present condition of their home landscapes, and to know something of the composition of the local biotic communities.

Such teaching would foster the hope that economic responsibility and ecological responsibility might become a single practice. Students would thus be prepared for the work of local adaptation, which, because the world changes, would be ongoing, never quite complete. They might learn at least to see what is most obvious: that the habitat of every creature in our home countryside is also *our* habitat, and to make it less inhabitable for other creatures makes it less inhabitable as well for us.

It has by now become my obligation to speak of these things as an elder. I have been collecting memories and observations of my home neighborhood in Henry County for seventy-five years, or about a third of the 235 years since the founding of Harrodsburg and Boonesborough. If I add to my own memory the voices of my grandparents, who also lived their lives in this place, telling me their memories of it, then I have a "living memory" of more than half the span of the modern history of Kentucky. My knowledge of this place, thus gathered, is entirely concordant with the plot of this book. It is the story, with a few uptilts, of "an unfortunate state of decline."

On the positive side, there are many more trees here now than there were at the time of my birth. Early in our history, the steep valley sides of the Kentucky River and its tributaries were cleared and row-cropped. The trees were cut, the litter burned, the slopes broken with "jumper" plows, the rocks piled, the crops planted and harvested. This cycle was repeated until erosion and depletion put an end to it, and then the trees were allowed to grow back—to restore sufficient fertility to the slopes to permit them to be cleared and cropped again.

This was the worst sort of farming, but the blame for it is hard to distribute justly. It was of course done in varying degrees of ignorance by the farmers, for almost nobody so far has tried to devise a conserving use for these "marginal" lands; but hard use was enforced by the usually adverse markets for agricultural products. Almost nobody so far has tried to understand how a bad agricultural economy affects the land. Desperate people would try the hopeless expedient of "plowing their way out of debt." Or they would overproduce row crops to compensate for low prices that were the result of overproduction. By about the time of World War II, probably because so many young men had gone to war or to factory jobs, this plowing of the steeper slopes was given up. The forest has been growing back now

for two generations or more. But if you walk those slopes today you will find under the trees the old cropland gullies, some healed, some still eroding.

With the return of the woods, there have been some significant returns of wildlife. Deer and wild turkeys, long gone before my time, have been reintroduced and are again present in large numbers. Beavers and otters, also absent in my early years, are here again. In the past few years bald eagles have been nesting a few miles upriver from my house, and sometimes I see one from my window.

Besides the reforestation of the slopes, the other great change in the landscape here has occurred in the pastures. From a time not long after arrival of the European settlers, the pasture grass predominant everywhere was bluegrass, which supplanted the canebrakes and the native grasses of the savannas. This seems to have been a fairly benign succession, for bluegrass and the naturalized European white clover that lived symbiotically with it, along with the many other wild plants that would come naturally to the pastures, were hospitable to the native animals and birds. The buffalo and elk and their predators were gone, but smaller creatures throve.

And then in the 1950s bluegrass began rapidly to be supplanted by fescue, introduced by the University of Kentucky. This was a taller, coarser grass, excellent for erosion control, but far less palatable and in some ways even dangerous to livestock, and not hospitable to wildlife. It makes a denser sod than bluegrass, and grants less passage to the runways of small mammals and ground-traveling birds such as the bobwhite. Though the bobwhite survives in some places, for many years I have not heard its much-loved voice at my own place in the river valley. Rotary mowing machines may be partly to blame for such diminishments, as also perhaps for an apparent decline in the populations of snakes such as the black ratsnake. Such changes inevitably accompany also the continuous cropping of corn and soybeans in the wider valley bottoms.

I am not a trained biologist or even a trained observer, and so I am speaking only of larger changes, obvious to anybody who has lived here so many years and remained fairly alert. During most of my life, for another example, the elm trees have been dying, and I have witnessed and regretted the disappearance of many a grand old landmark, just as generations before me witnessed the disappearance of the Carolina parakeets, the passenger pigeons, and the chestnut trees.

Maybe the biggest surprise to me in this history of disappearances was to learn of the disappearance, from everywhere but the oldest and largest forests, of the native earthworms. The "fishing worms" I used to dig, assuming they were as native as the ground itself, all are exotics, imported with potted plants or in the ballast of ships. Paul Kalisz, of the University of Kentucky Department of Forestry, told me this not too many years ago, and I was shocked. It is one of my most unfinished and troubling thoughts, for it shows how much I have taken the world for granted, and how little I have thought of what is not obvious.

To the weeds of cropland and pasture that people were complaining about when I was young, we have since added nodding thistle, Canada thistle, Johnson grass, multiflora rose, and, in the river bottoms, Japanese hops. Not so long ago, when you stepped from the open fields into the woods just about anywhere along the valley sides, you would be in the ancient community of the native plants. Now you will often find nearly solid stands of Japanese grass or garlic mustard. Among the native trees, vines, and shrubs you will now find Japanese honeysuckle, bush honeysuckle, tree-of-heaven, and (again) multiflora rose.

Among other animate exotics we have recently acquired Japanese beetles and a small ladybug-like beetle that lives exuberantly in people's houses, both serious pests. We have had European starlings and English sparrows since long before my time. More recently have come the house finch and the coyote. How all these newcomers, including us humans, will finally settle here, become integrated into the communities of native creatures, and so at last become native themselves, is a question involving many questions. We will be trying to answer them much longer than we have been here.

Two further disappearances are of particular interest to me because they show so well the carelessness of our economic life, and our consequent vulnerability to unintended consequences.

Fairly recently the black willows that used to be common along the banks of the Kentucky River have nearly disappeared. A few remain here and there, but always high up, at or near banktop. They have entirely disappeared along the low-water line, where they granted to the river a characteristic grace and beauty, and undoubtedly helped to control river bank erosion. I have found nobody who can explain their absence, and only the older fishermen seem to have noticed it. Something obviously is wrong. Is it a toxic pollutant in the water or the air? We need to know, but who is asking?

Another disappearance, also important, is that of the black dung beetles that we knew as "tumblebugs." Throughout my childhood and, I think, until the late 1940s or early 1950s, you would find these interesting creatures rolling their dungballs along the dusty paths of any cow pasture. They were burying the cow manure, in which they laid their eggs and on which their larvae fed. Why did they disappear? Though I had a sort of theory, I wanted scientific authority, and so I presented my question to an entomologist in the College of Agriculture at the University of Kentucky. I have been pondering his answer for the last thirty or so years:

"I don't know anything about them. But I can tell you this—they have no economic significance."

Well. That answer showed how conventionally submissive science can be to "economic significance," also how conventionally "economic significance" can be equated with "already known economic significance," and how conventionally indifferent agricultural science can be to ecological significance. I have yet to find someone who can tell me why the tumblebugs have disappeared. My own unscientific guess is that they disappeared because of some medication we were using on the cattle, probably a wormer.

But how can the disappearance of an insect that buries manure be economically insignificant? Again I am reduced to an unscientific guess, but, as I remember, the departure of the tumblebugs more or less coincided with an epidemic increase in the population of so-called face flies, which breed in manure piles. Face flies, in addition to their pestering of farm animals, are a major cause of pinkeye in cattle, which in turn can cause blindness, and which requires expensive treatment.

If I am guessing right, the tumblebugs were economically significant, and so was their disappearance. Furthermore, if I am right, this is an example not merely of an agriculturally caused agricultural problem but also of the impossibility of separating economic significance from ecological significance.

The cause of disappearance of the black willows I can't even guess at, but I attribute this generally and vaguely to the industrialization, and therefore the contamination, of nearly everything. The disappearance of the tumblebugs can be attributed more specifically, if still vaguely, to the industrialization of agriculture.

Both disappearances show us how inescapably we are members, for better or worse, of what Aldo Leopold called "the land-community." I have spoken of changes in the populations of nonhuman species in my neighborhood during my lifetime, but the changes in the human population have been at least as extreme. Through World War II, rural Kentucky was only marginally industrialized. The farms were mostly small, mostly solar powered by way of the bodies of people and animals, and highly diverse. Households in both town and country were sustained, this side of the corporate markets, by a variety of home manufactures and of foods raised and prepared at home. Most of the economic life was conducted at home or in local shops, stores, and offices. For the most part, people lived where they worked.

Now these rural places have become mostly "bedroom communities" for people who work in Louisville or Frankfort. Most economic life is conducted away from home. The old subsistence economy, with its many skills, has about vanished. The farms are larger and the farmers fewer. Much of the physical work is done by migrant laborers. The human population and all its activities are entirely dependent on purchased energy from fossil fuels. Milk cows and dairies are almost all gone, and so are almost all of the sheep, hogs, and poultry. The decline of wildlife diversity has been accompanied by the decline of domestic species and varieties. In sum, the land-community, in need more than ever of the attention of its human members, now has far fewer knowledgeable observers, users, and caretakers than it had fifty or sixty years ago.

My neighborhood, then, like neighborhoods all over Kentucky, is a naturally rich place long in decline toward ecological poverty—and, if it continues, toward economic poverty as well.

The publication of this book, as I hope my response to it shows, comes at a time when the need for hope has become urgent. The news from the land under our feet is not good, but the most hopeless thing we can do is ignore this news or pretend it is not so bad. As I have been thinking about this book, I have again been asking myself what our authentic reasons are for hope. Here is my list:

1. As this book suggests, we *can* learn where we are. We can look around us and see. If we see, by many observable signs, that during our history here we have lost much that we once had, we will see also that much remains.

2. We will see, furthermore, that we are not

helpless. Two great powers, if we will align ourselves with them and use them, are in our favor. They are land health and conservation. Land health, Aldo Leopold wrote, "is the capacity of the land for self-renewal." And "Conservation is our effort to understand and preserve that capacity."

3. Land health is still with us. In most places in our state we can prove this just by stopping a gulley. Leopold proved it by reforesting an exhausted farm. Wherever the ground is covered with perennial plants—and we can help with this—it is preserved from erosion, it conserves water, it offers year-round benefits to us and to other creatures. The ground has healed. It is well. If the ground is covered by *native* perennials, it is even better.

4. There is hope in seeing what we need to do, and in doing it. A part of our necessary work is conservation, and there is hope in knowing that conservation is already going on. Conservation in various forms has been an established effort in the United States since at least the beginning of the last century. But it was going on a long time before that wherever the land was used frugally, skillfully, and with affection.

5. There would be hope in effective public leadership, if we had it. But ecological degradation is not a political issue in Kentucky; it is not much more a political issue nationally. And I don't see help coming very soon from leaders in education. What I do see, and I see great hope in it, is what we could call leadership from the bottom: individuals and local groups who, without official permission or support or knowledge, are seeing what needs to be done and are doing it. Admirable work in sustainable agriculture, sustainable forestry, local economy, land preservation and restoration, and other kinds of conservation is being done all over the place unofficially by concerned people.

6. More formal citizens' organizations are also doing good work. They are worth contributing to, working for, and criticizing too when they need it.

7. A number of hope-giving efforts that individual citizens can join or undertake on their own are listed in this book's final chapter.

8. Some things are changing for the better, and there is hope in knowing this. Minds, lives, even policies can change for the better. History gives us some reason to think that a whole culture can change for the better. That is what we are hoping and working for.

9. Too much of the talk and politics of conservation consists of slogans such as "Think globally, act locally" or even single words, such as "green" or "sustainable" or "organic," that act like slogans. Such lazy language does harm. It becomes useful, in fact, to land-abusing corporations. What gives hope is actual conversation, actual discourse, in which people say to one another in good faith fully and exactly what they know, and acknowledge honestly the limits of their knowledge. This book is a capable, careful, generous offering to that kind of conversation.

10. Maybe the finest sources of hope are the people for whom the effort of conservation has ceased to be a separate activity and has come to be at one with their ways of making their living. Some foresters, farmers, and ranchers have achieved this. They have not achieved perfection, of course, but they have achieved a kind of unity of vision and work. For them, land health is not something added to their economy, but is at once their economy's basis and result.

THE INFORMATION IN THIS BOOK is a cumulation of the knowledge and work of many biologists and conservationists. We owe an enormous debt to numerous people, from the iconic figures of the past, like Constantine Rafinesque and John James Audubon, to the nature lovers from all walks of life who have contributed to our knowledge of Kentucky's flora and fauna. It is impossible to name them all here without overlooking some of them, so we have chosen not to take that risk. However, to all who have collected data or made observations on Kentucky's biota and have shared that information, we gratefully acknowledge your contributions.

Likewise, we acknowledge the legislators and other politicians at the state and national levels, conservation groups, state and federal agencies, and private citizens who contributed to the establishment of environmental laws, state and national parks and forests, nature preserves, and wildlife management areas, or who maintained private lands for the benefit of biodiversity. Many of these areas act as refugia (places that provide protection) for native species in otherwise heavily altered ecosystems. Without them, even more of our native species likely would have disappeared by now.

We are indebted to all of the individuals who generously shared their remarkable photographs and illustrations. Their images convey what a thousand words cannot. Special thanks are given to a few photographers who were particularly generous: Thomas Barnes, Lana Hays, Barry Howard, John MacGregor, Keith Mountain, and Chuck Summers. The artwork at the beginning of each chapter was adapted from original black-and-white paintings by talented artist Ann DiSalvo.

Thanks to Robert Butler, Donald Harker, William Martin, and an anonymous reviewer for their suggestions and comments on drafts of the manuscript that helped us resolve issues of organization and improve the content. Any errors that remain are the responsibility of the authors.

This book would not have been possible without the initial approval of the Board of Directors of the University Press of Kentucky and the support of their staff. The University Press's commitment to publishing books on the natural history of Kentucky is commendable.

We view this book as a celebration of the Commonwealth's native plants, animals, and natural communities. To all who have contributed to the conservation of biodiversity in Kentucky, even in the smallest way, we thank you and encourage you to continue your efforts. Finally, to all the citizens of our great state, we hope you enjoy and are inspired by Kentucky's biodiversity.

THIS BOOK IS A PRODUCT of the Kentucky State Nature Preserves Commission. The following authors are KSNPC staff (including retired[1] and former[2] staff), except where noted.[3]

EDITORS/AUTHORS

Greg Abernathy
Geographic Information Systems Specialist

Deborah L. White
Botanist/Natural Heritage Coordinator

Ellis L. Laudermilk
Invertebrate Zoologist

Marc Evans[1]
Ecologist

AUTHORS (listed alphabetically)

Joyce Bender
Nature Preserves Branch Manager

Ronald R. Cicerello[1]
Aquatic Zoologist

Shauna Dunham
Geographic Information Systems Specialist

Ryan Evans
Aquatic Zoologist

Martina Hines
Ecologist

Sara Hines
Heritage Database Manager

Heather Housman[2]
Ecologist

Tara R. Littlefield
Botanist

Brainard Palmer-Ball Jr.[1]
Terrestrial Zoologist

Ron Scott[2]
Land Protection Specialist

Brian Yahn
Ecologist

CONTRIBUTING AUTHORS (crayfishes section)

Guenter A. Schuster[3]
*Professor of Biological Sciences, Emeritus
Eastern Kentucky University*

Christopher A. Taylor[3]
*Research Scientist and Curator of Crustaceans
Illinois Natural History Survey*

MAPS AND GRAPHICS (except where noted)

Greg Abernathy
Geographic Information Systems Specialist

Chapter One

INTRODUCTION

*Every scrap of biological diversity is priceless,
to be learned and cherished, and never to be
surrendered without a struggle.*

—EDWARD O. WILSON[1]

THE DIVERSITY OF LIFE on our planet is astounding. From the lush rainforest of the Amazon to the seemingly barren arctic tundra, there is an abundance of life—and Kentucky is no exception. The state has a natural diversity of life so rich and complex that reality challenges the imagination. Fascinating and spectacular plants and animals such as the rainbow darter, golden mouse, cobra clubtail, three-birds orchid, and tiger salamander aren't found in the Amazon; they live among us in the remarkably rich prairies, rivers, and forests of Kentucky, along with thousands of other species.

If you walk into any natural area in Kentucky and look at the plants, turn over a few rocks in a creek and look for salamanders, listen to birds singing, or scan the air for insects, you will be overwhelmed with a profusion of life. Species and the natural communities they form are the biodiversity of the state. While this book provides only a glimpse of the state's many organisms and natural communities, perhaps it will be enough to give readers a new appreciation for the diversity of life within Kentucky. We are convinced biodiversity is worth protecting, and we hope this book will also convince you.

Less than an inch long, this dew-covered scarlet-and-green leafhopper makes a big impression with its stunning beauty. More than 2,500 leafhopper species occur in the United States and Canada, but this insect group is poorly known in Kentucky. © *Barry Howard*

BIODIVERSITY

Biodiversity is the variety of all living things and their roles and connections within ecosystems. Simply put, it is the web of life. All species fulfill a specific role or task, called a *niche*, in an ecosystem, and other species depend on this role. Remove one species and it may affect the entire natural community or ecosystem. Remove too many species and the community and ecosystem may be irretrievably changed or damaged. Ultimately, biodiversity is part of the earth's life-support system.

So why is it important to save biodiversity? Here are a few reasons to consider.

- **Support services.** We depend on biodiversity to support living systems. As inhabitants of Earth, we need stable ecosystems to perform ecological services like cleansing the air and water, production and preservation of soil, removal of waste products, pollution reduction, and climate regulation. We cannot live without these vital services.

- **Resources.** Many of the products people depend on are derived from natural sources. Natural disease resistance is often higher in

Unlike the pesky house mouse, the golden mouse is a Kentucky native. It lives in loosely knit social groups in thickets, forests, and field borders. *John R. MacGregor*

Each aster "flower" is actually made up of many small flowers, some forming the outer petals of the head and others densely packed in the center. New England aster (shown) is common along roadsides. *Thomas G. Barnes*

wild plants, and breeding them with related cultivated plants improves resistance. Also, we depend upon pollinators for one out of every four mouthfuls of food we eat. More than half of the medicines we use are derived from animals or plants. New medicines and other uses of natural resources are continually being discovered—and as species become extinct, the potential for these opportunities is lost.

- **Ecotourism.** In addition to the economic importance of food, medicine, and other natural resources, ecotourism and recreation are huge industries that provide a livelihood for many people. Ecotourism is the fastest-growing form of tourism[2] and depends upon the unique beauty of natural areas.

- **Aesthetics.** Nature is inspiring; its beauty enriches our lives. It is likely that pictures of natural scenes are hanging on your home or office walls. Wild places help us see beauty in the world, find relief from everyday stress, and appreciate our lives.

- **Ethics.** We share life with all other species on Earth, and the destruction of fellow species is a violation of the respect and fairness expected from members of a well-balanced society. From a religious perspective, it may be argued that we did not create life on Earth, so who are we to degrade or eliminate it? Ethically speaking, we have an obligation to preserve Kentucky's natural heritage.

- **Our legacy.** What is our responsibility to the future? How much do we care whether the next generation sees firebelly darters in their brilliant breeding colors? Do we care if they hear a common raven or see a Kentucky lady's-slipper? Should we decide that they can do without the zebra clubtail? Can we change the culture of environmental abuse and balance our use of land, air, and water with the need to preserve biodiversity?

Three Levels of Biodiversity

Genetic Diversity →	Species Diversity →	Ecosystem Diversity
The genetic makeup of each black-throated green warbler contributes to the overall health of a population; genetically diverse populations tend to be more viable and better able to adapt to environmental changes.	Eastern hemlock trees, American black bears, northern parulas, and other species collectively are part of a unique natural community called a hemlock-mixed forest. Each species plays a particular role in the community and its overall viability. The loss of a single species can have consequences for the entire community.	Hemlock-mixed forests, Cumberland Plateau gravel/cobble bars, and Appalachian bogs are a few of the natural communities found in the Appalachian Highlands physiographic province. Collectively, natural communities form diverse ecosystems across the landscape.

There are basically three levels of biodiversity: genetic, species, and ecosystem. The genetic makeup of each individual plant or animal contributes to the health of a population and the ability of that population to withstand the stress of life on Earth. These challenges may be as short-term as an exceptionally cold winter or as lasting as a decade-long drought. Species, the next level of biodiversity, are interconnected through their roles in each natural community. Building on this elaborate web of life is the third level, ecosystems, the connections among natural communities across the landscape.

How many species share the world with us? Estimates of the number of species living on Earth range from 3 to 30 million or more; however, the commonly accepted estimate is 10 to 15 million.[3-6] More than 200,000 species are known from the United States alone, but the real number may be twice that many.[7] Many groups of species are not well-known, and new species previously undescribed by scientists are still found each year. Like the rest of the planet, the exact number of species in Kentucky is unknown, though a reasonable estimate is that there are 19,400 species in the state (see Number of Species by Select Groups schematic, p. 5). This estimate does not include very poorly known groups such as worms, fungi, lichens, bacteria, and other microorganisms.

KENTUCKY'S PLACE IN THE WORLD

How does Kentucky's biodiversity compare to other states and the world? Several animal groups in the state are remarkably diverse. Salamanders, aquatic organisms, and cave-dwelling species attain some of their highest levels of diversity in the nation right here in Kentucky, primarily for two reasons. First, Kentucky is located in the southeastern United States, a global center of distribution for salamanders and a very rich area for various groups of aquatic organisms (e.g., fishes, mussels, crayfishes). Second, the combination of the state's climate and its extensive limestone geology created ideal conditions for cave formation and subsequent habitat for cave-dwelling species to evolve.

Number of Species by Select Groups

Group name	World	North America	Kentucky (native)
Fungi Kingdom			
• True fungi	56,200 [1]	34,000 [†1]	Unknown
• Lichens	13,500 [1]	3,800 [†1]	Unknown
Fungi subtotal	69,700	37,800	Unknown
Plant Kingdom			
• Mosses	10,000 [2,3]	1,400 [†2,3]	317 [4]
• Liverworts	6,000 [3,5]	700 [†3,5]	114 [4]
• Hornworts	100 [5]	11 [†5]	3 [4]
• Seed plants and ferns	247,786 [1]	15,990 [†1]	2,030 [6]
Plant subtotal	263,886	18,101	2,464
Animal Kingdom			
• Mollusks	28,918 [△]	2,179 [△]	380 [*△]
○ Freshwater snails	4,000 [1]	679 [7]	67 [*]
○ Land snails and slugs	24,000 [8]	1,005 [9]	210 [*]
○ Freshwater mussels	918 [10]	300 [11]	103 [11,12]
• Arachnids	41,141 [△]	3,890 [△]	501 [*△]
○ Spiders	39,882 [13]	3,807 [14]	500 [*]
○ Scorpions	1,259 [15]	83 [15]	1 [15,16]
• Crustaceans	45,000 [1△]	9,675 [†1△]	102 [*△]
○ Crayfishes	530 [17]	363 [18]	54 [17,19]
○ Other crustaceans	44,470 [1]	9,312 [1]	48 [*]
• Insects	900,000 [20△]	87,107 [21△]	15,202 [*△]
○ Mayflies	3,000 [20]	670 [20]	111 [22]
○ Dragonflies and damselflies	5,600 [23]	518 [24,25]	156 [26]
○ Stoneflies	2,000 [20]	690 [27]	110 [28]
○ True bugs	56,000 [20]	3,834 [21]	650 [*]
○ Beetles	350,000 [20]	27,000 [29]	4,000 [*]
○ Ants, bees, and wasps	161,500 [20]	17,777 [21]	3,000 [*]
○ Caddisflies	12,627 [30]	1,412 [31]	250 [32]
○ Butterflies and moths	160,000 [20]	13,000 [33]	2,400 [34]
○ True flies	124,000 [20]	16,914 [21]	2,875 [*]
○ Other insects	25,273 [20]	5,292 [21]	1,650 [*]
• Freshwater fishes	11,500 [35]	790 [36]	245 [12,37]
• Amphibians	5,918 [38]	258 [†39]	53 [12]
• Reptiles	8,240 [38]	295 [†39]	54 [12]
• Birds	9,964 [40]	783 [†39]	370 [41,42]
• Mammals	5,416 [38]	421 [†39]	67 [12]
Animal subtotal	1,056,072 [**]	105,191 [**]	16,974 [**]
Total number of species	1,389,658 [**]	161,092 [**]	19,438 [**]

† = United States only

△ = Sum of species groups included in this table only (numbers in green). This number is the best estimate based on references listed.

* = KSNPC estimate

** = Sum of major groups included in this table only. It does not include all species that occur in the world, North America, or Kentucky (e.g., algae, worms).

Note: Superscripts correspond to references listed in Sources of Maps and Graphics.

Select Species Groups in Kentucky
(Graphics scaled to represent number of species in group)

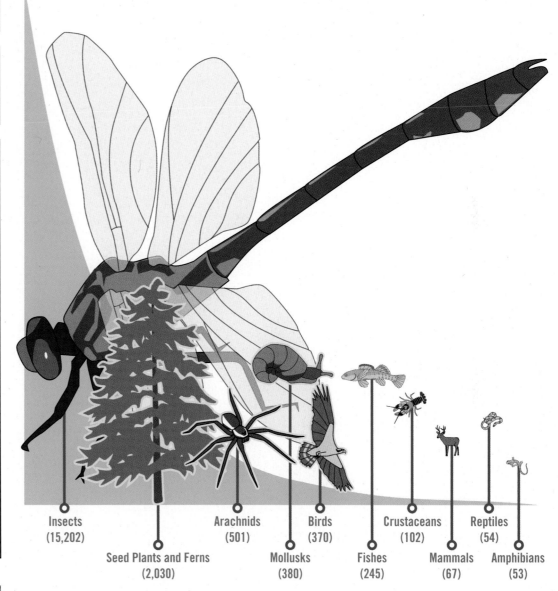

Insects (15,202)

Seed Plants and Ferns (2,030)

Arachnids (501)

Mollusks (380)

Birds (370)

Fishes (245)

Crustaceans (102)

Mammals (67)

Reptiles (54)

Amphibians (53)

The red salamander is a striking representative of the 33 salamander species known from the state. It is widely distributed throughout much of eastern Kentucky, but it occurs as far west as Graves County. *John R. MacGregor*

New species, including this colorful endemic Shawnee darter, are still being discovered in Kentucky. Described in 1997, this two-inch fish lives only in upland creeks of western Kentucky's Pond River watershed. *Matthew R. Thomas*

In fact, Kentucky is so rich in species that it ranks in the top five nationally for several groups. Below are some of the highlights of the state's rankings and overall contributions to national and global biodiversity.

◆ Kentucky's diverse aquatic fauna is of global and national significance. The state has more native fish species than all other states except Tennessee and Alabama, with approximately 30% of the North American total. It ranks fourth in the nation in native freshwater mussel species, with approximately 35% of the North American total, and fifth in the nation in number of crayfish (crawdad) species, with about 10% of the world's total.[8] The Green River watershed is nationally recognized as among the most ecologically significant rivers in the United States.[9]

◆ Kentucky ranks approximately fifth in the nation in total number of obligate cave-dwelling species, which are ecologically adapted to live in caves and their underground streams or groundwater.[10] Mammoth Cave, the longest known cave in the world, has more obligate cave species than any other U.S. cave.[11, 12]

◆ Kentucky is home to 102 taxa (species, subspecies, and varieties) believed to be endemic to the state or found nowhere else in the world.[13]

◆ In many regards, the southeastern United States has the greatest salamander diversity in the world.[14] Kentucky supports approximately 26% of the total U.S. salamander fauna.

◆ One of the largest prairie remnants east of the Mississippi River occurs on Fort Campbell (in Trigg and Christian counties), primarily in Kentucky.

- The mixed mesophytic forest in the mountains of eastern Kentucky is considered one of the most diverse temperate deciduous forests in the world.[15]

The state's geologic history and the resulting physical landscape have helped to shape its biodiversity. Located at a midlatitude of the North American continent, Kentucky has a temperate climate and is situated among several distinct ecoregions. Northern, southern, and midwestern influences are evident in the flora and fauna found here. A 12,000-year history of human activity in Kentucky has greatly influenced the state's biodiversity. Since European American settlement, human impacts have escalated until they now threaten many of the state's species and natural communities. Eighteen species that once lived in Kentucky are either possibly or presumed globally extinct, which is the ninth-highest total among states.[16] This number is so high primarily because of the number of aquatic animals that are now extinct. Even the one plant from Kentucky that is considered extinct, the stipuled scurf-pea, was associated with riverine habitat in an area altered by dam construction. These extinctions are a signal of profound changes in the landscape. Information on the state of the environment—from its soil, water, and air to its smallest creature—is critical to understanding and conserving our natural heritage.

Glades and prairies provide some of the showiest displays of wildflowers, like these pale purple coneflowers. *Thomas G. Barnes*

Chapter Two

PHYSICAL OVERVIEW

When we try to pick out anything by itself, we find it hitched to everything else in the universe.

—JOHN MUIR[1]

PLANTS AND ANIMALS are intimately tied to the physical landscape. Variations in climate, elevation, soil, geology, and hydrology influence species distribution and composition. This chapter provides an introduction to the major physical factors that affect species in Kentucky, and it explores their relationship to the state's rich natural heritage. The unique combination of physical features within Kentucky occurs nowhere else, much like the biodiversity that will be explored in subsequent chapters.

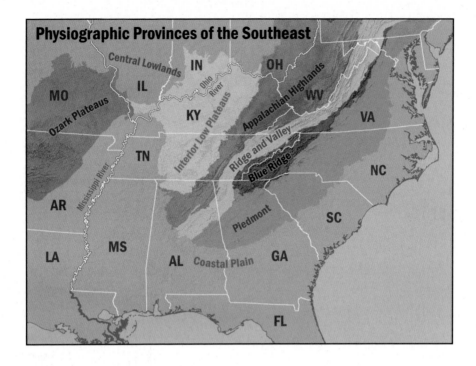

Physiographic Provinces of the Southeast

Bottomland forests, swamps, and oxbow lakes are characteristic communities of the nearly level, poorly drained lowlands found within the Mississippi/Ohio River floodplain region. © *John Brunjes*

NATURAL REGIONS

Natural regions are areas that share a general similarity in geology, topography, hydrology, soils, climate, and vegetation. The natural regions of Kentucky[2] are divisions of the three major physiographic provinces that occur in the state: the Coastal Plain, Interior Low Plateaus, and Appalachian Highlands.[3] The diversity within these physiographic provinces is one reason Kentucky supports a rich flora and fauna. The natural regions represent unique localized environmental and physical conditions within the physiographic provinces that affect the distribution of species and natural communities.

The Coastal Plain physiographic province occurs in far western Kentucky. Covered by the ocean as recently as the late Cretaceous Period, around 70 million years ago (hereafter abbreviated "mya"), the Coastal Plain is the youngest region in the state in geologic terms.[4] Kentucky is near the northern interior extent of this province, which stretches from coastal Texas to Massachusetts and inland along the Mississippi River valley to southern Illinois. The Coastal Plain is composed of two natural regions: (1) the Mississippi/Ohio River Floodplain, the broad, alluvial bottomlands of two of the largest rivers in the United States; and (2) the East Gulf Coastal Plain, a flat to rolling upland covered by windblown silt (loess) deposits. The eastern border of the province is defined by a hilly area composed of gravel and sand deposits that mark the different ancient shorelines of the Gulf of Mexico. The flora and fauna of this province are more typical of regions found farther south. Bald cypress swamps and many southern species reach their northern limits near here.

The Interior Low Plateaus physiographic province occupies the midsection of Kentucky. This province extends from northern Alabama through much of Tennessee and north through Kentucky to southern Illinois, Indiana, and Ohio. It is composed

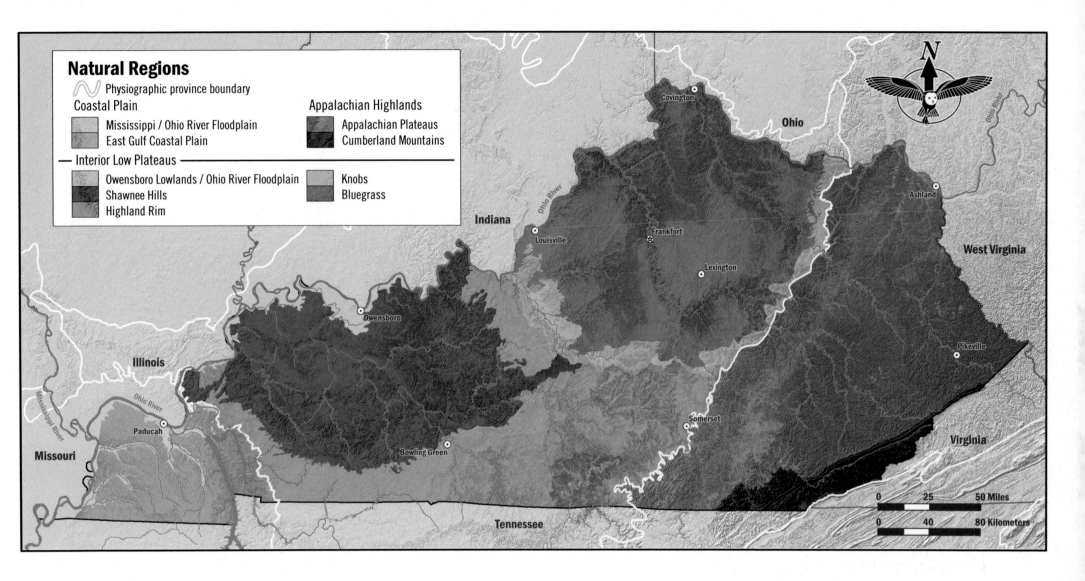

Natural Regions

〜 Physiographic province boundary

Coastal Plain
- Mississippi / Ohio River Floodplain
- East Gulf Coastal Plain

Appalachian Highlands
- Appalachian Plateaus
- Cumberland Mountains

— **Interior Low Plateaus** —
- Owensboro Lowlands / Ohio River Floodplain
- Shawnee Hills
- Highland Rim
- Knobs
- Bluegrass

of a series of plateaus, basins, and domes, often separated by distinct escarpments (steep slopes that separate two areas). Some parts of the province are hilly, while others are flat to rolling. This province contains five natural regions: the Owensboro Lowlands/Ohio River Floodplain, Shawnee Hills, Highland Rim, Bluegrass, and Knobs.

The Owensboro Lowlands/Ohio River Floodplain contains an extension of the southern floodplain forests of the Coastal Plain. The Shawnee Hills is a diverse area containing sandstone canyons and bluffs and vast limestone cave systems, including Mammoth Cave. Large wetlands also occur in the interior of this region. Karst (porous limestone) plains characterized by numerous sinkholes, caves, and underground streams are typical of the Highland Rim, as are hilly areas. The Bluegrass is associated with an ancient, eroded limestone dome in

Parts of the Highland Rim consist of flat limestone plains with sinkholes, caves, and few surface streams. *Gary Berdeaux*

Portions of the Shawnee Hills have sandstone bluffs and canyons similar to those found in the Appalachian Highlands, but on a smaller scale. *KSNPC photograph by Marc Evans*

The Knobs is a distinct region of isolated cone-shaped hills and ridge systems with intervening valley flats that partially encircles the Bluegrass Region. *Keith Mountain*

The steep hills and ridges of the Appalachian Highlands are heavily forested and provide a variety of habitats for native plants and animals. *KSNPC photograph by Marc Evans*

the central part of the state and is composed of gently rolling to steep hills and entrenched, cliff-lined rivers and streams. The Knobs, which partially encircles the Bluegrass, is a distinct region of isolated, conical hills and ridge systems with intervening flat valleys. Due to its large size and diversity of landforms, the flora and fauna of this province range from Coastal Plain to midwestern species, including many that are typical of prairie, glade, and oak–hickory forests.

Most of eastern Kentucky is in the Appalachian Highlands physiographic province, a large province that extends from New England to northern Georgia and Alabama. In Kentucky, this area consists of two natural regions, the Appalachian Plateaus and the Cumberland Mountains. The Appalachian Plateaus (which include the Cumberland and Allegheny plateaus) are composed of deeply eroded plateaus, steep hills, and narrow stream valleys. They include well-known sites such as the Red River Gorge Geological Area and Big South Fork National River and Recreation Area. The Cumberland Mountains, which occur in the southeast corner of the state, contain uplifted mountains and ridges. This region has the greatest topographic variation and highest elevations in the state, including Pine, Cumberland, and Black mountains. The biodiversity of this province in Kentucky is influenced by its central location in the Appalachian Mountain chain; it contains species typical of both the southern and northern Appalachians. This region was an important refugium for plants and animals during past periods of glaciation, and it continues to serve as an important migration corridor.

GEOLOGY, SOILS, AND TOPOGRAPHY

The physical character of Kentucky is as much a part of the state's biodiversity as the living creatures on its surface. Kentucky's geology, soils, and topography are closely related, and collectively they influence the distribution and biology of ecosystems.

GEOLOGY

The state's landscape is a product of both subtle and dramatic geologic events that submerged the land underwater for long periods, forced the Earth's crust upward into mountains and plateaus, and in some areas created extensive fault lines within the bedrock. The geologic formations created under these conditions have weathered and eroded for millions of years into Kentucky's landscape. With few exceptions (e.g., small amounts of igneous rock in western and eastern Kentucky), the rocks exposed at the surface in Kentucky are sedimentary, mostly limestones, sandstones, and shales.[5] Sedimentary rocks are formed when small fragments of rocks and minerals, dissolved minerals, or carbon-rich organic matter (decayed plants and animals) are deposited in horizontal layers in shallow seas, deltas, or swamps and subsequently compacted and hardened.

The state's oldest exposed rocks are Ordovician-age limestones formed 445 to 490 mya[6] when present-day Kentucky was located south of the equator and covered by a shallow tropical sea (see Natural History Timeline, pp. 28–29). These older rocks are deeply buried beneath most of the state but were pushed up closer to the surface by a massive regional uplift that locally bent the Earth's crust upward in central Kentucky, creating the Cincinnati Arch and shallow basins on either side of the arch. This uplift resulted in accelerated erosion of the younger rocks above, exposing the Ordovician rocks in the Bluegrass. The palisades of the Kentucky River are an outstanding example of this very old limestone.

Rocks formed later during the Silurian (415–445 mya) and Devonian (360–415 mya) periods are primarily dolomites and shales exposed in the hills of the Knobs that rings the Bluegrass.[7] Ordovician, Silurian, and early Devonian rocks contain abundant fossils, indicating the past presence of warm, shallow seas teeming with trilobites, brachiopods, corals, bryozoans, and other invertebrates. During the Devonian Period, organic-rich sediments were deposited and buried deep underground, where high pressure and temperature transformed them into oil and natural gas deposits.

Significant geologic change also occurred in the Mississippian (320–360 mya) and Pennsylvanian (300–320 mya) periods, collectively known as the Carboniferous Period. Marine organisms with calcium carbonate shells thrived in the tropical climate of the Mississippian Period. The shells of dead organisms, along with calcium carbonate precipitation from the seas, formed highly porous limestone beds hundreds of feet thick, exemplified by the Mammoth Cave system. The Carter Cave system also formed in this material, as did thousands of sinkholes, springs, and caverns across the state. During the Pennsylvanian Period, land was alternately

The distribution of several rare plants, such as cleft phlox, are curiously disjunct between the Kentucky River Palisades and north-central Tennessee. These two areas have similar types of Ordovician-age limestones. *John R. MacGregor*

The oldest exposed rock (445–490 million years old) in Kentucky occurs along the Kentucky River Palisades. *Greg Abernathy*

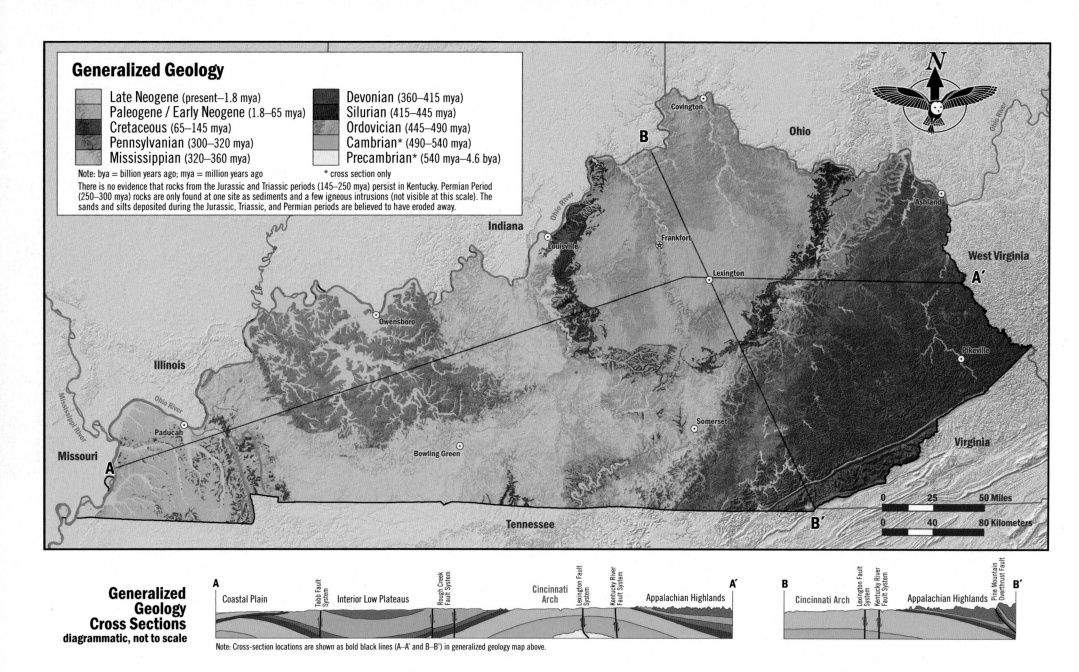

Generalized Geology

Late Neogene (present–1.8 mya)
Paleogene / Early Neogene (1.8–65 mya)
Cretaceous (65–145 mya)
Pennsylvanian (300–320 mya)
Mississippian (320–360 mya)

Devonian (360–415 mya)
Silurian (415–445 mya)
Ordovician (445–490 mya)
Cambrian* (490–540 mya)
Precambrian* (540 mya–4.6 bya)

Note: bya = billion years ago; mya = million years ago   * cross section only

There is no evidence that rocks from the Jurassic and Triassic periods (145–250 mya) persist in Kentucky. Permian Period (250–300 mya) rocks are only found at one site as sediments and a few igneous intrusions (not visible at this scale). The sands and silts deposited during the Jurassic, Triassic, and Permian periods are believed to have eroded away.

Generalized Geology Cross Sections
diagrammatic, not to scale

A — Coastal Plain — Tabb Fault System — Interior Low Plateaus — Rough Creek Fault System — Cincinnati Arch — Lexington Fault System — Kentucky River Fault System — Appalachian Highlands — A'

B — Cincinnati Arch — Lexington Fault System — Kentucky River Fault System — Appalachian Highlands — Pine Mountain Overthrust Fault — B'

Note: Cross-section locations are shown as bold black lines (A–A' and B–B') in generalized geology map above.

above and below sea level. This tropical period was characterized by vast swamps where plant remains accumulated as thick layers of peat. As sand and silt eroded from the uplands and filled the shallow basins on either side of the Cincinnati Arch, the peat deposits were buried. Under the pressure of these sediments, the peat was compacted, and with heat and time transformed into vast coal deposits within the Shawnee Hills and on the Appalachian Plateaus. The limestones, sandstones, and shales deposited during the Carboniferous Period are the most extensive formations exposed in the state, and numerous fossils document the marine and freshwater environments that existed during this time.

During the end of the Pennsylvanian Period and into the Permian Period, the landscape of eastern North America was dramatically changed. Land masses collided and compressed the Earth's crust, resulting in massive upthrusts that formed the extensive Appalachian Mountain range, which includes Cumberland and Pine mountains in Kentucky. It is believed that the Appalachians were originally as high as the Himalayan Mountains, but millions of years of erosion reduced them to the lower, less rugged mountains seen today.

Permian Period (250–300 mya) rocks are only represented by sediments at one site in western Kentucky and a few igneous intrusions in western and eastern Kentucky.[4] There is no evidence that rocks from the Jurassic and Triassic periods (145–250 mya) persist in Kentucky. Geologic information from surrounding states suggests that during the Permian, Triassic, and Jurassic periods, the seas receded, exposing the landmass of present-day Kentucky. These were times of significant geologic and climatic changes, and the sands and silts deposited during these periods are believed to have eroded away.[8]

Rocks formed during the Cretaceous (65–145 mya) and Paleogene (23–65 mya) periods are found primarily in extreme western Kentucky. Most of the sediments are gravels, shales, clays, or sands that were deposited in coastal or floodplain environments. The youngest sediments—mostly sand, clay, and gravel—were deposited in the floodplains during the Neogene Period, the current geologic period that began 23 million years ago. The Pleistocene and Holocene epochs of this period were a time when mammal species expanded, and fossils of American mastodons, wooly mammoths, and other behemoth-sized animals are found in these sediments. Recently scientists have suggested that since the Industrial Revolution—specifically, since the invention of the steam engine—a new geologic epoch has emerged: the Anthropocene, a time marked by anthropogenic global environmental change.[9, 10]

Limestone may outcrop where the bedrock is near the surface of the ground. Some of these outcrops, especially in the outer parts of the Bluegrass, form flat, open, rocky sites where glades and woodlands develop. *KSNPC photograph by Marc Evans*

The pretzel slime mold is a soil organism associated with decaying wood, feeding mostly on microorganisms by surrounding and digesting them. The pretzel part houses the reproductive spores. Slime molds are strange and colorful creatures, so poorly understood that they have at times been classified as fungi, plants, and even animals. *John R. MacGregor*

The splendid tiger beetle is strongly associated with sparsely vegetated red clay soils in the central United States. As a larva, its body just fits into a narrow burrow constructed at the surface of the soil, where it ambushes prey as they pass by. Adult beetles are most active in the spring and fall, and they are fast-moving predators of insects. *KSNPC photograph by Ellis L. Laudermillk*

SOILS

Healthy soil may be the most biologically diverse ecosystem on earth. Soil consists of water, air, mineral matter (e.g., sand, silt, or clay) and organic matter, but it also contains communities of living organisms. The numbers are almost unimaginable. For example, a teaspoon of productive soil generally contains between 100 million and 1 billion bacteria.[11] These bacteria can be remarkably diverse; a single gram of soil has been found to contain between 4,000 and 5,000 bacterial species.[12] While the diversity of soil organisms is still poorly known, an estimated 170,000 species have been identified.[13] Worldwide, bacteria and fungi account for about 84% of the biomass of living organisms in soil.[14] The remaining 16% comprises protozoa, nematodes, arthropods, earthworms, beetles, ants, termites, algae, protists, and small mammals.

Soil performs many functions, including decomposing organic matter and transforming it into humus, filtering pollutants, absorbing and storing water, converting nutrients into forms available to plants, and playing a critical role in the uptake and storage of carbon. Management practices, such as adding organic matter to the soil and avoiding the use of broad-spectrum pesticides that affect non-target species, can enhance the biological activity of soil organisms and help suppress pathogens.

Most of Kentucky's soils developed under similar climatic conditions and forested vegetation. Differences in soils are mainly attributable to the influence of soil parent materials, topography, and the length of time for which these factors have interacted; all of these factors, along with management practices, affect the number and diversity of organisms in the soil. A wide variety of soil parent materials occur throughout the state, including limestones, sandstones, and shales of different geologic ages, and sediments deposited by wind (loess) or water (alluvium). Topography and resulting landscape position, slope, and aspect greatly affect moisture, temperature, erosion, and drainage patterns, leading to diversity in soils formed from similar parent materials.

Like plants and animals, soils are classified into different types. The broadest classification is soil order (12 in the world), and the narrowest is soil series (23,000 in the United States). A named soil series can have a range of properties; some of the variations are based on differences in depth, slope, and erosion status. There are 331 different soil series mapped in Kentucky, representing six soil orders.[15]

The wide range of soils found in Kentucky significantly contributes to habitat and species diversity. The floodplains of the Coastal Plain predominantly have level, poorly drained alluvial soils derived from fine sediments deposited during frequent floods.[16] These soils are high in fertility and supported vast bottomland forests and swamps before these areas were cleared and drained for agriculture. The moderately fertile, highly erodible soils on gently sloping uplands to the east of the floodplain are formed mostly from thick, windblown loess deposits. Many of the soils in the upland areas of the Tennessee and Cumberland rivers formed in thin loess overlying sands, gravel, and clays of the Paleogene and early Neogene periods and are low in natural fertility.

The soils of the Interior Low Plateaus vary widely. Soils in the rolling uplands of the Shawnee Hills are generally of medium natural fertility and may be derived from loess or Pennsylvanian- and Mississippian-aged sandstones and shales, with some limestone along the southern region.[16] In the Owensboro Lowlands/Ohio River Floodplain, extensive areas of alluvial soils occur in broad river valleys. These soils are very fertile and support a mix of forested and marshy wetlands.

The Highland Rim is a rolling to level landscape underlain with extensive karst and containing moderately fertile, well-drained soils that are mostly developed from Mississippian-age limestones. This is the only region in Kentucky where extensive barrens and prairie vegetation occurred prior to settlement.

Ordovician-age limestones, found extensively in the center of the Bluegrass, are often rich in phosphorus and calcium. The phosphatic soils that developed in the region's karst topography are well-drained and very high in natural fertility. Outside the central Bluegrass, the soils are also formed from calcareous Ordovician-age deposits that include limestones, siltstones, and shales. As the Bluegrass approaches the Knobs, the topography becomes more rolling, and Silurian-age limestones and shales predominate. Soils formed here are relatively fertile but more erodible.

The hilly Knobs mainly has thin, acidic, very well-drained soils of low fertility. Valley soils between the hills are poorly drained and only somewhat more fertile. The soils of this region developed mostly from shales of Silurian and Devonian ages and from limestones, shales, and sandstone of Mississippian age.

Soils in the Appalachian Highlands, especially those on ridges and steep slopes, are thin, acidic, very well-drained, and rocky. They are derived mostly from Pennsylvanian-age sandstone, shale, and conglomerates that generally are low in fertility and very erodible if the forest cover is removed. Erosion in the uplands transports material to the lower slopes and floodplains, where soils that are somewhat more organic with higher fertility are formed in the accumulated material.

TOPOGRAPHY

Kentucky's elevation increases from west to east. The lowest elevation, 257 feet above sea level,[18] is along the Mississippi River in the extreme southwest corner of Fulton County. The highest elevation, 4,145 feet above sea level,[19] is the top of Black Mountain

Ben Begley

Lucy Braun described the soils of Pine Mountain in relation to the mountain's topography and vegetation.[17] She found that deep, nonacidic, mature soils with a distinct clay soil horizon developed in a broad trough near the crest of the mountain. The richest mesophytic forests on the south face developed within these areas of accumulation. Directly adjacent to the trough, on more exposed and steeper terrain, constant erosion prevented development of soil horizons, and thin, sandy, very acidic soils occurred that only supported a dry oak–pine forest.

The view from Knobby Rock in Blanton Forest State Nature Preserve, located on Pine Mountain in Harlan County, captures the ruggedness of the Cumberland Mountains.
© Chuck Summers

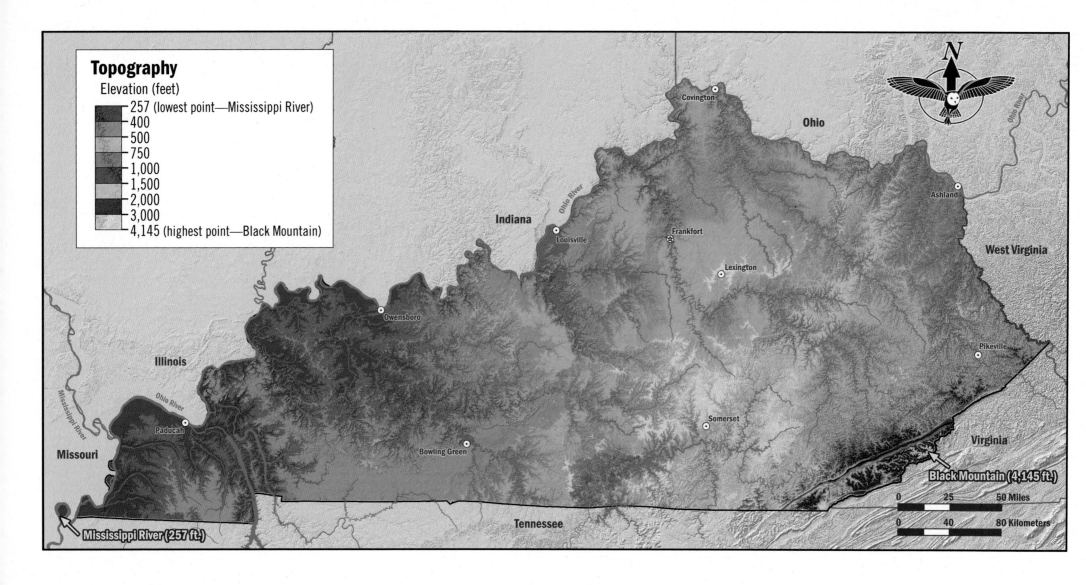

Topography

Elevation (feet)

- 257 (lowest point—Mississippi River)
- 400
- 500
- 750
- 1,000
- 1,500
- 2,000
- 3,000
- 4,145 (highest point—Black Mountain)

Missouri

Illinois

Indiana

Ohio

West Virginia

Virginia

Tennessee

Mississippi River

Ohio River

Ohio River

Paducah

Owensboro

Louisville

Bowling Green

Covington

Frankfort

Lexington

Somerset

Ashland

Pikeville

Black Mountain (4,145 ft.)

Mississippi River (257 ft.)

0 25 50 Miles

0 40 80 Kilometers

in Harlan County in extreme southeast Kentucky. The varied topography influences the development of numerous habitats. Alluvial floodplains border the Mississippi and Ohio rivers, while sandstone canyons and limestone caves occur in the Shawnee Hills. The western portion of the Highland Rim is a plain pockmarked with thousands of sinkholes, while the Bluegrass has rolling plains and steep hills with rich soils. The rugged forested hollows, gorges, and hills of the Appalachian Plateaus are surpassed only by the even higher and more rugged summits of the Cumberland Mountains.

WATER RESOURCES

Kentucky has abundant surface and groundwater resources. The state's surface waters include approximately 90,000 miles of streams[20] and more than 229,000 acres of lakes and reservoirs.[21] Along with groundwater, which includes extensive underground stream systems, these waters provide a diversity of habitats that support a wide variety of aquatic organisms.

Water resources are typically grouped based on watershed. A watershed is an area of land in which surface waters drain to a common point. Watersheds can be defined at varying scales, and like mixing bowls, smaller watersheds nest inside larger ones. Kentucky lies within the Ohio, Lower Mississippi, and Tennessee River watersheds, three of 21 regional watersheds that cover the nation.[22] Within Kentucky these three regional watersheds are divided into 17 major watersheds[23] that themselves are made up of even smaller watersheds. Large, regional watersheds tend to cross local, state, and national boundaries, illustrating the interconnectedness of large landscapes. The boundaries of the 17 major watersheds presented here are based on hydrology and the distribution patterns of freshwater fishes and mussels.

Geologic and climatic forces have shaped Kentucky's aquatic habitats and influenced species diversity. The state is centrally located in the eastern United States, placing it within the natural ranges of many aquatic organisms. Varied terrain including mountains, rolling hills, karst landscapes, and a flat coastal plain provides many different settings for the development of aquatic life. Species eliminated from areas to the north during the ice ages persisted here because the vast majority of the state was not glaciated. Although the last glacial advance did not scour Kentucky, glacial activity in the region was responsible for rerouting streams and changing their direction of flow. These radical hydrologic changes isolated some populations of a species from one another and caused the evolution of new species (speciation).

Further speciation occurred as populations were isolated from one another during periods of geologic uplift and faulting. For example, the formation of Cumberland Falls effectively separated areas above the falls from those below the falls. Natural erosion diverted streams to different watersheds through a process called "stream capture." This allowed the transfer of organisms between watersheds that were once separated from one another, further

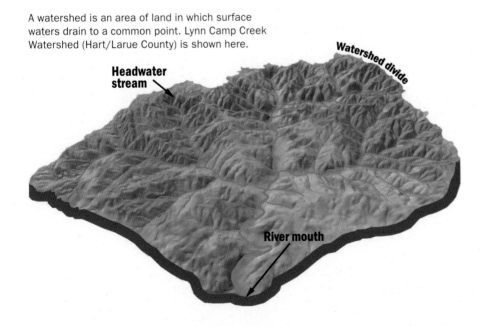

A watershed is an area of land in which surface waters drain to a common point. Lynn Camp Creek Watershed (Hart/Larue County) is shown here.

Watershed divide

Headwater stream

River mouth

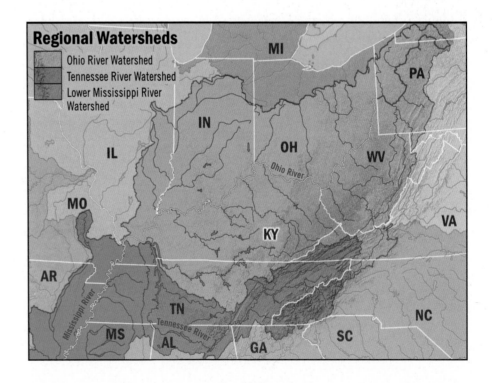

Regional Watersheds

- Ohio River Watershed
- Tennessee River Watershed
- Lower Mississippi River Watershed

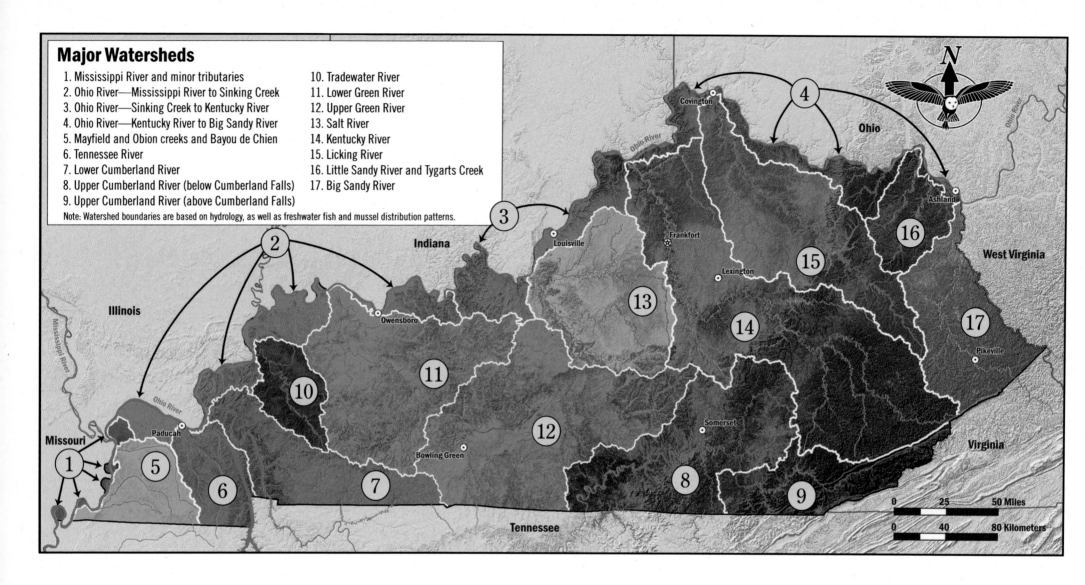

Major Watersheds

1. Mississippi River and minor tributaries
2. Ohio River—Mississippi River to Sinking Creek
3. Ohio River—Sinking Creek to Kentucky River
4. Ohio River—Kentucky River to Big Sandy River
5. Mayfield and Obion creeks and Bayou de Chien
6. Tennessee River
7. Lower Cumberland River
8. Upper Cumberland River (below Cumberland Falls)
9. Upper Cumberland River (above Cumberland Falls)
10. Tradewater River
11. Lower Green River
12. Upper Green River
13. Salt River
14. Kentucky River
15. Licking River
16. Little Sandy River and Tygarts Creek
17. Big Sandy River

Note: Watershed boundaries are based on hydrology, as well as freshwater fish and mussel distribution patterns.

contributing to aquatic diversification.[24] For example, there is evidence of species exchange through stream capture in the headwaters of Collins Fork in Knox County. This stream was once a part of the Cumberland River watershed but was captured by a tributary of the Kentucky River.[25]

In addition to the state's surface waters, Kentucky has abundant groundwater resources. Groundwater is water that lies beneath the surface of the earth, saturating the soil and filling up fractures in bedrock. In Kentucky, groundwater represents an important resource that supports rare subterranean organisms, particularly in the karst regions of the state. The area in and around Mammoth Cave National Park is dominated by karst terrain and has an extensive network of underground streams; it is one of the most unique and biologically diverse areas of the state and the world. Although surface

The largest rivers in or bordering Kentucky (and two of the largest in the United States), the Mississippi and Ohio, converge near Wickliffe. *KSNPC photograph by Heather Housman*

water typically passes through soil and rock prior to mixing with groundwater, which tends to filter out some pollutants, surface water can mix directly with groundwater in karst regions. The direct entry of unfiltered surface water into groundwater can severely affect the subterranean fauna and can contaminate drinking-water supplies.

CLIMATE

From tropical rainforests to polar ice caps, the diversity of life on Earth is partly attributable to responses by living organisms to varied climates. Weather conditions can change in minutes, but climate is the sum of all weather conditions—including wind, temperature, and precipitation—at a certain location over a period of years. Kentucky's climate falls within the temperate zone in which organisms have adapted to four distinct seasons that bring variable weather throughout the year.

Kentucky's location in the southeastern interior of North America creates a mild midlatitude climate with a large seasonal range of temperatures between summer and winter.[26] The relatively low elevations that surround Kentucky and its proximity to the Gulf of Mexico add a tropical marine

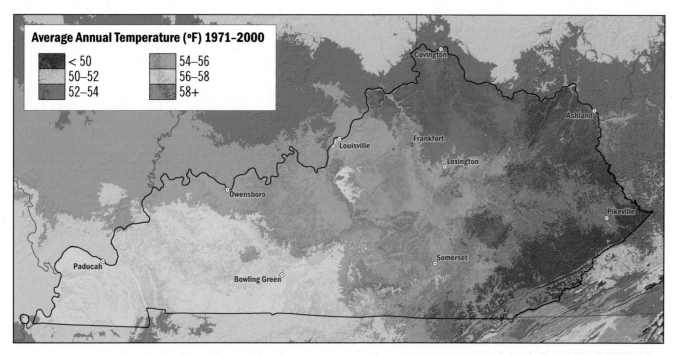

Average Annual Temperature (°F) 1971–2000

- < 50
- 50–52
- 52–54
- 54–56
- 56–58
- 58+

Covington
Ashland
Louisville
Frankfort
Lexington
Owensboro
Pikeville
Somerset
Paducah
Bowling Green

Data courtesy of PRISM Climate Group

The highest elevations of the Cumberland Mountains support a unique microclimate providing habitat for the Turk's cap lily, a favorite nectar source of the pipevine swallowtail. This northern hardwood forest is home to many species found nowhere else in Kentucky. *Thomas G. Barnes*

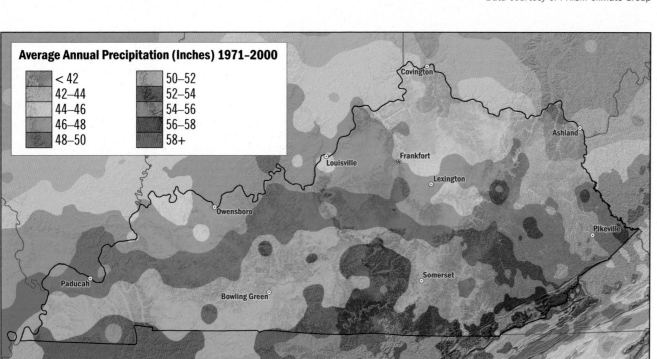

Average Annual Precipitation (Inches) 1971–2000

- < 42
- 42–44
- 44–46
- 46–48
- 48–50
- 50–52
- 52–54
- 54–56
- 56–58
- 58+

Covington
Ashland
Louisville
Frankfort
Lexington
Owensboro
Pikeville
Somerset
Paducah
Bowling Green

Data courtesy of PRISM Climate Group

influence that moderates temperature and increases precipitation. However, most weather systems in the state are pushed by strong upper-level winds from the west.

The growing season lengthens and the annual mean temperature increases from the northeast to the southwest, due in part to lower elevations and associated Gulf influences.[26] The last spring freeze usually occurs between early April and early May, and the first fall freeze occurs in October.

Annual precipitation in Kentucky is generally moderate (40–50 inches annually), with an increasing gradient from north to south. Spring is typically the wettest time of the year, and fall is the driest. Seasonal snowfall averages nearly 10 inches in the south and more than 20 inches in the north.

All organisms have adapted to seasonal changes in a variety of ways. To avoid cold temperatures, birds such as scarlet tanagers and indigo buntings migrate south. Other animals, such as woodchucks (groundhogs) and bats, hibernate until warmer temperatures arrive. Deciduous trees survive by dropping leaves to conserve moisture and energy. Other plants grow, flower, and fruit in the spring to avoid the hot, dry weather of summer.

EXTREME WEATHER

Extreme weather events such as tornadoes, ice storms, severe thunderstorms, flooding, droughts, and lightning-caused fire play a vital ecological role in shaping the natural landscape. These events typically are viewed from a human perspective in terms of loss of life and property destruction, but they also directly affect the composition and structure of plant and animal communities.

A weather event often only affects an area within a few square miles, but occasionally it may affect an area hundreds of miles across. Tornadoes, heavy winds, and ice storms may cause extensive damage to forests. Blown-down trees and broken limbs can disturb the soil and create openings in the forest that allow more sunlight to reach the forest floor. Some species take advantage of increased sunlight and disturbed soil conditions by colonizing these openings.

Older forests are susceptible to strong wind and ice damage. Older trees typically are taller, have large, heavy crowns, and may be hollow and weakened by age, fire damage, or disease. Fallen and standing dead trees (snags) contribute to habitat diversity and the number of species that live in an area. Woodpeckers, insects, mushrooms, salamanders, snails, bobcats, and soil organisms are all examples of species that may benefit from this kind of disturbance. However, some species, such as the shade-loving forest wildflowers, are negatively affected in the short term because of increases in sunlight and soil temperatures. Over centuries, repeated high-wind events and ice storms increase the number of fallen trees, which turns the soil and speeds

The effects of ice storm damage in a deciduous Kentucky forest. Light-colored patches represent toppled trees ripped out of the ground. *KSNPC photograph by Marc Evans*

Natural floods allow nutrient-rich sediments to be spread across the floodplain, replenishing nutrients in the soil and increasing the land's productivity. *Keith Mountain*

Hot, intense fires cause high rates of mortality in trees and shrubs, allowing fire-adapted species (mostly grasses and forbs) to thrive. *KSNPC photograph by Joyce Bender*

Easily mistaken for a snake, the eastern slender glass lizard thrives in fire-maintained habitats. This lizard is rare in Kentucky and is KSNPC-listed as threatened. *James Kiser*

nutrient uptake. Natural disturbances caused by weather events often result in the development of a forest with a wide range of tree ages and a diverse species composition.

Many species are adapted to flood or drought events. Heavy rains may cause soil erosion, deposition, and flooding. Species adapted to such disturbances—such as water willow, jewelweed, sycamore, and scouring rush—form unique communities that help stabilize stream banks. On the other extreme, droughts generally favor herbaceous (grasses and forbs) over woody vegetation. Natural communities such as dry prairies and open woodlands often expand when there are frequent severe droughts. Species such as little bluestem, pale purple coneflower, and Indian grass thrive under dry conditions.

Fires caused by lightning are rare in Kentucky. Historically, these fires played a significant role in shaping the landscape because they went unchecked and often burned vast areas. Fire-maintained habitats sustain grassland birds, such as bobolinks, grasshopper sparrows, and dickcissels, as well as reptiles such as corn snakes, pine snakes, eastern slender glass lizards, and six-lined racerunners. Many species that are dependent on fire-maintained communities have declined and are now considered rare.

Extreme temperatures can change the natural landscape. Native plants are adapted to seasonal changes and shifts in temperature, but extreme cold or heat (e.g., late freezes, early hot spells) can stress and sometimes kill organisms. Freezes in the late spring, when many plants are flowering, can disrupt flower development and cause low fruit and seed production. Consequently, wildlife that depends on these plants for food may decline. While extreme weather can be catastrophic, it is an integral part of ecosystem processes. Unpredictable natural events help maintain biodiversity.

LAND COVER

Kentucky's current land cover is an expression of land use; it is divided almost equally between forested land and human-modified areas (e.g., agricultural and developed land). In general, the rugged areas of the state, especially in the east, are more heavily forested, while level to rolling areas are predominately pasture, cropland, or developed rural and urban areas. Highly altered areas, such as agricultural and developed lands, offer little natural habitat and support few native species.

Forests cover nearly half of the state and are primarily composed of deciduous trees.[27, 28] Conifers (e.g., pines, eastern hemlock, and red cedar) dominate small areas of the state, with the largest tracts occurring mainly in the rugged cliff areas along the western edge of the Appalachian Highlands and on Pine Mountain. The majority of the remaining wetlands, primarily bottomland hardwood forest, occur in the lowlands of the Coastal Plain and Shawnee Hills, especially in the floodplains of the Mississippi and Ohio rivers and their tributaries. Other, smaller wetlands are scattered in upland depressions or in the floodplains of other rivers.

Pasture and cropland occupy more than a third of the state,[27, 28] with pasture much more abundant than cropland. Cropland is most common in the rich soils of the lowlands of the Shawnee Hills, the Highland Rim west of Bowling Green, and in the Coastal Plain. Pasturelands are scattered throughout western and central Kentucky, with a high concentration in the Bluegrass.

Urbanized areas—urban, suburban, and developed rural areas, along with associated roads and railroads—represent less than 10% of the landscape[27, 28] but are widely scattered throughout the state. Much of the state's large, high-density urban development is in the northern and central areas; however, many small to midsized communities

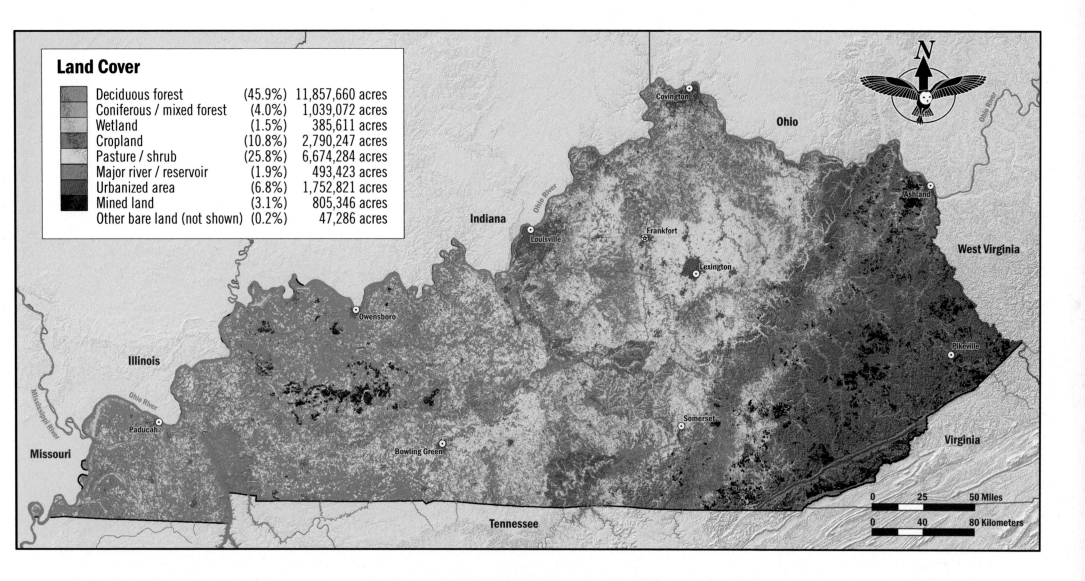

Land Cover

Deciduous forest	(45.9%)	11,857,660 acres
Coniferous / mixed forest	(4.0%)	1,039,072 acres
Wetland	(1.5%)	385,611 acres
Cropland	(10.8%)	2,790,247 acres
Pasture / shrub	(25.8%)	6,674,284 acres
Major river / reservoir	(1.9%)	493,423 acres
Urbanized area	(6.8%)	1,752,821 acres
Mined land	(3.1%)	805,346 acres
Other bare land (not shown)	(0.2%)	47,286 acres

Rugged topography has prevented many forests in eastern Kentucky from being converted to other land uses. *KSNPC photograph by Marc Evans*

Wetlands make up a small fraction of Kentucky's land area, but they provide invaluable services, such as unique wildlife habitat, water filtration, and flood control. *KSNPC photograph by Marc Evans*

Expansive croplands are most common in the western part of the state, while farms in eastern and central Kentucky tend to be smaller-scale operations. *Keith Mountain*

CHANGES IN LAND COVER OVER TIME

Compare current land cover with land cover prior to European American settlement (see Presettlement Land Cover map in Chapter 3, p. 37) to see how much land conversion and habitat loss have occurred in the last two centuries. Notable changes include the conversion of essentially all prairie and wetlands (mainly bottomland hardwood forests) to agricultural lands.

Strip mining denudes an area of virtually all vegetation, affects water quality, and alters the original topography. Although modern mining operations are legally required to reclaim stripped areas, it is impossible to return an area to its previous state of biodiversity. *KSNPC photograph by Marc Evans*

throughout the state are rapidly developing (e.g., Bowling Green and Somerset). More than 85,000 miles of roads connect these communities.[29]

Mined lands in Kentucky are primarily surface coal mines that account for more than 800,000 acres (3.5% of the state's land area).[27, 28] Surface coal mining is extensive in the Appalachian Highlands of eastern Kentucky and in the Shawnee Hills of western Kentucky. Though not shown on the accompanying map, vast underground mines are also present across these regions. Smaller limestone and sandstone quarries are also scattered across the state.

Kentucky is bordered by two major rivers, the Ohio and the Mississippi. Numerous smaller rivers and streams are scattered throughout the state.

The construction of dams on rivers and streams has formed large reservoirs that have flooded more than 229,000 acres.[21] In addition, hundreds of smaller reservoirs and ponds are scattered throughout the state.

Land cover is constantly changing. Recent land cover changes are being driven principally by urbanization, but other activities (such as mining and forest clearing) are also important factors. Changes in land cover greatly affect the health, distribution, and abundance of flora and fauna. Both state programs (Kentucky Landscape Snapshot) and federal programs (U.S. Geological Survey Gap Analysis Program) monitor changes in land cover. These programs provide vital data that aid management, planning, and protection activities.

Chapter Three

NATURAL HISTORY

After a long and fatiguing journey, through a mountainous wilderness . . . from the top of an eminence, we saw with pleasure the beautiful level of Kentucky.

—DANIEL BOONE, believed to be describing the view from Pilot Knob in Powell County, now a state nature preserve.[1]

KENTUCKY'S CULTURAL HISTORY is linked with the natural landscape. This chapter presents information on the influence of early human history, ancient peoples and early settlement, and the natural history of fire. Historical information provides a glimpse into the nature of unaltered natural communities and the plants and animals that lived in them—biodiversity as it was before the pervasive effects of civilization.

NATURAL HISTORY TIMELINE

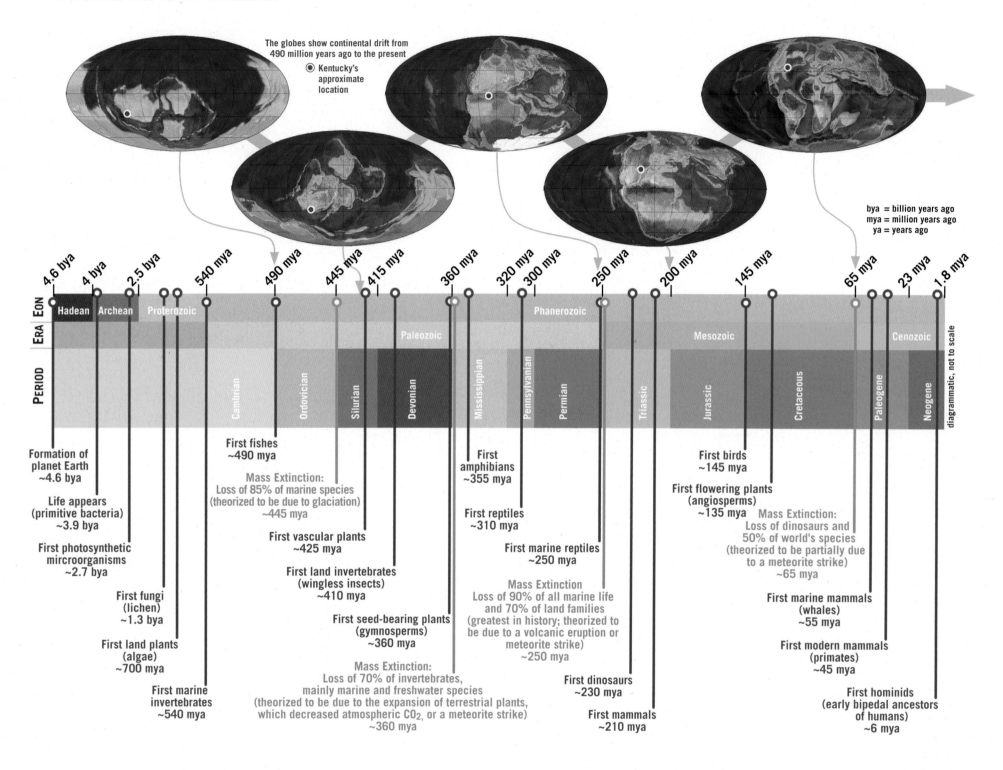

The globes show continental drift from 490 million years ago to the present

◉ Kentucky's approximate location

bya = billion years ago
mya = million years ago
ya = years ago

diagrammatic, not to scale

EON: Hadean | Archean | Proterozoic | Phanerozoic

ERA: Paleozoic | Mesozoic | Cenozoic

PERIOD: Cambrian | Ordovician | Silurian | Devonian | Mississippian | Pennsylvanian | Permian | Triassic | Jurassic | Cretaceous | Paleogene | Neogene

4.6 bya | 4 bya | 2.5 bya | 540 mya | 490 mya | 445 mya | 415 mya | 360 mya | 320 mya | 300 mya | 250 mya | 200 mya | 145 mya | 65 mya | 23 mya | 1.8 mya

Formation of planet Earth
~4.6 bya

Life appears
(primitive bacteria)
~3.9 bya

First photosynthetic mircroorganisms
~2.7 bya

First fungi
(lichen)
~1.3 bya

First land plants
(algae)
~700 mya

First marine invertebrates
~540 mya

First fishes
~490 mya

Mass Extinction:
Loss of 85% of marine species
(theorized to be due to glaciation)
~445 mya

First vascular plants
~425 mya

First land invertebrates
(wingless insects)
~410 mya

First seed-bearing plants
(gymnosperms)
~360 mya

Mass Extinction:
Loss of 70% of invertebrates,
mainly marine and freshwater species
(theorized to be due to the expansion of terrestrial plants,
which decreased atmospheric CO$_2$, or a meteorite strike)
~360 mya

First amphibians
~355 mya

First reptiles
~310 mya

First marine reptiles
~250 mya

Mass Extinction
Loss of 90% of all marine life
and 70% of land families
(greatest in history; theorized to
be due to a volcanic eruption or
meteorite strike)
~250 mya

First dinosaurs
~230 mya

First mammals
~210 mya

First birds
~145 mya

First flowering plants
(angiosperms)
~135 mya

Mass Extinction:
Loss of dinosaurs and
50% of world's species
(theorized to be partially due
to a meteorite strike)
~65 mya

First marine mammals
(whales)
~55 mya

First modern mammals
(primates)
~45 mya

First hominids
(early bipedal ancestors
of humans)
~6 mya

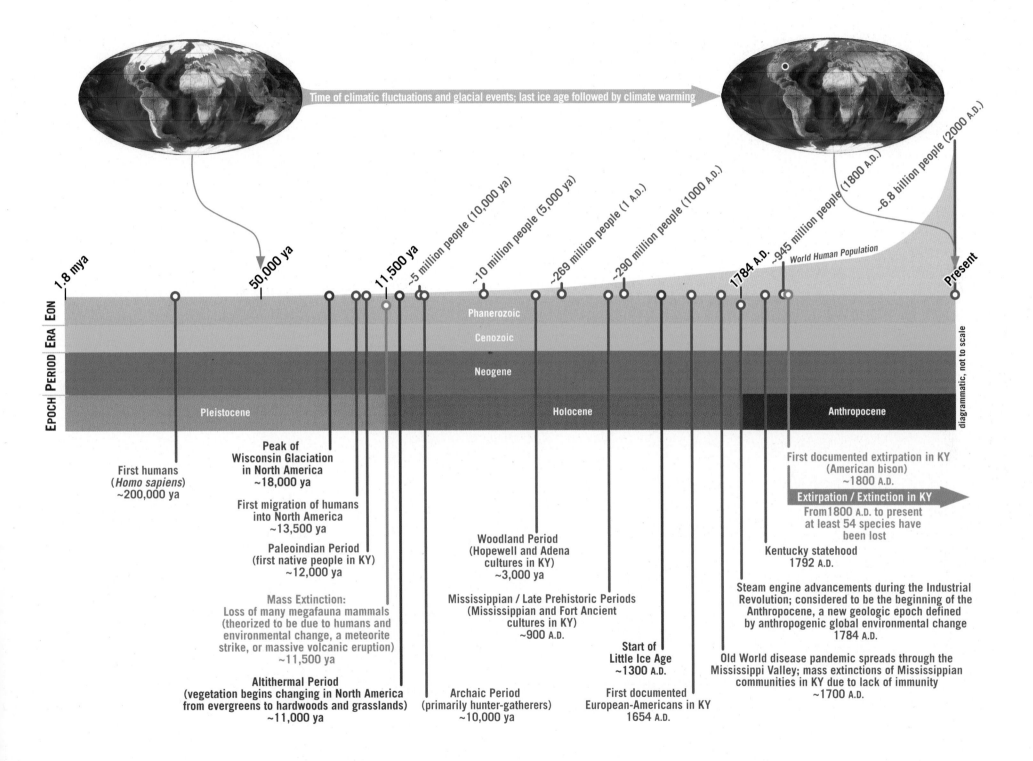

Time of climatic fluctuations and glacial events; last ice age followed by climate warming

~5 million people (10,000 ya)
~10 million people (5,000 ya)
~269 million people (1 A.D.)
~290 million people (1000 A.D.)
~945 million people (1800 A.D.)
~6.8 billion people (2000 A.D.)

1.8 mya
50,000 ya
11,500 ya
1784 A.D.
Present

World Human Population

diagrammatic, not to scale

EON | **ERA** | **PERIOD** | **EPOCH**

Phanerozoic
Cenozoic
Neogene

Pleistocene
Holocene
Anthropocene

First humans
(*Homo sapiens*)
~200,000 ya

Peak of
Wisconsin Glaciation
in North America
~18,000 ya

First migration of humans
into North America
~13,500 ya

Paleoindian Period
(first native people in KY)
~12,000 ya

Mass Extinction:
Loss of many megafauna mammals
(theorized to be due to humans and
environmental change, a meteorite
strike, or massive volcanic eruption)
~11,500 ya

Altithermal Period
(vegetation begins changing in North America
from evergreens to hardwoods and grasslands)
~11,000 ya

Woodland Period
(Hopewell and Adena
cultures in KY)
~3,000 ya

Mississippian / Late Prehistoric Periods
(Mississippian and Fort Ancient
cultures in KY)
~900 A.D.

Start of
Little Ice Age
~1300 A.D.

Archaic Period
(primarily hunter-gatherers)
~10,000 ya

First documented
European-Americans in KY
1654 A.D.

First documented extirpation in KY
(American bison)
~1800 A.D.

Extirpation / Extinction in KY
From 1800 A.D. to present
at least 54 species have
been lost

Kentucky statehood
1792 A.D.

Steam engine advancements during the Industrial
Revolution; considered to be the beginning of the
Anthropocene, a new geologic epoch defined
by anthropogenic global environmental change
1784 A.D.

Old World disease pandemic spreads through the
Mississippi Valley; mass extinctions of Mississippian
communities in KY due to lack of immunity
~1700 A.D.

NATIVE PEOPLES

Archaeological evidence suggests that the first people arrived in what is now known as Kentucky at least 12,000 years ago,[2] when much of the landscape is believed to have been open woodland with scattered groups of spruce and fir trees. These nomadic people, referred to as paleoindians, lived in small groups that hunted Pleistocene megafauna, such as American mastodon, giant bison, and giant sloth, and they collected wild plants to supplement their diets.[3] The first native people followed the traces (trails) created by the megafauna and later maintained by American bison, elk, and white-tailed deer. Early European American settlers continued to use this network of traces, several of which eventually became modern roads.

After the end of the Wisconsin Glaciation (~11,000 years ago), Kentucky's climate began to warm and became more like it is today. Spruce and fir trees were replaced by hardwood trees, and much of Kentucky was covered with forests. The extinction of the Pleistocene megafauna also occurred during this time. Scientists speculate the extinctions may have been the result of overhunting by early human hunters,[4] loss of habitat due to changing climate,[5] or even massive volcanic eruptions.[6] Regardless of what caused the extinctions, these environmental changes required adjustments in the paleoindian lifestyle, and it is believed that people divided into more specialized groups and developed cultural differences in response to local habitats and resources.[7]

While they continued to hunt large game animals such as bison, elk, and deer during the Archaic Period (~10,000–3,000 years ago), native people also started to develop more sophisticated tools and hunting methods for pursuing smaller game animals, including wild turkey, raccoon, rabbit, and squirrel. Fishes and mussels were also important parts of the diet of many groups, especially in western Kentucky.[3, 8] There is evidence that native people used fire to improve wildlife habitat and yields of food plants.[9] Some natural landscapes in Kentucky, particularly the extensive prairies of the southern Highland Rim and possibly open meadows and woodlands in the central Bluegrass, are believed to have been maintained primarily by fires set by native people.[10, 11]

Native people used nuts, berries, plums, pawpaws, grapes, persimmons, mushrooms, and many other plants for food, medicines, dyes, tools, and building materials. They spread these species by planting them and carrying them from place to place, and they expanded habitat for sun-loving plants by burning and clearing areas.[12]

Agriculture developed earlier in the Ohio River valley than in most other regions of North America, although hunting and gathering continued after

Artist's rendition of an archaic village in Kentucky. *Unknown artist, courtesy of the Kentucky Historical Society; KSNPC photograph by Martina Hines*

agriculture was developed. Kentucky is within one of five regions in the world where agriculture is believed to have developed independently. As early as 4,500 years ago, people here were clearing land with tools and fire to grow goosefoot, sumpweed, knotweed, sunflowers, and other native crops to supplement their diet.[13, 14]

During the Woodland Period (~3,000–1,100 years ago) native people became less nomadic, increasingly used agriculture, and began growing non-native crops like corn, acquired by trade with more southerly native peoples. Corn required the clearing and cultivation of large areas of bottomlands. It has been estimated that roughly one-tenth of an acre of corn was planted annually for each member of the village.[15] As cultivated areas declined in productivity, more lands were cleared for agriculture using slash-and-burn methods. In bottomlands, where almost all agriculture took place, floods were the primary means of fertilizing the soil, but periodic burning was used to extend soil fertility by increasing nitrogen and potash levels in heavily used croplands. Giant cane sometimes invaded the abandoned croplands, creating extensive thickets (canebreaks) noted by early European American pioneers.[16]

In the Mississippian/Late Prehistoric periods (~900–1700 A.D.), improved agricultural techniques yielded more food and resulted in a more stable lifestyle that allowed native people to prosper. As the

Kentucky is traversed by a network of trails created by animals thousands of years ago; some eventually became modern highways. This trail at Blue Licks State Park Nature Preserve has been used by American mastodon, bison, and people alike. *Greg Abernathy*

population grew, an increasing demand for food resulted in a more intense use of natural resources.[5] Settlements were located primarily in the floodplains of large streams and were often inhabited by several hundred and sometimes a few thousand people. The new lifestyle resulted in larger populations with complex social structures and new, distinct cultures, including the Mississippian culture in the southern and western parts of the state and the Fort Ancient culture in central, eastern, and northern Kentucky. In mountainous eastern Kentucky the impacts of native people on the landscape were probably minor and primarily restricted to the vicinities of their village sites.[15]

Infectious European diseases, such as smallpox, arrived in the Mississippi River Valley in the late 1600s. Native peoples lacked immunity to these diseases, resulting in the mass extinction of Mississippian communities in Kentucky.[2, 17, 18] By the time European American settlers arrived in Kentucky in 1750 A.D., most native people were gone, and the region was being used as a hunting ground.[19] In their absence, prairies and forest openings were invaded by trees, and abandoned fields became thickets. With the exception of a few plant distributions and perhaps the extent of prairie remnants in the state, very little evidence of land-use practices of these early inhabitants remains. The landscape known to native peoples was quickly and dramatically changed by the waves of new settlers.

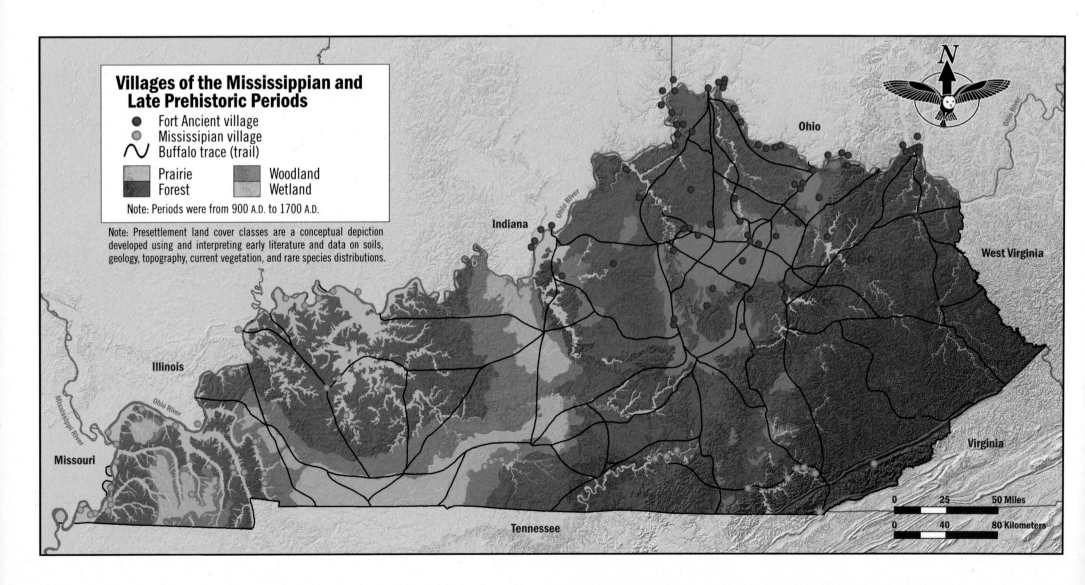

Villages of the Mississippian and Late Prehistoric Periods
- Fort Ancient village
- Mississippian village
- Buffalo trace (trail)
- Prairie
- Forest
- Woodland
- Wetland

Note: Periods were from 900 A.D. to 1700 A.D.

Note: Presettlement land cover classes are a conceptual depiction developed using and interpreting early literature and data on soils, geology, topography, current vegetation, and rare species distributions.

FIRE

Fire has had a significant impact on ecosystems throughout the world for millions of years. It influences where particular plants and animals live and ultimately the distribution of natural communities across the landscape. Prairies and woodlands expand when fire is frequent, and their areas shrink when it is suppressed. Forests, and even swamps, are adapted to periodic fire. It is an integral force in shaping the natural landscape, especially in the southeastern United States.[20]

Lightning is the only natural source of fire in Kentucky. The historical frequency and extent of fire caused by lightning is unknown. The extent to which native people used fire prior to European American settlement is debatable, but there is little doubt they used this powerful tool to manage the landscape. Fire was used to clear vegetation, hunt game, and improve forage for grazing animals. Settlers used fire to alter the land and thus indirectly shaped biodiversity in Kentucky, much the same as native peoples, and these activities continued throughout the 1700s and 1800s.[21] As settlers built more structures and permanent villages, concern about the destructive potential of fire grew. By 1921, the National Park Service and the U.S. Forest Service had developed a policy that advocated fire suppression, which strongly influenced land management for many decades.

Animals and plants that are adapted to tolerate and even take advantage of fire predictably occur in areas where fire is frequent, like ridge tops and grasslands. Prairie grasses, for instance, have a growing bud at the base of the plant, where it is protected from fire and can respond after the top leaves are burned. Some trees have thick bark that protects the tree's living tissue. Other species, like sugar maple and yellow poplar, are suppressed or eliminated by fire and occur in moist ravines where the influence of fire is minimal. Natural fire most commonly

occurs in the summer and fall in Kentucky, when vegetation is dry and more easily ignited.

Many animals have the ability to escape a fire. Large animals such as deer and fox simply outrun the flames, birds fly away, and small mammals and reptiles burrow to escape flames. Animals may even take advantage of fires and hunt at the edges for fleeing prey or scavenge recently burned areas. Some insects, such as ants, thrive following fires, and some beetle species with special infrared-detecting organs actively seek smoldering logs and stumps where they can nest and feed.[22]

As fire moves through the landscape, it releases nutrients that fertilize plants. Fire reduces shade and leaf litter, which exposes soil and existing plants to

A prescribed fire set by land managers to restore a prairie in Warren County, Kentucky.
KSNPC photograph by Joyce Bender

Species in the white oak group, such as this chestnut oak, possess a substance called tyloses that seals off injuries like those caused by fire and protects the tree from further damage. This substance is the reason why white oak barrels, such as those used to age wine and bourbon, are watertight. *KSNPC photograph by Heather Housman*

A gulf fritillary feeds on blazing star. Years of fire suppression can have unexpected results. For example, fire suppression in the eastern United States has resulted in a reduction of nectar resources available to migrating butterflies. *Thomas G. Barnes*

sunlight, stimulating germination and new growth. Fire may also reduce fungal pathogens and insects that threaten the health and vigor of plants.

S. J. Pyne said, "Fire can be as influential being withheld as it can by being applied."[23] Natural communities (e.g., oak–hickory forests or mixed oak forests and grasslands) that are maintained and influenced by fire will decline in extent and quality when natural fire frequency is reduced or eliminated from the landscape. After decades of suppression, however, the roles and benefits of fire in natural systems are better understood. Fire is increasingly used as a management tool to reduce the hazards of uncontrolled wildfire and improve the ecological health of natural ecosystems.

A map of Kentucky from actual survey of Elihu Barker, published 1973.

HISTORICAL ACCOUNTS

Knowledge about the landscape and natural communities that existed in Kentucky before European American settlement is imperative to protecting and managing the state's biodiversity today. Only small remnants remain of what once were vast prairies, ancient forests, and primeval swamps. Systematic land surveys were uncommon in the first states settled west of the Alleghenies, so descriptions by European American explorers provide the best information about the state's once-vast wilderness.

"When the lake burst on our view there were swans by hundreds, and white as rich cream, either dipping their black bills in the water, or stretching one leg out on its surface, or gently floating along. . . . It seems as if thousands of large, fat, and heavy swans were startled."

—JOHN J. AUDUBON describing Swan Lake in Ballard County in 1868[24]

". . . extensive plains, which stretch upwards of one hundred and fifty miles in a south-west course, and end only when they join the mountainous country. Some few clumps of trees, and a grove here and there, are the only obstructions to a boundless horizon."

—LETTER TO GILBERT IMLAY (late 1700s) describing the vast prairies east of Land Between the Lakes, author unknown[25]

"There are many canebrakes so thick and tall that it is difficult to pass through them. Where no cane grows there is abundance of wild rye, clover, and buffalo grass, covering vast tracts of country, and affording excellent food for cattle. The fields are covered with abundance of wild herbage not common to other countries."

—JOHN FILSON in 1784, describing the area around Elkhorn Creek[25]

"The mountains here are very steep and on some of them there is laurel and ivy. The tops of the mountains are very rocky and some parts of the rocks seem to be composed of shells, nuts and many other substances petrified and cemented together with a kind of flint. We left the river . . . and got to a rock by the side of a creek sufficient to shelter 200 men from rain."

—DR. THOMAS WALKER in 1750 describing the land along the Red River of eastern Kentucky[26]

35

PRESETTLEMENT LAND COVER

The Kentucky that early European American settlers saw is very different from the Kentucky of today. At the time of European American settlement, it probably was possible for a person to walk from the Cumberland Mountains to the Mississippi River and never leave the forest. On the other hand, in parts of the Highland Rim, one could ride a horse for days through treeless prairies with grasses as tall as a person on horseback. In western Kentucky, bald cypress and swamp tupelo towered over the wetlands, and all of the streams across the state were free-flowing and clean.

The Kentucky State Nature Preserves Commission's (KSNPC) presettlement land cover map[27] is a conceptual depiction of the presettlement land cover of Kentucky. The map was developed using and interpreting early literature and data on soils, geology, topography, current vegetation, and rare species distributions. The Coastal Plain was the only part of Kentucky that was systematically surveyed before settlement quickly altered the natural land cover.[28]

At the time of European American settlement, Kentucky was about 85% to 90% forested (including upland and wetland forests).[27] Although native people had an impact on the forest land, it is likely that the majority of forests were relatively undisturbed old growth. Prairie and woodland (a sparsely wooded area) made up most of the remainder of the state. Estimates of the extent of prairie in Kentucky range from 2.3 to 2.8 million acres.[29, 30] The largest area of prairie, named the "Big Barrens" by European American settlers, occurred in an arc from north

The first European American settlers encountered old-growth or primary forests with huge trees like these white oak, yellow poplar, and American chestnut. Today, few tracts of primary forest remain in Kentucky. *Karl Hodge, courtesy of the Kentucky Historical Society.*

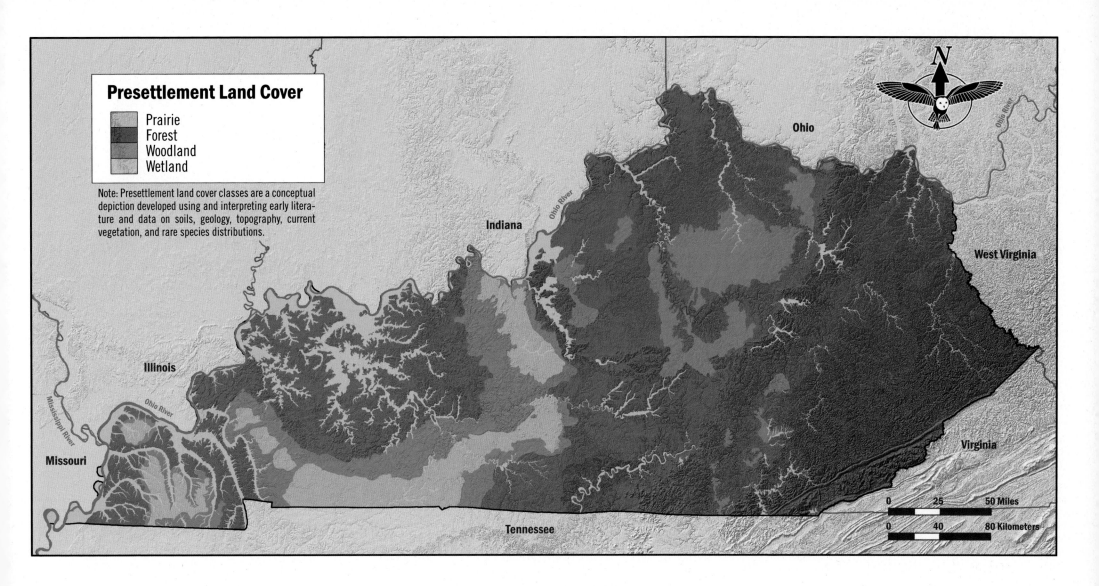

Presettlement Land Cover

- Prairie
- Forest
- Woodland
- Wetland

Note: Presettlement land cover classes are a conceptual depiction developed using and interpreting early literature and data on soils, geology, topography, current vegetation, and rare species distributions.

of what is now Elizabethtown, then south to Bowling Green, west to Hopkinsville, and northwest to the Ohio River. Smaller areas of prairie and woodland were scattered throughout the state. Wetlands, including swamps, bottomland hardwood forests, and marshes, covered from 1.5 to 2.3 million acres of Kentucky at the time of settlement.[27, 31] The largest wetlands occurred in western Kentucky, but many small wetlands were scattered throughout the state.

Chapter Four

SPECIES AND NATURAL COMMUNITIES

Each species, to put the matter succinctly,
is a masterpiece.

—EDWARD O. WILSON[1]

THE DIVERSITY OF KENTUCKY'S flora and fauna is fantastic: eyeless animals living in the dark, predators less than an inch long, and plants that "eat" animals. From the most common to the rarest, all plants, animals, and natural communities contribute to the biological variability across Kentucky. These are all part of the natural systems that support life in this state. While it may appear that a great deal is known about Kentucky's species, much is still unknown, especially the relationships among species and the consequences of extinction. One thing is clear: continued degradation of natural communities and loss of their associated species is expected. The more we learn, the more we realize how much we have to lose.

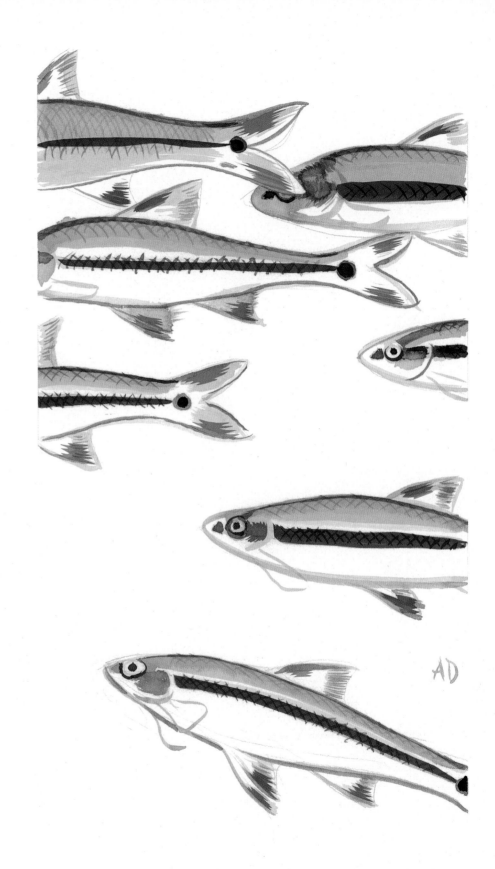

Fairy bonnet mushroom is found throughout Kentucky on decaying wood. *John R. MacGregor*

Species ranked G5S5, like the red fox, are considered secure both globally and in Kentucky. *Thomas G. Barnes*

SPECIES

Species and their genetic diversity are the bricks and mortar of biodiversity, the building blocks of ecological health. It is important to know how many species are found in the state, to assess whether they are common or rare, and to keep track of how many are being lost. Even in this era of knowledge, many organisms have not been counted or even discovered. The algae of Kentucky are an example. For more than 40 years Dr. Gary Dillard has been researching and cataloging the species of algae in the southeastern United States. Despite his dedicated efforts, there is still much to learn about the biology of this group.[2] There are also millions of microorganisms about which little is known, and all of them have a role in the ecology of natural systems.

If species are to be used as indicators of ecological health, it is important to be able to distinguish one from another. Taxonomists provide the method to do this. Taxonomy uses the differences, similarities, and evolutionary relationships among organisms to group them into categories. Each category is called a *taxon* (plural *taxa*, which for the purpose of this book refers to species and may include subspecies or varieties). Closely related species are grouped together into a larger category called a *genus*; closely related *genera* (plural for genus) are grouped into a *family*; and so forth.

Assessing the rarity of a species is also important

Taxonomy: The Five Major Kingdoms

Monera	Protista	Fungi	Plantae	Animalia
Includes all bacteria and cyanobacteria (blue-green algae). Sometimes split into two kingdoms, Eubacteria and Archaebacteria.	Probably the most vaguely defined kingdom because it includes many different kinds of unicellular and simple colonial organisms.	Includes mushrooms, yeasts, and many molds that absorb nutrients primarily from decaying material.	Multicellular photosynthetic organisms, including mosses, ferns, and seed-producing plants (both flowering and cone-bearing).	Kingdom with the greatest number of known species. All animals are multicellular and obtain food by eating other organisms or the products of other organisms.
Blue-green algae	Planktonic diatom	Fairy bonnet mushroom	Painted trillium	Black-throated green warbler

Taxonomy is a branch of biology that involves the describing, naming, and organization of organisms into a classification system, which takes into account the differences, similarities, and evolutionary relationships among organisms. Modern taxonomy uses the Linnaean System, which has been expanded to include seven major taxonomic categories:

Kingdom →	Phylum →	Class →	Order →	Family →	Genus →	Species
Animalia →	Chordata →	Aves →	Passeriformes →	Parulidae →	*Dendroica* →	*virens*
1,056,072 species	41,038 species	9,964 species	5,913 species	117 species	29 species	Black-throated green warbler

Global (G) and State (S) Conservation Ranks

G1 or S1	G2 or S2	G3 or S3	G4 or S4	G5 or S5
Critically Imperiled	Imperiled	Vulnerable	Apparently Secure	Secure
Very high risk of extinction or extirpation due to rarity (often five or fewer populations), very steep declines, or other factors.	High risk of extinction or extirpation due to very restricted range, very few populations (often 20 or fewer), steep declines, or other factors.	Moderate risk of extinction or extirpation due to restricted range, relatively few populations (often 80 or fewer), recent and widespread declines, or other factors.	Uncommon but not rare; some cause for long-term concern due to declines or other factors; or stable over many decades and not threatened but of restricted distribution or population size.	Common; widespread and abundant.

Rattlesnake-master borer moth

Gray squirrel

Additional ranks:
GX or SX = Presumed extinct/extirpated. Not located despite intensive searches; virtually no likelihood of rediscovery.
GH or SH = Possibly extinct/extirpated. Missing; known only from historical occurrences, but still some hope of rediscovery.

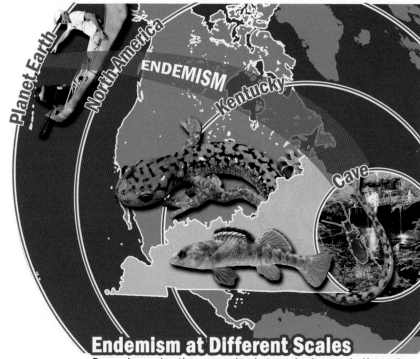

Endemism at Different Scales
Rogers' cave beetles are endemic to a single cave in Kentucky
↳Shawnee darters are endemic to Kentucky
↳Green salamanders are endemic to eastern North America
↳Humans are endemic to Planet Earth

to monitoring ecological health. In determining which species are secure (common) and which are in decline, a standardized method for assigning conservation status or rank has been established. Species are ranked for their vulnerability to extinction on a scale of 1 to 5. Species with ranks of G1 to G3 are vulnerable to extinction at the global level, and those with ranks of S1 to S3 are vulnerable to extirpation at the state or regional level (see the Conservation Science: Natural Heritage Methodology section in chapter 6). Species are designated endangered, threatened, or special concern based on their global and state conservation status. In Kentucky, state-level designations are assigned by KSNPC, and state-vulnerable species are referred to as KSNPC-listed.

With a few exceptions, this book highlights groups that are relatively conspicuous and for which a reasonable amount of information specific to Kentucky is available. Only a brief overview of each species group is provided; the reader is encouraged to seek more information about the biota of Kentucky.

ENDEMIC SPECIES

Endemic species are native and restricted to a defined area, such as a unique habitat, a watershed, or even a continent. Some species have narrow distributions as a result of ecological requirements (e.g., soil types for plants), limited mobility, physical barriers that prevent dispersal (such as waterfalls that may thwart upstream movement by fishes), or other chemical, biological, or physical factors. Although species distribution is not influenced by political boundaries, it is common for endemism to be reported using boundaries such as state lines.

Endemic Species

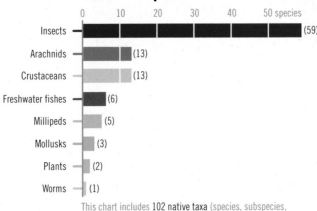

```
                  0    10    20    30    40    50 species
Insects          ████████████████████████████████ (59)
Arachnids        ████ (13)
Crustaceans      ████ (13)
Freshwater fishes ██ (6)
Millipeds        █ (5)
Mollusks         █ (3)
Plants           | (2)
Worms            | (1)
```

This chart includes 102 native taxa (species, subspecies, and varieties).

Of the 102 taxa currently considered endemic to Kentucky, 92% are invertebrates, and the remainder are fishes and plants (Appendix 1). Most of the endemics (80%) are obligate cave-dwellers (hereafter *subterranean*) that are ecologically adapted to live only in caves and their associated streams and groundwater. Caves and their fauna are often isolated from one another, like islands, so many subterranean animals are endemic to a single cave.

Rogers' cave beetle, an endemic species known from a single Kentucky cave, has one of the smallest distributions in the state. Kentucky's diverse subterranean fauna includes 59 cave beetle taxa, 92% of which are endemic. *KSNPC photograph by Ellis L. Laudermilk*

Insects make up the largest group of endemic species, followed by arachnids (mainly subterranean pseudoscorpions) and crustaceans (primarily crayfishes). Approximately 10% of Kentucky's endemic taxa are known exclusively from Mammoth Cave or other caves within Mammoth Cave National Park. No area of comparable size in the state exceeds this rich concentration of endemics.

Three Kentucky endemics are federally listed as endangered or threatened.[3] The Mammoth Cave shrimp, known only from the groundwater basins in or near Mammoth Cave National Park, is listed as endangered.[3,4] Contamination of groundwater and predation by exotic species threaten the existence of this tiny shrimp (adults measure up to one inch long).

The relict darter also is listed as endangered. Known only from the Bayou de Chien watershed in Graves and Hickman counties, this bottom-dwelling fish has a limited distribution and small population size. Additionally, it is threatened by habitat degradation and pollution related to agriculture (e.g., stream channelization, siltation, pesticide or herbicide runoff, and low stream flows due to irrigation).[5]

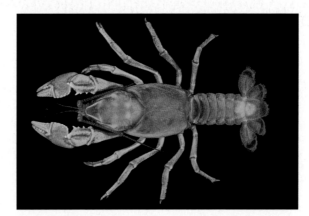

The Bluegrass crayfish, a Kentucky endemic, is known only from the Kentucky River watershed in Estill, Garrard, Madison, and Rockcastle counties. *Guenter A. Schuster*

About one inch long, the Mammoth Cave shrimp occurs only in the groundwater basins in or near Mammoth Cave National Park. It is federally and KSNPC-listed as endangered. *Chip Clark, National Museum of Natural History*

White-haired goldenrod, a plant known only from rock houses and ledges in the Red River Gorge Geological Area, is a threatened species.[3, 6] Popular recreational activities such as hiking, rock climbing, and camping have affected populations by trampling plants. Additionally, four endemic subterranean beetles are candidates for federal listing as threatened or endangered species.[7]

Endemic species are often associated with unique or isolated habitats. The geographic isolation of species on islands, in caves, or on mountaintops, for example, is one of the primary ways in which new species evolve through a process known as speciation. For example, during the Pliocene Epoch (5.3–1.8 mya), the Green River was a tributary to the lower Ohio River and was isolated from the present-day upper Ohio River watershed, which was part of a preglacial river that flowed north into Ohio.[8] During this period of isolation, several endemic species evolved in the Green River watershed, including the Kentucky and Shawnee darters.[8, 9]

Areas such as the Cumberland Mountains in southeastern Kentucky have peaks (e.g., Black Mountain) that isolate species much like islands. These mountains support unique flora and fauna not found elsewhere in the Commonwealth. For example, the only Kentucky occurrences of filmy angelica (a plant of upper elevations in the Appalachian Mountains) and several species of land snails are found at upper elevations on Black Mountain.[10, 11] When plants and animals are isolated, such as these examples from Black Mountain, it is more likely that they will evolve into new species.

FUNGI

Fungi include mushrooms, the most familiar group, as well as puffballs, single-celled yeasts, and sac fungi such as morels. One of their roles in natural systems is to break down all kinds of materials, from living things to rocks, into forms that are more usable within ecosystems. Imagining a world where wood, fallen leaves, dead animals, and plants are not decomposed fosters a keen appreciation for fungi, one of many groups serving as ecological recyclers. Fungal action builds and binds soil together and diversifies habitat by killing trees, thereby creating canopy gaps and cavities for animal use. The presence of certain soil fungi is essential for some plants, especially many orchids, to absorb nutrients and establish seedlings. Fungi that live within plants

NEARLY ENDEMIC SPECIES

Many species are nearly endemic to Kentucky, with some populations also occurring in bordering states. For example, the Cumberland sandwort is known only within a small area of the Cumberland River watershed in Kentucky and Tennessee.

Eugene Wofford

White-haired goldenrod, a plant known only from rock shelters in the Red River Gorge of Kentucky, is federally and KSNPC-listed as threatened. *John R. MacGregor*

The Kentucky darter is endemic to the upper Green and lower Barren River systems of Kentucky. *KSNPC photograph by Ellis L. Laudermilk*

The relict darter is known only from the Bayou de Chien watershed in Graves and Hickman counties. This rare darter is federally and KSNPC-listed as endangered. *J. Brent Harrel, U.S. Fish & Wildlife Service Kentucky Field Office*

Earth stars are a type of puffball mushroom common throughout the state. The fruiting body splits into rays, allowing the puffball to open and release millions of spores when struck by a drop of rain or otherwise disturbed. *John R. MacGregor*

British soldiers is a common lichen that gets its name from its resemblance to the red uniforms worn by English soldiers during the Revolutionary War. It can be found growing on decaying wood, soil, mossy logs, tree bases, and stumps. *Allen Risk*

may bolster the plant's defenses against herbivores. Nearly all antibiotics, such as penicillin, are derived from fungi. Taxol, a compound derived from fungi found in yews, has been used in the treatment of cancer.[12] Fungi are important in the food industry for products including yeast for bread and cheese, but they also cause disease in food and humans. It is estimated that only 5% to 10% of existing fungal species are known worldwide,[13] and even fewer are understood. A comprehensive inventory of fungi in Kentucky has never been completed, so there is not even a basic list of species. Considering their contribution to stable ecosystems, this is a huge gap in understanding natural systems.

LICHENS

Lichens are also poorly documented and understood. Lichens result from a complex relationship between a fungus and an alga or bacterium. They are found on many surfaces in natural areas, from the trunks of living and dead trees to rocks. Some forms of lichens hang from tree branches, and others are pioneers of bare, nutrient-poor soils where few other organisms can survive. One of the roles lichens serve in the ecosystem is to break down the substrate, the material on which they grow, which results in the slow accumulation of material that forms soil. A particularly important characteristic to people is lichen's sensitivity to air pollution; they are the "canary in the coal mine" of air quality and are used to measure air-pollution damage, including the detection of heavy metals. Lichens also are notoriously slow-growing, with estimates for some species at less than .1 or even .01 inch per year.[14] Lea's bog lichen, the only lichen known to be endangered in the state, is found on tree trunks in bottomland forests along the Ohio River and its tributaries. One possible reason for its decline is the changes in the duration and extent of flooding resulting from dam construction.

MOSSES, LIVERWORTS, AND HORNWORTS

Bryophytes, unlike fungi, are plants and use energy and light to make food. Their life cycles, especially their reproductive cycles, are different from other plants. Also, they do not have true roots or leaves (i.e., a vascular system) that transport water and nutrients. This is an important difference from seed plants and ferns, and it is the reason why there are no tree-size mosses. These little plants contribute to ecosystem functions such as water retention, nutrient cycling, and soil stability. Like fungi and lichens, they produce compounds that have potential as antimicrobial or anticancer pharmaceuticals. Each of the three bryophyte groups—mosses, liverworts, and hornworts—has unique ways to grow and reproduce. Mosses always have little leaves along a "stem." Liverworts are unique in having shiny oil bodies in each of the cells; unlike mosses, their spore-producing structures disappear quickly. Hornworts have distinctive green "horns" that house the spores and erupt from the leaves.

A preliminary list of 317 mosses has been compiled for the state.[15] This initial number compares to more than 380 species listed for Ohio and Tennessee each. Moss species were added to the list of rare plants for Kentucky in 1996 as a first attempt at focusing conservation attention on this group. Currently, 12 mosses meet the criteria for listing as vulnerable to decline and extinction in Kentucky. Several of the listed species occur on Black Mountain and within the Bad Branch watershed in Letcher County, emphasizing the importance of these botanically rich hotspots. In addition to the loss of habitat from land-use changes, mosses are under pressure from collectors who sell them in bulk to florists for use as soil covering and filler for hanging baskets.

Less is known about liverworts in Kentucky

than about mosses—so little, in fact, that it is difficult to be certain which species are rare. As more information becomes available on the distributions, habitats, and life histories of the 114 liverwort species found in the state to date,[15] no doubt species will be identified as vulnerable to decline.

Hornworts are less diverse than mosses and liverworts, with only three species known in Kentucky. Only about 100 species are known worldwide, compared to 10,000 moss species and 6,000 liverwort species.[16]

All bryophytes complete their reproduction outside the plant. Like frogs and other amphibians, they depend on water to be available to carry sperm to eggs. For this reason, egg production often occurs during the rainy season. While capable of nearly complete dehydration, the ability of these little plants to persist at a site is affected by long-term changes in the amount of moisture in their habitat, whether on land or in streams. For instance, timber removal, soil erosion, or excessive deer browsing can reduce moisture availability. Many species are highly sensitive to water pollution and serve as indicators of environmental health. Like fungi and lichens, new information on bryophytes and their function underscores their significance to the health of ecosystems.

SEED PLANTS AND FERNS

The flora of Kentucky is a living expression of the landscape—the physical features across the state. Other influences on plant distributions range from glacial events to animal behavior to plant genetics. A recent estimate of the number of native plant species (excluding algae, mosses, and their close relatives) found in Kentucky is 2,030.[17] While this number is not high compared to other states (30th in the nation[18]), the Kentucky flora is nevertheless unique and a melding of five different regional floras. The floras of the Appalachian Mountains, Gulf Coastal

floodplain, Mississippi river floodplain, and the Great Plains, as well as a few species from northern forests, all influence the makeup of the state's flora.

The seed plants include plants that flower and the cone-bearing trees (pines, junipers, cypress, and hemlock). Some of the most familiar plants in the Kentucky flora are deciduous trees, such as sugar maple and sycamore; showy seasonal perennials, such as bloodroot, which signals the beginning of spring; and ironweed and goldenrod, reminders of

Lizard skin liverwort is relatively common throughout much of the Northern Hemisphere. It grows on damp forest floors and along shaded streams, and it produces a distinctive scent when crushed. *Allen Risk*

In Kentucky this endangered sphagnum moss occurs on seeping sandstone outcrops in the Cumberland Mountains, the southernmost extent of its northern Appalachian range. Its red hue distinguishes it from other sphagnum mosses. *Allen Risk*

Rose moss is named for the flowerlike appearance of the upper leaves; it is commonly found in shaded areas on rich soil, rocks, old logs, and tree bases. It also is found in Asia, Canada, and Europe. *Allen Risk*

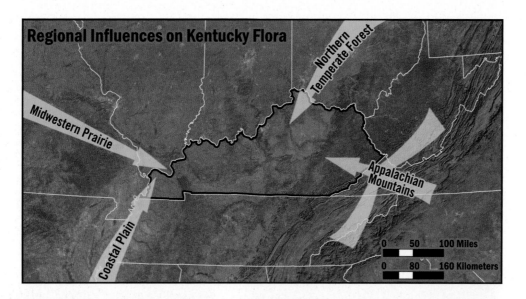

Regional Influences on Kentucky Flora

Northern Temperate Forest

Midwestern Prairie

Coastal Plain

Appalachian Mountains

0   50   100 Miles
0   80   160 Kilometers

Common milkweed is an important food plant for butterflies. Monarch butterfly caterpillars feed on the plant, and the poison in the plant passes to the butterfly, making it an undesirable meal for predators. © Barry Howard

Bloodroot is one of the earliest plants to flower in the spring, often as early as March. © Barry Howard

summer's end. Each native plant occupies an ecological niche influenced by factors including soil, light, and water availability. For instance, flowering dogwood, a plant often associated with alkaline soils, occurs in the filtered light of open forests on middle to lower slopes. Blueberries, on the other hand, require dry, thin, acidic soils commonly found on ridgetops. Pale green orchid also needs acid soils, but it occurs where groundwater flows to the surface, forming a seep, or in low, flat areas. While pale green orchid is found in habitat where moisture is predictable but temporary, yellow pond lily requires deeper, more permanent water. Plant by plant, species adapt to different conditions and sort into natural communities across the landscape.

Plants depend upon other plants and animals. They may share pollinators or depend upon one another to create floral displays to attract pollinators. Appalachian bugbane, for example, depends upon other, more showy flowering plants to attract pollinators; as these decline, so does the bugbane.[19] Plants may share nutrients or parasitize one another for them. In the competition for resources and space, plants such as walnut trees can release compounds that prevent other plants from growing around them. Plants may also create habitat for other plants, such as the tussocks (mounds) of land created in wetlands by cypress trees, which allow upland plants to live essentially above the wetland. Kentucky's flora is the sum of complex relationships between plants; but while many of the species have been cataloged, less is known about their interactions. These relationships are as important to the success of a species as their physical habitat.

Plants are categorized according to their growth form (e.g., trees, shrubs, and forbs), but in reality, some shrubs can have a tree-like form (or vice versa), and some herbs may tend to twine, looking much like vines. Despite these categorization pitfalls, the flora may be divided into plant types (see chart). The most common plant families (groups of related plants) are the same for Kentucky as for most of the nation: asters, grasses, and sedges.

There are also some surprising and unusual habits and characteristics among Kentucky's plants. Some of the oddest are the sundews; they are carnivorous. But think small. Sundews are the size of a quarter, and their animal victims are roughly the size of gnats. The unlucky victim sticks to the sundew and slowly is digested, probably providing a source of nitrogen in an otherwise nutrient-poor environment. Another surprise is that there are 41 orchid species in Kentucky. Although orchids are commonly thought of as a tropical group, they are known throughout the state in marshes, prairies, and all forest types. Kentucky orchids differ from many tropical species in that they are terrestrial rather than epiphytic (anchored in trees). Cactus, another plant associated with hot climates, is also native to Kentucky; the eastern prickly pear cactus occurs statewide. Another unusual group of plants are those that are parasitic, such as mistletoe, a familiar plant in tree canopies, and squawroot, a fleshy, cob-looking plant of the forest floor. Nearly every plant adaptation, however unusual, contributes to a species' survival and its connection with the surrounding ecosystem.

Rare plants represent many different groups among the flora, from mosses to trees. They are found throughout the state and in many different habitats; many are found in habitats that are rare themselves. The presence or concentration of rare plants (hotspots) identified in the Plant Rarity Hotspot map often correlates with habitats that are limited in Kentucky, such as rockhouses or wetland seeps. Red River Gorge, the Kentucky River Palisades, Bad Branch, Black Mountain, and the East Gulf Coastal Plain are hotspots important to rare plant conservation. Another especially important area is along the southern Kentucky border in McCreary and Whitley counties, a biogeographically unique region on the Cumberland Plateau.

Sneezeweed and mistflower, both common fall-blooming plants, in an early frost. © *Barry Howard*

Swamp rose is one of four native roses in Kentucky.
© *Barry Howard*

Flora by Select Plant Types

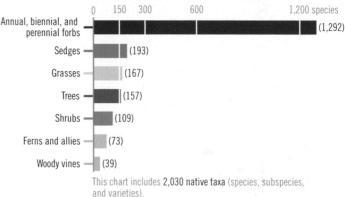

This chart includes **2,030 native taxa** (species, subspecies, and varieties).

Yellow pond-lily occurs in standing water and has adapted to this habitat by producing long stems with leaves and flowers at the water surface. *Thomas G. Barnes*

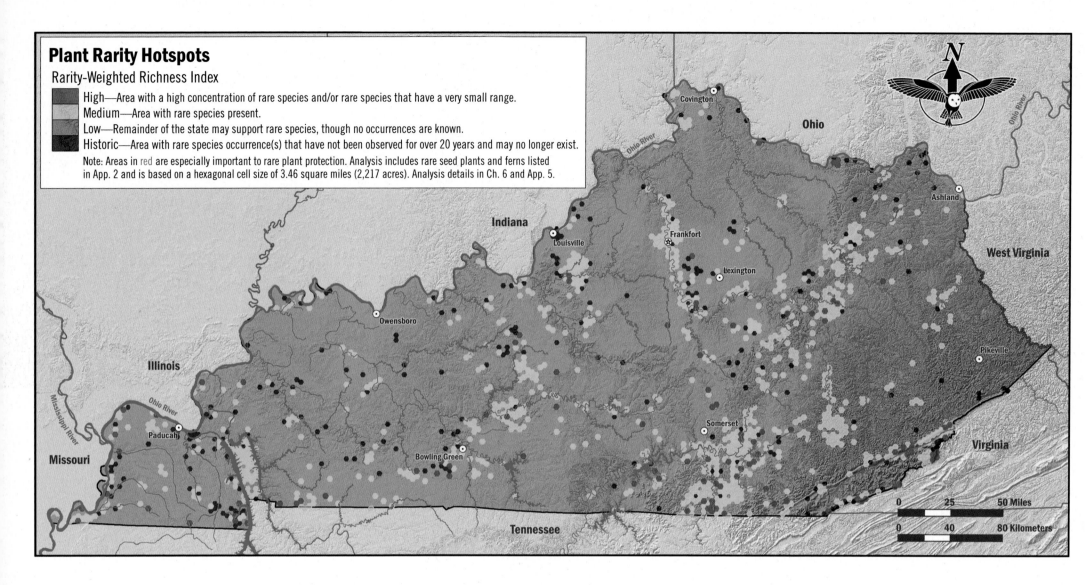

Plant Rarity Hotspots

Rarity-Weighted Richness Index

High—Area with a high concentration of rare species and/or rare species that have a very small range.

Medium—Area with rare species present.

Low—Remainder of the state may support rare species, though no occurrences are known.

Historic—Area with rare species occurrence(s) that have not been observed for over 20 years and may no longer exist.

Note: Areas in red are especially important to rare plant protection. Analysis includes rare seed plants and ferns listed in App. 2 and is based on a hexagonal cell size of 3.46 square miles (2,217 acres). Analysis details in Ch. 6 and App. 5.

Currently, 275 plants are state-listed as endangered or threatened through the Rare Plant Recognition Act.[20] Another 57 appear to be declining and are KSNPC-listed as special concerns.[11] Forty-eight plants, including eight that are federally listed, are globally rare (G1–G3) and are of the highest conservation priority.

A chain is only as strong as its weakest link; likewise, a flora is only as resilient as its most vulnerable plants. Evidence indicates that many vulnerable species continue to decline, despite conservation efforts:[11]

♦ About 725 documented occurrences of listed plants—no doubt a small portion of the actual number—are either extinct or historical (not seen in 20 years or more).

- The number of plant species that are designated historical has increased from 21 in 1993 to more than 60 in the last few years, a possible indication that native plants are disappearing from the state.

- About 30% of the KSNPC-listed plants are known from only one county, and 70% are known from five or fewer counties.

- Sixty-two listed plants do not occur on either private land that is managed for conservation or public lands.

Habitat loss is the take-home message from the decline in Kentucky's flora. Excess nutrients from fertilizers and sedimentation affect aquatic plants. Exotic pest plants can replace not only rare plants but the entire herbaceous flora. Introduced diseases have endangered trees such as American chestnut and white walnut. Plants are generally resilient enough to adapt to change, but the dramatic changes in the environment in recent decades are outpacing their abilities. Provided here are a few examples of rare plants associated with different habitat types and the kinds of habitat degradation that have led to their decline.

Eggert's sunflower requires periodic fire. Like many dry grassland and woodland species, this plant is adapted to the conditions created by burning and has responded well in sites managed with fire. Eggert's sunflower was federally listed and then subsequently removed from national listing when more populations were found in Tennessee. Eggert's sunflower remains KSNPC-listed as threatened in Kentucky because there are so few populations in the state, and woodland and glade habitat continues to decline.

Grassland habitat not only occurs under dry conditions; fire also creates natural grassy openings in mesic and wet areas. Wood lily is associated with open grassy forests, from dry to very moist sites. The grassy groundcover in these habitats disappears

if natural disturbance cycles, such as periodic fire, are disrupted. When this habitat declines, wood lily may be relegated to forested edges, the only remaining habitat with sufficient light for this species.

Some openings are maintained by fire, but others are a result of soil and geologic conditions. Fameflower, a beautiful little plant that is best seen by lying belly to the ground, is adapted to small pockets of soil on expanses of flat rock outcrops, a type of glade. Its succulent leaves and threadlike flowering stem conserve water in this harsh environment. Numerous other rare plants have adapted to geologic features like rockhouses and clifflines. These habitats are detrimentally affected by erosion and excessive use. All-terrain vehicles, for instance, can cause severe damage to the thin soils in glades, in particular; once the habitat is altered, weedy plants become dominant, and the native flora declines.

Kentucky lady's-slipper orchid is typically found in floodplains where alteration of surface or under-

left to right:

Limestone fameflower blooms at about four o'clock in the afternoon. *Thomas G. Barnes*

Wood lily has declined as a result of habitat loss and may also be overcollected by plant enthusiasts and sellers. *Julian Campbell*

Southern maidenhair fern, one of 80 species of fern in Kentucky, is found in limestone seeps. *Thomas G. Barnes*

left to right:
Price's potato bean is one of eight federally listed plants in Kentucky. It has a large underground tuber that may have been used as food by pioneers and Native Americans. Habitat loss in recent centuries has led to its rare status, perhaps along with collection of this tuber. *Brainard Palmer-Ball Jr.*

Many sedges are small and inconspicuous, but Fraser's sedge is an exception. It has strap-like leaves and conspicuous fuzzy heads (the flower cluster). It is one of 36 sedges on Kentucky's rare plant list. *Thomas G. Barnes*

ground water availability is likely to result in its decline. It stands out even in these lush, moist places because its flowers are as large as a fist. Like most floodplain and wetland plants, this orchid is sensitive to changes in hydrology that can result from clearing of trees, increased surface runoff from paving or construction, or water channelization.

INVERTEBRATES

Invertebrates are animals without backbones and include such familiar groups as insects, mussels, snails, and spiders. More than 70% of all known species in the world and approximately 99% of all known animals are invertebrates.[21–23] Simply stated, Earth's biological diversity is dominated by invertebrates, especially insects, and life here would drastically change without their enormous contributions. Invertebrates play extremely important roles in fundamental processes such as decomposition, soil production, pest control, and pollination. They are an important food source for many animals and even for a few plants, such as the sundews.

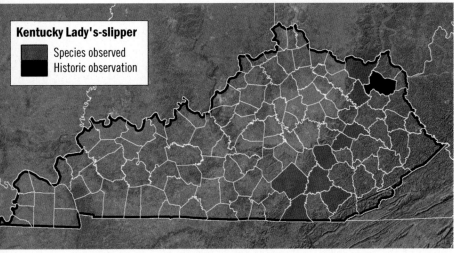

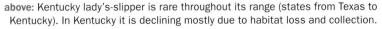

Kentucky Lady's-slipper
■ Species observed
■ Historic observation

above: Kentucky lady's-slipper is rare throughout its range (states from Texas to Kentucky). In Kentucky it is declining mostly due to habitat loss and collection.

right: Kentucky lady's-slipper has large flowers, with the larger ones as big as baseballs. The plant has a complex pollination mechanism to attract bees and other pollinators down into the flower's pouch or "slipper," where it deposits pollen on them. *Thomas G. Barnes*

Hoary puccoon flowers are a favorite nectar choice of the Olympia marble butterfly. Adults fly only in spring, usually the last three weeks of April. *KSNPC photograph by Ellis L. Laudermilk*

Mollusks

Approximately 24,000 terrestrial mollusk species have been described in the world, but an estimated 11,000 to 40,000 additional species may exist.[27] Furthermore, approximately 7,000 freshwater mollusk species are known, with an estimated 3,000 to 10,000 species still unknown.[27] Unfortunately, mollusks also have the highest number of documented extinctions for any major group of animals in the world and in Kentucky (see Extirpated and Extinct Species section).[27]

Terrestrial Snails and Slugs

Approximately 1,000 land snails and slugs are known from North America, and about 210 species of native land snails and slugs have been reported from Kentucky.[11, 28] Two primary conditions are responsible for this diversity. First, the Appalachian Mountains, including the Appalachian Highlands Physiographic Province of eastern Kentucky, are very old. Their age has allowed plenty of time for land snails, and other groups such as salamanders, to diversify in rich mesic forests. Consequently, the Appalachian region is the North American center of land snail diversity.[29] Second, much of the state is underlain with limestone.[30] Snails use calcium carbonate from limestone for construction and maintenance of their shells, so an abundant supply contributes to a diverse fauna.

Most terrestrial snails can be identified by the color, size, and shape of their shells. Some species also have one or more toothlike structures within the shell's aperture (the opening of the shell used by the snail) that helps distinguish species. Kentucky's smallest snails, the pupillids, are longer than they are wide and are spiral-shaped, with a total length as short as one-sixteenth of an inch.[31] The queen crater, Kentucky's largest land snail, is broader than it is long and is more than an inch and a half in diameter.[31] Slugs, on the other hand, lack shells, but they may be identified by color patterns or internal characteristics.

Nearly 400 mollusk species, such as this kidneyshell, are known from Kentucky. *Guenter A. Schuster*

Shells of the glassy grapeskin snail are thin, as demonstrated by the obvious crack in this individual's shell. In Kentucky, this threatened species is found only on Pine and Black mountains. *KSNPC photograph by Ellis L. Laudermilk*

The queen crater's shell may exceed 1.5 inches in diameter, making it Kentucky's largest land snail. This rare mollusk is found in only McCreary and Wayne counties. *KSNPC photograph by Ellis L. Laudermilk*

INVERTEBRATE FACTS

- An estimated 99% of all human and animal waste is probably decomposed by invertebrates.[24]
- Ground-dwelling invertebrates, such as earthworms and ants, produce an estimated $5 billion worth of topsoil in the United States each year ($25 billion worth of topsoil worldwide) in addition to aerating the soil and recycling nutrients.[25]
- According to the Xerces Society, insects pollinate 75% of crop plant species, providing humans with about one out of every four mouthfuls of food and drink consumed.
- Insect-pollinated crops in the United States exceed $9 billion in value annually, and insect products, such as honey and wax, contribute millions more.[26]

Unlike the glassy grapeskin, the rare striped whitelip occurs only at some of the lowest elevations in the state along the Ohio and Mississippi rivers. *KSNPC photograph by Ellis L. Laudermilk*

Physid snails, a type of pulmonate, can trap air in their shells for breathing instead of using gills, enabling them to escape aquatic predators and find food outside of water. *KSNPC photograph by Ryan Evans*

Armored rocksnails are found on rocky shoals of large rivers, such as the Ohio and Tennessee, in Kentucky. *KSNPC photograph by Ellis L. Laudermilk*

KSNPC considers 17 terrestrial snails rare in the state; two of these are found only in subterranean habitats. The Kentucky range of one KSNPC-listed threatened species, the glassy grapeskin, is limited to Pine and Black mountains, among the highest elevations in the state. Some rare snails prefer high elevations, while others are found only at the lowest. For example, the striped whitelip, also KSNPC-listed threatened, lives in bottomland hardwood forests and swamps along the floodplains of Kentucky's largest rivers, the Ohio and Mississippi. These habitats are disappearing at an alarming rate as the forests are cleared and swamps drained, primarily for agricultural purposes, and the striped whitelip is disappearing as well. Most land snails and slugs prefer moist environments, but a few species, such as the increasingly rare whitewashed rabdotus, surprisingly prefer the xeric (very dry) habitats of glades or prairies.

Freshwater Snails

Freshwater snails are a rich, unique, and often-overlooked part of our native aquatic fauna. They are found in habitats ranging from small springs to big rivers as well as lakes and reservoirs. North America is home to approximately 679 species, and the southeastern United States has more species than any other region.[32, 33] This group has received little attention from scientists, and a definitive species list for Kentucky is lacking. Approximately 67 species inhabit Kentucky,[34, 35] which ranks about 12th nationally.[36]

Two major groups of freshwater snails are found in the state: gill-breathing and lung-breathing. Gill-breathing, or operculate, snails have the greatest number of species and are some of the rarest. Gill-breathing snails extract oxygen from the water to respire. They require higher water quality and oxygen levels than lung-breathing snails, which may limit their distribution.

Lung-breathing, or pulmonate, snails are generally better adapted to a wide range of conditions. Some species are able to withstand periods of drying or low water due to their ability to breathe air. Individual snails also possess both male and female sexual organs (hermaphroditism), which allows for greater reproductive success and a broader geographic distribution than species with gills.

Snails are important grazers in aquatic ecosystems. They typically feed on algae, diatoms, and

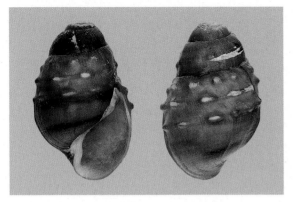

bacteria found on various hard and soft substrates. Snails use a rasping mouthpart called a *radula* to scrape and graze food from these surfaces. Interestingly, some species have adapted ways to filter food from water that are similar to those used by freshwater mussels. In high densities, gill-breathing snails play an important role in energy cycling in streams.[37] When dense colonies of these snails graze on rocky and woody substrates, they help stimulate the production of carbon, which in turn can be taken up by other organisms downstream.

Freshwater snails are also an important food source for birds, crayfishes, turtles, and other animals. Fishes, such as sturgeon, freshwater drum, and some sunfishes, have molar-like mouthparts that allow them to feed on snails by crushing their shells.

A lack of overall knowledge about the diversity and distribution of freshwater snails has led to very little protection for the group in general; only three species are federally listed as endangered in the southeastern United States, and none of these occur in Kentucky. Currently, 10 species are KSNPC-listed as special concerns, with several others under review. Kentucky is home to the majority of all known occurrences of one of these species, the shaggy cavesnail. It is known only from the upper Green, Barren, and Rough river watersheds

of Kentucky and the Blue River system of Indiana. The shaggy cavesnail is restricted to springs or cave streams.[35]

Freshwater Mussels

The United States is the world's center of freshwater mussel species richness, with about 300 species.[32, 38] Most species are from the southeastern United States, where only Alabama, Tennessee, and Georgia supported more than the 103 species historically found in Kentucky. Kentucky mussels are members of two faunal groups: the Mississippian, whose species are distributed throughout the Mississippi River basin (including the Ohio River), and the Cumberlandian, with species restricted to most of the Cumberland and Tennessee River drainages.[39, 40]

Most mussel species occupy a variety of habitats, ranging from big rivers, such as the Ohio and Mississippi, to upland streams, such as the Rockcastle and South Fork Kentucky rivers.[39, 41] Other species are restricted to lowland streams and wetlands (e.g., pondmussel and Texas lilliput), big rivers (fat pocketbook and white wartyback), or small streams (slippershell and Cumberland papershell).

Mussel species richness varies among watersheds and is determined by watershed area, geologic history, habitat diversity, fish species richness,

left to right:
The varicose rocksnail is a large river species found in the lower Tennessee and middle to lower sections of the Ohio River in Kentucky. *KSNPC photograph by Ellis L. Laudermilk*

Found only in the lower Ohio and Mississippi rivers and their lowland tributaries in western Kentucky, the bleufer is KSNPC-listed as endangered. *KSNPC photograph by Ronald R. Cicerello*

Once occurring nearly statewide, the purple lilliput is now KSNPC-listed as endangered. Only three populations in the Green and upper Cumberland river watersheds remain. *KSNPC photograph by Ronald R. Cicerello*

The plain pocketbook is a common inhabitant statewide, from small streams to large rivers. This individual is anchored to the bottom with its muscular foot. It uses siphons (upper right edge of shell) to imbibe water, which contains oxygen and food, and to release waste products. *KSNPC photograph by Ronald R. Cicerello*

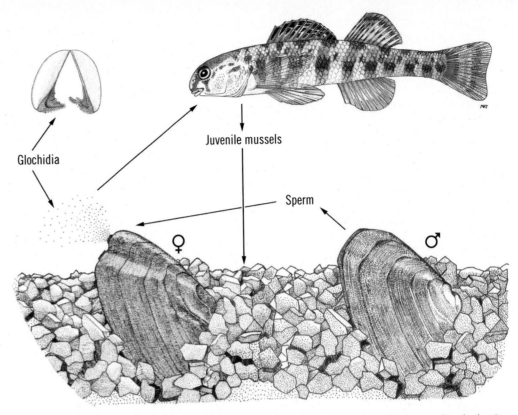

Generalized life cycle of freshwater mussels, as exemplified by the littlewing pearlymussel and a host fish, the emerald darter. Following the fertilization of eggs within the female, parasitic larval mussels called glochidia develop. The glochidia are released into the water, attach to a host fish, and encyst. The glochidia transform into juvenile mussels after a few weeks, drop from the fish, and fall to the bottom. *Courtesy of Matthew R. Thomas*

and other factors.[39, 42, 43] The Cumberland, Ohio, and Green river watersheds support the most diverse faunas, with 88, 79, and 73 species, respectively. Only 10 mussel species are known from the watershed above Cumberland Falls, a 60-foot-high barrier to the upstream movement of aquatic organisms. Most mussels are distributed nearly statewide, but about 30, mainly Cumberlandian species, inhabit three or fewer watersheds. Only the Kentucky creekshell found in the Green River drainage is endemic to the state.

Freshwater mussels range in length from one to 10 inches and live partially or completely buried in gravel, sand, or mud bottoms of streams, wetlands, and lakes.[40] They live between paired shells (valves),

often beautifully decorated and colored. Anchored to the bottom with a muscular foot, mussels move little or not at all and feed by filtering organic debris and microscopic plants and animals from the water.

Mussel reproduction is highly complex and unusual.[41] In most species the sexes are separate, but a few species are hermaphroditic. In either case, fertilization occurs when sperm filtered from the water is united with eggs in the female's gills. The resulting microscopic larvae, called *glochidia*, must parasitize a host, typically a fish, to continue the life cycle. The glochidia of some mussel species parasitize many fish species, but others use only one or a limited number of species as hosts. Mussels employ a range of strategies to infect a host. Some produce

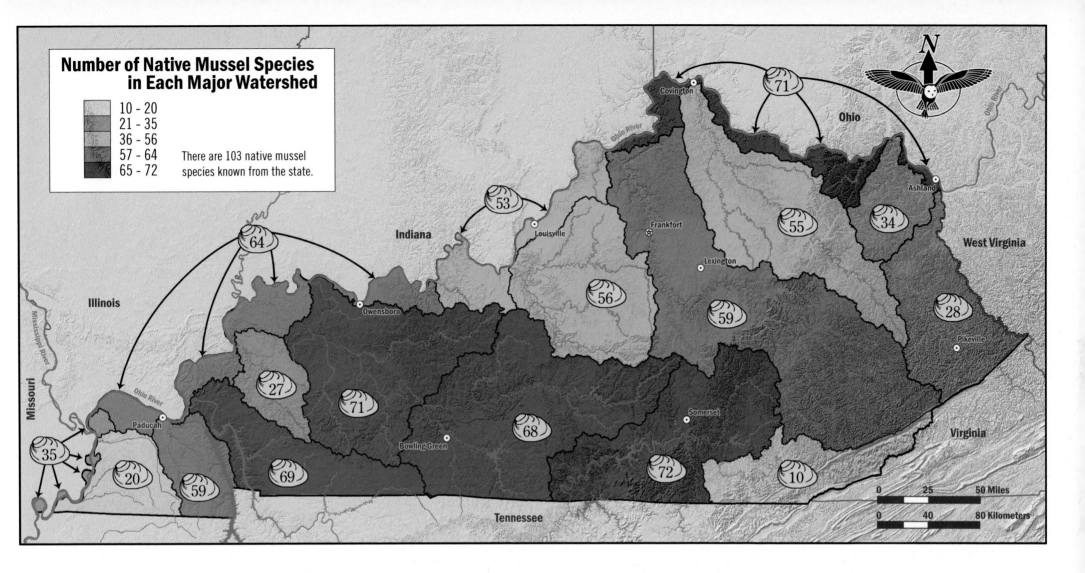

Number of Native Mussel Species in Each Major Watershed

Legend:
- 10 – 20
- 21 – 35
- 36 – 56
- 57 – 64
- 65 – 72

There are 103 native mussel species known from the state.

and broadcast millions of glochidia and gamble that they will encounter the host. Others produce packets of glochidia, called *conglutinates*, that resemble fishes or other animals and are ejected from the mussel in the presence of potential hosts. Still others have "lures" that look like worms, insects, or fishes. Hosts attracted to the lures are parasitized when they approach or attempt to eat the lure. Over several weeks the glochidia develop into juvenile mussels that drop from the host and continue the life cycle if their home in the stream or lake bottom is suitable and if they can avoid predators.

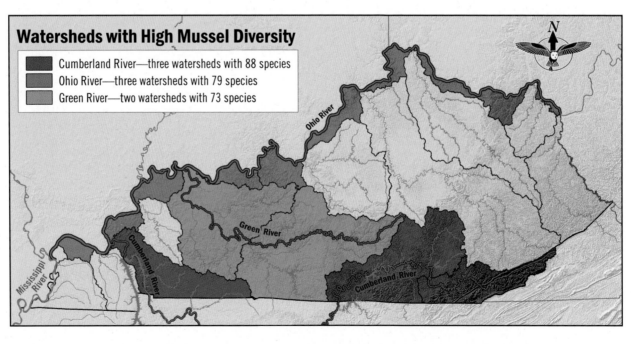

Watersheds with High Mussel Diversity

- Cumberland River—three watersheds with 88 species
- Ohio River—three watersheds with 79 species
- Green River—two watersheds with 73 species

Kentucky's rich mussel diversity has declined significantly in the last 200 years.[39, 41] Freshwater mussels are one of the most endangered groups of organisms in the United States and Kentucky.[27, 44] Habitat alteration and destruction from stream channeliza-

The Cumberland elktoe is a federally and KSNPC-listed endangered species endemic to the upper Cumberland River watershed of Kentucky and Tennessee. Only five populations are known in Kentucky, all from small tributaries. *KSNPC photograph by Ronald R. Cicerello*

tion and impoundment, pollution, wetland drainage, declines in host fish species, and other factors have all contributed to their decline. Twenty-one species (20% of all Kentucky mussel species) have been extirpated (lost from the state) or are extinct.[3, 7, 11] Of the remaining 82 species, 34 (41%) are considered rare by KSNPC, and 18 of these are federally listed or are candidates for listing. Even species that remain relatively common have experienced major reductions in the number or extent of drainages they inhabit. Activities that increase silt and sediment or change flow in streams can adversely affect mussels. Silt and sediment can degrade or smother habitat. Altering flow by impounding streams can eliminate mussels or host fishes that require flowing water. Members of the mussel genus *Epioblasma* typically inhabited gravel and sand riffles in medium to large rivers, but much of this habitat has been lost to impoundment in Kentucky, and 13 of 19 *Epioblasma* species are extinct or have been extirpated from the state. Without concerted efforts to conserve mussels, fishes, and their habitats, more mussel species will become imperiled or lost.

Arachnids

Resembling insects, spiders are actually arachnids, a diverse group that also includes scorpions, pseudoscorpions, whip scorpions, ticks, chiggers, mites, and daddy longlegs, among others. Of the approximately 39,000 spider taxa known in the world,[45] more than 3,800 are found in North America.[46] Most of Kentucky's arachnid fauna is very poorly known, because the state has never had a comprehensive inventory of the group. In fact, the number of spider species in the state is unknown; however, based on the spider fauna of other states (e.g., Alabama, Connecticut, and Illinois), Kentucky probably has more than 500 species.[47-49]

Only three spider species found in Kentucky—the brown recluse, northern black widow, and southern black widow—have especially potent venom that

The six-spotted fishing spider is adept at walking on water or diving below the surface in search of prey. This efficient predator feeds on small fishes, insects, or other invertebrates that share its habitat. © *Barry Howard*

may be dangerous to humans, but all are very shy and not inclined to bite. Despite their notoriety, bites that cause major health problems or death are rare even though many people live in very close proximity to brown recluse and black widow spiders. Learning to identify these spiders and avoiding contact with them is the key to preventing bites.

The adult brown recluse may be identified by its uniform yellowish-brown color with no stripes or patterns on the legs or abdomen, six pairs of eyes in three groups, and a dark brown violin- or fiddle-shaped pattern on the top of the cephalothorax (fused head and thorax, where the legs attach).[50] The neck of the violin points towards the spider's abdomen. Brown recluse spiders are typically found in dark, undisturbed sites indoors, such as basements, cellars, closets, or garages, and outdoors under logs, rock piles, or lumber. Depending on the amount of venom and sensitivity of the individual, venom from the brown recluse may destroy tissue surrounding the bite. A very serious wound may develop and range in size from an adult's thumbnail to the size of a hand. The wound could take six to eight weeks to heal; for some people, full recovery can take months, and scarring can occur.[51]

Black widow spiders are some of the most notorious and feared spiders of all, but their reputation is largely unfounded. While it is true that black widows possess dangerous venom, their first instinct is to flee rather than attack when disturbed by humans. They often are found under rocks or logs or inside holes of dirt embankments, but they also may be encountered in garages, barns, or other outbuildings. The adult northern and southern black widows are very similar in appearance and were considered a single species for many years. The southern black widow female may be identified by a red hourglass-shaped pattern, which is usually fully developed, on the underside of the abdomen. The rear half of the hourglass is generally a rounded rectangle or anvil shape rather than a true triangle.

Typically, the top middle of the abdomen also has a row of red spots. In the northern black widow female, the red hourglass is usually not joined in the middle but is present in two parts. In addition to the row of red spots, this species also has diagonal white stripes on top of the abdomen. Males of both species are much smaller than the female and usually have more red and white markings. The females of some black widow species occasionally kill and eat the males after mating, but this is not a common practice, contrary to popular belief. If the female is well fed, males usually escape to mate again.[50]

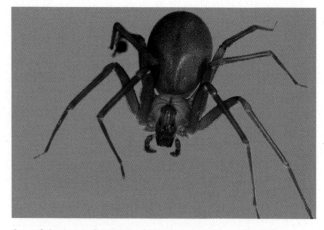

One of the most distinguishing characteristics of the brown recluse is the dark brown violin-shaped pattern on its cephalothorax. Brown recluse venom is potentially dangerous, but as its common name implies, this spider prefers seclusion and rarely bites humans unless it is harassed. *Ric Bessin, University of Kentucky*

The southern black widow is one of the most feared spiders in North America. In reality, this timid and reclusive species uses its potent venom to subdue small prey and is not aggressive towards humans if left undisturbed. *KSNPC photograph by Ellis L. Laudermilk*

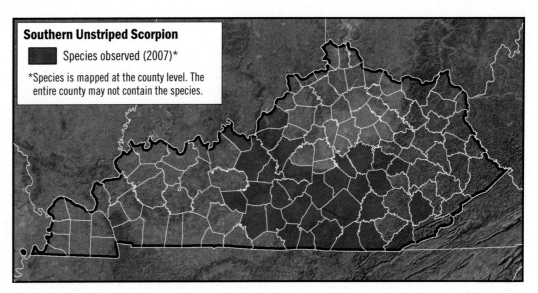

Southern Unstriped Scorpion

　　Species observed (2007)*

*Species is mapped at the county level. The entire county may not contain the species.

The southern unstriped scorpion is widely distributed in eastern Kentucky, but it also occurs as far west as Edmonson County. This native species is the only scorpion known from Kentucky. *KSNPC photograph by Ellis L. Laudermilk*

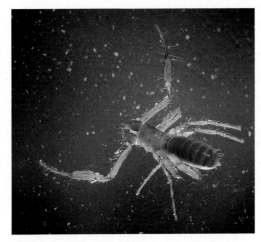

All of Kentucky's rare subterranean pseudoscorpions resemble this *Kleptochthonius* sp. These "false scorpions" look like tiny or baby scorpions without stingers. *Julian J. Lewis*

Nearly 1,300 scorpion species are known in the world, with about 83 species known from North America.[52] Only one species, the southern unstriped scorpion, is found in the state. While most Kentuckians have never encountered this shy and reclusive native scorpion, it has been confirmed in 32 (27%) Kentucky counties.[53, 54] Typically found in association with decaying pine logs, it may also be found under rocks or inside buildings, including houses.[53] The southern unstriped scorpion's sting generally is considered slightly less painful than a paper wasp's sting.[54]

Twelve arachnid taxa known from Kentucky are considered rare by KSNPC.[11] All are found exclusively in subterranean habitats, and seven of the 12 are pseudoscorpions. Resembling scorpions without a tail or stinger, pseudoscorpions are extremely small, generally one-sixteenth to one-eighth of an inch long; they are flat-bodied and have a short, usually oval-shaped abdomen. They also have a pair of pincerlike claws that project forward from the body. Pseudoscorpions normally are found where moisture is present, and some species are particularly beneficial to humans because they prey on booklice,

the larvae of clothes moths and carpet beetles, and other pests found in the home. They are also one of the top predators in leaf litter and soil.

Crustaceans
The most well-known crustaceans in the state are the crayfishes; however, Kentucky has more than 40 noncrayfish crustacean species that are typically very small and not easily observed.[4, 11, 55-60] Fairy shrimps, amphipods, fish lice, water fleas, copepods, isopods, and seed shrimp often are overlooked, but they are important elements of the state's native biodiversity. New crustacean species are being discovered in the state, illustrating there is much to learn about the diversity and distribution of these poorly understood animals.

Crustaceans provide an abundant food source for other animals in the food chain. While the state has several taxa restricted to cave environments, noncrayfish crustaceans may be found in a variety of aquatic environments, such as wetlands, streams, lakes, and temporary water bodies, some of which completely dry out. Their ability to survive in environments that periodically dry out is

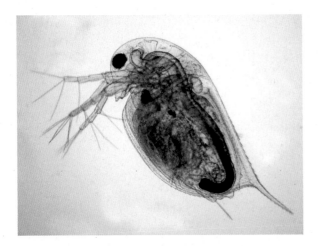
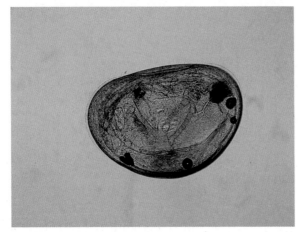
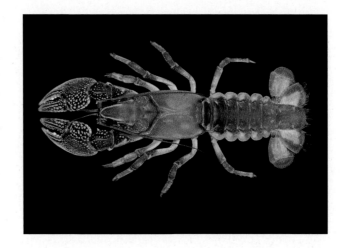

due in part to eggs that are able to withstand desiccation and freezing, and to the ability to burrow into moist sediments (e.g., isopods) until more favorable conditions return. Fairy and clam shrimps are often only found in temporary pools or ponds devoid of fish, but they are prey for aquatic beetles and amphibians.

These crustaceans mostly share similar reproductive patterns for survival. They tend to produce a large number of young hatched from eggs that are brooded by females in external egg pouches or within the adult (e.g., seed shrimp). Alternatively, some of these small crustaceans, such as water fleas, can reproduce asexually by cloning themselves (a process called *parthenogenesis*). While many species typically filter-feed (taking algae, bacteria, and smaller zooplankton with specially designed mouth parts), some copepods prey on small fly larvae and even larval fish.

Isopods and amphipods are typically associated with more permanent waters such as springs, sloughs, ponds, seeps, and rivers. Upstream colonization is difficult due to their limited mobility.

Some of the state's noncrayfish species are *commensal* (deriving resources from another species yet causing no apparent harm). Several seed shrimp species, for example, require a crayfish as a host but cause them little or no harm. They use crayfishes to reproduce, rear young, and disperse, because they are only capable of swimming short distances. On the other hand, fish lice are typical parasites, burrowing into the gills or flesh of certain fishes.

Crayfishes

There are 363 native crayfish species known from North America.[61] Kentucky is home to 54 species of crayfishes, all belonging to a single family (Cambaridae).[62] Species in two genera (*Cambarus* and *Orconectes*) make up 87% of the crayfishes in the state. Kentucky is fifth nationally—behind Alabama (85 species), Tennessee (80), Georgia (72), and Mississippi (64)—in the total number of species by state and supports about 10% of the world's total.[61, 62]

There are several important reasons for the high number of species in Kentucky. First, the southern Appalachians are believed to be the center of evolution for both *Cambarus* and *Orconectes* species. Secondly, from east to west there is a complete change of species composition in Kentucky—from the mountains to the Mississippi River floodplain—which is indicative of the changes in geology, physiography, and natural regions. The most important

left to right:
A water flea is a common type of cladoceran. Microscopic cladocerans are an important part of many food chains. *Howard Webb*

Ostracods or seed shrimps are microscopic animals found in a variety of aquatic habitats, including cave waterbodies, lakes, and reservoirs, as well as permanent and temporary wetlands. Like cladocerans, ostracods serve an important link in food webs. *Howard Webb*

Crayfishes sometimes have common names as colorful as their bodies, like this paintedhand mudbug known from Louisville to the Land Between the Lakes. *Guenter A. Schuster*

At least five color forms of the upland burrowing crayfish are known, including this spectacular version. *Guenter A. Schuster*

watersheds for crayfish diversity in the state are the Cumberland (29 species), Green (26), Ohio (26), and Kentucky (17).

The life cycle of crayfishes consists of an annual pattern during which adult males change from reproductively active forms during the fall, winter, and spring to reproductively inactive forms during the summer. Generally, females begin copulating in early fall and continue through the spring, depositing their eggs onto their swimmerets under their abdomens from early spring to midsummer. Once the eggs are deposited on the swimmerets, they develop and hatch in approximately three weeks. After they hatch, the young stay attached to the female through two or three molts (approximately one to three weeks). Most crayfishes probably live three to five years.

Crayfishes can be classified into several groups based on their habitats. In general, crayfishes are classified as living either underground (in caves or burrows) or in surface waters. Those living in surface waters can be further categorized as inhabiting *lentic* (still water) environments, such as lakes, or *lotic* (moving water) environments, such as streams.

Some crayfishes may live in either habitat. Most (72%) Kentucky crayfishes can be classified as living in lotic environments. Three species live in Kentucky caves, while three other species are restricted to lentic environments such as sloughs, swamps, and marshes. All crayfishes have the capacity to burrow, but nine species spend most of their time in burrows. The latter species may be placed into two broad categories: primary burrowers and secondary burrowers. The primary burrowers rarely leave the burrow, and then only to forage on the land and to look for mates. The secondary burrowers routinely leave burrows to forage in nearby waters.

No Kentucky crayfish species are federally listed; however, a recent conservation assessment of North American crayfishes indicated that 11 (20%) of Kentucky's species are globally rare and in need of protection.[61] Furthermore, KSNPC lists 18 species (33% of fauna) as globally or state rare (Appendix 2). Of these, all three cave species are included, and the remaining 15 species share one or more of the following characteristics: endemism, restricted range, or unique habitat requirements.

Preservation of water quality and habitat are

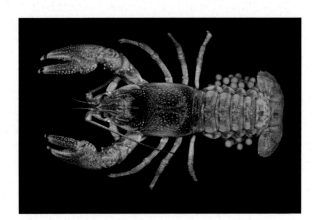

A female Kentucky River crayfish carries a bundle of eggs under her abdomen, a condition known as "in berry." This species is primarily found in the upper Cumberland, Kentucky, and Salt river watersheds. *Guenter A. Schuster*

The beautifully colored valley flame crayfish is a primary burrower. Their burrows are located in fields, usually where the water table is close to the surface, across southeastern and central Kentucky. *Guenter A. Schuster*

Lacking eyes and pigment, this rare ghost crayfish lives only in cave streams along a narrow band of counties from Green and Hart northwest to Breckinridge and Meade. *Guenter A. Schuster*

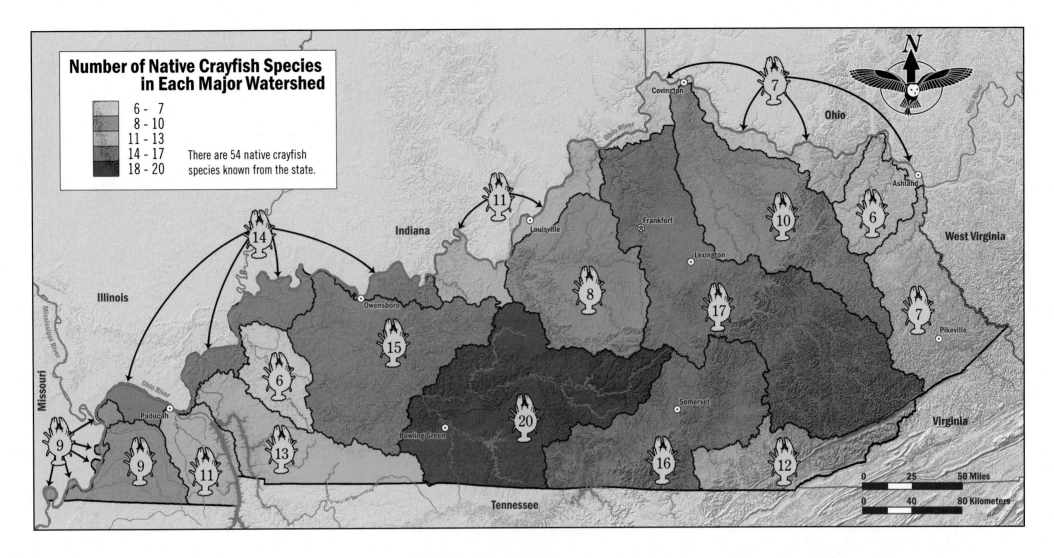

Number of Native Crayfish Species in Each Major Watershed

6 - 7
8 - 10
11 - 13
14 - 17
18 - 20

There are 54 native crayfish species known from the state.

important to the protection of native crayfishes. The main problems in crayfish conservation fall under the large umbrella of habitat degradation and loss and the introduction of non-native crayfishes. In Kentucky, the primary culprits appear to be reduced water quality and habitat alteration. Reduction of water quality is caused by urbanization and increased siltation from poor mining, logging, and agricultural practices. Habitat alteration is often the result of channelization and loss of wetlands, especially in western Kentucky.

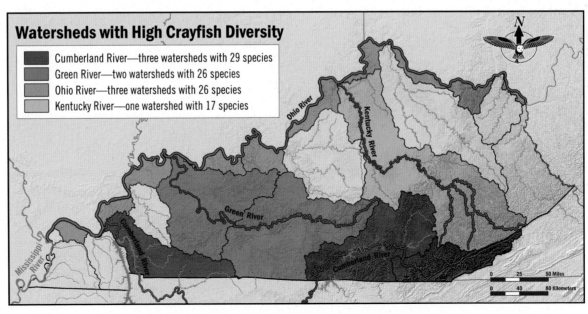

Watersheds with High Crayfish Diversity

Cumberland River—three watersheds with 29 species
Green River—two watersheds with 26 species
Ohio River—three watersheds with 26 species
Kentucky River—one watershed with 17 species

The regal moth is common in Kentucky. More than 2,300 moth species, including exotics, have already been documented in the state, but species previously unrecorded are found every year. *KSNPC photograph by Ellis L. Laudermilk*

This bumblebee mimic isn't even a bee; it's a robber fly, an efficient predator and member of the insect order Diptera or "true flies." *KSNPC photograph by Ellis L. Laudermilk*

Insect Species

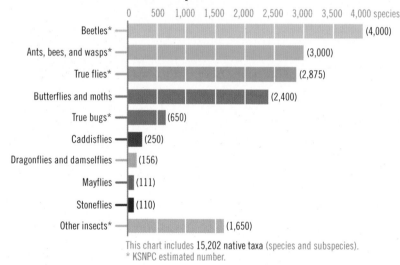

Beetles*	(4,000)
Ants, bees, and wasps*	(3,000)
True flies*	(2,875)
Butterflies and moths	(2,400)
True bugs*	(650)
Caddisflies	(250)
Dragonflies and damselflies	(156)
Mayflies	(111)
Stoneflies	(110)
Other insects*	(1,650)

This chart includes **15,202 native taxa** (species and subspecies).
* KSNPC estimated number.

Three very similar species make up Brood XIV of the 17-year periodical cicada. Adults of all three emerged during 2008, but this brood will not be seen again until 2025. *Sabrina Christian*

Insects

Documenting insect diversity is no easy task, for several reasons. First, the sheer number of species is overwhelming. Second, insects are often small, inconspicuous, and difficult to find. Third, a relatively small number of biologists study insects, compared to other major groups. Fourth, insects' life cycles may include stages (e.g., larvae and pupae) that are difficult to distinguish from closely related species or that are very brief (some adult insects live only one day). Finally, insects may live underground or in other places (e.g., tree canopies, rock piles) that are not easily accessible to humans. For example, nymphs of the 17-year periodical cicada live underground for most of their life cycle, and the adults make an appearance for only a few weeks—once every 17 years! In spite of these impediments, several important facts regarding insect diversity are known.

Insects are the most species-rich group of organisms on the planet, with more than 900,000 known species worldwide.[26] In fact, more than 60% of all known species are insects.[26] Furthermore, an estimated five to 10 million species may be undiscovered.[26] Thirty-one orders representing nearly 90,000 insect species are known in North America north of Mexico.[63] The number of insect species in Kentucky is unknown due to a lack of or inadequate surveys for many groups; however, KSNPC estimates that more than 15,000 species live in the state, based on extrapolations from Kentucky's more well-known insect groups, such as mayflies, dragonflies and damselflies, stoneflies, caddisflies, tiger beetles, and butterflies and moths.

The four insect groups (orders) with the largest number of known species in the world, in order from greatest to least, are the beetles (order Coleoptera); butterflies, skippers, and moths (Lepidoptera); bees, wasps, and ants (Hymenoptera); and flies (Diptera) (see Number of Species by Select Groups schematic in chapter 1). Except for the

Lepidoptera, relatively little is known about these insects in Kentucky; however, KSNPC estimates that these four orders account for more than 80% of Kentucky's insect fauna. Beetles are probably the most diverse, with more than 4,000 species possible in Kentucky. Through millennia, beetles have evolved to take advantage of many niches in the natural world, which partly explains their tremendous diversity. Terrestrial, aquatic, and subterranean habitats are all well represented, and 54 (53%) of Kentucky's 102 endemic taxa are subterranean beetles (see Endemic Species section).[11]

Many insects are primarily found in terrestrial environments, but aquatic habitats such as temporary pools, natural lakes, wetlands, seeps, creeks, and rivers are also vital to a number of insect species. Some species reproduce only in streams, while others prefer stationary water such as marshes and swamps. Thirteen of North America's 31 insect orders have members that are at least semiaquatic, and several orders are predominantly aquatic (e.g., mayflies, stoneflies, dragonflies and damselflies, and caddisflies).[64] The life cycle of a typical aquatic insect begins when adult females lay eggs in or near the water. After hatching, larvae live in the water for a few days to several years, depending on the species and climate, before changing into an adult. Adults of most orders (e.g., dragonflies, stoneflies, and caddisflies) continue their life cycle in a terrestrial setting, while adults of others, such as aquatic beetles, continue life in the water. Adults in some groups, such as mayflies, do not feed but simply mate, lay eggs, and die. In other groups, such as dragonflies and damselflies, adults may live for several weeks, foraging, mating, and even migrating (e.g., the common green darner). Aquatic insects are an important component of food webs in both aquatic (larvae) and terrestrial (adult) ecosystems.

The United States is one of the most diverse regions in the world for many aquatic insect orders such as caddisflies, mayflies, and stoneflies. In fact,

The northern barrens tiger beetle is among 21 tiger beetle taxa found in Kentucky. Unfortunately, this iridescent beauty is uncommon in the state. *KSNPC photograph by Ellis L. Laudermilk*

the United States supports approximately 13% of the world's known caddisfly fauna, about 30% of its mayflies, and about 40% of its known stoneflies.[23] More inventories are needed, but to date approximately 250 caddisfly species,[65-67] 111 mayfly species,[68] and 110 stonefly species[69] have been recorded in Kentucky. These three groups of insects are also the most sensitive to water pollution. In general, the number of species and the abundance within each species decline as water quality declines. Documenting the presence or absence of species and determining their abundance and distribution within watersheds are excellent ways to assess water quality in streams.

Dragonflies and damselflies (Odonata) are probably the best known of Kentucky's aquatic insects. These acrobatic, aerial predators were among the first insect groups to appear on Earth, about 300 million years ago.[70] At least 156 species have been reported from the state, which represents about 30% of the North American total.[71,72] Some species (e.g., most clubtails) reproduce exclusively in streams, while others, such as the skimmers and pond damsels, complete their life cycle in lakes, ponds, or

Aquatic insect larvae, such as this caddisfly (top), stonefly (middle), and mayfly (bottom), are excellent indicators of stream health and are important components of food webs in aquatic ecosystems. *Guenter A. Schuster*

A dew-covered eastern pondhawk roosts beside a Franklin County wetland. Streams and wetlands are important habitats for these beneficial insects. *Ellis L. Laudermilk*

The brilliantly colored Baltimore checkerspot is found in wetland and seep habitats where turtlehead, its larval food plant, grows. *KSNPC photograph by Ellis L. Laudermilk*

Larvae of the caddisfly genus *Pycnopsyche* use twigs, leaf discs, or other plant materials to build a "case" in which they live. Look closely at the right side of the case to see the caddisfly's head. *Guenter A. Schuster*

wetlands. Both adult and larval Odonata are predators that benefit humans by preying on mosquitoes and other pest insects that sometimes carry diseases. Odonata are harmless and do not bite, sting, or transmit diseases that affect humans. The adults of many species have striking blue, red, green, or yellow colors that rival the beauty of butterflies.

Caddisflies (Trichoptera) are among the most creative insects. Larvae of many species construct "cases" or portable homes made of sand grains, bits of leaves, wood, or tiny rocks bound together with silk they produce. The cases provide protection, aid in respiration in their aquatic habitats, and serve as the chamber for pupation before the adult emerges. Some caddisfly species are predators and don't use cases, while others build silk capture nets to filter microscopic food particles from the water. Along with freshwater mussels, they are part of the biological cleansing system of streams.

Butterflies, skippers, and moths (Lepidoptera) are one of the most diverse and best known of the state's insect groups. Primarily found in terrestrial habitats, more than 2,400 native lepidopteran species have been documented in the state;[73–75] however, a few species new to Kentucky are found each year. In fact, more than 100 additional species have been recorded since the last comprehensive state checklist was published in 1999.[73–75] Most of the new finds are moths, and these primarily nocturnal insects account for the overwhelming bulk of Lepidoptera diversity, with more than 2,300 species recorded from the state. Almost all butterflies and moths are dependent upon plants to complete their life cycle because the larval stage, or caterpillar, feeds on some part of a plant. Some caterpillar species are specialists and feed on only one plant species, called the host or food plant, while others are generalists and feed on a variety of plants. Females typically seek host plants and deposit eggs on or near the leaves or stem. After hatching, a larva feeds on the host plant until it pupates and begins transformation into an adult. The survival of butterfly and moth species is dependent upon the conservation of habitats supporting their host plants.

In general, adult lepidopterans obtain nectar from flowers using their proboscis, which exceeds 10 inches in length in some sphinx moths. Some adults don't feed but simply mate and die. In most cases, adults live only a few weeks, but a few species defy the rules and are relatively long-lived, often enduring what would appear to be insurmountable odds. Foremost among these is the familiar monarch butterfly. In one of the greatest migration events in nature, each fall millions of these delicate butterflies flutter their way up to 3,000 miles from eastern North America to overwintering sites, primarily in the Sierra Madre Mountains of Mexico. Survivors begin the trip back the following spring, and subsequent generations continue the journey to their northern breeding grounds. Even though the offspring have never been to Mexico, as fall arrives they inherently know how to navigate back to the same mountains their ancestors used.

Seventy-eight insect taxa known from Kentucky are considered rare by KSNPC (Appendix 2). Furthermore, one species, the American burying beetle, has been extirpated from the state, and the robust pentagenian burrowing mayfly is now extinct. Kentucky's rare insects are found in a variety of habitats, including (but not limited to) mountain peaks, prairies, cypress swamps, springs, seeps, and deep inside the subterranean passages of caves. Black Mountain and Mammoth Cave are examples of the most important sites supporting concentrations of rare insects. Many other caves are extremely important because they contain rare endemic species restricted to only one cave. Kentucky's prairie, barren, and glade habitats also support a rich diversity of rare insects that have evolved with the plants upon which they depend.

Edward O. Wilson, a renowned author on biodiversity, once famously said invertebrates are the

One of the most well-known and phenomenal migration events staged by an insect takes place each fall when huge numbers of monarchs leave their breeding grounds in the United States and Canada to overwinter in the Sierra Madre Mountains of Mexico. © *Barry Howard*

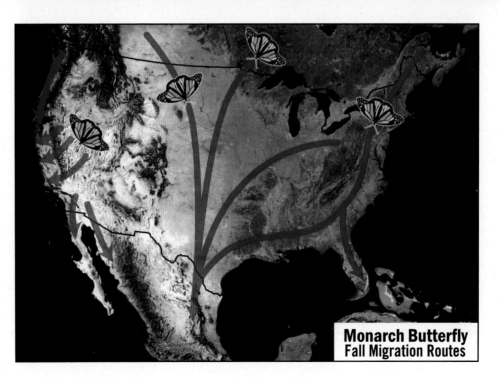

Monarch Butterfly Fall Migration Routes

The dainty eastern red damsel is endangered in Kentucky, where it lives in spring-fed bogs or seeps, habitats that are also very rare in the state. *KSNPC photograph by Ellis L. Laudermilk*

The regal fritillary may have been abundant in Kentucky prior to European American settlement, but now it has nearly disappeared from eastern North America. The loss and fragmentation of prairies probably doomed this showy butterfly. *KSNPC photograph by Ellis L. Laudermilk*

Vertebrate Species

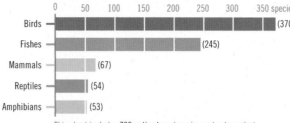

	species
Birds	(370)
Fishes	(245)
Mammals	(67)
Reptiles	(54)
Amphibians	(53)

This chart includes **789 native taxa** (species and subspecies).

Bats, such as this Rafinesque's big-eared bat, are extremely beneficial mammals because they are major predators of night-flying insects. A single bat may eat 3,000 or more insects each night, so a colony of 1,000 bats could consume more than 21 million insects every week!
John R. MacGregor

Freshwater Fish Species

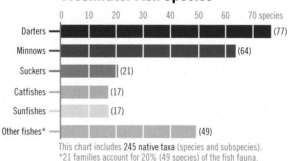

	species
Darters	(77)
Minnows	(64)
Suckers	(21)
Catfishes	(17)
Sunfishes	(17)
Other fishes*	(49)

This chart includes **245 native taxa** (species and subspecies).
*21 families account for 20% (49 species) of the fish fauna.

"little things that run the world."[76] While often small and inconspicuous, invertebrates play extremely critical roles in ecosystem function. Like other groups, habitat conservation and control of non-native species are the keys to their survival.

VERTEBRATES

Vertebrates (animals with backbones) are the largest, most conspicuous, and complex of animals. They are also the most highly evolved animals and include fishes, amphibians, reptiles, birds, and mammals. Although the overall number of vertebrate species accounts for only about 1% of the world's animals, their diversity and life histories are much more completely known than those of invertebrates. It is remarkable when a new vertebrate species is discovered, whereas new species of invertebrates are discovered often. Even though mammals are relatively well-known, there is still much to learn about their behavior, interactions, and tolerance for changing environments.

Freshwater Fishes

Kentucky's freshwater fish and lamprey fauna historically included 245 native species, approximately 30% of the North American fauna and more than all other states except Tennessee and Alabama.[8, 9, 77–79] Another 23 non-native fishes have been introduced into the state, mainly for sport fishing. The species richness of the state's native fish fauna is a result of many factors, including drainage evolution (e.g., formation of the Appalachian Mountains, inundation by ancient seas, glaciation of northern North America), the presence of large rivers (e.g., the Mississippi and Ohio), habitat diversity, and the absence of glaciation during the last 10,000 to 15,000 years.[8, 42]

Darters (77 species) and minnows (64) account for nearly 60% of the fauna. Generally, these fishes are abundant and small (less than 4 inches), and their common names, such as firebelly darter and rosefin shiner, often describe the brightly colored breeding males characteristic of many species. Along with suckers (21 species), catfishes (17), and sunfishes (17), these five families account for 80% of the Kentucky fauna.

Five groups of fishes occur in Kentucky: big river, lowland, upland, subterranean (cavefishes), and Terrapin Creek.[8, 80] Big-river species mainly inhabit the Mississippi and Ohio rivers and lower reaches of major tributaries and include the lake, pallid, and shovelnose sturgeons. Lowland fishes, such as the lake chubsucker and slough darter, are found in wetlands and associated habitats in and west of the lower Green River. Upland streams with permanent flow, high gradient, and coarse bottoms, such as sections of the Green and Kentucky rivers, are inhabited by the speckled darter and elegant madtom. Three species of cavefishes, the northern, southern, and spring (spring cavefish are often found in caves but are not an obligate cave species), inhabit cave streams and springs in the extensive sinkhole region of central and western Kentucky. Terrapin Creek, a spring-fed coastal plain stream, has Kentucky's most unusual fauna, with seven species found nowhere else in the state and several others with limited state ranges.

Fish diversity among watersheds is determined by watershed size, geologic history, habitat diversity, and other factors.[8, 42, 79, 81] The Cumberland, Green, Kentucky, and Tennessee river watersheds are the largest in Kentucky and support the most diverse faunas with 171, 154, 126, and 125 species, respectively. Within the Cumberland River drainage, Cumberland Falls is a 60-foot-high barrier to the upstream movement of fishes, and the watershed above the falls has the least diverse fauna in the state. Above the falls, only 39 native fishes are known, plus 13 additional species introduced from elsewhere in the state, primarily for sport fishing. Approximately 14 species are distributed statewide, whereas 48 species (mainly darters) only inhabit one watershed and sometimes only a short stream segment. Six species are endemic to Kentucky, but

several others occur only in the Cumberland River, Tennessee River, or Terrapin Creek watersheds and are shared with Tennessee.

Life-history characteristics, such as reproduction and feeding, vary widely among fishes.[8, 80] Western mosquitofish grow to about 2.5 inches long and can reach sexual maturity in the first year of life, whereas lake sturgeon can grow to nine feet long and can take up to 30 years to reach maturity. Sunfishes, catfishes, and others invest considerable energy and effort in their offspring by building and spawning in nests and protecting fertilized eggs and young. Other species, such as the walleye, provide no parental care and scatter eggs and sperm over shoals of gravel, sand, and boulders in flowing water. Feeding habits are equally diverse and include predators (e.g., gar), grazers (bluegill), strainers (gizzard shad), food suckers (sturgeon and suckers), and parasites (lampreys).

Kentucky's native fish fauna has been negatively affected by 200 years of habitat alteration and destruction from stream channelization and

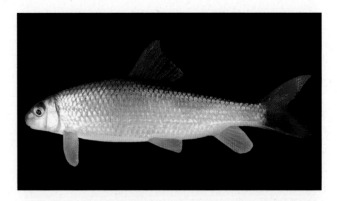

top to bottom:
The smallmouth redhorse is a bottom-dwelling fish that may reach two feet in length. It inhabits medium to large rivers nearly statewide. *KSNPC photograph by Ronald R. Cicerello*

The speckled darter lives in riffles or pools with gravel and sand bottoms and moderate current in the Tennessee River watershed of western Kentucky. *KSNPC photograph by Ronald R. Cicerello*

The golden topminnow is restricted to the Running Slough drainage in Fulton County and is KSNPC-listed as endangered. Topminnows are dorsally flattened, live just beneath the surface of the water, and graze on mosquito larvae and other aquatic invertebrates and algae. *KSNPC photograph by Ronald R. Cicerello*

The blackside dace is a Cumberland River endemic that inhabits small, well-forested upland streams with clean bedrock and bottoms of gravel or sand. It is federally and KSNPC-listed as threatened because of habitat degradation and loss associated with poor land-use practices. *KSNPC photograph by Ellis L. Laudermilk*

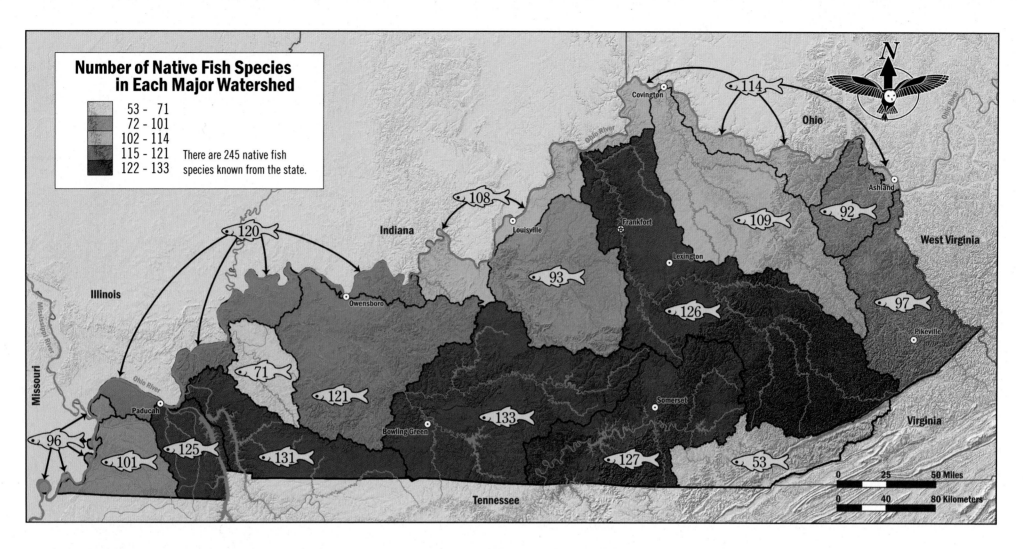

Number of Native Fish Species in Each Major Watershed

53 - 71
72 - 101
102 - 114
115 - 121
122 - 133

There are 245 native fish species known from the state.

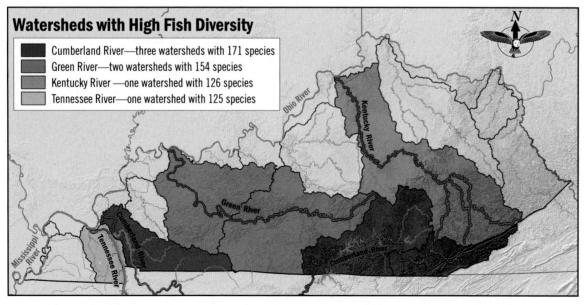

Watersheds with High Fish Diversity

Cumberland River—three watersheds with 171 species
Green River—two watersheds with 154 species
Kentucky River—one watershed with 126 species
Tennessee River—one watershed with 125 species

impoundment, pollution, wetland drainage, and other activities. Nine (4%) species have been extirpated from the state, including the extinct harelip sucker. Of the remaining 236 species, 60 (25%) are considered rare and are KSNPC-listed, six of which also are federally listed or listing candidates.[3, 7, 11] Most imperiled fishes are darters (16 species) and minnows (15), followed by lampreys (5), suckers (4), and catfishes (4). Imperiled fishes are rare because habitat alteration and pollution negatively affects the stream bottom where these fishes live, feed, or nest. Habitat protection and restoration are the keys to conservation of Kentucky's diverse fish fauna.

Amphibians

Kentucky has a diverse amphibian fauna that includes a total of 53 species; within the group are 20 frogs and toads and 33 salamanders,[11] the latter of which represents about 26% of the total U.S. fauna.[82] All of Kentucky's amphibians are native, a quality that is unique among the state's vertebrate groups.

Kentucky's frogs and toads are classified into several groups, including cricket frogs, true toads, narrowmouth toads, tree frogs, chorus frogs, true frogs, and spadefoots. Members of these groups differ in a number of characteristics including size, habitat, and breeding strategy. True toads typically have rough skin and often live in drier areas. Tree frogs have enlarged pads on the tips of their toes that allow them to climb vertical surfaces to forage for insects. Spadefoots have hardened ridges on their heels that allow them to burrow into soft soil.

Like all amphibians, those occurring in Kentucky are at least partially dependent upon water to complete their life cycle. However, four salamander species live their entire lives in water: the three-toed amphiuma and lesser siren live in swamps, while the mudpuppy and eastern hellbender live in streams. Most of the remaining 29 species split their time between water and land, typically associating with streams and ponds only during the breeding season. However, several species of woodland salamanders in the genus *Plethodon* are found in forested areas away from water year-round, and they only require damp crevices in clifflines or under rocks to reproduce.

All of Kentucky's amphibians lay eggs. Frog eggs typically are laid in pools of water, while some terrestrial salamanders lay their eggs in cool, moist habitats like clumps of moss along pond margins, the undersides of rocks along streams, and damp crevices in clifflines and caves. Many of Kentucky's frogs are referred to as "explosive" breeders, suddenly emerging from hiding places all at once and in large numbers to lay eggs in pools of water following heavy rains.

The tadpole is a widely recognized stage in the life cycles of frogs and toads. Tadpoles hatch from eggs, and after growing several weeks to many months in water they transform into adult frogs. Hatchling salamanders are known as larvae instead of tadpoles.

The red-spotted newt is the exception to the general rule that amphibian larval stages live in water or moist environments. These small salamanders live in ponds as adults, but most larvae transform into a terrestrial land form called the "red eft," which lives out of water. Efts forage on the forest floor for about a year and then reenter the water to live out the remainder of their lives.

Most of Kentucky's terrestrial amphibians feed on insects and other invertebrates, including earthworms. Aquatic forms eat a variety of small invertebrates such as caddisfly and mayfly larvae. Tadpoles and larvae often graze on algae and aquatic plants.

The males of Kentucky's 20 frog and toad species all have unique calls that they primarily use to attract females for breeding. These sounds are as varied as the frogs' appearance and include the long, melodious trills of American toads, the resonating grunts of bullfrogs, the loud snores of crawfish frogs, and the high-pitched whistles of tiny spring peepers.

Some amphibian populations have declined dramatically in the past few decades in many scattered regions around the world, and similar declines have been noted in a few of Kentucky's amphibians. It is currently believed that these declines cannot be blamed on one particular cause but that a combination of factors—including habitat loss and modification, environmental pollution from a variety of chemicals, ozone depletion, and introduced diseases—is responsible.[83] Pollution and introduced diseases affect local amphibian populations, especially frogs, typically halting eggs from hatching or larvae from developing properly.

Many consider the first tree buds and wildflowers to be the earliest harbingers of spring in

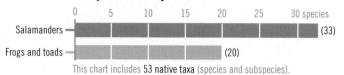

Amphibian Species

	0	5	10	15	20	25	30 species
Salamanders							(33)
Frogs and toads					(20)		

This chart includes **53 native taxa** (species and subspecies).

Barking treefrogs are "explosive" breeders that are found only in a limited range in the western Highland Rim. When abnormally heavy rainfall occurs from late spring to early summer, males and females suddenly gather at temporary pools of water to breed. *Mark W. Gumbert*

The bright orange-red color of the terrestrial stage of the red-spotted newt, or eft, advertises toxins in the salamander's skin that will sicken unsuspecting predators. *John R. MacGregor*

One of Kentucky's most spectacular—but strange—amphibians is the eastern hellbender, a bizarre-looking aquatic salamander that grows up to two feet in length. The hellbender's closest relative lives in southeast Asia.
John R. MacGregor

Kentucky, but herpetologists (scientists who study amphibians and reptiles) know the earliest organisms to stir are actually certain species of frogs and salamanders. Late winter rains bring these creatures from beneath the surface of the forest floor, where they have spent many months; then they march to thawing ponds to pair, mate, and lay eggs.

While evolutionary relationships among the amphibians of our region are relatively well-known, scientific studies based on more highly refined techniques continue to identify new species. For this reason, the most recent additions to Kentucky's amphibian fauna are newly recognized species like the southern zigzag salamander and the northern ravine salamander. These small amphibians were

formerly considered forms or subspecies within more widespread species.

The presence or concentration of rare amphibians identified in the Amphibian Rarity Hotspot map often correlates with increasingly uncommon habitats in Kentucky, such as pristine mountain ridges, forested stream corridors, and wetlands. Natural areas such as Pine Mountain; undeveloped forest lands and stream corridors near Cincinnati; wetlands in the Jackson Purchase area; and the Blood River, Obion Creek, and Terrapin Creek corridors are important to amphibian conservation.

Eleven (21%) of Kentucky's amphibians are considered rare and are KSNPC-listed; this total includes 25% of Kentucky's frogs and toads (six

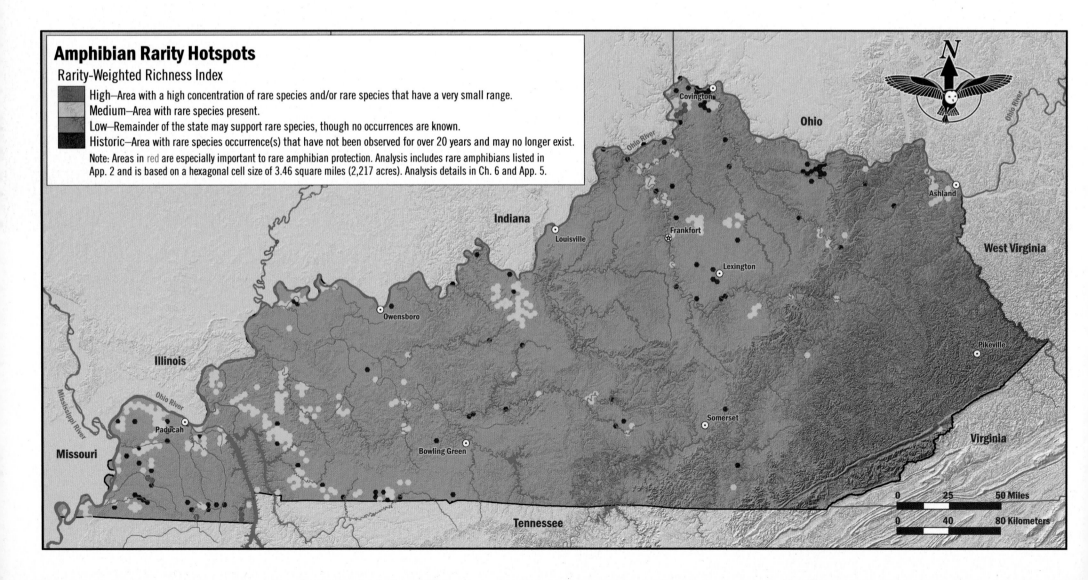

Amphibian Rarity Hotspots

Rarity-Weighted Richness Index

High—Area with a high concentration of rare species and/or rare species that have a very small range.
Medium—Area with rare species present.
Low—Remainder of the state may support rare species, though no occurrences are known.
Historic—Area with rare species occurrence(s) that have not been observed for over 20 years and may no longer exist.

Note: Areas in red are especially important to rare amphibian protection. Analysis includes rare amphibians listed in App. 2 and is based on a hexagonal cell size of 3.46 square miles (2,217 acres). Analysis details in Ch. 6 and App. 5.

Wehrle's salamander is probably Kentucky's rarest amphibian. It is known from only a few rock outcrops in the southeastern part of the state. *John R. MacGregor*

species) and 15% of the state's salamanders (five species).[11] None of Kentucky's amphibians are federally listed. Destruction and alteration of intact forested areas and wetlands are the most significant impacts on amphibian populations in Kentucky.

Reptiles

Kentucky's reptile fauna is composed of 55 species, all but one of which are native, and includes 14 turtles, nine lizards, and 32 snakes.[11] In addition, there are several species that consist of two or more recognizable subspecies, each with unique characteristics and sometimes occupying specific ranges with little overlap.

Turtles were placed in the taxonomic class Reptilia for many years and are included within this section of the book. However, recent evolutionary studies have found turtles to be quite different from other reptiles, and most authorities now place turtles in their own taxonomic class, called Chelonia.

Most turtles have a bony layer covering their bodies, referred to as the carapace (on the back) and the plastron (under the belly). However, there are two species referred to as "softshells" because a leathery carapace protects their bodies. Kentucky's

The alligator snapping turtle is a denizen of floodplain sloughs and large, slow-moving rivers in the western part of the state. Weighing in at up to 200 pounds, it is by far Kentucky's largest turtle. Despite its size, little is known about the life history of this secretive species. *John R. MacGregor*

largest turtle is the alligator snapping turtle, a rare species that may weigh more than 200 pounds. While most turtles are associated with water, the most familiar member of the group is a terrestrial species, the eastern box turtle. This species is really a tortoise, similar to the ancient relicts of the Galapagos Islands. Unlike turtles, tortoises can retract completely into their shells.

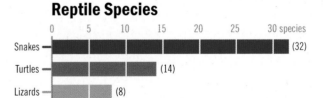

Reptile Species

	0	5	10	15	20	25	30 species
Snakes							(32)
Turtles			(14)				
Lizards	(8)						

This chart includes **54 native taxa** (species and subspecies).

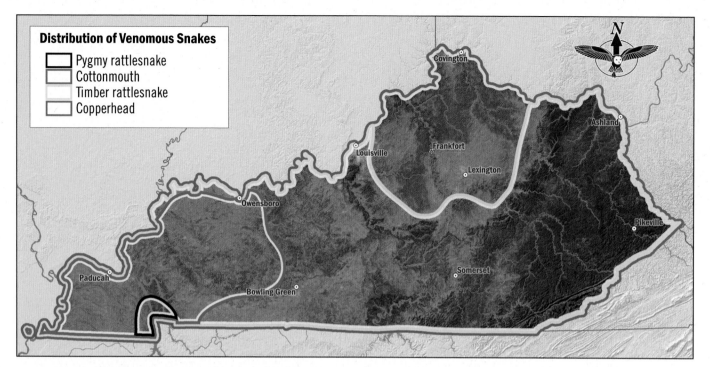

Distribution of Venomous Snakes
- Pygmy rattlesnake
- Cottonmouth
- Timber rattlesnake
- Copperhead

N

Covington

Ashland

Frankfort

Louisville

Lexington

Owensboro

Pikeville

Somerset

Paducah

Bowling Green

The copperbelly water snake occurs throughout much of the Shawnee Hills region of Kentucky, inhabiting shallow-water marshes and sloughs. The species is threatened by wetland loss and degradation. *John R. MacGregor*

Lizards and snakes are relatively similar, with coarse or smooth scales covering their long, slender bodies. However, lizards have legs; in one case, the slender glass lizard, the legs are mere vestiges (skeletal remnants) contained inside the body. Lizards also have moveable eyelids and external ear openings. Many species have tails that easily break free from the main body, allowing them to escape the grasp of would-be predators. Loss of the tail is only temporary, because it can be regenerated.

Snakes are covered with scales, like lizards, but they are legless and have immovable eyelids and no external ear openings. As snakes grow in size, they periodically shed their outer layer of skin.

The majority of reptiles lay eggs, although some lizards and snakes (e.g., skinks, eastern garter snake, water snakes, and our venomous species) bear live young. Some reptile eggs are hard-shelled, but others are covered by a leathery skin. Turtles lay clutches of eggs in nests that are dug into soft soil or sand, but most lizards and snakes lay their clutches of eggs beneath rocks or in rotten logs.

Most reptiles have excellent eyesight that allows them to detect the slightest movement and secure prey. However, snakes can also obtain sensory information about their surroundings with their forked tongue, which is rapidly flicked back and forth in the air to detect odors. Kentucky's venomous snakes also have heat-sensing abilities that allow them to search out warm-blooded prey at night. Although many species of reptiles bite, only a few of Kentucky's snakes have venom that can be harmful or fatal to prey or humans. Kentucky is home to four species of venomous snakes: the copperhead, cottonmouth, timber rattlesnake, and pygmy rattlesnake. The cottonmouth is found only in western Kentucky wetlands, and the rare pygmy rattler is found only in the Land Between the Lakes area. Timber rattlesnakes are found across much of the state but are distributed very locally, and they are absent in the north-central portion. The copperhead is the only relatively widespread venomous species.

Reptiles are cold-blooded, so all of them essentially hibernate in protected places during the winter. Aquatic turtles retire to the bottoms of rivers, lakes, and ponds, while terrestrial species retreat into burrows. Some species, including eastern garter snakes, timber rattlesnakes, and cottonmouths, sometimes gather into underground dens in sizable groups to overwinter.

All reptiles obtain oxygen by breathing air into lungs; however, most turtles are also able to absorb oxygen through their skin, allowing them to remain below the surface of the water for long periods.

Reptile diets are about as diverse as the group

Five-lined skinks are highly adaptable, thriving in a variety of natural and human-created semiopen habitats. The tails of skinks can snap off if bitten by a predator; the tail is then regenerated, and the animal lives on.
John R. MacGregor

The western ribbon snake is an attractive serpent of marshy wetlands in far western Kentucky. These slender reptiles prey primarily on tadpoles, small frogs, and fish. *John R. MacGregor*

itself. Turtles eat a variety of animal and plant life, including carrion, while tortoises eat fungi and fruits. Most lizards feed primarily on insects and other invertebrates. Small terrestrial snakes typically feed on invertebrates, but some are highly specialized, with diets consisting primarily of ant eggs (southeastern crowned snake) or small lizards (scarlet kingsnake). Most larger snakes prey on small mammals, especially rodents. The black rat snake is an adept climber and has evolved to prey on bird eggs and nestlings in addition to small rodents. Water snakes generally feed on fish and tadpoles, but the queen snake feeds primarily on crayfish. A few species have very specialized diets; the hognose snake preys primarily on toads, and the mud snake feeds mainly on aquatic salamanders, primarily lesser sirens.

Only one introduced reptile has become established in the state: the European wall lizard. A small number of these lizards apparently escaped from a captive population in the Cincinnati area, and some now live in cliffs and rock walls along the Ohio River in north-central Kentucky.

The presence or concentration of rare reptiles identified in the Reptile Rarity Hotspot map often correlates with habitats that are limited in Kentucky, such as intact floodplains and dry woodland. The most significant sites for conservation of reptiles in Kentucky are the floodplain corridors of the Mississippi River, lower Ohio River, and Tennessee River in the western part of the state. Also of great importance are dry woodland systems in the vicinities of the Land Between the Lakes, Mammoth Cave, and the far northern and southern portions of the Daniel Boone National Forest. Finally, remnant wetland habitats in the Louisville area and across the Shawnee Hills are critical for the survival of rare reptiles.

KSNPC considers 17 (31%) of Kentucky's reptiles to be rare; this total includes three (21%) of the state's turtles, three (33%) of Kentucky's lizards, and 11 (34%) of the snakes.[11] None of Kentucky's reptiles are federally listed. Destruction and alteration of natural grassland, woodland, and wetland habitats are the most significant impacts negatively affecting reptile populations in Kentucky.

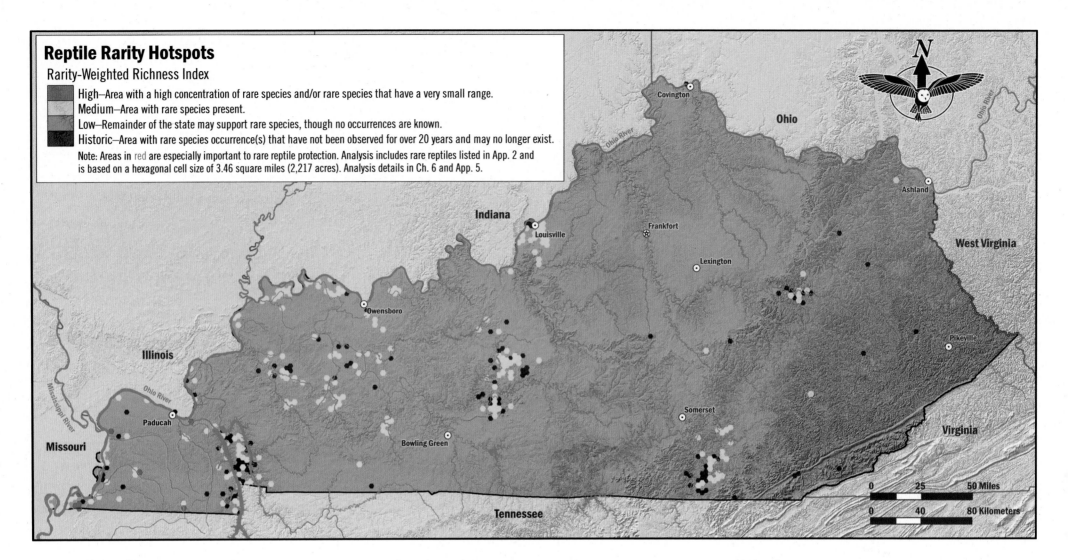

Reptile Rarity Hotspots

Rarity-Weighted Richness Index

High—Area with a high concentration of rare species and/or rare species that have a very small range.
Medium—Area with rare species present.
Low—Remainder of the state may support rare species, though no occurrences are known.
Historic—Area with rare species occurrence(s) that have not been observed for over 20 years and may no longer exist.

Note: Areas in red are especially important to rare reptile protection. Analysis includes rare reptiles listed in App. 2 and is based on a hexagonal cell size of 3.46 square miles (2,217 acres). Analysis details in Ch. 6 and App. 5.

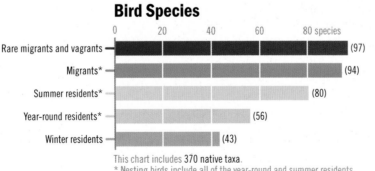

Bird Species

	0	20	40	60	80 species
Rare migrants and vagrants					(97)
Migrants*					(94)
Summer residents*				(80)	
Year-round residents*			(56)		
Winter residents		(43)			

This chart includes 370 native taxa.
* Nesting birds include all of the year-round and summer residents, as well as some migrants. There are 14 birds in the state that are primarily considered migrants even though they have small populations that actually nest.

Birds

Birds are the most highly mobile group of terrestrial vertebrates; only bats share birds' ability to quickly travel long distances. For this reason, many more bird species have been found in Kentucky—at least 377, of which 370 are considered native—than any other terrestrial vertebrate group.[84, 85] Of the 275 species that occur here regularly, approximately 150 routinely nest in the state.[86] Approximately 100 species are rarely reported migrants or vagrants (e.g., oceanic birds driven inland by hurricanes).

Five bird species introduced into the United States from Eurasia (the Eurasian collared-dove, European starling, house sparrow, mute swan, and rock pigeon) and one western U.S. species (house finch) have become established in Kentucky. The rock pigeon, European starling, and house sparrow are among the most conspicuous birds in settled areas.

Compared to most states, Kentucky's bird list is relatively modest, due largely to the state's interior position in the eastern part of the country (away from coastlines) and its greater length longitudinally (east-west) than latitudinally (north-south). Bird ranges in the interior eastern United States generally vary more in a north-south direction, so states like Indiana and Illinois typically have a greater diversity of birds.

All of Kentucky's birds are capable of flight. The group is remarkably diverse, including waterbirds such as swans, geese, ducks, loons, grebes, pelicans, herons, cranes, plovers, sandpipers, gulls, and terns; scavenging vultures; predators such as hawks, falcons, and owls; marsh-loving birds including rails and moorhens; tree-loving woodpeckers; tiny hummingbirds; and a vast array of songbirds, such as flycatchers, shrikes, vireos, swallows, crows, nuthatches, wrens, kinglets, thrushes, warblers, tanagers, sparrows, blackbirds, and finches. Birds known from Kentucky vary in size from the tiny ruby-throated hummingbird (which weighs as much as a few pennies) to the American white pelican, which weighs in at more than 15 pounds and has a wingspan of more than eight feet. Birds communicate largely by sound, utilizing complex repertoires of calls and songs to defend territories, attract mates, and warn others of danger. The males of many species are brightly colored or have bold patterns that help make them more conspicuous to potential mates.

Birds occur in virtually all habitat types. From the larger lakes and rivers in the western part of the state to the forested mountains of the east, most habitats have characteristic species. Bird diversity increases slightly from east to west in Kentucky, primarily due to the increase in habitat diversity, including the larger areas of grassland and wetlands in western Kentucky that are largely absent in the east.

Many birds adapt to habitat changes easily, moving readily into man-made environments. Due to this high level of mobility and adaptability, the distribution and abundance of some birds has changed since European American settlement. In a relatively short time, some birds that were common in the state (e.g., forest songbirds) have become much less numerous and widespread, while others favoring open and edge habitats have become the most abundant (e.g., the northern cardinal, indigo bunting, and song sparrow).

Birds utilize both plants and other animals for food. Raptors, such as hawks and owls, prey on a variety of small animals including insects, frogs, snakes, birds, and mammals. Carrion-eating vultures play a role in recycling dead animals. Most songbirds are either insectivorous (i.e., they eat insects) or frugivorous (i.e., they eat berries and seeds). By eating insects, birds provide a significant amount of pest control in both settled areas and forested landscapes, benefiting humans immeasurably. Some birds switch from eating insects during summer to seed diets in winter; others survive the winter by migrating to warmer climates, including the tropics.

Some birds stay in Kentucky year-round, but many spend only the summer or winter here, and others simply migrate through in spring or fall. A few of the more noticeable migratory movements include the *V* formation of bugling sandhill cranes in February and December, flocks of common nighthawks in late August and early September, and colorful woodland warblers in early May. Some of the most conspicuous birds that nest in

Red-headed woodpeckers inhabit open woodlands and have adapted to human alteration of the landscape, now occupying many artificial openings. *Lana Hays*

The brilliantly colored scarlet tanager is one of several dozen songbirds that spend the summer in Kentucky or migrate through the state in spring and fall, but overwinter in the tropics of Central and South America. *Lana Hays*

Kentucky include the northern cardinal, American robin, mourning dove, and indigo bunting. Common forest and forest-edge nesting birds that winter primarily in the tropics include red-eyed vireo, wood thrush, hooded warbler, and indigo bunting.

Many migratory birds exhibit a high degree of site fidelity. Individuals that nest or overwinter in a specific location one year often return to the same exact spot in succeeding years after spending the rest of the year at a corresponding summering or wintering site hundreds or even thousands of miles away. How birds navigate with such extraordinary precision remains somewhat of a mystery. However, it has been demonstrated that many birds use patterns of stars and the movements of the sun to accurately return to home ranges. At least some birds also appear to use the magnetic field of the Earth for navigation, while others may simply use geographic features.

Nine breeding species (meaning they rear young in the state) have become extinct or extirpated since European settlement, including some of the state's more notable birds (Appendix 3). The greater prairie-chicken, a large, grouse-like bird, was once found in the native prairies, and the Carolina parakeet, ivory-billed woodpecker, and Bachman's warbler all formerly inhabited bottomland forests and swamps in western Kentucky. The passenger pigeon was at one time so abundant in central Kentucky forests and woodlands that passing flocks made day

above and below:
Barred owls are one of several species of nocturnal raptors that occur in Kentucky year-round. These large owls are most common in lowland forests of the western portion of the state. *Lana Hays*

The northern pintail is one of nearly 30 waterfowl species known from Kentucky. This species overwinters here after migrating south from nesting grounds in the northern United States and Canada. *Lana Hays*

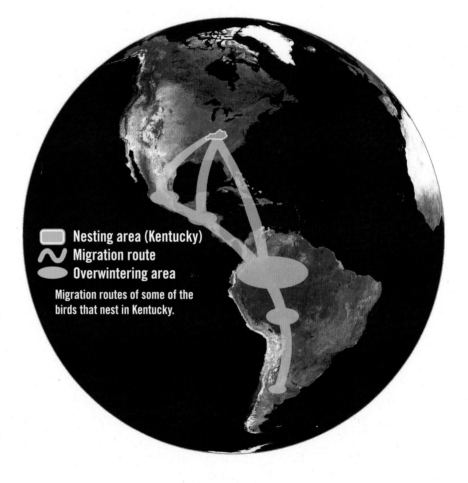

Nesting area (Kentucky)
Migration route
Overwintering area
Migration routes of some of the birds that nest in Kentucky.

seem like night![87] Other former breeders are the anhinga, black tern, swallow-tailed kite, and red-cockaded woodpecker. The trumpeter swan and whooping crane also once regularly visited Kentucky, but only as a winter visitant and a migrant, respectively. Both species are still considered extirpated, although individuals originating from recent reintroduction efforts in other parts of the eastern United States are being seen with increasing regularity.

The presence or concentration of rare nesting birds identified in the Nesting Bird Rarity Hotspot map often correlates with habitats that are limited in Kentucky, such as extensive blocks of relatively mature forest along mountain ridges and floodplain corridors, as well as expansive grasslands. Natural areas like the Cumberland Mountains of the southeastern part of the state, the floodplain corridors of the Mississippi and lower Ohio rivers of the west, and the grasslands of north-central Kentucky and the Shawnee Hills are important to the conservation of rare nesting birds.

Forty-eight (32%) of Kentucky's nesting birds are considered rare and are KSNPC-listed;[11] two of these are also federally listed. Of the nesting bird species listed by KSNPC, 25 (52%) are associated with wetland habitats, while 12 (25%) are associated with grasslands. Habitat destruction and alteration are the most significant negative impacts on nesting bird populations in the state. Several species

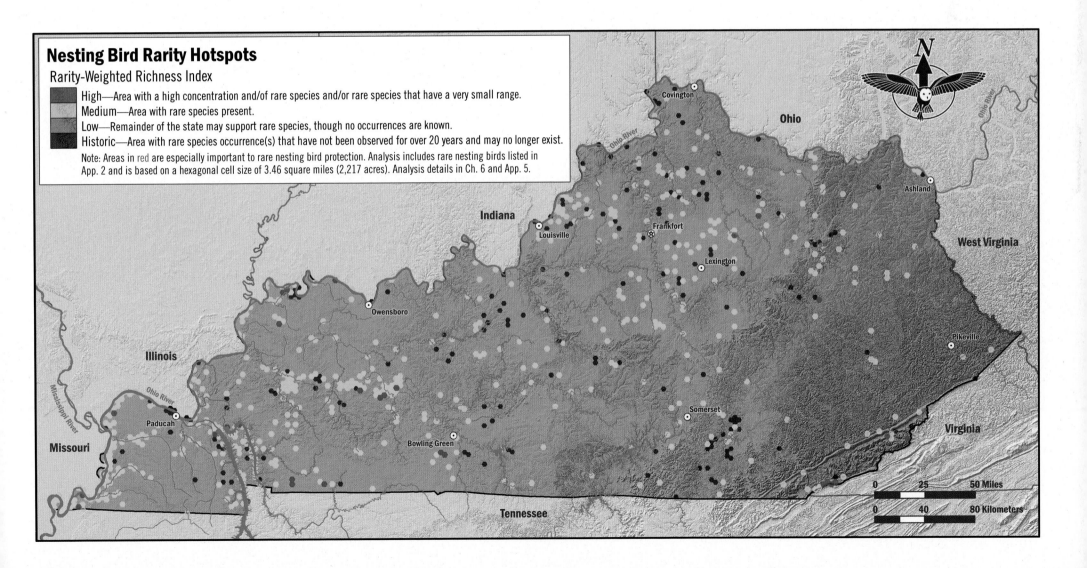

Nesting Bird Rarity Hotspots

Rarity-Weighted Richness Index

- High—Area with a high concentration and/of rare species and/or rare species that have a very small range.
- Medium—Area with rare species present.
- Low—Remainder of the state may support rare species, though no occurrences are known.
- Historic—Area with rare species occurrence(s) that have not been observed for over 20 years and may no longer exist.

Note: Areas in red are especially important to rare nesting bird protection. Analysis includes rare nesting birds listed in App. 2 and is based on a hexagonal cell size of 3.46 square miles (2,217 acres). Analysis details in Ch. 6 and App. 5.

Absent during the "DDT era" of the mid-20th century, the nesting population of the peregrine falcon has increased steadily in Kentucky during the past 15 years. There are now at least nine nesting pairs along the Ohio River corridor, and the species was removed from federal listing in 1999. *Lana Hays*

that experienced great declines (e.g., the great blue heron, bald eagle, and peregrine falcon) have rebounded in response to regulatory actions and conservation programs. All three species were harmed by the accumulation of pesticide residues in the environment during the middle of the 20th century. However, environmental regulations helped remove harmful chemicals from the landscape and are primarily responsible for a reversal of these downward trends.

Little is known about the life history of the least weasel, a tiny predatory mammal that occurs in grassland areas, including farmland. *John R. MacGregor*

Mammal Species

Rodents	(22)
Bats	(16)
Carnivores	(12)
Shrews and moles	(10)
Rabbits	(3)
Ungulates	(2)
Marsupials	(1)
Armadillos	(1)

This chart includes **67 native taxa** (species and subspecies).

Mammals

Kentucky's present-day mammal fauna is composed of 71 species, all but four of which are native. This diverse group includes one marsupial (opossum), one armadillo, 10 shrews and moles, 16 bats, three rabbits, 24 rodents, 12 carnivores, and four ungulates (hoofed mammals).[11] All of the state's mammals bear live young; however, the Virginia opossum, like all marsupials, carry their tiny, naked young in their mother's pouch for the first several weeks of life.

Kentucky's mammal fauna has changed dramatically since European American settlement. Large herbivores, such as elk and American bison, and carnivores that preyed upon them, such as wolves and eastern cougars, were abundant before the forests were cleared and prairies tilled. Hunting pressure and bounties placed on predators (e.g., the gray wolf) also played a role in their demise (see the Overcollection and Overharvesting section in chapter 5).

Several species have been introduced from Eurasia, either accidentally (the Norway rat and house mouse) or intentionally (the wild boar and fallow deer). Most have become nuisances; the first two have cost humans significantly due to damages in food storage, and the latter two have negatively affected native flora and fauna.

A few species are known from Kentucky only as wandering individuals, including the Mexican free-tailed bat, Seminole bat, and badger. One recent arrival from the southern United States, the nine-banded armadillo, is now believed to be established in small numbers in the western part of the state.

Of Kentucky's 16 bat species, more than half inhabit caves. Several species spend the winter in caves where temperatures stay above freezing and allow the bats to survive in a state of hibernation. A few, such as the gray myotis and Virginia big-eared bat, use caves year-round, although they seldom use the same cave for both hibernation and summer roosting. If bats do not use the stable environments of caves during winter, they typically migrate farther south, where warmer temperatures allow them to continue to feed on insects. Like many migratory animals, bats show a very high level of site fidelity. They typically use the same cave or summer home range each year after spending a large portion of the year hundreds of miles away at a wintering or summering site.

Bats use a variety of roosting sites in addition to caves. Human structures, such as house attics, barns, and bridges, are commonly used by big brown bats and little brown bats, but these species and others also use hollow trees, crevices in clifflines, the flaking bark of dead trees, or "shaggy–barked" species of oaks and hickories. Members of the genus *Lasiurus* (e.g., the red bat) simply roost in clusters of leaves in trees.

Many bats are colonial, but some generally are solitary. Bats do not see well; they use a type of sonar (echolocation) to navigate and find prey. Calls emitted by the bats reflect off surfaces around them, including prey. Their sensitive ears detect the returning echos. All Kentucky bats feed primarily on flying insects captured in flight. Larger species forage on beetles and moths, while smaller species primarily catch smaller moths, aquatic insects, flies, and mosquitoes.

Shrews and moles are a distinctive group of small mammals distinguished by their glossy gray or brown fur, pointed snouts, and poor eyesight. They all spend most of their time underground. Eastern moles are the bane of many homeowners, tunneling beneath the turf in search of grubs.

Kentucky's three rabbit species are in a distinct group referred to as the Lagomorpha. The group name is derived from Greek and refers to the hare-like shape of most species: long, floppy ears and enlarged back feet. Lagomorphs' enlarged hind feet allow them to hop rather than walk like other mammals. They also have relatively large ears for temperature regulation and hearing. The most common rabbit in Kentucky is the eastern cottontail.

Rodents are a diverse group that includes familiar species such as the gray squirrel, fox squirrel, eastern chipmunk, woodchuck or groundhog, beaver, muskrat, and white-footed mouse. The group also includes two vole species and the southern bog lemming, all tiny, short-tailed mammals found in grasslands. Woodlands are inhabited by several species of mice and one vole. The Allegheny woodrat is a native rodent that lives primarily along clifflines and in caves. Most rodents eat a variety of small invertebrates, seeds, and foliage.

Kentucky's carnivores include the coyote, two foxes, American black bear, raccoon, river otter, two skunks, two weasels, mink, and bobcat. Many are reclusive species, active only at night and seldom seen. Prior to the 1970s, the coyote was seldom seen in the state; however, in recent years it quickly spread statewide and is now common. American black bears, once common across the state, are rebounding in the southeastern mountains after many years of absence.

Kentucky's ungulates were once much more common, but today the group is represented by only one native species, the white-tailed deer. Bison are now found only in captivity, including a large

Black bears once again roam the eastern Kentucky mountains. While they typically avoid humans, never approach or attempt to feed these magnificent animals, and keep all trash in bear-proof containers! *Steve Maslowski, U.S. Fish & Wildlife Service; courtesy of U.S. Fish & Wildlife Service National Digital Library*

The prairie vole is one of several common Kentucky mammals. These abundant inhabitants of grassland areas are sought by many predators, including hawks, owls, snakes, and foxes. *John R. MacGregor*

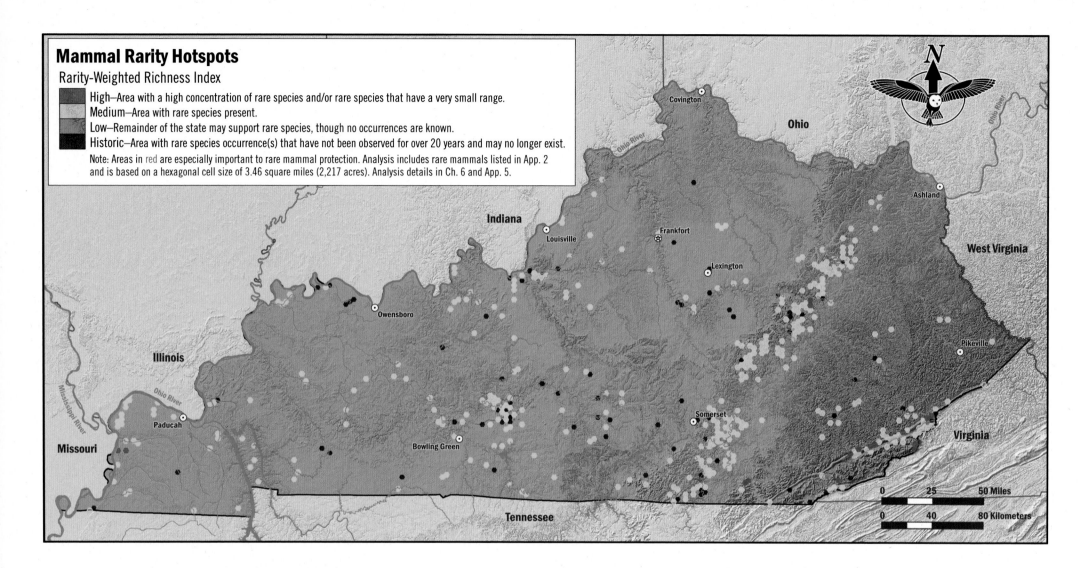

Mammal Rarity Hotspots

Rarity-Weighted Richness Index

High—Area with a high concentration of rare species and/or rare species that have a very small range.

Medium—Area with rare species present.

Low—Remainder of the state may support rare species, though no occurrences are known.

Historic—Area with rare species occurrence(s) that have not been observed for over 20 years and may no longer exist.

Note: Areas in red are especially important to rare mammal protection. Analysis includes rare mammals listed in App. 2 and is based on a hexagonal cell size of 3.46 square miles (2,217 acres). Analysis details in Ch. 6 and App. 5.

Big brown bats have adapted well to human settlement. They are commonly found in suburban areas, cities, and farmland, roosting in attics and abandoned buildings. They feed on insects, including many agricultural pests. *John R. MacGregor*

demonstration area in the Land Between the Lakes. After the elk's long absence from the state, individuals captured in Utah were introduced on reclaimed mine land in eastern Kentucky in 1998.

Among Kentucky's mammals, some of the bats are the most threatened; in fact, seven (44%) bat species are considered rare by KSNPC.[11] A combination of bats' specific habitat requirements and their vulnerability while hibernating in caves has resulted in significant declines in the population of the federally listed Indiana bat. The closely related gray myotis also declined, but conservation measures, including protection of caves and improved pesticide regulations, resulted in a reversal of this trend.

In 2006, a new, mysterious illness appeared in the northeastern United States that began killing bats while they hibernated. This illness has emerged as a significant threat to bats that hibernate to pass the winter all across North America. Called "white-nosed syndrome" because a white fungus typically appears around the nose of affected bats, this unknown pathogen has already killed hundreds of thousands of bats. Affected species include the big brown bat, eastern pipistrelle, eastern small-footed myotis, Indiana bat, little brown bat, and northern myotis. Infected hibernating bats either die and fall to the cave floor, or they arouse in winter and emerge from their caves, using up critical body-fat stores and eventually starving. While the syndrome has been confined to the northeast so far, it continues to spread farther south and recently appeared in West Virginia. It is very likely that by the time this book is published, Kentucky will be among the states with confirmed white-nosed syndrome caves. Cavers should avoid the potential transfer of this unknown pathogen from cave to cave by thoroughly disinfecting all clothing and gear after exiting any cave.

Three small mammals found in moist, older forests—the long-tailed shrew, cinereus shrew, and Kentucky red-backed vole—are found only in limited regions of the state; logging and forest fragmentation threaten their presence in Kentucky.

The presence or concentration of rare mammals identified in the Mammal Rarity Hotspot map often correlates with habitats that are limited in Kentucky, such as forested mountains and floodplains and undisturbed cave systems. The most significant sites for conservation of mammals in Kentucky are the Cumberland Mountains, including Pine Mountain, the Cliff section along the western margin of the Cumberland Plateau, the Mammoth Cave region, and the Mississippi River and lower Ohio River floodplain corridors in the far west.

Fourteen (20%) of Kentucky's mammals are considered rare by KSNPC, including seven bats.[11] Three of Kentucky's bats are also federally listed. Habitat destruction and alteration are the most significant threats to mammal populations in Kentucky.

EXTIRPATED AND EXTINCT SPECIES

Not too long ago, huge herds of American bison roamed the prairies and woodlands of Kentucky, moving between grazing grounds, salt licks, and calving grounds. Trumpeter swans and ivory-billed woodpeckers soared among expansive cypress swamps. Colorful flame chubs and yellow blossom mussels lived in clear, free-flowing streams. Flocks of beautiful Carolina parakeets darted between trees, while millions of passenger pigeons darkened the sky in nomadic flights. Sadly, native populations of these species have been eradicated from the state (i.e., extirpated), and the latter two species no longer exist anywhere in the world.

Six plant and 48 animal taxa that once lived in Kentucky have been extirpated (Appendix 3). Of these 54 taxa, 18 (33%) are presumed or possibly globally extinct, which is the ninth-highest total among the states.[18] Animals that depend on aquatic ecosystems (e.g., mussels, fishes, and insects) make up 57% of Kentucky's extirpated or extinct species, illustrating the grave threat to these habitats. Even Kentucky's one extinct plant, the stipuled scurf-pea, was associated with riverine habitat in an area altered by dam construction.

Nine fish species have disappeared, but freshwater mussels have been particularly affected, with 21 species lost. Most of these mussels, especially

An inhabitant of springs and spring-fed streams in southeastern Kentucky, the flame chub is among nine fishes that have disappeared from the Commonwealth. © *Noel Burkhead and Howard L. Jelks*

The oddly shaped forkshell mussel once lived in the Cumberland River downstream from Cumberland Falls, but it has not been observed in Kentucky since 1947. Male (top) and female. *Guenter A. Schuster*

Recent reports of the ivory-billed woodpecker from other states have stirred the birding community, but this regal bird disappeared from western Kentucky swamps in the early 1870s. *Artwork by Guy Coheleach*

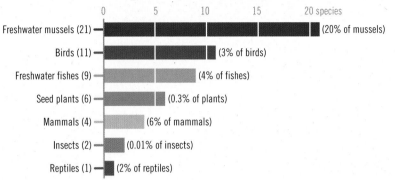

Extirpated and Extinct Species

Freshwater mussels (21) — (20% of mussels)
Birds (11) — (3% of birds)
Freshwater fishes (9) — (4% of fishes)
Seed plants (6) — (0.3% of plants)
Mammals (4) — (6% of mammals)
Insects (2) — (0.01% of insects)
Reptiles (1) — (2% of reptiles)

This chart includes **54 native taxa** (species and subspecies). Percentages are based on the total number of native species known from Kentucky for each species group.

members belonging to the riffleshell genus *Epioblasma,* require relatively unpolluted, large, free-flowing rivers to survive. All of Kentucky's large rivers have been altered by impoundment and degraded by water pollution. Consequently, species that live only in the largest rivers (e.g., the Ohio and Mississippi) were among the first to disappear.

With a range that extended from eastern Texas to North Carolina and from southern Illinois down through Florida and all the way to Cuba,[88] the ivory-billed woodpecker seemed secure. However, extensive loss of old-growth bottomland hardwood forests and swamps resulted in a major rangewide population crash of this magnificent bird. The last reports of ivory-billed woodpeckers in Kentucky came from Fulton County in the early 1870s.[11] In 1944, what was believed to be the last documented U.S. population of the ivory-billed woodpecker was lost when a lone female died in northeastern Louisiana.[89] In 2004, however, several reported sightings, as well as video and audio recordings, of at least one ivory-billed woodpecker were made in the Cache River National Wildlife Refuge in Monroe County, Arkansas.[89–91] Despite these observations and post-1950 reports in other southeastern states and Cuba,[89–91] the return of this majestic bird to Kentucky is unlikely because of habitat loss and fragmentation.

While several species disappeared from Kentucky many years ago (e.g., Carolina parakeet, passenger pigeon, and gray wolf), other species, such as the red-cockaded woodpecker, recently were lost from the state. Small populations of this bird were found in the mixed-pine woodlands of southeastern Kentucky. This pineland ecosystem was extensively altered by disturbance and loss of natural processes like periodic fire, so the birds continued to dwindle, despite management efforts. The final blow came from a massive loss of pine trees resulting from a southern pine beetle outbreak in 1999 and 2000 that killed many of the older trees the birds used for nesting. As a result, state and federal agencies decided that the remaining birds in Kentucky could not survive. The last red-cockaded woodpecker in Kentucky was captured in Laurel County on March 23, 2001, and relocated to South Carolina.

Burying beetles were given this intriguing common name because they bury the carcasses of small dead animals about the size of a mouse, robin, or quail. Adults remove the carcass's fur or feathers, roll the carcass into a ball, and treat it with secretions to prevent decomposition. Females lay eggs near the buried carcass. The eggs hatch in a few days, and larvae move to the carcass where the adults guard them and feed them regurgitated food until they are able to feed on the carcass independently. Parental care of any kind is very unusual among insects.

The American burying beetle is the largest carrion beetle in North America and was once widespread across much of temperate eastern North America, including Kentucky. However, it has disappeared from most of its historical range and is now federally listed as endangered. The decline seems to have taken place from the late 1800s to the early 1970s. Several factors may have contributed to the decline, but habitat fragmentation or loss that led to changes in carrion size or availability and increased competition from other scavengers is the leading theory for this beetle's rapid collapse. Other factors, such as insecticides, herbicides, disease, artificial lighting that attracts and kills insects (e.g., bug zappers) or otherwise interferes with their nocturnal activity (streetlights), and reproductive limitations may have contributed to the decline. The last American burying beetle observed in Kentucky was seen in Trigg County in 1974.

Wild populations of five mammal species (the American bison, eastern cougar, elk, gray wolf, and red wolf) were eliminated from Kentucky, primarily because of habitat loss and excessive hunting. However, in 1998 elk captured in Utah were introduced on reclaimed mine land and now roam across several counties in eastern Kentucky. American bison and elk were the two largest animals native to Kentucky at the time of European American settlement. Because of their size and relatively large numbers, they had a major influence on vegetation and vegetation structure. Large herds of grazing bison and elk helped maintain the open conditions of prairies and woodlands, and they trampled large areas along traces (trails) and around salt licks. In the forests they helped maintain trails and clearings.

The eastern cougar is an enigma. In all likelihood, this magnificent cat is extinct in the wild, but reports of cougar continue to pour in across the eastern United States, including Kentucky. Do these reports really represent eastern cougars that somehow managed to survive, hidden away in remote areas? Could they be once-captive western cougars that have escaped or been released into the wild, or are they young western cougar males seeking new territories in the east? It is very difficult to substantiate these reports, so the existence of the eastern cougar remains unconfirmed.

Kentucky continues to lose plants and animals. The red-cockaded woodpecker managed to survive in the state until 2001, but future generations will no longer see this woodpecker peering out of its nest cavity in Kentucky. *Danny Bales*

The American burying beetle is the only Kentucky insect federally listed as endangered. This large, beautiful beetle was last observed in Kentucky in 1974. *Courtesy of Nebraska Game and Parks Commission*

The reclusive eastern cougar, similar to the western cougar shown here in a controlled setting, once roamed Kentucky's forests. Wolves and cougars are refined predators that play important roles in maintaining healthy, balanced ecosystems. *Larry Master*

Smallscale darter males acquire brilliant colors in the spring to attract females. This gorgeous species is critically imperiled in Kentucky.
Matthew R. Thomas

SPECIES ON THE BRINK

Hundreds of taxa are perilously close to joining Kentucky's list of extirpated species. Currently, 727 (one lichen, 392 plants, and 334 animals) taxa are rare and KSNPC-listed (Appendix 2); however, more species are added to the list nearly every year. Of the 727 KSNPC-listed taxa, 381 (52%) are critically imperiled (S1), and 190 (26%) additional taxa are imperiled (S2). Furthermore, 76 of the 727 (10%) have not been seen in the state in 20 or more years (SH) and may have already been extirpated. The highest priority for conservation efforts should be given to critically imperiled species. Each population has the potential to contribute to the species' genetic diversity and may ultimately be vitally important to its survival.

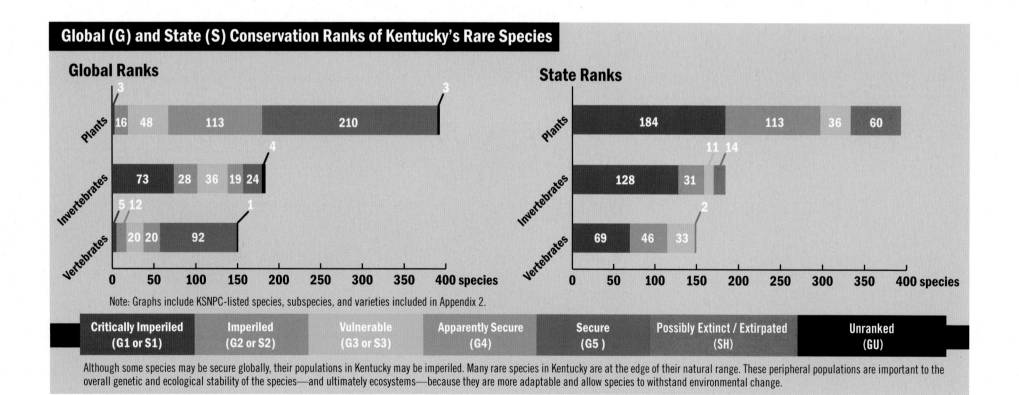

Global (G) and State (S) Conservation Ranks of Kentucky's Rare Species

Global Ranks

Plants: 3, 16, 48, 113, 210, 3
Invertebrates: 73, 28, 36, 19, 24, 4
Vertebrates: 5, 12, 20, 20, 92, 1

State Ranks

Plants: 184, 113, 36, 60
Invertebrates: 128, 31, 11, 14
Vertebrates: 69, 46, 33, 2

Note: Graphs include KSNPC-listed species, subspecies, and varieties included in Appendix 2.

Critically Imperiled (G1 or S1)	Imperiled (G2 or S2)	Vulnerable (G3 or S3)	Apparently Secure (G4)	Secure (G5)	Possibly Extinct / Extirpated (SH)	Unranked (GU)

Although some species may be secure globally, their populations in Kentucky may be imperiled. Many rare species in Kentucky are at the edge of their natural range. These peripheral populations are important to the overall genetic and ecological stability of the species—and ultimately ecosystems—because they are more adaptable and allow species to withstand environmental change.

NATURAL COMMUNITIES

Kentucky's rich biological diversity is also expressed by the variety and variability of the natural communities in the state. Simply defined, natural communities are distinct assemblages of plants, animals, and other organisms that tend to be repeated across the landscape where similar environmental conditions occur. The major natural community systems are terrestrial, wetland, aquatic, and subterranean.[92-94] Terrestrial communities range from dry, rocky glades to rich mesic forests, while wetland communities include bald cypress swamps and bottomland hardwood forests. Aquatic communities range from shallow floodplain lakes to high-gradient mountain streams. Subterranean communities include underground streams, huge caverns, and small caves.

Many factors are used to classify natural communities. Terrestrial and wetland communities are classified by factors such as vegetation, hydrology, soils, and geology. These communities usually are

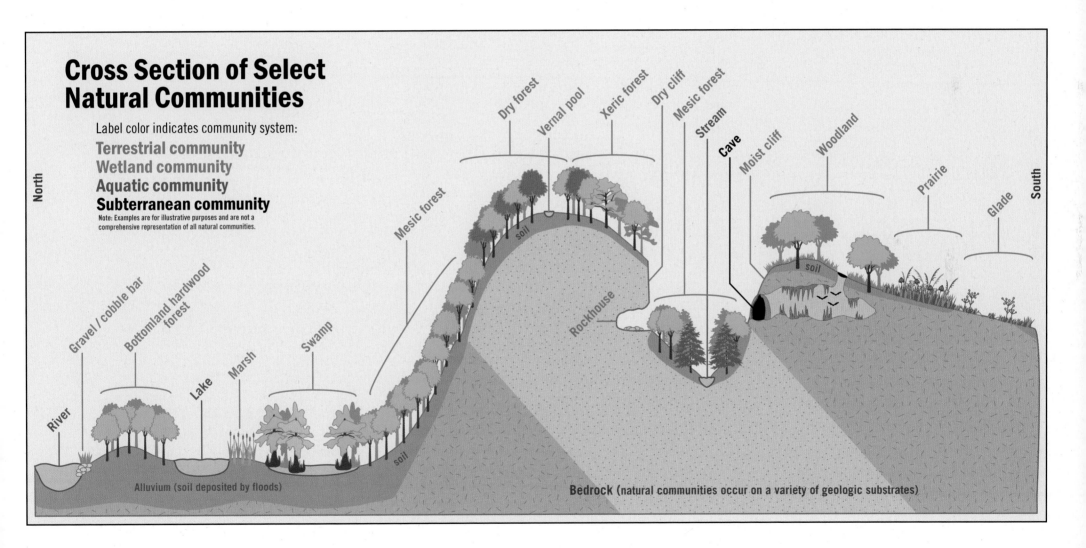

Cross Section of Select Natural Communities

Label color indicates community system:

Terrestrial community
Wetland community
Aquatic community
Subterranean community

Note: Examples are for illustrative purposes and are not a comprehensive representation of all natural communities.

North

South

Dry forest
Vernal pool
Xeric forest
Dry cliff
Mesic forest
Stream
Cave
Moist cliff
Woodland
Prairie
Glade

Mesic forest
soil
Rockhouse
soil

Gravel / cobble bar
Bottomland hardwood forest
Swamp
Lake
Marsh
River

soil
soil

Alluvium (soil deposited by floods)

Bedrock (natural communities occur on a variety of geologic substrates)

Classifications of natural communities are based on many factors. Rich, moist soil, sandstone bedrock (and boulders), deciduous canopy trees, and moisture-loving ferns help define this acidic mesophytic forest. *KSNPC photograph by Brian Yahn*

described in terms of the dominant vegetation because it is easily visible. Aquatic and subterranean communities may be classified by factors such as physical features and faunal groups. Thirty-seven terrestrial natural communities and 25 wetland natural communities are recognized as occurring in Kentucky (Appendix 4). Currently, there are no commonly accepted aquatic and subterranean community classification systems specifically for the state.

More than half of Kentucky's terrestrial natural communities and more than 80% of its wetland natural communities have been converted to land uses dominated by non-native species (primarily pasture, cropland, and lawn).[95, 96] Nearly all natural communities in the state have been altered by impacts such as logging, mining, fire, grazing, invasive species, hydrological changes, or erosion. In addition, many are fragmented by agriculture and development. As a result, high-quality natural communities of any type are rare.

TERRESTRIAL COMMUNITIES

Terrestrial communities occur primarily in upland areas with well-drained soils that do not flood or remain saturated for a prolonged period. They are classified as either forested or non-forested.

Terrestrial Forest Communities

Forests are communities dominated by trees with a more or less closed canopy cover (>75% canopy closure), where the branches of most adjacent trees meet or overlap. Kentucky has a great diversity of forest types because of the states' varied topography, geology, soils, and climate. KSNPC estimates that at the time of European American settlement, 85% to 90% of the state was covered in old-growth forests. Today, Kentucky is approximately 50% forest, with only about half of forests occurring as large forest tracts (see Large Forest Tracts map in chapter 6, p. 135).[95, 96]

Unfortunately, today's forests bear the scars of many decades of abuse. Repeated logging, overgrazing, invasive species and diseases, pollution, and frequent fires have taken a sad toll. Non-native fungi, insects, and other pathogens have attacked chestnut, elms, ashes, dogwoods, eastern hemlock, and oaks.

Most of Kentucky's forests are classified as temperate deciduous. Trees in deciduous forests lose their leaves in autumn and go dormant during the winter. Evergreen forests of pine, eastern hemlock, or cedar are more limited but also occur in the state. Upland and wetland forests are primarily classified based on soil conditions (dry or mesic) for upland forests, and duration and degree of wetness for wetland forests. They may be further divided by the substrate upon which they grow (e.g., limestone, sandstone, or shale).

Dry forests are common in Kentucky and are generally found on slopes facing south and west, narrow ridgetops, and other areas with poor or rocky soils that are very well drained. These forests are often referred to collectively as oak-hickory forests. Depending upon the substrate, characteristic trees of dry forests include white, Chinkapin, black, chestnut, scarlet, and southern red oaks, as well as pignut hickory, red maple, and sourwood. The driest sites with the poorest soil (i.e., xeric forest) usually have post and blackjack oaks.

Although dry forests are mainly deciduous, they often have evergreen trees as constituents or dominants, especially in xeric (very dry) areas. Pitch and shortleaf pine primarily are restricted to sandstone and shale on the Appalachian Plateau, Cumberland Mountains, and eastern Knobs, whereas red cedar and Virginia pine occur statewide in dry forests, often on limestone and sandstone.

Mesic forests occur throughout Kentucky wherever rich, moist soils have developed. They are associated with sites protected from direct sun, such as deep ravines and hollows or hillsides facing north and east. Common trees in mesic forests include sugar maple, American beech, white ash, northern red oak, yellow poplar, black walnut, and shagbark hickory. Typical trees and shrubs found below the canopy include spicebush, pawpaw, and wild hydrangea. These forests have the best display of spring wildflowers. Trilliums, bloodroot, wood poppy, jack-in-the-pulpit, and many others may carpet the forest floor.

The Appalachian mesophytic forests in eastern Kentucky are richer and more diverse than the typical mesic forests in the rest of the state. In fact, these forests, called mixed mesophytic forest, are among the most diverse temperate forests in the world. Many species of trees may codominate, and any one stand may commonly have yellow poplar, basswood, American beech, sugar maple, yellow buckeye, and many others. Deep gorges or valleys often have eastern hemlock and sometimes white pine. Great rhododendron can form dense, almost impenetrable thickets in these gorges. Disjunct, less diverse examples of these forests can be found in a few scattered locations in the Knobs and Shawnee Hills.

The Cumberland highlands forest is a rare type of northern hardwood forest that only occurs in the Cumberland Mountains at elevations above 3,400 feet, primarily on Black Mountain in Harlan County. This forest type is extremely lush and rich, partly because of high precipitation (more than 60 inches per year) and cooler temperatures due to elevation. Characteristic trees include yellow birch, black cherry, sugar maple, and mountain magnolia.

Prairie, Glade, Woodland, and Cliff Communities

Although Kentucky was mostly forested at the time of European American settlement, KSNPC estimates that 10% to 15% of the state was composed of nonforested communities like prairies, glades, woodlands, and cliffs. Historically, fire and grazing

above: Black Mountain in Harlan County supports the Cumberland highlands forest, a type of northern hardwood forest that is home to numerous rare plants and animals. *KSNPC photograph by Marc Evans*

left: The hemlock-mixed forest is a type of Appalachian mesophytic forest that occurs in the Cumberland Mountains and Appalachian Plateaus of eastern Kentucky. This forest has the highest diversity of tree species (up to 28) in North American temperate forests and is one of the earth's most diverse temperate forests. *KSNPC photograph by Martina Hines*

Glades, such as this limestone glade, usually occur as small natural openings in a forest. *KSNPC photograph by Brian Yahn*

Native prairie once covered millions of acres in western Kentucky. Today, only small remnants exist. *Thomas G. Barnes*

by bison, elk, and deer were critical in maintaining the open conditions of prairies and woodlands. Today, these communities are very rare and only occur as scattered remnants due to habitat destruction (agriculture and development), fire suppression, and invasion by non-native species.

Prairies are open grasslands with little or no woody cover (<25% canopy closure). KSNPC estimates that at the time of settlement, Kentucky had 2.5 to 3.0 million acres of prairie, mostly in the Highland Rim and Coastal Plain. Early accounts described vast prairies that were 60 to 70 miles long and 60 miles wide, with tall grasses and few trees or shrubs. Early settlers called them "barrens" because they thought the soil was too poor to support trees. Today, only a few thousand acres of prairie are left in widely scattered and mostly degraded remnants. An exception is Fort Campbell Military Reservation, which contains one of the largest prairie remnants east of the Mississippi River (~20,000 acres in Kentucky and Tennessee). This prairie has persisted because it is part of the Fort Campbell weapons firing range, and it frequently burns as a side effect of exploding munitions.

There are two broad types of upland prairie communities in Kentucky. Tallgrass prairie, or mesic prairie, occurs on deep, rich, well-drained soils and is dominated by big bluestem and Indian grass. The deep root systems of the tallgrass prairie and its associated soil organisms have created some of the most productive soil in the world. Dry prairie occurs on sites that have thinner and drier soil, where rock is sometimes exposed. They are often called midgrass prairies due to the dominance of shorter grasses, such as little bluestem and tall dropseed.

Glades are small, naturally open areas with bedrock at or near the surface. In Kentucky, glades are very uncommon and small (usually less than 2 acres). Typically located on slopes facing south and west and exposed to sun and heat, glades are predominately xeric, and soils are thin and droughty.

They occur on sandstone, limestone, and shale and may either be level or sloping. Although glades are usually dry, winter and spring precipitation often saturates and pools on level glades, sometimes for a period of weeks. Because this wet period is so brief, many species that live in glades have adapted to harsh, dry conditions. Glade species are either very drought-tolerant or are annuals that flower and set seed before the heat of the summer. Glades are surprisingly diverse for their size and serve as isolated refugia for many species. Some typical glade plants include false aloe, eastern prickly pear cactus, poverty dropseed, pale purple coneflower, widow's-cross stonecrop, orange grass, and rushfoil.

Woodlands are communities composed of widely spaced trees that form a canopy that is open to partially closed (25%–75% canopy closure), which allows enough light through to support grass and shrubs in the understory. Woodlands are transition zones between forests and grasslands, and they support species from both types of communities. Their open structure is maintained by drier site conditions and periodic disturbance like fire or grazing. Today, woodlands are rare, and most that once existed have been cleared for pasture or have grown back into closed-canopy forest due to a lack of fire or other natural disturbances that helped maintain their open aspect.

Extremely dry pine or oak woodlands occur on exposed ridgetops and adjacent hillsides. The associated ground cover is sparse due to rocky, thin soils. Oak woodlands of blackjack, post, chinkapin, and chestnut oak are scattered throughout the state. Pine woodlands of pitch and shortleaf pine occur in the Appalachian Highlands and Cumberland Mountains. Most dry woodlands include red cedar and Virginia pine. More mesic woodlands occur on rolling plains and lower slopes where soils are deeper and droughts have less impact.

Limestone and sandstone cliff communities are common throughout the state. Cliffs provide

above: The Bluegrass woodland, a very rare type of woodland, was only known to occur in the Bluegrass region and is now essentially extirpated. It is thought that grazing by large herds of bison, elk, and deer, as well as infrequent fire, helped maintain the woodland's open, savanna-like appearance. The exact composition and extent of this community are not known because the Bluegrass was settled early, and the community was destroyed before it was well-documented. The Bluegrass woodland was dominated by huge, spreading bur oaks, chinkapin oaks, and blue ash. *Neil Pederson, EKU*

right: Natural rock shelters called rockhouses are interesting features that occur in some cliffs. Rockhouses have overhanging roofs and are more or less protected from weather. Many are small, but others are huge and cavelike (hundreds of feet wide and almost as deep). Some are desert-dry and barren, and others are wet and covered with liverworts and ferns. A number of rare species are associated with cliffs and rockhouses. *KSNPC photograph by Brian Yahn*

Cliff communities occur along the hundreds of miles of cliff lines in the state. *KSNPC photograph by Marc Evans*

a variety of habitats for plants and animals. Many cliffs are exposed and xeric, while some are sheltered and range from moist to wet. Natural rockhouses, also called rock shelters, are interesting features of some cliffs.

Lacustrine wetlands occur in lakes, defined as deep water bodies that have a wave-swept shoreline. Metropolis Lake, a state nature preserve along the Ohio River in McCracken County, is one of Kentucky's few remaining natural lakes. © *Chuck Summers*

Palustrine wetlands, like this cypress swamp, are periodically to semipermanently flooded. They include swamps, bottomland hardwood forests, marshes, and seeps. *KSNPC photograph by Marc Evans*

WETLAND COMMUNITIES

Wetlands are areas that have shallow standing water or saturated soils for at least part of the year, and support plants, animals, and other organisms that are adapted to living under these conditions. The majority of wetlands are found within floodplains of medium to large rivers, but isolated wetlands in sinkholes and depressions (i.e., vernal pools) also may be found in upland areas. Most upland wetlands result from the development of a hard, essentially impermeable soil layer called a fragipan or hardpan.

The vast majority of Kentucky's wetlands occur in the western half of the state. Wetlands may be forested or nonforested, and they range from deep-water cypress and tupelo swamps to infrequently flooded bottomland terrace forests. Nonforested wetlands range from seasonally wet meadows to marshes and shrub swamps that are wet year-round. At the time of settlement, Kentucky had more than 1.5 million acres of diverse wetlands. Today, after major drainage projects, less than 300,000 acres of wetlands remain, and many of these are in poor condition.[97]

Wetland Forest Communities

A swamp is a hardwood, conifer, or mixed-forest wetland that is permanently or semipermanently flooded or saturated, deterring the growth of most trees and shrubs. Plants that live in swamps are adapted to grow in or on the water or epiphytically (i.e., on other plants or floating logs). Swamps range from closed canopy to very open and often occur in a mosaic of swamp, shrub swamp, and marsh. Swamps occur primarily in the floodplains of rivers but also occur in upland depressions.

Typical deep-water swamps in Kentucky usually are dominated by bald cypress, often with swamp tupelo, and are restricted to the western half of Kentucky. Other common swamp trees include overcup oak, swamp chestnut oak, swamp white oak, and willow oak as well as black willow, red maple, and swamp cottonwood.

Bottomland hardwood forests typically have a shorter hydroperiod (period of water saturation) than swamps, and they usually develop a more diverse hardwood canopy and sometimes a well-developed understory. Characteristic trees, which often grow to huge size, include pin oak, overcup oak, swamp chestnut oak, sweet gum, American elm, silver maple, sycamore, and green ash.

Flatwoods are scattered across Kentucky but are uncommon. They occur on level terrain where a fragipan—which restricts drainage and causes water to pool at or near the surface—has developed. Flatwoods are usually wet in the winter and spring, but some may be very dry during summer months,

creating xero-hydric (dry-wet) habitat conditions. Post oak is the characteristic tree of the xero-hydric flatwoods, often occurring in pure stands. Other trees of flatwoods include shagbark hickory, southern red oak, willow oak, white oak, and pin oak.

Marsh, Seep, Wet Prairie, and Shrub Swamp Communities

A marsh is an open, treeless wetland usually dominated by sedges, rushes, and grasses. Water depth influences the distribution and kinds of plants and results in distinct vegetation zones within a marsh ranging from deep water with submerged aquatics to shallow water with emergent aquatics. Wet meadows, somewhat similar to marshes, are usually drier and support more mesic forb species than marshes. Wet prairies, also similar to marshes, often contain a mixture of species from mesic upland prairie and wetland marsh communities. They occur on deep, poorly drained soils and are dominated by cord grass, gamma grass, switch grass, and big bluestem. Marshes and wet meadows are scattered throughout the state, but only a few remnant wet prairies are known to exist.

Seeps are usually small, open- to closed-canopy wetlands that form where groundwater percolates to the surface. They often are carpeted with a dense covering of sphagnum or other mosses, which in turn support an interesting assemblage of ferns and wildflowers adapted to grow in the saturated substrate. Two characteristic ferns of this habitat are cinnamon and royal ferns. Other typical plants include cardinal flower, turtlehead, smooth phlox, and arrow-leaved tear thumb. Seeps are among the most fragile and rarest communities in the state.

A shrub swamp is a wetland dominated by shrubs and small trees such as buttonbush, sandbar willow, Virginia willow, and swamp rose. Shrub swamps usually occur around the edges of floodplain sloughs and in other shallow-water areas. Although usually small in extent, some shrub swamps may cover many acres.

Riverine wetlands include areas within the channel of a river or stream, including natural communities such as gravel/cobble bars, mud flats, and sandbars. These communities and the species that live in them are adapted to frequent disturbances, both from scouring by fast-moving floodwaters and from silt deposition by slow-moving floodwaters.

Old-growth forests (see sidebar for definition)

An unusual and very rare type of wetland is the seep, often called a bog. Most are very acidic, but some that occur over limestone are quite calcareous. Cinnamon ferns, often growing more than six feet tall, are characteristic of this habitat. © Chuck Summers

Cumberland Plateau gravel/cobble bar is a rare riverine wetland community that occurs in several streams in the Cumberland Plateau of southeastern Kentucky. The bars here are well-developed and are composed of boulders mixed with sand and gravel. Instead of the weedy plants of typical cobble bars, the flora is rich in prairie plants and other unusual species. The open areas of the bars have grasses such as big bluestem, Indian grass, and little bluestem. Blazing stars, false dragonhead, and rockcastle asters add to the prairie-like appearance. Thomas G. Barnes

OLD-GROWTH FORESTS

Old-growth forests are much more than groups of large, old trees. KSNPC recognizes two basic kinds of old-growth forest: those that have never been logged (primary forests), and second-growth forests with limited disturbance for at least a century. Some experts suggest 150 to 200 years as a minimum age indicator of old growth.[98,99] Old-growth forests are characterized by a scattering of old trees of relatively large diameter with spreading crowns, a good representation of unevenly aged younger trees, undisturbed soil, and an understory of native species. Over time, natural disturbances and maturity result in an increasing number of large snags, pits, and mounds from fallen trees; rotting logs in various stages of decay; natural gaps; and generally a more complex forest structure.[98,100]

of any type are rare. Today, only 7,200 acres of old-growth forest are known in 67 scattered tracts in Kentucky.[11] Less than half of Kentucky's forest and woodland communities (15 of 34) have at least one known representative old-growth stand.[11] Most of these are small stands of old trees, but a few larger examples still exist. Blanton Forest State Nature Preserve in Harlan County, with approximately 2,300 acres of old growth, is the largest old-growth remnant known in Kentucky. Other large, protected old-growth tracts include Lilley Cornett Woods in Letcher County, Big Woods in Mammoth Cave National Park, Obion Creek Wildlife Management Area in Hickman County, and several stands scattered throughout Daniel Boone National Forest.

The majority of Kentucky's native freshwater species are found in natural, free-flowing streams. The Big South Fork Cumberland River supports a diverse aquatic community upstream from the impounded section of Lake Cumberland, including several rare fishes and mussels. *Sabrina Christian*

AQUATIC COMMUNITIES

Aquatic systems are classified as running water (lotic), such as creeks and rivers, or standing water (lentic), which includes ponds, lakes, and wetlands.[101] Aquatic animal communities are found in similar habitats within each system, occurring within the bottom sediments (worms and water mites), upon the bottom (many macroinvertebrates), among vegetation (dragonflies and beetles), in the water column (fishes), and on the surface (water striders). However, different physical and chemical characteristics in each system lead to distinct plant and animal communities. Some species (e.g., large-mouth bass) are generalists capable of living in either system, but the majority of darters, freshwater mussels, stoneflies, and many others can live only in streams. Native species that live in natural (i.e., unimpounded, unchannelized) stream communities are the primary reason for Kentucky's exceptional aquatic biodiversity.

Running Water

Streams may be roughly classified as temporary or permanent (perennial).[101, 102] Temporary streams flow intermittently (after a rain), or they sink below ground at some point. Small streams with no tributaries (other streams flowing into the original stream) are called first-order streams. Two first-order streams unite to form a second-order stream, two second-order streams combine to make a third-order stream, and so on. They can further be classified into three sizes or segments within a river system: small headwater streams, medium-sized streams, and large rivers.

Species in creeks and rivers have adapted to a unidirectional water flow, high dissolved oxygen levels, and lower water temperatures, especially in the headwaters (first- or second-order segments). Constant flow transports food from upstream to downstream, so the animals in each stream or river

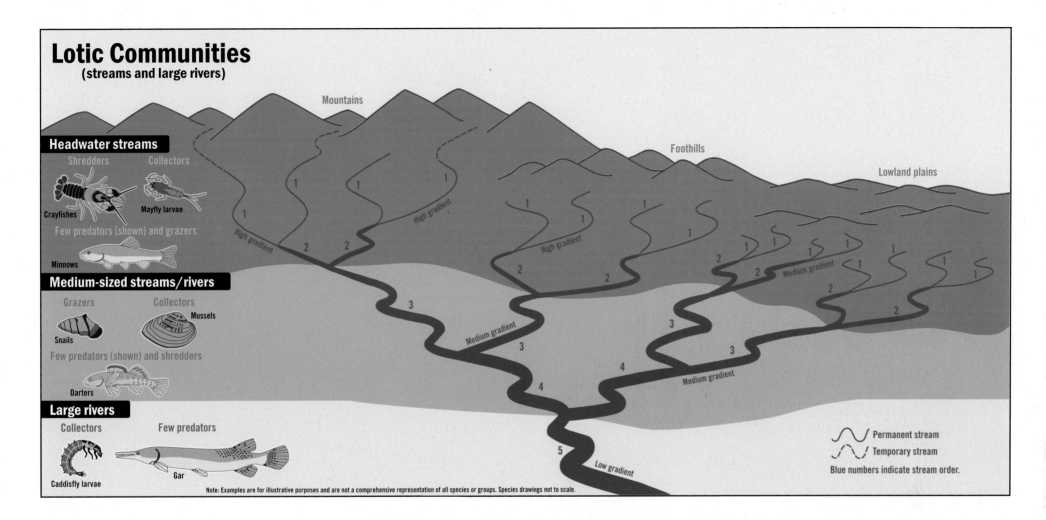

Lotic Communities
(streams and large rivers)

Headwater streams

Shredders   Collectors

Crayfishes   Mayfly larvae

Few predators (shown) and grazers

Minnows

Medium-sized streams/rivers

Grazers   Collectors
                   Mussels

Snails

Few predators (shown) and shredders

Darters

Large rivers

Collectors   Few predators

Caddisfly larvae   Gar

Note: Examples are for illustrative purposes and are not a comprehensive representation of all species or groups. Species drawings not to scale.

Mountains

Foothills

Lowland plains

Permanent stream
Temporary stream
Blue numbers indicate stream order.

High gradient · Medium gradient · Low gradient

segment use specialized feeding mechanisms to perform a role or function based on available food resources (see text box). For example, some caddisflies are "collectors" because they filter minute food particles carried in slower currents by constructing tiny, fine-mesh nets made of silk. From a river's headwaters to its mouth, physical and chemical changes occur that lead to a continuous change in the aquatic community. This interaction, as described in more detail below, is called the river continuum concept.[103]

In general, first-order or headwater streams have cool- or cold-water-adapted species that rely

GENERAL CLASSES OF AQUATIC SPECIES

Here is a general classification of aquatic species by feeding method and ecological role in an aquatic system:[64]

- **Shredders** shred organic material (e.g., plants, leaves, and sticks) into smaller sizes.
- **Collectors** collect or filter small organic particles.
- **Scrapers** or **grazers** graze on algae or plant material attached to surfaces such as rocks and logs.
- **Plant piercers** pierce plants and suck out their fluids.
- **Predators** are carnivores that eat other animals.
- **Parasites** live on or in other organisms and feed on the host's tissues.
- **Scavengers** eat dead and decaying organic matter.

above and below:
Appearing in the fossil record before dinosaurs, paddlefish are among the oldest fishes on Earth. They live in large rivers, where their diet consists of zooplankton filtered from the water.
John R. MacGregor

Hellgrammites, the larval stage of dobsonflies (order Megaloptera), are well-equipped to live in the swift currents of riffles. Individuals have paired claws on their legs and terminal appendages (prolegs) that help them hold on to the bottom. *Guenter A. Schuster*

above right:
Riffles, the shallow, turbulent areas of streams, support a rich assemblage of aquatic organisms. They also make great ambush points for predators, such as this black-crowned night-heron feasting on gizzard shad at the Falls of the Ohio River near Louisville. © *John Brunjes*

primarily on leaf drop and other organic material from the terrestrial environment. Organisms capable of collecting, tearing, or shredding leaves, sticks and other organic material for food (e.g., crayfishes, mayflies, and stoneflies) and small insectivorous fishes (creek chub is the prototypical species) dominate headwaters. Coarse organic material is broken down into smaller particle sizes and carried by the current downstream, where the stream widens and drainage area increases. Headwater streams are critically important to the well-being of downstream communities, and disturbances therein may have profound negative effects on biodiversity throughout the watershed.

Aquatic communities in medium-sized streams are less reliant on food from the adjacent terrestrial environment because the stream is wider and the canopy above it is open. This allows for more sunlight and greater in-stream photosynthesis (i.e., food production) that exceeds terrestrial input. As the stream width begins to increase, velocity slows, and the water begins to warm, with more sunlight penetrating to the bottom. The animal community shifts from collector and shredder species to predominantly grazers and collectors. Grazers scrape algae off rocks with specialized mouthparts. Aquatic plants, snails, mussels, and larger predatory fishes (such as smallmouth bass) that are not found in the headwaters begin to appear. Species diversity increases with increasing stream size, drainage area, food availability, moderate water temperatures, and habitat variability.

Another shift occurs in the physical, chemical, and biological characteristics of a stream as it continues downstream, receives the input of many tributaries, and becomes a large river. Due to the erosional powers of water, the river generally meanders more, and its width significantly increases, allowing more sunlight to warm the water. Current slows, and river plankton communities, both animal and plant species, become more common. Fine organic particles suspended in the water column are a major food component of large river communities. The aquatic community changes to species adapted to warmer water, and overall diversity begins to decline due to uniformity of habitat, food, and temperature. Plankton and other filter feeders, such as paddlefish, mussels, and caddisflies, and predators, such as gar and catfish, are the norm.

Habitats within stream segments include riffles, runs, and pools.[6] Riffles have the most turbulent, highly oxygenated, and swift water, with coarse rock and gravel bottoms. Species that live in riffles have physical adaptations or behaviors that help them hold on in fast current, such as burrowing into the bottom (mussels), lack of or reduced air bladders (darters), flattened bodies (water penny beetle larvae), or hooks and suckers (mayfly, stonefly, and dobsonfly larvae). Runs are transitional areas between riffles and pools. Species that live here prefer slower currents and take advantage of food washed downstream from the turbulent riffles. Pools have the slowest current and deepest water in streams, and scavengers (such as suckers and catfish) and plankton feeders are common. Only the finest sediments remain suspended in slow currents, and the aquatic community more closely resembles a lentic system.

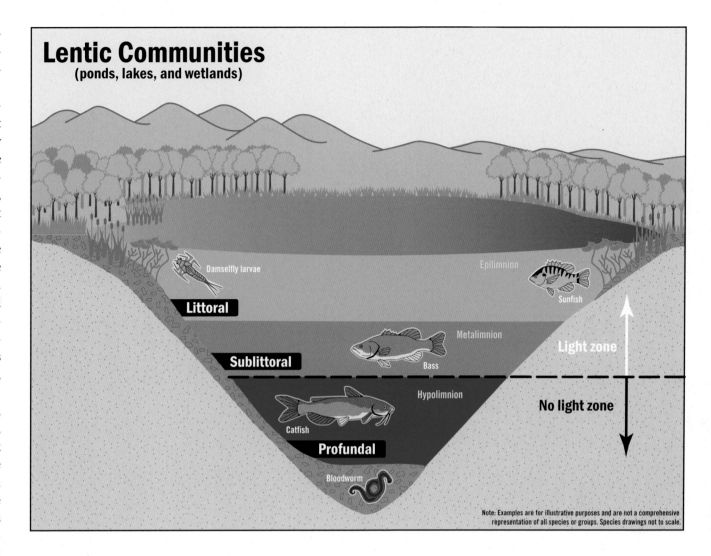

Note: Examples are for illustrative purposes and are not a comprehensive representation of all species or groups. Species drawings not to scale.

Standing Water

Lentic systems differ from lotic systems in that they lack a unidirectional current. Food sources, substrate composition, temperature profiles, oxygen levels, and species assemblages are also different.[101] Food production primarily comes from within the system. Typically bowl-shaped, lentic habitats are classified according to the amount of light that reaches the bottom. Lentic habitats may also have temperature stratification zones if the water is deep.

Species that live in lentic systems, such as this cypress swamp in Ballard County, do not require flowing water, and many have developed strategies to deal with oxygen depletion. © *Chuck Summers*

Damselfly larvae, including this American rubyspot, have large gills at the end of their abdomen to extract oxygen from the water. *KSNPC photograph by Ellis L. Laudermilk*

The warmest water occurs at or near the surface; the coldest is at or near the bottom.

Three zones of lentic habitats are recognized according to the amount of light that strikes the bottom.[101] The littoral zone occurs along the shallow edges of lentic habitats. Light penetrates all the way to the bottom in this zone, allowing photosynthesis to occur, and vegetation may be abundant. The aquatic community revolves around light and photosynthesis, and species diversity (e.g., dragonflies, damselflies, beetles, and sunfishes) is greatest in this zone. The sublittoral zone includes deeper water; while light typically reaches the bottom, this zone is dimly lit, and vegetation is absent. The deepest water habitats compose the profundal or dark zone. No light reaches the bottom in this zone, and decomposition of organic material is prevalent. Decomposition uses the limited oxygen in the water, so dissolved oxygen levels may reach very low levels. It is difficult for species to tolerate these harsh conditions, but a few have adapted and may even be abundant.

Unlike most of their stream counterparts, lentic species often cope with lower dissolved oxygen levels, which seasonally may become extremely low.[101] Consequently, many species are equipped to circumvent this problem. For example, some fishes, such as topminnows, live near the surface and have upturned mouths so they can breathe air if needed.[104] Some beetles trap an air bubble under their body while at the surface and then use air from the bubble while feeding underwater. Other insects have very large gills to extract oxygen (e.g., damselflies), or they extend respiratory tubes (e.g., water scorpions) above the surface to breathe air.[64] Bloodworms, the larvae of midge flies, live in the oxygen-depleted profundal zone. They are called bloodworms because they possess and rely upon hemoglobin, a red pigment that enhances their ability to use available oxygen.[105] In small, isolated wetlands that dry periodically, fairy shrimp have adapted by producing drought-resistant eggs that are laid prior to the onset of dry conditions.

Like other organisms, aquatic species have specific habitat requirements. Physically altering or polluting an aquatic system may completely change its physical and chemical characteristics, thus eliminating some or most of the species that live there.[102] For example, all of Kentucky's large rivers have been impounded, and some of these (e.g., the Ohio and Kentucky) were impounded by a series of locks and dams that allow navigation. Dams impede normal flow patterns and migration of aquatic organisms and create a series of connected reservoirs, so impounded rivers function more like hybrids between rivers and lakes. Consequently, many aquatic organisms—especially freshwater mussels that are adapted to live only in unimpeded big-river habitats—have disappeared from impounded rivers. Like the bloodstream of a human, unpolluted, free-flowing streams are the life-support system for many plants and animals.

SUBTERRANEAN COMMUNITIES

Karst landscapes are areas of land sculpted by the dissolution and erosion of limestone,[106] and most of Kentucky's caves are formed in these regions. Constant weathering of limestone leads to the development of sinkholes, sinking streams, underground rivers, springs, and caves. Obligate cave-dwelling organisms (hereafter subterranean) are ecologically adapted to live only in caves and their associated streams and groundwater.[107, 108] Little is known about Kentucky's obligatory deep-soil-dwelling fauna (edaphobites) and species found in deep wells or slowly moving groundwater (phreatobites), so they are not addressed here.

Caves are normally defined as natural openings in the ground that extend beyond the light zone and are large enough for human entry.[109] Kentucky's caves primarily form in limestone as slightly acidic, slowly moving groundwater or underground streams abrade, dissolve, and carry away rock, leaving behind passages. Most caves in the world, especially the largest, form during this process and are called solution caves.[109]

Several criteria are used to classify caves, including rock type (e.g., limestone), stream type (influent, effluent), and cave origin (solution).[109] Dry caves do not have streams, and wet or active caves are further classified by three types of streams: influent, effluent, or through. Influent caves have streams that flow into them, while effluent caves have streams flowing out of them. Through caves contain streams

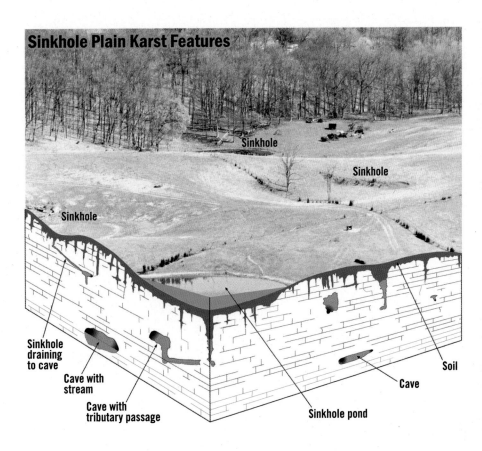

Sinkhole Plain Karst Features

Sinkhole

Sinkhole

Sinkhole

Sinkhole draining to cave

Cave with stream

Cave with tributary passage

Sinkhole pond

Cave

Soil

right: Kentucky's caves contain some amazingly beautiful formations, and collectively they support one of the richest subterranean faunas in the nation. Tiny pseudoscorpions, beetles, and white, eyeless fishes and crayfishes are among the species that live exclusively in caves. © *Chuck Summers*

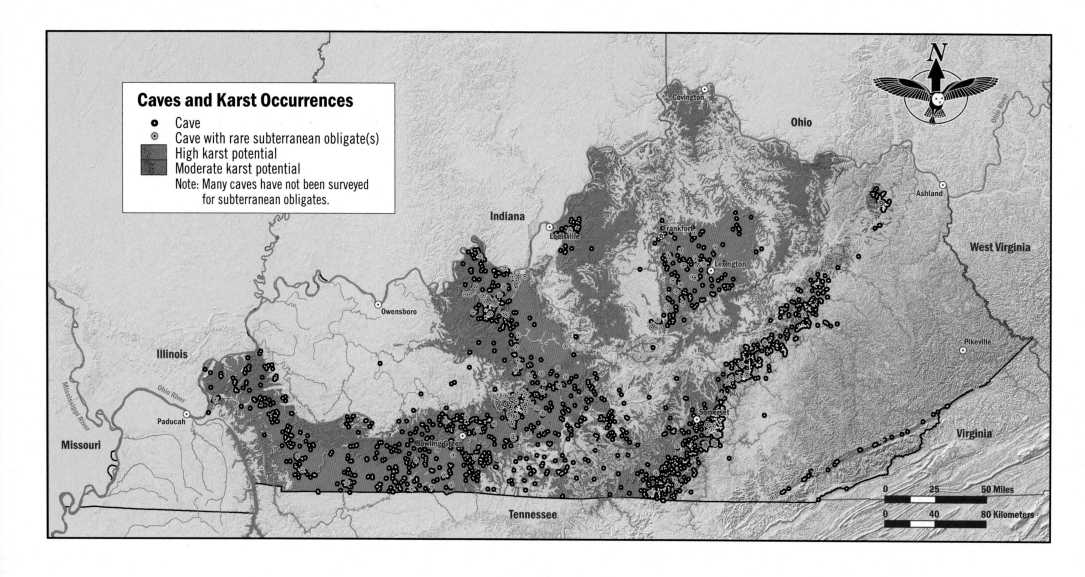

Caves and Karst Occurrences

- ○ Cave
- ◉ Cave with rare subterranean obligate(s)
- High karst potential
- Moderate karst potential
- Note: Many caves have not been surveyed for subterranean obligates.

flowing both into and out of the cave. Kentucky's caves vary in size from small tubes or rooms to the extensive passages of Mammoth Cave.[106]

Subterranean organisms, also known as troglobites (terrestrial) or stygobites (aquatic), have several advantageous adaptations for life underground: (1) specialized sense structures for touch, taste, and smell; (2) longer appendages for energy-efficient movement or sensory enhancement; (3) behavior and reproductive modifications needed for nutrient-

poor environments, such as those often found in caves; and (4) much longer life spans than their surface counterparts, probably because of a slower metabolism and fewer predators.[110] Conversely, life underground also means that some body parts or functions, such as eyes, pigment, or flight, are not needed, so they slowly become nonfunctional or are completely lost.

Cave communities ultimately are supported by food (organic materials) brought in from the surface in two primary ways.[111] Food (e.g., sticks and leaves) may be transported by water, either from a stream flowing into the cave or by percolation of water from the surface. Alternatively, food may be directly transported into caves by animals (e.g., bats and cave crickets) in the form of feces, as the eggs of cave crickets, or by animals that fall into or enter caves and subsequently die there. Subterranean species also may be harmed or killed by pollution that washes in from sinkholes, sinking streams, or groundwater. Bioaccumulation (i.e., the accumulation of toxins such as pesticides or herbicides) is a major concern for cave organisms and all species with long life spans. Predators from above ground, especially introduced non-native species, may invade caves and decimate subterranean populations, because cave species are not adapted to coexist with their surface counterparts.

The United States harbors more known subterranean species than any other country in the world.[112] Approximately 1,000 subterranean species have been described from the United States,[112] but as many as 6,000 additional species may await discovery.[113] On the basis of the best information available, it is estimated that Kentucky's subterranean fauna is about the fifth most diverse in the nation,[114] with more than 130 species and subspecies. Remarkably, 82 (62%) are endemic to the state, and most have very limited distributions. In fact, many are known from a single location, such as Rogers' cave beetle, which is found only in one Kentucky cave. The restricted distribution of subterranean species means they are particularly vulnerable to extinction, and 78% of the state's fauna is globally imperiled or vulnerable (G1–G3).[115]

Two subterranean fishes, the northern and southern cavefishes, occur in the state.[8] Both have limited distributions and are KSNPC-listed as special concern. The overwhelming majority of subterranean species are invertebrates, especially insects. Beetles account for approximately 45% of the fauna,

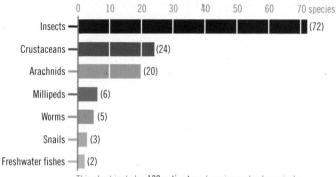

Subterranean Obligate Species

Insects (72)
Crustaceans (24)
Arachnids (20)
Millipeds (6)
Worms (5)
Snails (3)
Freshwater fishes (2)

This chart includes 132 native taxa (species and subspecies).

above and below:
The northern cavefish is one of two rare Kentucky fishes (the other is the southern cavefish) adapted to live only in caves. It occurs from Edmonson and Hart counties to Breckinridge and Meade counties. *John R. MacGregor*

Three rare subterranean obligate crayfishes occur in Kentucky, including this Appalachian cave crayfish. *Guenter A. Schuster*

and an astounding 92% are endemic to Kentucky. Three rare subterranean crayfishes are known from Kentucky caves.[62] The ghost crayfish occurs in caves in the upper Green and Nolin river watersheds and in Breckinridge, Hardin, and Meade counties. The Mammoth Cave crayfish is known from caves in the lower Cumberland and Green river watersheds, most notably the Mammoth Cave system. The Appalachian cave crayfish is found in upper Cumberland River watershed caves. One of the rarest invertebrates is the Mammoth Cave shrimp, a federally

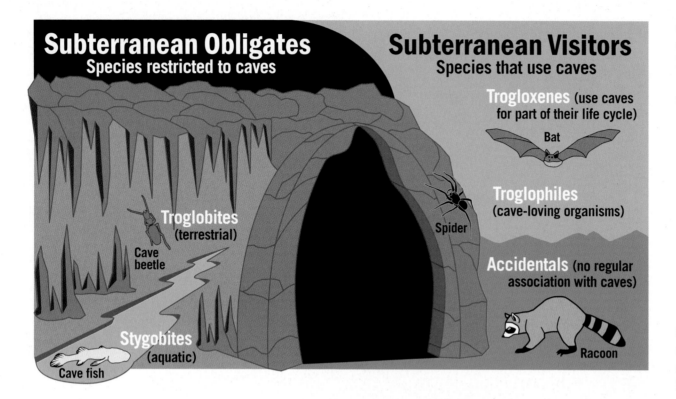

Subterranean Obligates
Species restricted to caves

Troglobites (terrestrial)
Cave beetle

Stygobites (aquatic)
Cave fish

Subterranean Visitors
Species that use caves

Trogloxenes (use caves for part of their life cycle)
Bat

Troglophiles (cave-loving organisms)
Spider

Accidentals (no regular association with caves)
Racoon

The Virginia big-eared bat, a federally endangered species, has ears more than an inch long. *John R. MacGregor*

and KSNPC-listed endangered species that is endemic to subterranean groundwater in and around Mammoth Cave.[4]

In addition to subterranean species, other animals use caves and are classified as follows:

- Troglophiles are cave-loving organisms that can complete their entire life cycle in caves, but they also use cavelike habitats (e.g., some spiders and salamanders)

- Trogloxenes use caves for part of their life cycle (e.g., bats), but they return to the surface or cave entrance to obtain food.

- Accidentals have no regular association with caves (e.g., raccoons).[107, 108]

Bats are perhaps the most familiar of Kentucky's trogloxenes. Of the state's 16 bat species, 10 depend on the warm and relatively stable temperatures of caves to survive harsh winter weather. While some bats migrate south to avoid winter, most hibernate in caves, where cool temperatures slow their metabolism. A few of these species also inhabit caves at other times of the year to raise their young in the protected confines of underground passages.

There is still much to learn about Kentucky's subterranean habitats and fauna. In fact, while *Caves and Karst of Kentucky* reported 3,770 caves in 1985,[106] the precise number of caves in the state is still unknown. The Kentucky Speleological Survey has mapped approximately 3,100 unique caves and estimates that more than 5,000 will eventually be catalogued.[116] Lying beneath portions of Barren, Edmonson, and Hart counties, Mammoth Cave is Kentucky's—and arguably the nation's—crown jewel, with more subterranean species than any other U.S. cave.[117, 118] Most caves in the state still await comprehensive biological inventories that will undoubtedly yield new species; nevertheless, Kentucky already supports one of the most diverse subterranean faunas in the world.

Chapter Five

THREATS

Like wind and sunsets, wild things were taken for granted until progress began to do away with them. Now we face the question whether a still higher "standard of living" is worth its cost in things natural, wild, and free.

—ALDO LEOPOLD[1]

KENTUCKY'S BIODIVERSITY is in an unfortunate state of decline. Although the causes of this decline are varied, virtually all of them can ultimately be traced to people and our use of resources. Habitat loss has clearly had the most adverse impact on biodiversity in Kentucky and continues to be the most significant threat to it. Loss of habitat results from conversion of natural areas to other land uses (e.g., forest cleared for a building site) and degradation of habitat quality due to invasive species, pollution, and climate change. Additionally, overexploitation of species is a threat that has resulted in species loss. This chapter explores human impacts on Kentucky's biodiversity.

HABITAT CONVERSION AND LAND-USE CHANGE

The initial settlement of Kentucky by European Americans more than 200 years ago was the beginning of significant loss of natural habitat. Land clearing for agriculture and housing has continued since settlement and has expanded as the state's population has grown. Agriculture, urban development, and natural resource extraction collectively have resulted in the conversion of natural habitat at ever-increasing rates. From 2001 to 2005, an estimated 105 acres of forest were lost every day in Kentucky due to land-cover conversion.[2] As natural habitat is converted and lost, the remaining habitat becomes fragmented and degraded, which weakens the overall stability of an ecosystem.

URBANIZATION

By the 2000 Census, Kentucky's population had grown to more than 4 million people, and it is projected to rise to nearly 5 million by 2030.[3] Population increases have led to significant loss of habitat and have resulted in greater urbanization (urban growth and sprawl), expansion of infrastructure (roads and utility lines), and alteration of waterways, all of which have negative impacts on biodiversity. Urban areas account for nearly 7% of the

Suburban areas are expanding at unprecedented rates, resulting in the loss of farms and green space. *Keith Mountain*

GLADECRESS

Kentucky gladecress is an example of a species in danger of extinction primarily due to urban sprawl. This small spring wildflower, endemic to the state, is known only from Bullitt and Jefferson counties, where it is restricted to dolomitic limestone outcrops. Interstate connections with Louisville have brought more people to that area, and now homes and roads are replacing pastures, woodlands, and glades. Kentucky gladecress sites have declined 64% since monitoring began in 1980.[4]

Thomas G. Barnes

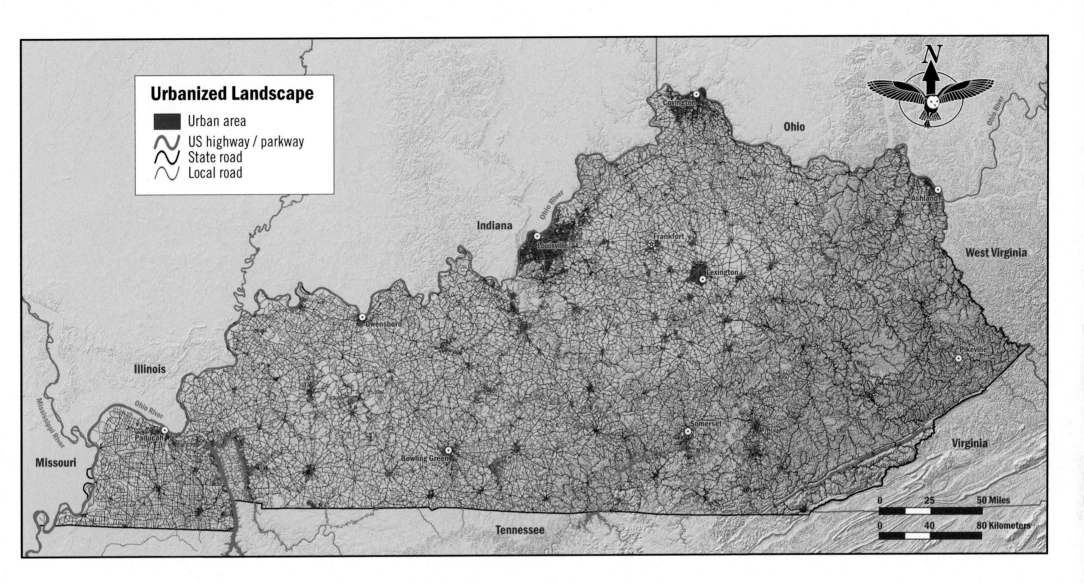

Urbanized Landscape

- ■ Urban area
- ∿ US highway / parkway
- ∿ State road
- ∿ Local road

state,[5, 6] more than 85,000 miles of roads[7] and 11,500 miles of power lines[8] traverse the state, and at least 1,000 dams have been built statewide.[9] Urban areas are typically covered with asphalt and concrete, impervious surfaces that reduce the ground's ability to absorb and filter rainwater, which results in increased flooding, erosion, and pollution.

Urban areas in Kentucky continue to develop and expand. Although most urban areas offer shopping, dining, entertainment, and employment opportunities, many people choose to commute from suburban or rural areas rather than live in the city. People move to the fringes of town to escape traffic, noise, crime, and other urban issues and to take advantage of cheaper land. Schools, retail centers, and other associated infrastructure tend to follow the populace, and soon the fringe becomes urbanized and a new fringe appears; this is urban sprawl. Beyond the fringes of existing cities, urban sprawl is occurring along interstates and major

DAMS' IMPACT ON BIODIVERSITY

While dams provide beneficial services to an ever-increasing population, their negative effects on aquatic habitats and species are devastating. Upstream of dams, sedimentation increases, oxygen decreases, and the habitat changes from shallow running water with alternating pools and riffles to deep standing water. Downstream impacts of dams may extend for miles. Depending on dam height, water temperature might be colder, oxygen levels could be lower, the flow rate may be more erratic, and bank erosion may increase. Dams may create barriers to aquatic species dispersal, isolating populations from one another. For mussels, dams may prevent contact with the host fishes necessary for reproduction.

All of the large lakes (reservoirs) in the state were artificially created by impounding rivers. Lake Barkley (pictured here) and Kentucky Lake were formed by damming the Cumberland and Tennessee rivers, respectively. *KSNPC photograph by Marc Evans*

GREENING UP URBAN AREAS

Urban planning efforts, advancements in building design, and shifting attitudes toward urban living are transforming the urban landscape. Investments in urban revitalization efforts are beginning to attract more people back to city centers, which ultimately slows the pace of sprawl. New building practices promote the use of reclaimed and recycled materials and reduce impacts through techniques that mimic natural systems, such as "green rooftops" to moderate building temperatures and constructed wetlands for sewage treatment. Green ideas are blossoming into a lucrative industry. As these ideas begin to permeate the public consciousness, cultural attitudes about the relationship between the natural world and the urban environment may also be transformed.

transportation networks, around small towns in close proximity to larger metropolitan areas, and around desirable natural features such as lakes and public forests.

A vast infrastructure network supports the urbanized landscape. The tens of thousands of miles of roads, railways, and power lines that cross the state fragment habitat and can act as barriers to movement for some species. Each year in Kentucky thousands of wildlife deaths are associated with vehicle collisions. Fragmentation provides an avenue for invasive species to enter and expand into natural habitats. Collectively, these impacts lessen the ecological significance and functionality of natural communities.

As the state's population grows and urbanization spreads, water resources are affected. All of Kentucky's major rivers, as well as a significant number of smaller rivers and streams statewide, have been drastically transformed by impoundment and channelization over the last 80 years. Dams were constructed to provide energy, flood control, a secure water supply, and recreational areas.[9] The state's rivers are also occasionally dredged to maintain sufficient depth for navigation, provide flood control, or obtain gravel or sand. These alterations affect or eliminate the natural flow and habitat in streams throughout a watershed.

AGRICULTURE

Nearly 36% of Kentucky is agricultural land.[5,6] Historically, a greater portion of the state was converted for agricultural purposes, but many farm fields have been abandoned and have grown back to forest. The growth of agriculture has led to the loss of nearly all of the state's prairies and a significant reduction in the acres of upland forests and wetlands. Conventional agricultural lands offer minimal habitat for native species and may be a source of runoff laden with sediment and pesticides, which degrades the surrounding habitat.

Many of Kentucky's first European American settlers emigrated from farms in the eastern United States, drawn by reports of bountiful land resources. The earliest settled land in the state was the fertile areas of the Bluegrass, which is highly productive for crops and livestock. Settlers used agricultural practices suited to conditions in Europe. Native grassland and woodland plants were adapted to intermittent grazing by large, free-roaming mammals

Fields planted in corn under conventional tillage are particularly susceptible to erosion during rainfall events. This not only results in the loss of valuable topsoil; it also degrades water quality when runoff transports large amounts of sediment, nutrients, and pesticides into streams. *Tim McCabe, USDA Natural Resources Conservation Service; courtesy of U.S. Fish & Wildlife Service Digital Library System*

(e.g., American bison); as settlers confined livestock and implemented year-round grazing, native plants began to decline. Native grasses were eventually replaced by non-native, cool-season grasses better adapted to continuous grazing for a longer growing season. In the mountains of eastern Kentucky, settlers cleared trees on steep, forested slopes for farming and allowed livestock to graze the forest understory. These practices had devastating results. The land often only supported crops for a few years, because soils were quickly exhausted, and sedimentation from these lands severely degraded the aquatic habitats of mountain streams.

Engineering advances, such as the John Deere steel plow in the 1830s, resulted in the conversion of additional natural areas to agriculture. Industrial agriculture began in earnest in the mid-1900s

MODERN AGRICULTURE

One consequence of modern agriculture is that about 15 plant and eight animal species supply 90% of our food, compared with about 7,000 plants that humans have cultivated and collected for food since agriculture began.[10] While a focus on a few crops is efficient, it also reduces options for managing the food supply in response to environmental challenges and change.

This 1920 Breathitt County farm was typical of eastern Kentucky at the time, with the surrounding hills extremely eroded as a result of logging, cropping, and grazing. *Willard Rouse Jillson Photo Collection/Kentucky Geological Survey County Photographs, 1920*

SUSTAINABLE AGRICULTURE

Many new farming practices reduce soil erosion, chemical use, and negative impacts on biodiversity. These techniques are becoming more widely implemented through government-sponsored landowner incentive programs. Farmland can be managed to benefit long-term productivity while also reducing impacts on biodiversity. Increasingly, agricultural areas function as corridors for animal movement between natural areas and as stopover sites for migrating birds.

BEFORE

AFTER

Restricting livestock access to streams reduces the amount of sediment and nutrients reaching the stream from adjacent pastures and bank erosion. Farm Bill programs provide cost-share funding to address some of the environmental impacts of farming. *Bridgett Costanzo, courtesy of U.S. Fish & Wildlife Service Digital Library System*

when advances in machinery production, fertilizers, and chemicals became available to farmers. In the 1970s, the belief that the world's ability to supply food would fall short of the projected need resulted in rapid expansion of U.S. food production and exports. Remnant natural areas were further reduced as more land was converted to row-crop farming. In western Kentucky channelization and drainage projects severely affected wetlands such as the extensive bottomlands in the Mayfield Creek and Bayou de Chien watersheds. These changes are typical of wetland conversion in other areas of the state.

NATURAL RESOURCE EXTRACTION

Throughout Kentucky's history, the state's abundant natural resources have been heavily utilized through mining and logging, with limited regard for environmental impact. Although early European American settlers cleared large areas of forest, significant, widespread extraction did not occur until industrialists from the East Coast purchased timber and mineral rights and built railroads to ship out the resources. Forestry and mining continue to be major industries, to the detriment of

Extensive logging occurred in eastern Kentucky in the late 1800s and early 1900s. Due to the primitive techniques used, many of the forests regenerated and retained a diversity of tree species, one indicator of quality in mesophytic forests. *Courtesy of Kentucky Historical Society*

biodiversity. Virtually all of the primary forests have been cleared (less than 7,500 acres are documented[11]), more than 800,000 surface acres of land have been mined,[5, 6] and more than 1,400 miles of streams have been buried[12, 13] or significantly damaged for the extraction of coal.

Forestry

Kentucky is nearly 50% forested[5, 6] and ranks second in the nation in hardwood production.[14] Most of the state's forests have been logged at least once, and in most cases multiple times. Large, intact tracts of forest are critically important to forest health and biodiversity. With 89% of the state's forests privately owned,[14] the role of private landowners is crucial to biodiversity protection. In Kentucky, wood is harvested from both publicly and privately owned forests to meet the high demand for lumber. While wood and associated products are important economically, many harvest techniques conflict with long-term protection of biodiversity.

In addition to the loss of trees, logging practices often change the number and diversity of other organisms in an ecosystem. One particularly destructive harvest technique is "high-grading," which removes the best hardwood trees and leaves poorer-quality trees and less-marketable species, such as maples. The shift in tree species composition on high-graded sites causes changes throughout the forest ecosystem, ranging from microorganisms in the leaf litter all the way up to mammals.[15]

Reforestation (e.g., tree planting) and natural regeneration address some of the adverse impacts of logging, but they alone will not ensure a healthy, diverse forest ecosystem. For instance, some forest plants are reduced or eliminated when a forest is completely cleared of trees or "clear-cut." Doll's eye and purple trillium are much less likely to occur in (and may never recolonize) clear-cut or heavily thinned forests.[16] Forest management techniques that reduce the impacts on biodiversity before and

during logging are needed, as well as a balance between preservation of natural forests and the use of forest resources.

Forest clearing converts large tracts into patchworks of ever-smaller forests. Large mammals, such as the American black bear, need continuous expanses of forest to have enough resources and seclusion to survive. Also, the smaller the forest, the less interior forest habitat for native species such as the cerulean warbler. The edges around fragmented forests are exposed to more wind and sun, harsh conditions that are different from those deep inside the

Today, the industrial size and methods of commercial logging have the potential to change the physical features of the land and markedly reduce forest species diversity. Also, invasion of invasive plants after logging has become a serious impediment to forest recovery, which was not a problem a century ago. *Keith Mountain*

forest. Also, edges of fragmented forests are more accessible to weedy, invasive species such as bush honeysuckle and tree-of-heaven, plants that then spread throughout the forest. Opportunistic species, such as the brown-headed cowbird, notorious for depositing their eggs in the nests of smaller, native forest birds, also establish in forest-edge habitat. Once the eggs of these intruders hatch, the host birds use energy and resources to rear the large demanding cowbird chicks, and the eggs or young of the native birds are often displaced.

Minerals and Fuels

Nationally, Kentucky ranks third in production of coal, 14th in oil, and 20th in natural gas.[17, 18] The extraction (mining and drilling) of fuel and mineral resources alters and degrades natural habitats,

Adapted from Kentucky Geological Survey map.

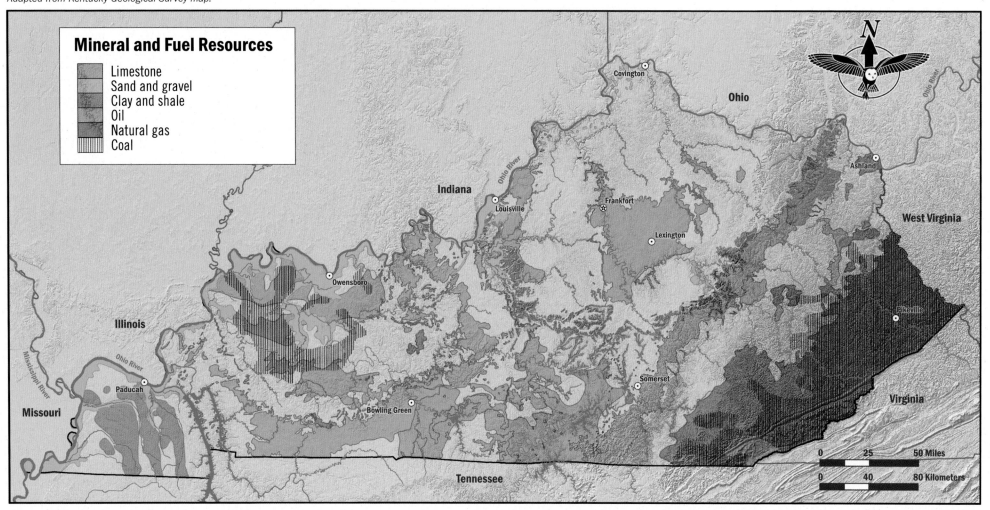

resulting in habitat loss and fragmentation, invasive species infestation, and pollution. These activities permanently alter the landscape, detrimentally affecting native species and reducing overall biodiversity.

Currently, coal is the most heavily utilized energy resource in the state. In addition to providing 97% of the state's electricity, it is also exported to 25 states and four foreign countries.[17] Coal is extracted via surface mining (e.g., mountaintop removal and contour mining) and underground mining. Surface mining eliminates or degrades and fragments forests.[19] Since the Surface Mining Control and Reclamation Act of 1977, many surface-mined lands have been converted to open grasslands of non-native grasses and forbs,[18, 20] although tree planting is more common for new initiatives.[21] If soil is compacted during reclamation, few, if any, forest species (including trees) are able to recolonize. Even on former mining sites where soil is not compacted, native species richness remains generally low.[22, 23]

Mountaintop removal mining involves removing the summit of a mountain to access coal and filling adjacent valleys with excess soil and rock (overburden). These operations change vast expanses of land; in fact, one of the largest coal mines in Kentucky encompasses 17,000 acres.[24] This form of mining has considerable impact on the flora, fauna, water quality, and scenic beauty of the Appalachian region.

More than 800,000 surface acres (3.1%) of Kentucky's landscape have been mined primarily for coal (see Land Cover section, chapter 2).[5, 6] More than 1,400 miles of streams, mostly headwater streams, in eastern Kentucky have been buried or significantly damaged by the deposition of overburden.[12, 13] Burying the upper reaches of streams eliminates unique aquatic habitat and causes impacts, such as sedimentation and loss of food, to waterways and aquatic organisms downstream from the mining operation.

Other surface-mined minerals include limestone and sandstone, which are used for a variety of purposes, including construction of roads and golf courses. Mining rocks and minerals also permanently alters the landscape, although these operations are less extensive and are somewhat scattered throughout the state. Siltation from the mining of gravel and sand from streams, even from small mining operations, can adversely affect the local stream fauna.

Of an estimated 250,000 wells drilled in the state in search of oil and gas, 31,000 are still active.[25] Construction of access roads, pipelines, and drilling sites for these operations contribute to forest fragmentation and soil erosion. Water quality also can be threatened by brine from abandoned wells and radioactive material from leaking oilfield wastes.[18]

Surface mining may be so extensive and destructive that ecosystem functions are obliterated. *KSNPC photograph by Marc Evans*

MINIMIZING MINING'S IMPACT

New programs and research through the state's regulatory programs focus on improving postmining conditions and the natural rehabilitation of mined lands. The Kentucky Reforestation Initiative is an effort to develop techniques that reduce soil compaction and create conditions more conducive to reforestation with hardwood species.

Reducing dependence on nonrenewable energy and resources will in turn reduce the impact of mining on Kentucky's biodiversity. Interest in alternative energy sources, such as solar and wind power, has increased due in part to tax incentives. Only about 34% of the energy generated by large power plants is delivered to consumers;[18] with improved efficiency of power plants, less coal would be needed to meet energy demand. On the consumer side, reducing home energy use also plays a role. Balancing energy needs and conservation is a challenge for Kentucky, a state with well-established fuel and mining industries and a rich natural heritage.

DEFINITIONS

- ♦ **Native:** A species that naturally occurs in an area.
- ♦ **Non-native/exotic:** A species introduced, either intentionally or inadvertently, that does not naturally occur in an area.
- ♦ **Invasive:** A non-native/exotic species that aggressively outcompetes native species.

The native cecropia moth is under attack by an exotic tachinid fly that was introduced to control yet another exotic species, the gypsy moth. Unfortunately, the beautiful cecropia moth, like other members of the silkmoth family, appears to be declining across its range. © *Barry Howard*

INVASIVE SPECIES

The spread of invasive species in ecosystems worldwide is one of the most significant threats to biodiversity. Forty-two percent of the federally listed animals and plants in the United States are at risk primarily due to non-native species.[26] European starlings, kudzu, and Asiatic clams occupy increasingly scarce habitat and compete with native species for resources (food and water). Invasive species are prolific reproducers and have the ability to quickly colonize and adapt to native ecosystems; without natural predators or biological controls, they can be extremely difficult to control or eradicate. As habitat quality is degraded by invasive species, native species diversity suffers.

Since Europeans first settled North America, a tremendous influx of non-native species has occurred, either accidentally or intentionally. These species stowed away in the ballast water of large ships and arrived in crate packing material; some were even welcome guests in gardens and yards. Not all non-native species adapt to their new environments, but some adapt so well that they invade natural areas, proliferate, and displace native species. Invasive species are now spreading at unprecedented rates, often with the assistance of humans.

INVASIVE ANIMALS AND PATHOGENS

Invasive animals are causing havoc among the state's flora and fauna and are affecting the quality of natural areas. These species range from tiny insects and microscopic pathogens to birds and mammals. State and federal agencies have recently identified the most problematic aquatic and terrestrial species in Kentucky and have developed plans for their control.[27, 28]

The hemlock woolly adelgid is a tiny invasive insect that feeds on the needles of Carolina hemlocks and eastern hemlocks. Native to Asia, this insect was accidentally introduced to western North

Hemlock woolly adelgids can lay as many as 300 eggs twice per year. The ability to reproduce rapidly is characteristic of pest species. *Connecticut Agricultural Experiment Station Archive, Bugwood.org*

The loss of eastern hemlock trees will likely jeopardize the black-throated green warbler too. In Kentucky, breeding pairs use large hemlocks to raise their young, often building nests high in trees that are 60 to 80 feet tall. *Michael Butler, Trent University*

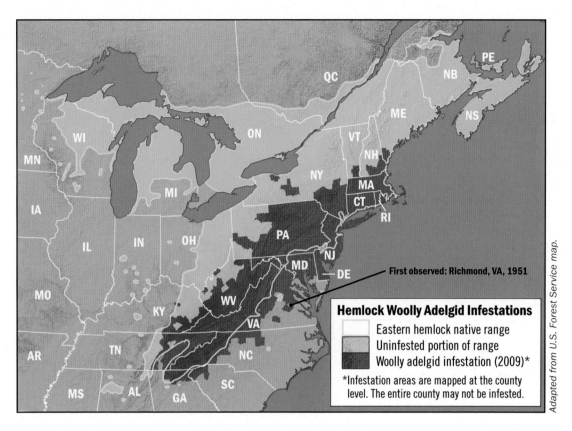

First observed: Richmond, VA, 1951

Hemlock Woolly Adelgid Infestations
◻ Eastern hemlock native range
▦ Uninfested portion of range
◼ Woolly adelgid infestation (2009)*

*Infestation areas are mapped at the county level. The entire county may not be infested.

Adapted from U.S. Forest Service map.

America in the 1920s and again in the Richmond, Virginia, area in the early 1950s.[29] In 2006 the adelgid was first documented in eastern Kentucky,[30] an area where eastern hemlock is a major forest component. Adult adelgids are less than one-sixteenth of an inch long. They are called "woolly" because they are covered by wool-like projections made of wax. They feed on the sap in hemlock needles and typically cause an infested tree to die within two to 12 years.[31-33] This tiny insect has already killed 80% of the hemlock trees along the Blue Ridge Parkway and in Virginia's Shenandoah National Park.[34]

The loss of hemlock creates stands of dead and dying trees, resulting in an ecological disaster for species dependent upon this habitat. Streams formerly shaded by hemlocks will warm, which may cause declines in some aquatic species. Habitat will be reduced for birds that use hemlock forests for nesting and foraging, such as black-throated green warblers. This tiny insect has the potential to dramatically alter Kentucky's landscape.

The Asiatic clam gets less attention than its notorious cousin, the zebra mussel, but it is an extremely invasive animal in many Kentucky streams.

The Asiatic clam, an exotic aquatic pest, is abundant in Kentucky's rivers and streams. This small mussel can be detrimental to native freshwater mussels. *KSNPC photograph by Heather Housman*

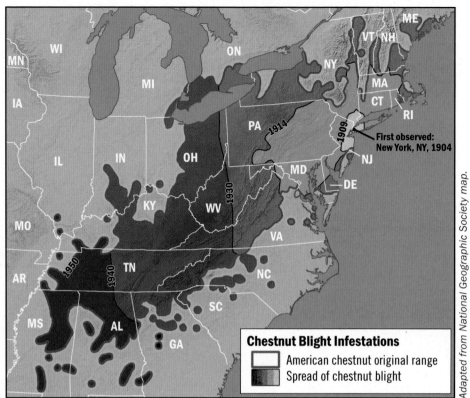

First observed: New York, NY, 1904

Chestnut Blight Infestations

☐ American chestnut original range
■ Spread of chestnut blight

Adapted from National Geographic Society map.

This nickel- to quarter-sized bivalve is gold or light brown in color and may be found by the thousands in sandy and gravelly substrates of streams and reservoirs. First introduced to the West Coast in the 1920s, it has moved across the country to become a major problem in the eastern United States. Its range expansion is due in part to its use as bait by fishermen; it is also sold in the pet trade as pygmy or gold clams. In addition, juveniles may be transported worldwide in the ballast water of large ships. Asiatic clams compete with native mussels for habitat and resources. They have the potential to affect fishes by disrupting food chains, and they may affect the early life stages of some native freshwater mussels. Asiatic clams are capable of achieving populations dense enough to clog water-intake pipes, causing millions of dollars worth of damage.[35, 36]

Non-native pathogens also threaten biodiversity. One of the best examples of the potential of such pathogens to dramatically and overwhelmingly change an ecosystem is chestnut blight, a fungal pathogen that essentially eliminated the American chestnut. This massive tree was once a major component of eastern forests and a common street tree. Wildlife and free-ranging livestock relied on its nuts as a rich food source. The wood was used extensively for building material due to its rot-resistant properties.

Chestnut blight was inadvertently introduced in North America in the late 1800s by way of Japanese chestnut nursery stock and later by Chinese chestnuts.[37] These non-native chestnut trees were sold by mail order, providing an easy way for the fungus to spread rapidly throughout the entire native range of American chestnut. By the 1940s, the blight had passed through most of Kentucky.[38] The fungus grows in and under the bark, essentially girdling the tree by killing the living cells just beneath the bark. Once the tree's main stem dies, the chestnut sends up stump sprouts. The sprouts survive for several years, occasionally maturing enough to flower and produce fruit, before succumbing once again to the blight.

INVASIVE PLANTS

Approximately 24% (570 species) of Kentucky's flora is non-native.[39] Currently, the Kentucky Exotic Pest Plant Council lists 92 of these species as warranting concern.[40] Several species represent serious threats to biodiversity due to their abundance, distribution, and rate of spread.

Asian bittersweet and winter creeper are vines that were introduced as ornamentals from Asia in 1736 and 1907, respectively.[41] They aggressively wrap around trees and sometimes break limbs due to their weight. Their dense growth shades tree seedlings and chokes out native ground cover. Asian bittersweet hybridizes with native American bittersweet, which could lead to the elimination of the native species. The heaviest concentrations of Asian bittersweet are in the southeastern mountains, but the vine is spreading due to its growing use in wreath-making and other crafts. Discarded wreaths often have seeds that may germinate. Winter creeper is widely sold as a ground cover and escapes from yards to surrounding natural areas.

Another invasive from Asia, bush honeysuckle, was introduced in the 1700s and 1800s as an ornamental and wildlife food plant.[41] It forms dense thickets and shades out other native plants. The abundant, brightly colored berries are rich in

above and right:
Thick mats of winter creeper choke out native vegetation on the forest floor and eliminate habitat for ground-dwelling species. *James H. Miller, USDA Forest Service, bugwood.org*

Bush honeysuckle—the green shrub dominating this hillside in early spring—invades woodlands, especially in the Inner Bluegrass region. The shrub's red berries are dispersed by birds, making it easier for this exotic to invade forests. *KSNPC photograph by Tara Littlefield*

KENTUCKY'S LEAST WANTED: THE TOP 20 MOST INVASIVE EXOTIC PLANTS[40]

Asian bittersweet	Japanese knotweed
Autumn olive	Kudzu
Burning bush	Miscanthus
Bush honeysuckle	Multiflora rose
Chinese yam	Poison hemlock
Common chickweed	Privet
Crown vetch	Purple loosestrife
Garlic mustard	Sericea lespedeza
Japanese grass	Tree-of-heaven
Japanese honeysuckle	Winter creeper

The overwhelming growth of garlic mustard eliminates critical habitat for several rare plants as well as more common native wildflowers in Kentucky's forests.
KSNPC photograph by Tara Littlefield

carbohydrates, but they do not offer migrating birds the high-fat, nutrient-rich food sources needed for long flights.

Garlic mustard was introduced in about 1868 by northern Europeans who used this species for food and medicine.[42] This herbaceous plant forms a dense ground cover that excludes native forest plants, such as Braun's rockcress, which is federally listed. Each mustard plant can produce more than 800 seeds, making it very difficult to control once established. Garlic mustard is found primarily in the Bluegrass, with scattered populations elsewhere.

Tree-of-heaven, native to China, was introduced to the United States via Europe in 1784 as an ornamental and is now found statewide.[41, 42] Its roots exude chemicals that inhibit the growth of other plants. The trees produce large quantities of seeds that can drift on the wind for great distances, enabling them to establish in tree gaps of otherwise closed-canopy forests. This species resprouts from damaged roots, making it difficult to control.

POLLUTION

Air, land, and water are the dumping grounds for waste of all kinds, from industrial to personal. The large volume of pollution dumped into the environment can overwhelm the Earth's capacity to absorb, transform, or break down these materials. Some pollutants may take thousands of years to decay, resulting in long-term ecological damage. Unfortunately, pollutants such as heavy metals and pesticides do not just disappear or remain suspended in the air and water; they enter the tissues of living organisms and increase in toxicity as they are passed up the food chain, a process known as bioaccumulation. Other pollutants, such as sediment and carbon dioxide (CO_2), indirectly harm plants and animals by altering their habitats.

AIR

Air pollution results from the release of chemicals and particulates into the atmosphere. In Kentucky, air pollution is mainly caused by burning fossil fuels, either for electricity (e.g., coal-burning power plants) or transportation (vehicle emissions). The Kentucky Division of Air Quality regulates several thousand sources of air pollution. Regulated pollutants include volatile organic compounds, nitrogen oxides, ground-level ozone, sulfur dioxide, carbon monoxide, heavy metals (e.g., mercury), particulate matter, and CO_2. Although the Clean Air Act of 1963 has greatly improved air quality, its grandfathering provision allows older coal-powered plants to avoid meeting the requirements that new facilities must adopt. Hundreds of grandfathered power plants, some in Kentucky, continue to emit 10 times more pollutants than new facilities do.[43]

Once pollutants are released into the atmosphere, they eventually are deposited onto the land or water. For example, sulfur compounds create acid deposition that can change soil chemistry and ultimately affect flora and fauna both above ground and

Older coal-burning power plants, such as the Paradise plant in Muhlenberg County, are exempt from the improved pollution-control standards new facilities must meet. This plant may contribute to poor air quality at Mammoth Cave National Park. *Keith Mountain*

below it. Acid deposition can also alter the chemistry of rivers and lakes, which can have devastating effects on aquatic organisms.[44] For instance, excess aluminum that leaches from soils into waterways can be toxic to fish.

LAND

Soil contamination occurs when chemicals are spilled, leached from underground storage tanks or landfills, applied as pesticides and herbicides, or directly released as industrial waste into the soil.[18] Among the most significant soil contaminants are heavy metals, herbicides, pesticides, and polychlorinated biphenyls (PCBs). Pesticides and herbicides,

widely used across Kentucky on agricultural crops, lawns, roadsides, power lines, and railroads can be toxic to native flora and fauna, especially aquatic organisms.[18, 45]

Some pesticides (e.g., DDT) decrease the production, fertility, and hatchability of bird eggs and can cause weight loss or even death among birds.[46] Atrazine, the most commonly used herbicide in Kentucky, negatively affects many terrestrial and aquatic nonvascular plants, and may be linked to reductions in species richness and biomass of aquatic invertebrates and fish.[18, 45] Pesticides can negatively affect amphibians such as frogs and salamanders.[47, 48] Some progress has been made in eliminating pesticides

PESTICIDE CASE STUDY

In 1962, Rachel Carson's book *Silent Spring*[53] made the public aware of the devastating effects of unrestrained use of dichloro-diphenyl-trichloroethane (DDT) and other chemicals used at the time. DDT is a highly effective, long-lasting, indiscriminate pesticide that kills not just the targeted species but other insect species; ultimately, DDT affects an entire ecosystem. DDT was specifically linked to the decline of the bald eagle, osprey, and other birds when it was discovered that DDT reduced their ability to form viable eggs. In 1972, DDT was banned for crop use in the United States, though it continues to be used in other countries. This new awareness led to government regulation and development of chemicals that are less dangerous to the environment and humans.

During the 1960s, osprey numbers in Kentucky declined, probably due mostly to the accumulation of DDT in the ecosystem. Numbers remained low even after the federal ban on the use of DDT was implemented in 1972, but ospreys began to increase during the 1980s, in part as a result of "hacking" programs by state and federal agencies. Since the mid-1980s, the osprey nesting population has gradually increased, especially in the Land Between the Lakes area. © *Tom Fusco*

that affect nontarget organisms. For example, the insecticide carbofuran (also known as Furadan), a chemical widely used across Kentucky to control insects on alfalfa crops, has recently been banned by the Environmental Protection Agency because of its toxicity to wildlife.

WATER

Water pollution occurs indirectly through surface runoff and underground leaching (nonpoint-source pollution) or through direct release into streams (point-source pollution). Nonpoint-source pollution is mainly caused by runoff from agricultural, urban, and mined lands. Point-source pollution is regulated by law. For example, municipal wastewater treatment plants and industries must obtain

permits allowing direct discharge of pollutants into streams. A study by the Kentucky Division of Water revealed that 611 river miles have been affected by point pollution sources.[54] Catastrophic events, such as the 2001 Martin County coal slurry spill into the Tug Fork river and the 2000 Wild Turkey Distillery bourbon spill in the Kentucky River—which was the largest fish kill from a single spill in Kentucky[18]—can completely decimate aquatic organisms until stream health recovers.

Sedimentation and siltation contribute to the loss of aquatic biodiversity. Soil, fertilizer, manure, and other wastes from farms, mining areas, construction sites, and septic systems may wash into nearby waterways during rain events.[18] Removing trees, shrubs, and other vegetation from riparian areas increases erosion of soil or sediment into streams. Excessive sedimentation smothers freshwater mussels and eggs of aquatic organisms, causing decline in the diversity of fishes, invertebrates, and plants in streams. For example, the KSNPC-listed aquatic plant threadfoot is especially sensitive to sedimentation in rivers, and it declines or disappears as sedimentation increases.

GLOBAL CLIMATE CHANGE

The last 10,000 years have been a period of climatic stability under which human civilization has developed and ecosystems have adapted.[55] However, the planet's climate is now rapidly changing. The

Although trace levels of mercury naturally occur in many Kentucky waterbodies, concentrations that pose an environmental threat appear to be the result of releases from anthropogenic activities, such as coal mining and burning. Toxic chemicals are absorbed by bacteria and tiny plants, such as plankton, becoming more concentrated and toxic as they travel up the food chain. Dangerously high mercury levels have been found in species such as bats, eagles, and otters. *Robert Dunlap*

primary cause of this change is the accumulation of greenhouse gases in the atmosphere, particularly CO_2, from burning fossil fuels (coal, oil, and natural gas) and clearing forests (e.g., burning trees, which releases the carbon they store). Elevated CO_2 levels lead to the alteration of long-term weather patterns, including more intense heat and cold in some locations, and more extreme weather events such as floods, droughts, and ice storms.[56]

A warmer climate will stress some native plants and animals, increase species extinctions, and cause disruptions in ecosystem processes.[55, 57] Ecosystems are beginning to transform and may ultimately disassemble as the life cycles of coexisting and interdependent species change.[55] Pest species will likely have an increased advantage, because these species are notorious for rapidly adapting to new conditions.[57] Although the speed and long-term effects of climate change are not fully known, research is demonstrating that as ecosystems and species are stressed, they have the potential to further accelerate climatic warming. For example, rising temperatures are thawing permafrost worldwide, creating a landscape of ponds and lakes.[55, 58] These water bodies contain bacteria that feed on and convert previously frozen carbon into methane gas, which is 23 times more efficient at trapping heat than CO_2.[58]

In the United States, hundreds of studies have already documented changes in species' ranges, behavior, and composition due to global climate change. Range-restricted species, particularly polar and mountaintop species, are undergoing severe habitat reductions and likely will be some of the first species to go extinct as a result of climate change.[57] Declines in amphibians, coral reefs, polar bears, and many other groups have been documented. Range shifts may also disrupt plant–insect or predator–prey interactions. The range of the red fox, for example, has shifted northward into territories of the arctic fox, threatening the latter's survival.[59] Similar shifts in range have been documented for birds,

mammals, intertidal invertebrates, and plants.[60–63] Plant flowering and animal breeding times have also been changing.[57] The cumulative impacts of global climate change may result in approximately 24% of temperate deciduous forest species going extinct by 2050.[64]

Climate change is affecting Kentucky. A recent revision of the U.S. Department of Agriculture's plant hardiness zones map shows that since 1990, approximately 80% of the state has shifted a complete zone, which represents an increase in the average annual minimum temperature.[65] A warming climate will adversely affect species and natural communities that require specific climatic conditions. For example, rising temperatures likely will cause the decline or loss of the rare plants and animals that thrive in the cool climate on top of Black Mountain.

The race to address climate change is on as governments, industries, private organizations, and citizens attempt to find ways to reduce greenhouse gas levels. The United Nations Framework Convention on Climate Change agreement was signed 16 years ago; since then, 192 nations have joined this international agreement, which is aimed at creating cooperation and developing strategies to address

Rosy twisted-stalk is a high-elevation species found on Black Mountain that may be especially vulnerable to decline as a result of climate change. *KSNPC photograph by Marc Evans*

GLACIAL RETREAT

In most parts of the world, glaciers are rapidly retreating. It is estimated that glaciers in the high elevations of the tropics will be gone by 2020.[55] In the continental United States, glacial retreat is evident at Glacier National Park, which is projected to no longer contain glaciers by 2030.[55] The park's Grinnell Glacier illustrates the extent of glacial retreat since 1940.

Unknown photographer, USGS, courtesy of Glacier National Park Archives

Karen Holzer, USGS, courtesy of Glacier National Park Archives

SPECIES AT RISK DUE TO CLIMATE CHANGE

Species that live on low-lying islands or in high altitudes are particularly vulnerable to climate change.[55, 57] These species have few options for adapting to rising sea levels and temperatures. Polar bears were federally listed as Threatened in 2008 due to loss of sea ice habitat.[66] The American pika is a high altitude species of the Rocky Mountains that may become the first species federally listed as Endangered due to habitat loss associated with climate change.[67]

© Jenny Huang

In describing the Red River region of eastern Kentucky, Daniel Boone commented: "The buffalo were more frequent than I have seen cattle in the settlements, browsing on the leaves of the cane, or cropping the herbage of those extensive plains, fearless because ignorant of the violence of man. Sometimes we saw hundreds in a drove, and the numbers about the salt springs were amazing." *The Adventures of Colonel Daniel Boone, woodcut courtesy of the Kentucky Historical Society*

climate change.[68] Switching from fossil fuels to more sustainable alternative energies, conserving forests, and using more sustainable agricultural methods are essential steps for reducing greenhouse gas emissions in an effort to address climate change.

OVERCOLLECTION AND OVERHARVESTING

The most devastating era in wildlife exploitation, both in Kentucky and nationally, occurred more than 100 years ago, when little or no regulation of commercial harvesting or hunting existed. The American bison, passenger pigeon, and Carolina parakeet were hunted or otherwise collected to the point of extinction or extirpation from the state. The populations and distributions of other game species were significantly reduced by the beginning of the 20th century. For example, Kentucky's white-tailed deer population had fallen to an estimated 2,000 individuals by 1940, and only 800 wild turkey existed in the state as late as 1959.[69] The end of large-scale commercial harvesting and the regulation of recreational hunting beginning in the early 1900s substantially reduced the excessive harvesting of wildlife. Some game species, such as deer and turkey, have been restored to viable populations through wildlife management.

THE PASSENGER PIGEON

The passenger pigeon, now extinct, is believed to have been the most abundant land bird in North America, with an estimated 3 to 5 billion individuals.[70] The life history of the passenger pigeon was unlike that of any other bird. Huge nomadic flocks roamed across North America, feeding and nesting in groups or colonies. In 1813, John James Audubon observed a large flock near Louisville. After unsuccessfully attempting to count the birds because of their overwhelming numbers, he estimated that a flock of this size could be one mile wide, pass by at one mile per minute for three hours, contain two pigeons per square yard, and reach a total length of 180 miles. Based on these figures, he estimated the flock he observed would contain 1,115,136,000 pigeons![71] Overhunting, random shooting, constant disturbance of roosting and nesting colonies, and deforestation doomed this once-abundant bird. The last known passenger pigeon, "Martha," died on September 1, 1914, at the Cincinnati Zoological Garden. The last documented sighting of a passenger pigeon in Kentucky was in 1898.

Courtesy of Kentucky Historical Society

In 1947, Aldo Leopold eloquently wrote: "There will always be pigeons in books and museums, but these are effigies and images, dead to all hardships and to all delights. Book-pigeons can not dive out of a cloud to make the deer run for cover, nor clap their wings in thunderous applause of mast-laden woods. They know no urge of seasons; they feel no kiss of sun, no lash of wind and weather; they live forever by not living at all. . . . The pigeon was no mere bird, he was a biological storm. He was the lightning that played between two biotic poles of intolerable intensity: the fat of the land and his own zest for living. Yearly the feathered tempest roared up, down, and across the continent, sucking up the laden fruits of forest and prairie, burning them in a travelling blast of life. Like any other chain-reaction, the pigeon could survive no diminution of his own furious intensity. Once the pigeoners had subtracted from his numbers, and once the settlers had chopped gaps in the continuity of his fuel, his flame guttered out with hardly a sputter or even a wisp of smoke."[72]

Goldenseal is among the many commercially valuable medicinal native plants that are gathered to supply an expanding foreign and domestic market for herbal remedies. Increased collection of American ginseng, slippery elm, black cohosh, and other plants has led to growing concern regarding the viability of their populations in Kentucky. *John R. MacGregor*

Although the abuses of the past no longer pose the same degree of threat to Kentucky's biodiversity, negative effects from both legal and illicit commercial harvest of plants and animals have continued. For example, prior to World War II and the advent of plastic buttons, many native mussel species were commercially harvested to supply shells for the pearl-button industry. Beginning in the 1950s and increasing through the late 1980s, commercial harvest provided mussel shells to the Japanese cultured-pearl industry. However, harvest volume declined significantly following a massive disease outbreak that affected Akoya oysters in Japan, killing more than 50% of them in 1996 and 1997[73] and ultimately decimating the industry.

Several plants (e.g., goldenseal and American ginseng) are gathered in the wild for herbal and medicinal purposes, substantially diminishing their populations and distribution. Other examples of overcollecting include the killing of American black bears to sell their organs on the black market, collection of eastern box turtles for the pet trade, and harvest of orchids for the horticultural trade.

Animals have been overhunted out of fear. As early as 1795, the Kentucky legislature passed a law offering a bounty for killing wolves. Gray and red wolves and eastern cougars were systematically eradicated from the landscape, and numerous other predator species were substantially diminished in numbers. These species were not hunted for food or direct profit but were deemed "harmful" or "nuisance" species that should be killed for the public good. Unfortunately, countless snakes, bats, and birds of prey are still killed in the mistaken belief that these animals pose some danger or have no useful purpose.

Chapter Six

CONSERVATION

Now I truly believe that we in this generation must come to terms with nature, and I think we're challenged, as mankind has never been challenged before, to prove our maturity and our mastery, not of nature but of ourselves.

—RACHEL CARSON[1]

UP TO THIS POINT, information on the state of Kentucky's biodiversity has mostly painted a bleak picture of loss and decline. However, there are conservation efforts that are forging ahead with the hope of protecting and restoring the state's natural heritage. Information gathered through inventory and monitoring is used to assess the status of species and natural communities. Land preservation and species-recovery efforts are diverse and growing, as are other more indirect but equally important efforts, such as recycling, treating wastewater, and improving air quality. This chapter presents information on some of the ways biodiversity conservation is taking place.

CONSERVATION SCIENCE: NATURAL HERITAGE METHODOLOGY

Effective biodiversity conservation depends on scientific information on ecosystems. The Natural Heritage Program Network, which operates primarily in North, Central, and South America, is focused on gathering information on elements of biodiversity (mostly species and natural communities) and applying standardized techniques to map and manage this information. KSNPC is a member of the network, which was originally created by The Nature Conservancy in 1974 and is now administered by NatureServe. The natural heritage methodology is the framework used to identify and protect the best occurrences of species or natural communities vulnerable to extirpation (i.e., elimination from an area, such as Kentucky) or extinction. To accomplish this task, each program follows the same methodology to assign global and state ranks based on the total number of populations or individuals in each region.

One remarkable aspect of this method is that all information on a species or natural community, from Manitoba to Maui, is available in one place. This standardized methodology allows each natural

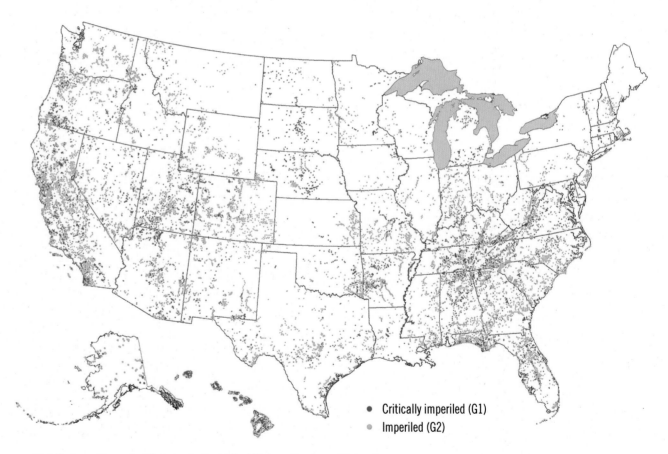

Distribution of Imperiled Species in the United States. *Courtesy of NatureServe*

- ● Critically imperiled (G1)
- ● Imperiled (G2)

heritage program to determine the most important plant and animal populations, communities, or natural areas within their political boundaries. Collectively, this information is used to make global assessments. For instance, these data helped determine that more than 90% of the Braun's rockcress populations worldwide, and 100% of the Shawnee darters, occur in Kentucky. For some species and communities, such as the fanshell mussel and Cumberland pine barrens, respectively, Kentucky has the best known occurrences in the world.

Another tenet of the natural heritage methodology is that protection of species and communities vulnerable to extinction also results in protection of species and communities that are more common. If one thinks of biodiversity as a fabric, with the threads being the species and ecosystems that support life on Earth, then reinforcing the individual threads—especially those threads or species that appear vulnerable to breaking—will ensure that the fabric as a whole remains intact.

Natural heritage programs maintain species and natural community data that are collected during field surveys conducted by biologists or retrieved from both published and unpublished literature. Heritage program staff collect much of the data; however, universities, government agencies, companies, and individuals also contribute. Data are mapped and stored using Biotics, NatureServe's biodiversity data management software. Data in the system are stored with a spatial reference (i.e., coordinates associated with the surface of the earth). Natural Heritage Program Network data are widely used by state and federal agencies, as well as private consultants, and the network has become a key source of data on rare species and natural communities. Several of the maps in this book were created using Natural Heritage Program Network data.

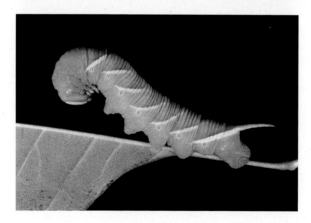

top to bottom:
The harmless scarlet kingsnake mimics the venomous harlequin coralsnake, with one telltale difference: on the scarlet kingsnake's body, the red bands touch the black bands, whereas on the harlequin coralsnake red touches yellow. A secretive, skilled, and very beneficial predator, the scarlet kingsnake feeds on small snakes, lizards, mice, and invertebrates. *John R. MacGregor*

With a wingspan of 1.5 inches or less, the small coral hairstreak is often found nectaring on butterfly milkweed. The plant also benefits, because the butterfly aids in pollination. *KSNPC photograph by Ellis L. Laudermilk*

Waved sphinx moth caterpillars and adults are still common in Kentucky, but most sphinx and silk moth species are declining statewide. *John R. MacGregor*

CONSERVATION LANDS

Conservation lands are either public (lands owned by federal, state, or local governments) or private (lands owned by individuals, nongovernmental organizations, or foundations) areas that offer some designated or recognized degree of natural-area protection. These lands are essential to the protection of Kentucky's biodiversity. There are more than 1.6 million acres of conservation lands in Kentucky,[2, 3] which account for approximately 6.4% of the state's land area. Management of these lands may be solely the landowner's responsibility, or it may be shared through partnerships that provide additional expertise and funding. Management objectives vary considerably due to different legislative mandates,

philosophies, or land-use policies; these objectives may focus on multiple uses, or they may be specific to a particular purpose, such as protection of habitat or rare species. The common thread is that all of these lands directly or indirectly protect Kentucky's biodiversity to some degree and therefore have conservation value.

Federal conservation lands include national parks, national wildlife refuges, national recreation areas, national forests, military installations, and private lands under federal easements. Federal conservation lands were established with widely different intents. National Park regulations require the protection of species, land, water, and their associated natural processes. The U.S. Forest Service manages lands such as the Daniel Boone National Forest

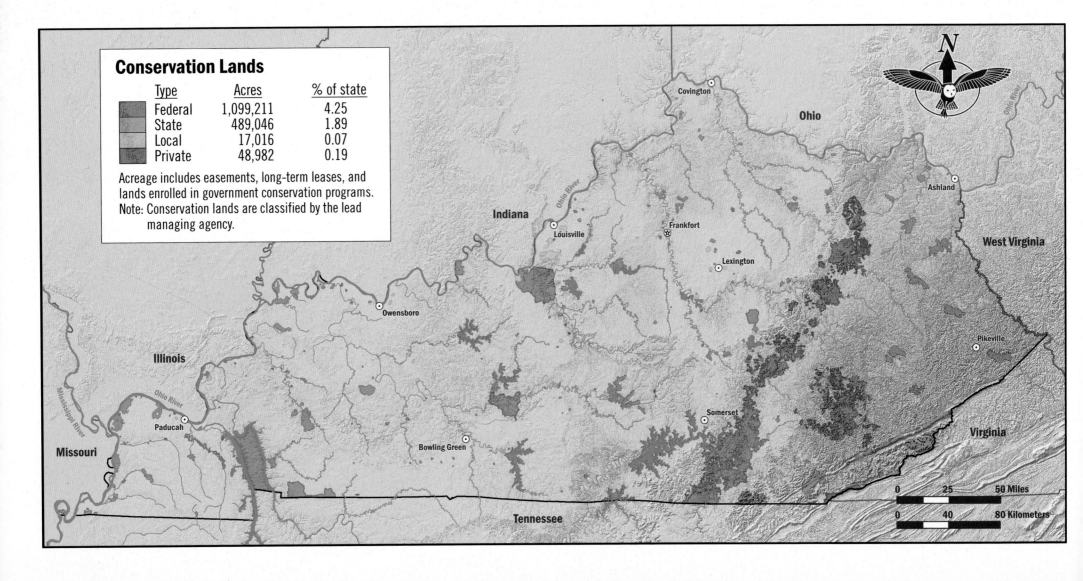

Conservation Lands

Type	Acres	% of state
Federal	1,099,211	4.25
State	489,046	1.89
Local	17,016	0.07
Private	48,982	0.19

Acreage includes easements, long-term leases, and lands enrolled in government conservation programs.
Note: Conservation lands are classified by the lead managing agency.

for sustainable multiple uses. Two federal properties in Kentucky, Land Between the Lakes National Recreation Area and Mammoth Cave National Park, are designated as Biosphere Reserves by the United Nations Educational, Scientific and Cultural Organization (UNESCO).[4] The stated intent for these reserves is to establish ecosystem-scale biodiversity protection zones that integrate sustainable land-use practices for the benefit of local communities. Additionally, Mammoth Cave National Park is included on UNESCO's World Heritage List.[5]

State lands include wildlife management areas managed principally for hunting and fishing, state parks managed for recreation and cultural heritage, state forests primarily managed to demonstrate proper forest stewardship practices for timber production, and state nature preserves specifically managed for preservation of rare species and natural communities. Additional state lands include state university properties, such as research forests and natural areas (e.g., Lilley Cornett Woods, Griffith Woods, Robinson Forest) and state wild river corridors that protect some of the state's highest-quality rivers. Some state properties, such as Stone Mountain Wildlife Management Area and State Natural Area (Harlan County), are jointly managed by multiple agencies. Not all lands managed by state agencies are state-owned; in some cases state agencies manage private lands under lease and easement agreements.

Local conservation lands include city and county government properties as well as private lands under local government easements. Many of these

left: Thompson Creek Glades is a dedicated state nature preserve in Larue County. Dedication provides some of the strongest legal conservation safeguards in Kentucky. *Thomas G. Barnes*

below: Daniel Boone National Forest is the largest area of conservation land in Kentucky. Within its 707,000 acres are nearly 1,000 occurrences of 160 different KSNPC-listed species and 12 federally listed species. The forest is especially renowned for the number of cliffs, rockhouses, and arches it contains (Princess Arch shown here). *Thomas G. Barnes*

right: Stone Mountain Wildlife Management Area and State Natural Area in Harlan County is jointly owned by two state agencies (the Kentucky Department of Fish and Wildlife Resources and KSNPC) that cooperate in its ownership and management. Many conservation lands benefit from such partnerships. *KSNPC photograph by Marc Evans*

Prairie species, like this royal catchfly, have adapted to the natural fire cycles of prairie systems. Fire stimulates germination of royal catchfly seed. *Thomas G. Barnes*

Corn snakes spend a lot of time hunting rodents or resting in underground burrows, so humans rarely see them. The Red River Gorge Geological Area provides habitat for this beneficial species. *John R. MacGregor*

Protection of Kentucky's biodiversity depends on land conservation. Although many conservation lands are distributed across the state, their cumulative acreage is inadequate for long-term biodiversity protection. To maintain the ecological systems that sustain the state's rich natural heritage, corridors must be established between existing conservation lands, landscape fragmentation must be minimized, and more land needs to be protected and actively managed.

RESTORATION MANAGEMENT

Few natural areas in Kentucky remain pristine; most have been altered, and restoration is needed. Natural-area management tools and strategies, such as prescribed fire, are used to restore ecological processes; to mitigate the effects of development and past land use, such as erosion, habitat fragmentation, or pollution; and to protect the ecological value of natural lands.

Fire is an important natural disturbance. Its influence on the landscape has been diminished due to a century of active fire suppression and fragmentation of the landscape. When fire is excluded, woody species increase. Prairies, for instance, are quickly transformed to shrubland and forest. To restore the open, grassy conditions of prairies and other communities, fire is "prescribed" under a very specific set of weather conditions, including temperature, relative humidity, and wind speed. These controlled burns reestablish some of the natural effects of fire and prevent wildfires by reducing materials that fuel a fire.

Invasive plants and animals can displace native species, and their control is increasingly important. Depending on the site and extent of the invasion, pest plants are hand-pulled, sprayed with herbicide, mowed, or burned. The removal process can cause a decline in native species, such as sensitive rare plants or butterflies, so managers must apply

lands have been acquired with assistance from the Kentucky Heritage Land Conservation Fund, a program that provides state grants for perpetual protection of natural areas. Jefferson Memorial Forest (Jefferson and Bullitt counties) and Raven Run Nature Sanctuary (Fayette County) demonstrate community commitments to providing nature-related recreation while protecting natural areas.

Private conservation lands include properties owned by foundations, land trusts, and private colleges as well as lands under land-trust easements. These lands include large holdings such as the 14,000-acre Bernheim Arboretum and Research Forest (Bullitt and Nelson counties), one of the largest private forests in the state. The Nature Conservancy is another large conservation landowner that protects rare species and natural communities statewide. Land trusts play a role in protecting biodiversity through land purchases and partnerships with government and conservation groups. For example, the Kentucky Natural Lands Trust works with government agencies, private industry, and local citizens to protect the biologically diverse Pine Mountain ecosystem in southeastern Kentucky.

Fire is prescribed in prairies to stimulate native grasses and forbs and eliminate woody species. *KSNPC photograph by Joyce Bender*

the right technique at the right time of year to protect sensitive species.

Management of wetlands and streams may involve both revegetation and restoration of natural drainage patterns. In some cases, original stream channels are reengineered to recreate natural flow. Bottomlands are replanted with tree species that occurred in these ecosystems prior to deforestation. These efforts increase wetland functions, such as water filtration and groundwater recharge, and reduce erosion and excess drainage.

RARE-SPECIES MANAGEMENT SUCCESS FOR SHORT'S GOLDENROD

Short's goldenrod is a federally and KSNPC-listed endangered species. It was discovered in 1840 at the Falls of the Ohio River by Charles W. Short, a Kentucky physician and botanist. Lock and dam construction eliminated this population, but in 1939, Short's goldenrod was discovered 100 miles east near Blue Licks Spring in Robertson County. Short's goldenrod is curiously restricted to the Blue Licks area in Kentucky and one site in Indiana, and it is believed that the plant adapted to trampling and grazing associated primarily with bison. Historically, Blue Licks Spring was a source of minerals for mammals from mastodons to bison. Short's goldenrod likely declined following extirpation of the bison and land-use changes.

The federally endangered Short's goldenrod has responded well to prescribed fire and brush-removal management. *KSNPC photograph by Nicholas Drozda*

Short's goldenrod is protected in several nature preserves and parks in the Blue Licks area. On dedicated state lands, KSNPC has a multifaceted approach to managing Short's goldenrod. Exotic invasive species, such as sweet clover, nodding thistle, crown vetch, and tall fescue, threaten to displace the plant. Mechanical removal of these non-native plants (e.g., mowing and pulling) and the judicious use of herbicides are reclaiming some of the lost habitat.

Encroaching hardwood trees, shrubs, and red cedars shade Short's goldenrod and reduce flowering. Prescribed fire has been used to reduce woody cover, control invasive species, and enhance conditions that stimulate goldenrod growth and flowering. With the aid of volunteers from the Sierra Club and the Kentucky Native Plant Society, areas overridden with red cedars too large to be affected by fire are being cleared. As a result, stem counts of Short's goldenrod increased three- to 10-fold over several years, confirming that management has been effective in restoring this species.

GOVERNMENT REGULATION

Beginning in earnest during the mid-1960s and peaking during the 1970s, a flurry of new state and federal laws were enacted to address diminished environmental quality and loss of natural resources, and to impose more environmental oversight. These statutes regulate harmful activities such as air and water pollution, which not only endanger human health but also degrade habitat and threaten plant and animal species.

During this time, the public and policy-makers began to realize the magnitude of the ecological impacts of surface mining for coal in Kentucky. In 1966, Kentucky updated strip-mining laws with provisions for enforcement and reclamation. Slightly more than a decade later, Congress weighed in by passing the landmark Surface Mining Control and Reclamation Act of 1977.[6] Prior to this law, surface mines were simply abandoned and left unreclaimed. These laws and their preceding versions, as well as the Clean Air Act and Clean Water Act, were the first federal regulations aimed at reducing environmental impacts from abandoned mines.

Also in the late 1960s, the Kentucky General Assembly enacted legislation enabling local governments to adopt planning and zoning ordinances to manage and control development. Although many counties and cities have yet to adopt such ordinances, a number have implemented them. Although habitat loss due to development continues at unprecedented rates, planning and zoning ordinances have the potential to slow and reduce the impact of development.

State and federal laws to regulate hunting and fishing were instrumental in curbing rapid declines in many game species and migratory birds. In 1973, Congress passed the Endangered Species Act, the first comprehensive law aimed at conserving imperiled species that were not considered commercially or recreationally valuable. The purpose of the law is

New techniques are constantly being added to the arsenal of tools used in restoration. Land managers assess the condition of a natural area, including threats and existing degradation, and develop strategies to maintain, revive, or enhance ecosystem health. Successful management usually requires a significant amount of capital, scientific knowledge, and time.

TIMELINE OF SELECTED REGULATORY MILESTONES BENEFITING KENTUCKY BIODIVERSITY

1861 Kentucky passes law prohibiting killing of certain songbirds and establishing the first closed seasons for select game bird and waterfowl species.

1900 Lacey Act, prohibiting interstate transportation of wildlife taken in violation of state law, enacted by Congress.

1912 Kentucky Game and Fish Commission (now the Kentucky Department of Fish and Wildlife Resources) created.

1918 Migratory Bird Treaty Act signed.

1940 Federal Bald Eagle Protection Act enacted (amended in 1962 to also cover the golden eagle).
U.S. Fish and Wildlife Service established.

1947 Congress passes Federal Insecticide, Fungicide, and Rodenticide Act (FIFRA).

1948 Federal Water Pollution Control Act passed by Congress.
Ohio River Valley Water Sanitation Commission created to protect water quality in the Ohio River.

1950 Kentucky Water Pollution Control Commission (now the Kentucky Division of Water) established.

1953 Kentucky Strip Mining and Reclamation Commission formed.

1963 Congress passes the Clean Air Act.

1965 Federal Water Pollution Control Administration created; forerunner of the U.S. Environmental Protection Agency (EPA).

1966 Kentucky passes revised strip-mining bill with provisions for enforcement and reclamation practices.
Legislation authorizing county planning and zoning enacted.

1968 National Wild and Scenic Rivers Act passed by Congress.

1969 National Environmental Policy Act passed by Congress.

1970 EPA created.
Significant strengthening amendments to the Clean Air Act passed by Congress.

1972 Clean Water Act passed by Congress.
Kentucky Wild Rivers Act enacted.
Clean Air Act substantially amended and strengthened.
Kentucky Natural Resource and Environmental Protection Cabinet established (now the Energy and Environment Cabinet).
Federal Environmental Pesticide Control Act, amending FIFRA, passed by Congress.
Use of the pesticide DDT banned by the EPA.

1973 Endangered Species Act enacted by Congress.
Phaseout of leaded gasoline begins.

1974 EPA bans the pesticide dieldrin for agricultural use (use for mothproofing and termite control continues until 1987).

1976 Resource Conservation and Recovery Act and Toxic Substances Control Act passed by Congress.

1977 Surface Mining Control and Reclamation Act of 1977 passed by Congress.

1979 EPA bans manufacture of polychlorinated biphenyls (PCBs).

1980 Comprehensive Environmental Response, Compensation, and Liability Act (Superfund) legislation passed by Congress.

1990 Kentucky Heritage Land Conservation Act passed (funding established 1994).

1990 Congress passes major amendments to the CAA, leading to significant reduction in acid-rain-forming sulfur dioxide emissions.

1994 Kentucky Agriculture Water Quality Act passed.

1995 Kentucky Biodiversity Task Force Report issued.

1998 Kentucky Forest Conservation Act passed.

2006 EPA bans most uses of the pesticide carbofuran (Furadan).

Bald eagle populations have rebounded during the last several decades, largely because the pesticide DDT—which weakened eggshells and greatly reduced reproductive success—was banned in 1972. In 2006 there were 50 breeding pairs nesting in Kentucky, and the U.S. Fish & Wildlife Service removed the species from the federal endangered species list in 2007. *Steve Hillebrand, courtesy of U.S. Fish & Wildlife Service Digital Library System*

"to provide a means whereby the ecosystems upon which endangered species and threatened species depend may be conserved."[7] This law significantly influenced biodiversity protection and contributed to national and international conservation efforts.

Additional statutes and regulations were created in the ensuing years, and many previously enacted laws were further refined. Although regulations are important to biodiversity conservation, alone they are insufficient to prevent habitat loss or declining populations of many imperiled plant and animal species.

CONSERVATION PLANNING

Conservation planning is focused on long-term support for all native species, both rare and common, and sustaining biodiversity at all levels. Effective planning involves field surveys and data gathering; analysis of species distributions and existing protected areas; evaluation of threats and identification of additional areas in need of protection; and ongoing monitoring of protected areas to assure they continue to support biodiversity.[8, 9] The goal of conservation planning is the use of sound science to identify priority areas for the protection of biodiversity.[9]

Geographic information systems (GIS) are being widely used by conservation organizations to aid with planning efforts. GIS is a system of software, hardware, and data that allows for the creation, modification, and analysis of information that has a spatial reference (i.e., coordinates associated with the surface of the earth). The mapping and modeling capabilities of GIS assist with everything from species tracking and monitoring to inventory and management. GIS provides a means of developing predictive models that help identify potential rare species habitat and target field surveys. In addition, GIS helps with improving environmental review and data sharing, and it enables the creation of

high-quality maps for planning, management, and outreach. The following case studies are examples of conservation applications of GIS in Kentucky.

RARITY HOTSPOT ANALYSIS

The distribution and concentrations of rare species are of particular interest for developing conservation strategies that target biodiversity. Records of species locations provide insight into how widely or narrowly a species is distributed and whether it occurs in close proximity to other rare species. GIS greatly assists with the analysis of species observation data and the identification of biologically important areas.

One approach used by conservation planners is to identify "biodiversity hotspots": areas with the greatest number of rare species.[10] A problem with this approach is that it does not account for rarity, such that widely distributed species, which are a conservation concern only in portions of their range (e.g., fringe populations), disproportionally weight the resulting hotspots,[11] and species that are very rare carry no special significance. To assess rare species in Kentucky, a rarity hotspots analysis was conducted using extant rare species occurrences in the Kentucky Natural Heritage Program database. Rarity hotspots are areas with rare species present that have been ranked based on the number and individual rarity of each species present. The methodology for this analysis is based on a rarity-weight richness index developed by the Association for Biodiversity Information, now known as NatureServe.[11]

KSNPC used GIS to create rarity hotspots for particular species groups (see the sections for seed plants and ferns, amphibians, reptiles, nesting birds, and mammals in chapter 4 to view maps of the results, and Appendix 5 for analysis details). A hexagonal grid was used to divide the state into equal areas. Each species used in the analysis was given a species rarity score based on its distribution and total number of populations in the state (i.e., widely distributed species have lower rarity scores). Each cell within the hexagonal grid was ranked based on the total number of rare species present and their cumulative rarity, which is the sum of the individual species rarity scores. Rarity hotspots were defined on three levels:

- **High:** Area with a high concentration of rare species and/or rare species that have a very small range.

- **Medium:** Area with rare species present.

- **Low:** Area that may support rare species, though no occurrences are known.

- **Historic:** Area with rare species occurrence(s) that have not been observed for over 20 years and may no longer exist.

PRIORITY WATERSHEDS FOR CONSERVATION OF IMPERILED FISHES AND MUSSELS

Kentucky's native freshwater fish and mussel faunas are among the most diverse in North America, the center of worldwide freshwater mussel and temperate freshwater fish biodiversity.[12-14] There are 103 native mussels and 245 native fishes known from Kentucky.[15-19] During the last century, habitat destruction and degradation (e.g., dams and pollution) caused the extirpation or extinction of 20% (21 species) and 4% (nine species) of Kentucky's mussels and fishes, respectively. Of those species remaining, 41% (34 species) of mussels and 25% (60) of fishes are considered imperiled.[20-23]

The identification of priority areas for the conservation of these imperiled aquatic species is necessary to ensure that the most important areas are protected and limited funds are expended wisely. The state was divided into 616 watersheds, a modified version of U.S. Geological Survey delineations,

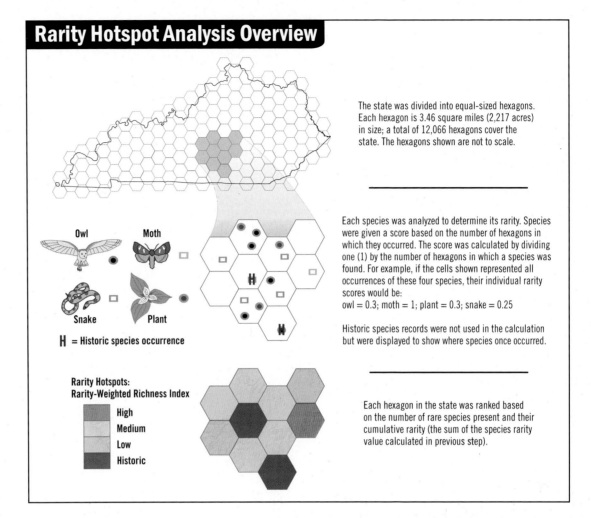

Rarity Hotspot Analysis Overview

The state was divided into equal-sized hexagons. Each hexagon is 3.46 square miles (2,217 acres) in size; a total of 12,066 hexagons cover the state. The hexagons shown are not to scale.

Each species was analyzed to determine its rarity. Species were given a score based on the number of hexagons in which they occurred. The score was calculated by dividing one (1) by the number of hexagons in which a species was found. For example, if the cells shown represented all occurrences of these four species, their individual rarity scores would be:
owl = 0.3; moth = 1; plant = 0.3; snake = 0.25

Historic species records were not used in the calculation but were displayed to show where species once occurred.

Owl   Moth

Snake   Plant

H = Historic species occurrence

Rarity Hotspots:
Rarity-Weighted Richness Index

High
Medium
Low
Historic

Each hexagon in the state was ranked based on the number of rare species present and their cumulative rarity (the sum of the species rarity value calculated in previous step).

and GIS was used to assign each a value based on the presence and rarity of imperiled fishes and mussels (post-1986 records of species in appendices 2 and 6). Watersheds were ranked based on the total number of imperiled fish and mussel species present and their cumulative rarity (sum of the individual species rarity scores).[13, 24] Only 190 (31%) watersheds in the state contain imperiled fish or mussel species. Of these, 53 watersheds with an area totaling 3,684,700 acres (14% of the state) were identified as priorities for conservation. All imperiled fish and mussel species are represented in at least two

The taillight shiner inhabits oxbow lakes, low-gradient streams, and wetlands along the lower Ohio and Mississippi rivers. This uncommon fish is KSNPC-listed as threatened because of stream and wetland alteration and loss.
KSNPC photograph by Ronald R. Cicerello

The clubshell once inhabited rivers nearly statewide. It now is restricted to a short segment of the upper Green River and is federally listed as endangered. *KSNPC photograph by Ronald R. Cicerello*

of these priority watersheds (except for species restricted to one watershed).

The top priority watershed identified is Terrapin Creek, a spring-fed Coastal Plain stream in western Kentucky that supports the most unique fish fauna in the state. Abundant wetlands, springs, spring runs, and clear gravel and sand-bottomed riffles and pools in the watershed are home to 12 imperiled fish species (e.g., goldstripe darter, blacktail redhorse, and brighteye darter), almost one-third of the stream's total fish fauna. Many of these fishes typically are found south of Kentucky in the lower Mississippi River basin. The Terrapin Creek watershed is the only place where six of these species are found in the state, and three others are known only from one additional watershed.

The Mississippi River watershed extending from Mayfield Creek to Obion Creek is the second most important priority watershed. Nine imperiled species (six fishes and three mussels) typical of big rivers are known from this watershed, including the only known Kentucky populations of sturgeon and sicklefin chubs.

The Green River watershed from Lynn Camp Creek to Ugly Creek in Mammoth Cave National Park is the third most important priority watershed. Twenty-five imperiled mussel and fish species, including eight federally listed species, inhabit this watershed. The Green River is nationally recognized as being among the most ecologically significant rivers in the United States and Kentucky.[14] Green River is significant because it supports: (1) one of

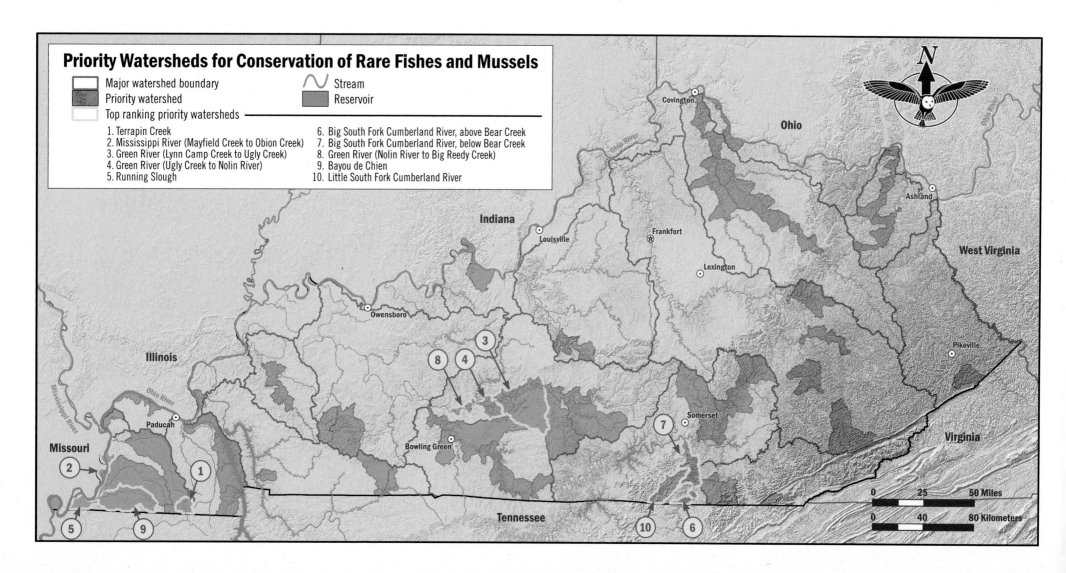

Priority Watersheds for Conservation of Rare Fishes and Mussels

- Major watershed boundary
- Priority watershed
- Top ranking priority watersheds
- Stream
- Reservoir

1. Terrapin Creek
2. Mississippi River (Mayfield Creek to Obion Creek)
3. Green River (Lynn Camp Creek to Ugly Creek)
4. Green River (Ugly Creek to Nolin River)
5. Running Slough
6. Big South Fork Cumberland River, above Bear Creek
7. Big South Fork Cumberland River, below Bear Creek
8. Green River (Nolin River to Big Reedy Creek)
9. Bayou de Chien
10. Little South Fork Cumberland River

only three reproducing populations of the fanshell, (2) the only known Kentucky population of several species (e.g., clubshell), and (3) the most viable Kentucky populations for several species (e.g., rabbits-foot and western sand darter).

Conservation efforts focused on the 53 priority watersheds would help protect key populations of all imperiled fish and mussel species in the state, but the effort would be challenging. Some watersheds are highly developed (e.g., the Mississippi, Ohio, and lower Tennessee rivers), and conservation competes with agriculture, waterway navigation, and other land-use practices. The large number and average size (69,533 acres) of the priority watersheds overwhelm the resources required to fully protect them. Despite these and other challenges, efforts to protect several priority watersheds, including the Green River Bioreserve Project, are already under way.

LARGE FOREST TRACTS

Large tracts of relatively unbroken forest provide essential ecosystem services and play an important role in conservation of biodiversity. Some forested tracts are large enough to have deep forest interiors that are more ecologically stable than smaller forests with little or no interior. These tracts are buffered from forest edge effects such as increased susceptibility to invasive species infestations and greater fluctuations in temperature, humidity, and wind. Many native plants and animals require large interior forest areas to successfully reproduce and maintain stable population levels. For example, the hooded warbler, black-throated green warbler, and black-throated blue warbler, as well as the ovenbird and veery, prefer forests with deep interior, and they decline in small forests with little or no interior available.[25]

The Kentucky Large Forest Tracts Project was initiated to determine the location and quantity of large tracts of forest remaining in the state. Although approximately 50% of Kentucky remains

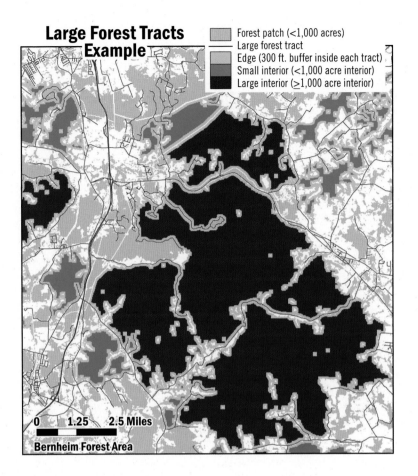

Large Forest Tracts Example

■ Forest patch (<1,000 acres)
— Large forest tract
■ Edge (300 ft. buffer inside each tract)
■ Small interior (<1,000 acre interior)
■ Large interior (≥1,000 acre interior)

0   1.25   2.5 Miles

Bernheim Forest Area

forested, these forests are fragmented by roads, railroads, utility corridors, and agricultural fields. Nearly half of the forests statewide average only 30.4 acres in size[26] and have limited ecological value. Recent land-use trends illustrate the rate of forest loss and fragmentation. Every day in Kentucky from 2001 to 2005, an estimated 105 acres of forest were converted to other land uses (e.g., mining, agriculture, and development),[27] resulting in severely fragmented forests.[28]

Large forest tracts were identified using GIS modeling techniques. Data on roads, railroads, utility lines, and land cover were analyzed to identify large forested areas. Forests were classified as either large forest tracts (areas of at least 1,000 acres) or

Martin's Fork Watershed is part of a 33,500-acre block of forest that stretches across Brush and Cumberland mountains into Virginia. The headwaters of Martin's Fork originate in Cumberland Gap National Historical Park, and portions of the remainder of the upper watershed are collaboratively managed by several state agencies. *KSNPC photograph by Marc Evans*

forest patches (areas of less than 1,000 acres). This process identified more than 2,650 large forest tracts totaling more than 7.2 million acres, or 54% of all forest in the state.[29] The largest tract is 66,500 acres in and around Big South Fork National River and Recreation Area, which stretches into Tennessee. About 22,000 acres of this tract are in Kentucky.

The largest forested tract wholly within Kentucky is 46,300 acres located primarily within Fort Knox Military Reservation in central Kentucky.

Large forest tracts were further analyzed to assess the extent of interior forest within each tract. Although 54% of forests were identified as large forest tracts, these tracts are composed of edge and

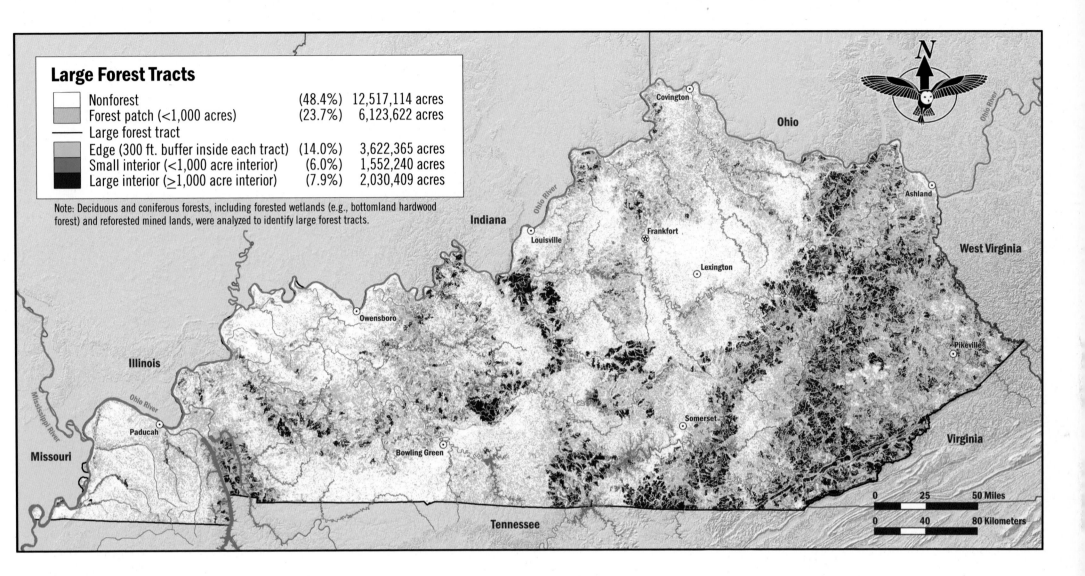

Large Forest Tracts

☐ Nonforest	(48.4%)	12,517,114 acres
▨ Forest patch (<1,000 acres)	(23.7%)	6,123,622 acres
— Large forest tract		
▨ Edge (300 ft. buffer inside each tract)	(14.0%)	3,622,365 acres
▨ Small interior (<1,000 acre interior)	(6.0%)	1,552,240 acres
■ Large interior (≥1,000 acre interior)	(7.9%)	2,030,409 acres

Note: Deciduous and coniferous forests, including forested wetlands (e.g., bottomland hardwood forest) and reforested mined lands, were analyzed to identify large forest tracts.

interior. Forest edge was identified using a 300-foot buffer[30] inside each tract, with the remaining forest classified as either "large interior" (interior forest of at least 1,000 acres) or "small interior" (interior forest of less than 1,000 acres). The interior forests associated with large forest tracts account for only 27% of forests statewide, and only slightly more than half of these are considered large interior forests.[29]

The greatest concentration of the largest forest tracts is in the rugged hills and mountains of eastern Kentucky. Throughout the rest of the state, large forest tracts are typically smaller and much less common. The largest tracts outside of eastern Kentucky are mainly public lands such as Mammoth Cave National Park. Most of the state's core interior forests occur in the Cumberland Mountains and Appalachian Plateaus, though there are scattered concentrations through the Knobs, Highland Rim, and Shawnee Hills.

Forested corridors are important for the movement of animals and plants. They often follow watercourses such as the Palisades of the Kentucky River, depicted here. *Brian Yahn*

diversity.[31] Cores and the ecological corridors that connect them are critical to long-term biodiversity protection.

Without a network of corridors, most core areas of natural habitat are like islands in an ocean, and it is difficult or impossible for animals and plants to leave the "island." This can result in a genetically inferior population over time and can eventually result in local extirpation of species. Larger islands of core habitat support larger populations and greater biodiversity, while smaller islands support smaller populations and fewer species of plants and animals. Also, several closely spaced islands will support higher populations and more species. These biological principles direct how cores and corridors are identified.

Ecological corridors can be as simple as a wooded fencerow that connects two woodlots, or a wide, forested stream valley. As with cores, larger (wider) corridors provide greater interior habitat and afford more room for movement of plants and animals. In the urbanized landscape, corridors often intersect roads, and many states have built wildlife over- or underpasses to facilitate wildlife movement and reduce wildlife-related accidents.

GIS is being used to analyze species observations, land cover, conservation lands, and topography to help identify, evaluate, and monitor cores and corridors. Defining corridors requires an assessment of the physical structure of the landscape (e.g., the degree of fragmentation) and an understanding of functional connectivity of individual species (how a species uses the landscape).[32] Species movement patterns vary widely; in a fragmented landscape, generalist species have fewer restrictions to movement than forest specialists that are restricted to specific habitats.[32]

A number of ecological corridor projects are in progress in Kentucky involving federal, state, and local agencies, as well as private organizations and individuals. Project areas include Pine Mountain,

CORES AND CORRIDORS

Protecting the largest remaining areas of isolated natural habitat and connecting them by means of a network of ecological corridors is an important method for the conservation of many native plants and animals. Ecological corridors (also called wildlife corridors or landscape linkages) are pathways of natural habitat, either existing or restored, that connect "cores," large areas of natural habitat within a fragmented landscape. Habitat connectivity allows plants and wildlife to move between core areas that are needed for food, mating, and shelter, thus increasing survival rates and maintaining genetic

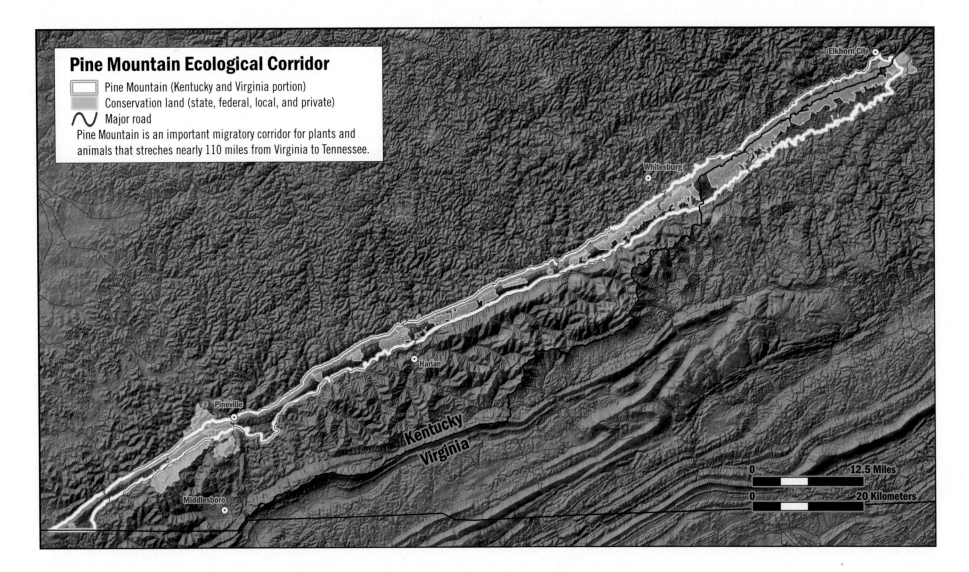

Kentucky River Palisades, Clark's River, Terrapin Creek, Obion Creek, Floyds Fork, and Green River. These projects protect critical mountain and river habitat in some of the most biologically diverse areas of the state.

CITIZEN CONTRIBUTIONS

Biodiversity conservation is not the exclusive responsibility of government. With more than 90% of the state in private ownership, conservation of natural lands and imperiled species cannot be achieved without the efforts of private citizens. The contributions of citizens include amateur naturalists who contribute their knowledge, volunteers who participate in conservation projects across the state, and landowners voluntarily protecting rare species on their property.

Amateur naturalists contribute to the knowledge of flora and fauna and increase public awareness.

SIMPLE THINGS CITIZENS CAN DO TO HELP PRESERVE BIODIVERSITY

• Consume less gasoline: use mass transportation, bike, drive a more fuel-efficient vehicle, carpool, make fewer trips by car.

• Reduce, recycle, and reuse consumer goods.

• Decrease energy use at home: turn off lights and appliances when not in use; replace incandescent bulbs with long-lasting, compact fluorescent bulbs; insulate and seal drafts; raise the thermostat in the summer, and lower it in the winter.

• Join a national, state, or local conservation organization.

• Volunteer for projects that improve habitat or reduce threats to biodiversity.

• Purchase a state nature license plate or donate to the Nature and Wildlife Fund on the tax refund check-off section of your Kentucky income tax form.

• Reduce or eliminate the use of herbicides, pesticides, and fertilizer.

• Improve habitat for native plants and animals on your property: install bat boxes or bird houses, establish butterfly gardens with locally native plants, restore riparian areas by planting native trees.

• Grow a garden and consume easily accessible locally produced food.

• Continue to learn about the natural world throughout your life; the more you know, the more you will appreciate and understand how our actions individually and collectively influence biodiversity.

Volunteer water-quality monitors with the Kentucky Division of Water's Water Watch program help keep track of the biological condition of many Kentucky streams. These volunteers also help raise public awareness of the importance of clean water and healthy aquatic ecosystems. *Ken Cook, Kentucky Water Watch*

Citizen volunteer efforts, such as the U.S. Geological Survey North American Breeding Bird Survey or the annual National Audubon Society Christmas Bird Count, provide information on the status and distribution of native species in Kentucky. Some citizens volunteer their time and effort as members of a conservation organization for on-the-ground conservation projects. Examples of these projects include members of a Ducks Unlimited chapter constructing and installing wood duck nest boxes, a Boy Scout troop helping Soil Conservation District staff install erosion-control measures, or a group of Sierra Club volunteers removing invasive bush honeysuckle. In addition to volunteering, many citizens have made significant financial contributions to conservation organizations and causes that have benefited biodiversity.

Individual landowners who manage their property for the benefit of native plants and animals also make important contributions to the preservation of Kentucky's biodiversity. A number of state and federal programs provide technical and financial assistance to eligible landowners to improve habitat conditions on their land. For many private landowners, however, stewardship of their property is a result of a personal relationship with their land. A prime example of a conservation ethic is illustrated by landowners who donate conservation easements on high-quality natural areas. These easements permanently protect property and help conserve plants, animals, and natural communities.

Citizen contributions come in many forms and are truly the means to progress in the conservation struggle. Although governmental, private, and

The landowners of a significant gray myotis maternity cave donated a conservation easement around the cave, ensuring permanent legal protection from development or other harmful land uses. *John W. Newman*

nonprofit programs are engaged in conservation efforts, the future of our state's natural heritage lies with the choices each of us makes. We hope that you now have a new appreciation and understanding of Kentucky's biodiversity, and our ultimate wish is that you are encouraged to contribute to its protection.

LITERATURE CITED

DEDICATION

1. Berry, W. 1977. The unsettling of America: culture & agriculture. Sierra Club Books, San Francisco, California, USA.

CHAPTER 1. INTRODUCTION

1. Wilson, E. O. 1999. The diversity of life. Second edition. W. W. Norton & Company, New York, New York, USA.
2. Anonymous. 1997. Ecotourism takes off. The Economist 344:62.
3. Watson, R. T., V. H. Heywood, I. Baste, B. Dias, R.Gámez, T. Janetos, W. Reid, and G. Ruark. 1995. Global biodiversity assessment. Cambridge University Press, Cambridge, UK.
4. Pullin, A. S. 2002. Conservation biology. Cambridge University Press, Cambridge, UK.
5. Townsend, C. R., M. Begon, and J. L. Harper. 2003. Essentials of ecology. Second edition. Blackwell Publishing, Malden, Massachusetts, USA.
6. Resh, V. H., and R. T. Cardé. 2003. Encyclopedia of insects. Academic Press, San Diego, California, USA.
7. Stein, B. A., L. S. Kutner, and J. S. Adams, editors. 2000. Precious heritage: the status of biodiversity in the United States. Oxford University Press, New York, New York, USA.
8. Taylor, C. A., and G. A. Schuster. 2004. The crayfishes of Kentucky. Illinois Natural History Survey Special Publication 28, Champaign, Illinois, USA.
9. Master, L. L., S. R. Flack, and B. A. Stein, editors. 1998. Rivers of life: critical watersheds for protecting freshwater biodiversity. The Nature Conservancy, Arlington, Virginia, USA.
10. Culver, D. C., pers. comm., September 24, 2007.
11. Culver, D. C., and B. Sket. 2000. Hotspots of subterranean biodiversity in caves and wells. Journal of Cave and Karst Studies 62:11–17.
12. Culver, D. C., L. Deharveng, A. Bedos, J. J. Lewis, M. Madden, J. R. Reddell, B. Sket, P. Trontelj, and D. White. 2006. The mid-latitude biodiversity ridge in terrestrial cave fauna. Ecography 29:120–128.
13. Kentucky State Nature Preserves Commission. 2007. Natural Heritage Database. Kentucky State Nature Preserves Commission, Frankfort, Kentucky, USA.
14. Petranka, J. W. 1998. Salamanders of the United States and Canada. Smithsonian Institution Press, Washington, D.C., USA.
15. Braun, E. L. 1950. Deciduous forests of eastern North America. Blakiston Books, Philadelphia, Pennsylvania, USA.
16. NatureServe. 2002. States of the union: ranking America's biodiviersity. NatureServe, Arlington, Virgnia, USA.

CHAPTER 2. PHYSICAL OVERVIEW

1. Muir, J. 1911. My first summer in the Sierra. Houghton Mifflin Company, New York, New York, USA.
2. Evans, M., and G. Abernathy. 2008. Natural regions of Kentucky map. Kentucky State Nature Preserves Commission, Frankfort, Kentucky, USA.
3. Fenneman, N. M. 1938. Physiography of the eastern United States. McGraw-Hill, New York, New York, USA.
4. McDowell, R. C., editor. 1986. The geology of Kentucky: a text to accompany the geologic map of Kentucky. United States Geological Survey Professional Paper 1151-H. United States Geological Survey, Washington, D.C., USA. Available at http://pubs.usgs.gov/prof/p1151h/index.html. Accessed August 14, 2009.
5. Kentucky Geological Survey. 2005. Igneous rocks. Available at www.uky.edu/KGS/rocksmn/igneousRocks.htm. Accessed September 22, 2008.
6. Kentucky Geological Survey. 2006. Strata of Ordovician age. Available at www.uky.edu/KGS/geoky/ordovician.htm. Accessed August 14, 2008.
7. McGrain, P. 1983. The geologic story of Kentucky. University of Kentucky Geological Survey, Special Publication 8, Series 11, Lexington, Kentucky, USA.
8. Kentucky Geological Survey. 2005. Ancient times in Kentucky: kinds of fossils found in Kentucky organized by time (age). Available at www.uky.edu/KGS/fossils/fossils_age.htm. Accessed September 22, 2008.
9. Crutzen, P. J., and E. F. Stoermer. 2000. The "Anthropocene." Global Change Newsletter 41:17–18. Available at www.igbp.net/documents/resources/NL_41.pdf. Accessed August 14, 2008.
10. Zalasiewicz, J., M. Williams, A. Smith, T. L. Barry, A. L. Coe, P. R. Bown, P. Brenchley, D. Cantrill, A. Gale, P. Gibbard, F. J. Gregory, M. W. Hounslow, A. C. Kerr, P. Pearson, R. Knox, J. Powell, C. Waters, J. Marshall, M. Oates, P. Rawson, and P. Stone. 2008. Are we living in the Anthropocene? GSA Today 18:4–8.
11. Soil and Water Conservation Society. 2000. Soil biology primer. Soil and Water Conservation Society, Ankeny, Iowa, USA.
12. Wilson, E. O. 1999. The diversity of life. W. W. Norton, New York, New York, USA.
13. Wall, D. H., G. Adams, and A. N. Parsons. 2001. Soil biodiversity. Pages 47–82 in F. S. Chapin III, O. E. Sala, and E. Huber-Sannwald, editors. Global biodiversity in a changing environment: scenarios for the 21st century. Springer-Verlag, New York, New York, USA.
14. Gobat, J. M., M. Aragno, and W. Matthey. 2004. The living soil: fundamentals of soil science and soil biology. Science Publishers, Enfield, New Hampshire, USA.

15. Soil Survey Staff, Natural Resources Conservation Service. 2009. Soil series classification database. Natural Resources Conservation Service, United States Department of Agriculture, Lincoln, Nebraska, USA. Available at http://soils.usda.gov/technical/classification/scfile/index.html. Accessed March 31, 2009.

16. Bailey, H. H., and J. H. Windsor. 1964. Kentucky soils. University of Kentucky Agricultural Experiment Station Miscellaneous Publication 308, Lexington, Kentucky, USA.

17. Braun, E. L. 1935. The vegetation of Pine Mountain, Kentucky: an analysis of the influence of soils and slope exposure as determined by geological structure. American Midland Naturalist 16:517–565.

18. United States Geological Survey. 2004. Kentucky [map]. The National Atlas of the United States. United States Geological Survey, Reston, Virginia, USA. Available at http://www.nationalatlas.gov/printable/images/pdf/reference/pagegen_ky.pdf. Accessed September 22, 2008.

19. McGrain, P., and J. C. Currens. 1978. Topography of Kentucky. Kentucky Geological Survey Special Publication 25, Series X, Lexington, Kentucky, USA.

20. United States Geological Survey. 1999. National hydrography dataset. United States Geological Survey, Reston, Virginia, USA. Available at http://nhd.usgs.gov. Accessed April 13, 2009.

21. Kentucky Division of Water. 2006. 2006 integrated report to Congress on water quality in Kentucky, Vol. I. 305(b): assessment results with emphasis on the Kentucky River basin management unit and Salt-Licking rivers basin management unit. Environmental and Public Protection Cabinet, Frankfort, Kentucky, USA.

22. United States Geological Survey. 2005. 1:2,000,000-scale hydrologic unit boundaries. National Atlas of the United States, Reston, Virgnia, USA. Available at http://nationalatlas.gov/mld/hucsoom.html. Accessed April 13, 2009.

23. Cicerello, R. R., and G. Abernathy. 2008. Major watersheds of Kentucky. Kentucky State Nature Preserves Commission, Frankfort, Kentucky, USA.

24. Burr, B. M., and M. L. Warren Jr. 1986. A distributional atlas of Kentucky fishes. Kentucky Nature Preserves Commission Scientific and Technical Series 4, Frankfort, Kentucky, USA.

25. Kuehne, R. A., and R. M. Bailey. 1961. Stream capture and the distribution of the percid fish *Etheostoma sagitta,* with geologic and taxonomic considerations. Copeia 1961:1–8.

26. Kentucky Climate Center. 2007. Climatography of Kentucky. Kentucky Climate Center, Western Kentucky University, Bowling Green, Kentucky, USA. Available at http://kyclim.wku.edu/climatography.htm. Accessed August 14, 2007.

27. Kentucky Division of Geographic Information. 2004. Kentucky 2001 Anderson level III land cover. Kentucky Division of Geographic Information, Frankfort, Kentucky, USA. Available at http://kygeonet.ky.gov. Accessed September 14, 2009.

28. Kentucky GAP Analysis Program. 2002. Kentucky Gap Analysis Program land cover map. Mid-America Remote Sensing Center, Murray State University, Murray, Kentucky, USA. Available at http://kygeonet.ky.gov. Accessed September 14, 2009.

29. Kentucky Transportation Cabinet. 2007. All roads. Kentucky Transportation Cabinet, Frankfort, Kentucky, USA. Available at ftp://ftp.kymartian.ky.gov/trans/statewide/shape/. Accessed September 14, 2009.

CHAPTER 3. NATURAL HISTORY

1. Imlay, G. 1797. A topographical description of the western territory of North America: containing a succinct account of its soil, climate, natural history, population, agriculture, manners, and customs. Third edition. Augustus M. Kelley Publishers, New York, New York, USA [reprint 1969].

2. Lewis, B. R. 1996. Kentucky archaeology. The University Press of Kentucky, Lexington, Kentucky, USA.

3. Jennings, D. 1989. Prehistory of North America. Mayfield Publishing, Mountain View, California, USA.

4. Alroy, J. 2001. A multispecies overkill simulation of the end-Pleistocene megafaunal mass extinction. Science 292:1893–1896.

5. Diamond, J. 1997. Guns, germs, and steel: a short history of everybody for the last 13,000 years. Jonathan Cape, London, UK.

6. Erwin, D. G. 2006. Extinction: how life on Earth nearly ended 250 million years ago. Princeton University Press, Princeton, New Jersey, USA.

7. Waldman, C. 1985. Atlas of the North American Indian. Facts on File, New York, New York, USA.

8. Webb, L. S. 1998. The significance of late prehistoric/early historic utilization of bison by aboriginal populations of the eastern prairie peninsula and the Ohio River Valley. Ph.D. dissertation, University of Kentucky, Lexington, Kentucky, USA.

9. Cronon, W. 1983. Changes in the land: indians, colonists, and the ecology of New England. Hill and Wang, New York, New York, USA.

10. Campbell, J. 1980. Present and presettlement forest conditions in the Inner Bluegrass of Kentucky. Ph.D. dissertation, University of Kentucky, Lexington, Kentucky, USA.

11. Wells, P. 1970. Historic factors controlling vegetation patterns and floristic distributions in the Central Plains region of North America. Pages 221–224 *in* W. Dort Jr. and L. K. Jones Jr., editors. Pleistocene and recent environments of the central Great Plains. Special publication 3. University Press of Kansas, Lawrence, Kansas, USA.

12. Henderson, A. G. 1998. Middle Fort Ancient villages and organizational complexity in central Kentucky. Ph.D. dissertation, University of Kentucky, Lexington, Kentucky, USA.

13. Flannery, T. 2001. The eternal frontier: an ecological history of North America and its peoples. Grove Press, New York, New York, USA.

14. Delcourt, P. A., H. R. Delcourt, C. R. Ison, W. E. Sharp, and K. J. Gremillion. 1998. Prehistoric human use of fire, the eastern agricultural complex, and Appalachian oak-chestnut forests: paleoecology of Cliff Palace Pond, Kentucky. American Antiquity 63:263–268.

15. Davis, D. E. 2000. Where there are mountains: an environmental history of the southern Appalachians. University of Georgia Press, Athens, Georgia, USA.

16. Platt, S. G., and C. G. Brantley. 1997. Canebrakes: an ecological and historical perspective. Castanea 62:8–21.

17. Kelton, P. 2002. The great southeastern smallpox epidemic, 1696–1700: the region's first major epidemic? Pages 21–27 *in* R. Ethridge and C. Hudson, editors. The transformation of the southeastern Indians: 1540–1760. University Press of Mississippi, Jackson, Mississippi, USA.

18. Ramenofski, A. F. 1987. Vectors of death: the archaeology of European contact. University of New Mexico Press, Albuquerque, New Mexico, USA.

19. Henderson, A. G. 1992. Dispelling the myth: seventeenth- and eighteenth-century Indian life in Kentucky. Register of the Kentucky Historical Society 90:1–25.

20. Martin, W. H., S. G. Boyce, and A. C. Echternacht, editors. 1993. Biodiversity of the southeastern United States: upland terrestrial communities. John Wiley and Sons, New York, New York, USA.

21. Williams, M. 2003. Deforesting the Earth: from prehistory to global crisis. The University of Chicago Press, Chicago, Illinois, USA.

22. Trabaud, L. 1987. Fire and survival traits of plants. Pages 65–89 in L. Trabaud, editor. The role of fire in ecological systems. SPB Academic Publishing, The Hague, The Netherlands.

23. Pyne, S. J. 1982. Fire in America: a cultural history of wildland and rural fire. Princeton University Press, Princeton, New Jersey, USA.

24. Buchanan, R. 2005. Life and adventures of Audubon the naturalist. Cosimo Classics, New York, New York, USA.

25. Imlay, G. 1797. A topographical description of the western territory of North America: containing a succinct account of its soil, climate, natural history, population, agriculture, manners, and customs. Third edition. Augustus M. Kelley Publishers, New York, New York, USA [reprint 1969].

26. Johnston, J. S. 1898. First explorations of Kentucky: Doctor Thomas Walker's journal of an exploration of Kentucky in 1750, being the first record of a white man's visit to the interior of that territory, now first published entire, with notes and biographical sketch: also Colonel Christopher Gist's journal of a tour through Ohio and Kentucky in 1751, with notes and sketch. Filson Club, Louisville, Kentucky, USA.

27. Evans, M., and G. Abernathy. 2008. Presettlement land cover of Kentucky. Kentucky State Nature Preserves Commission, Frankfort, Kentucky, USA.

28. Bryant, W. S., and W. H. Martin. 1988. Vegetation of the Jackson Purchase of Kentucky based on the 1820 General Land Office Survey. Pages 264–276 in D. H. Snyder, editor. Proceedings of the first annual symposium on the natural history of lower Tennessee and Cumberland River valleys. Center for Field Biology of the Land Between the Lakes, Austin Peay State University, Clarksville, Tennessee, USA.

29. Dickens, S. N. 1935. The Kentucky barrens. Bulletin of the Geographical Society of Philadelphia 43:42–51.

30. McInteer, B. B. 1946. A change from grassland to forest vegetation in the "Big Barrens" of Kentucky. American Midland Naturalist 35:276–282.

31. Dahl, T. E. 1990. Wetlands losses in the United States 1780s to 1980s. United States Fish and Wildlife Service, Washington, D.C., USA, and Northern Prairie Wildlife Research Center, Jamestown, North Dakota, USA. Version 16, July 1997. Available at www.npwrc.usgs.gov/resource/wetlands/wetloss/index.htm. Accessed March 31, 2009.

CHAPTER 4.
SPECIES AND NATURAL COMMUNITIES

1. Wilson, E. O. 1995. E.O. Wilson to the defense— biologist fights for the protection of endangered species. National Wildlife 34:10–17.

2. Dillard, G. E. 1989–2007. Freshwater algae of the Southeastern United States. Part 1 (1989); part 2 (1989); part 3 (1990); part 4 (1991); part 5 (1991); part 6 (1993); part 7 (2000); part 8 (2007). E. Schweizerbart'sche, Stuttgart, Germany.

3. United States Fish and Wildlife Service. 2005. Endangered and threatened wildlife and plants. 50 CFR 17.11 and 17.12. United States Fish and Wildlife Service, Washington, D.C., USA.

4. Leitheuser, A. T. 1988. Recovery plan for Kentucky cave shrimp (Palaemonias ganteri Hay). United States Fish and Wildlife Service, Atlanta, Georgia, USA.

5. Warren, M. L., Jr., B. M. Burr, and R. G. Biggins. 1994. Technical/agency draft recovery plan for the relict darter (Etheostoma chienense). Report prepared for the United States Fish and Wildlife Service, Southeast Region, Atlanta, Georgia, USA.

6. White, D., and N. Drozda. 2006. Status of Solidago albopilosa Braun (white-haired goldenrod) [Asteraceae], a Kentucky endemic. Castanea 71:124–128.

7. United States Fish and Wildlife Service. 2007. Endangered and threatened wildlife and plants; review of native species that are candidates for listing as endangered or threatened; annual notice of findings on resubmitted petitions; annual description of progress on listing actions; proposed rule. Federal Register 72:69034–69106.

8. Burr, B. M., and M. L. Warren Jr. 1986. A distributional atlas of Kentucky fishes. Kentucky Nature Preserves Commission Scientific and Technical Series 4, Frankfort, Kentucky, USA.

9. Ceas, P. A., and L. M. Page. 1997. Systematic studies of the Etheostoma spectabile complex (Percidae; Subgenus Oligocephalus), with descriptions of four new species. Copeia 1997:496–522.

10. Petranka, J. G. 1982. The distribution and diversity of land snails on Big Black Mountain, Kentucky. Master's thesis, University of Michigan, Ann Arbor, Michigan, USA.

11. Kentucky State Nature Preserves Commission. 2007. Natural heritage database. Kentucky State Nature Preserves Commission, Frankfort, Kentucky, USA.

12. Stierle A., G. Strobel, and D. Stierle. 1993. Taxol and taxane production by Taxomyces andreanae, an endophytic fungus of Pacific yew. Science 5105:214–216.

13. Hawksworth, D. L. 2000. The magnitude of fungal diversity: the 1.5 million species estimate revisited. Paper presented at the Asian Mycological Congress 2000, July 9–13, 2000, University of Hong Kong, China.

14. Brodo, I. M., S. D. Sharroff, and S. Sharroff. 2001. Lichens of North America. Yale University Press, New Haven, Connecticut, USA.

15. Risk, A. 2007. Unpublished data.

16. Stotler, R. E., and B. Crandall-Stotler. 1977. A checklist of the liverworts and hornworts of North America. Bryologist 80:405–428.

17. Jones, R. L. 2005. Plant life of Kentucky: an illustrated guide to the vascular flora. The University Press of Kentucky, Lexington, Kentucky, USA.

18. NatureServe. 2002. States of the union: ranking america's biodiviersity. NatureServe, Arlington, Virginia, USA.

19. Pellmyr, O. 1986. The pollination ecology of two nectarless Cimicifuga sp. (Ranunculaceae) in North America. Nordic Journal of Botany 6:713–723.

20. Kentucky Revised Statutes 146.600–619.

21. Wilson, E. O., editor. 1988. Biodiversity. National Academy Press, Washington, D.C., USA.

22. Ponder, W., and D. Lunney, editors. 1999. The other 99%: the conservation and biodiversity of invertebrates. Transactions of the Royal Zoological Society of New South Wales, Mosman, Australia.

23. Stein, B. A., L. S. Kutner, and J. S. Adams, editors. 2000. Precious heritage: the status of biodiversity

in the United States. Oxford University Press, New York, New York, USA.

24. Black, S. H. 2001. Why should we care about invertebrates, anyway? Xerces News 1:1, 4–5.

25. Vaughan, M. 2002. The economic importance of insects. Xerces News 2:1, 4–5.

26. Resh, V. H, and R. T. Cardé. 2003. Encyclopedia of insects. Academic Press, San Diego, California, USA.

27. Lydeard, C., R. H. Cowie, W. F. Ponder, A. E. Bogan, P. Bouchet, S. A. Clark, K. S. Cummings, T. J. Frest, O. Gargominy, D. G. Herbert, R. Hershler, K. E. Perez, B. Roth, M. Seddon, E. E. Strong, and F. G. Thompson. 2004. The global decline of nonmarine mollusks. BioScience 54:321–330.

28. NatureServe. 2006. Central databases. Arlington, Virginia, USA.

29. Ricketts, T. H., E. Dinerstein, D. M. Olson, C. J. Loucks, W. Eichbaum, D. DellaSalla, K. Kavanagh, P. Hedao, P. Hurley, K. Carney, R. Abell, and S. Walters. 1999. Terrestrial ecoregions of North America: a conservation assessment. Island Press, Washington, D.C., USA.

30. McFarlan, A. C. 1943. Geology of Kentucky. University of Kentucky, Lexington, Kentucky, USA.

31. Pilsbry, H. A. 1940. Land Mollusca of North America (north of Mexico). The Academy of Natural Sciences of Philadelphia Monographs No. 3, Vol. 1, Part 2, Philadelphia, Pennsylvania, USA.

32. Neves, R. J., A. E. Bogan, J. D. Williams, S. A. Ahlstedt, and P. W. Hartfield. 1997. Status of aquatic mollusks in the southeastern United States: a downward spiral of diversity. Pages 43–85 in G. W. Benz and D. E. Collins, editors. Aquatic fauna in peril: the southeastern perspective. Southeast Aquatic Research Institute Special Publication No. 1. Lenz Design & Communications, Decatur, Georgia, USA.

33. Johnson, P. D., A. E. Bogan, C. E. Lydeard, K. M. Brown, and J. R. Cordeiro. 2007. Finalizing a conservation assessment for North American freshwater gastropods. Presentation at the biennial symposium of the Freshwater Mollusk Conservation Society, March 12–15, 2007, Little Rock, Arkansas, USA.

34. Branson, B. A., D. L. Batch, and S. Call. 1987. Distribution of aquatic snails (Mollusca: Gastropoda) in Kentucky with notes on fingernail clams (Mollusca: Sphaeriidae: Corbiculidae). Transactions of the Kentucky Academy of Science 48:62–70.

35. Burch, J. B. 1989. North American freshwater snails. Malacological Publications, Hamburg, Michigan, USA.

36. Johnson, P. D., A. E. Bogan, K. M. Brown, J. T. Garner, P. D. Hartfield, and J. R. Cordeiro. In prep. Conservation status of North American freshwater gastropods. American Fisheries Society, Bethesda, Maryland, USA.

37. Morales, J. B. T., and A. K. Ward. 2000. Snail grazers affect the fate of labile dissolved organic C in streams. Journal of the North American Benthological Society 19:659–669.

38. Turgeon, D. D., J. F. Quinn, Jr., A. E. Bogan, E. V. Coan, F. G. Hochberg, W. G. Lyons, P. M. Mikkelsen, R. J. Neves, C. F. E. Roper, G. Rosenberg, B. Roth, A. Scheltema, F. G. Thompson, M. Vecchione, and J. D. Williams. 1998. Common and scientific names of aquatic invertebrates from the United States and Canada: mollusks. Second edition. American Fisheries Society Special Publication 26, Bethesda, Maryland, USA.

39. Cicerello, R. R., M. L. Warren, Jr., and G. A. Schuster. 1991. A distributional checklist of the freshwater unionids (Bivalvia: Unionoidea) of Kentucky. American Malacological Bulletin 8:113–129.

40. Parmalee, P. W., and A. E. Bogan. 1998. The freshwater mussels of Tennessee. The University of Tennessee Press, Knoxville, Tennessee, USA.

41. Cicerello, R. R., and G. A. Schuster. 2003. A guide to the freshwater mussels of Kentucky. Kentucky State Nature Preserves Commission Scientific and Technical Series 7, Frankfort, Kentucky, USA.

42. Burr, B. M., and L. M. Page. 1986. Zoogeography of fishes of the lower Ohio–upper Mississippi basin. Pages 287–324 in C. H. Hocutt and E. O. Wiley, editors. The zoogeography of North American freshwater fishes. John Wiley and Sons, New York, New York, USA.

43. Morey, D. F., and G. M. Crothers. 1998. Clearing up clouded waters: paleoenvironmental analysis of freshwater mussel assemblages from the Green River shell middens, western Kentucky. Journal of Archaeological Science 25:907–926.

44. Williams, J. D., M. L. Warren, Jr., K. S. Cummings, J. L. Harris, and R. J. Neves. 1993. Conservation status of freshwater mussels of the United States and Canada. Fisheries 18:6–22.

45. Platnick, N. I. 2007. The world spider catalog, version 7.0. American Museum of Natural History. Available at http://research.amnh.org/entomology/spiders/catalog/. Accessed October 6, 2007.

46. Ubick, D., P. Paquin, P. E. Cushing, and V. Roth, editors. 2005. Spiders of North America: an identification manual. American Arachnological Society.

47. Kaston, B. J. 1981. Spiders of Connecticut. Revised edition. State Geological and Natural History Survey of Connecticut Bulletin 70, Hartford, Connecticut, USA.

48. Folkerts, D. R. 2006. A preliminary checklist of the spiders of Alabama. Available at www.auburn.edu/~folkedr/spiders/index.html. Accessed July 28, 2008.

49. Moulder, B. 2006. Checklist of Illinois spiders. Illinois State Museum, Spider Collection Online. Available at www.museum.state.il.us/ismdepts/zoology/spiders/checklist.html. Accessed July 28, 2008.

50. Kaston, B. J. 1972. How to know the spiders. Third edition. Wm. C. Brown Company Publishers, Dubuque, Iowa, USA.

51. Jones, S. C. 2004. Brown recluse spider. The Ohio State University Extension Fact Sheet, Columbus, Ohio, USA.

52. Fet, V., W. D. Sissom, G. Lowe, and M. E. Braunwalder. 2000. Catalog of the scorpions of the world (1758–1998). The New York Entomological Society, New York, New York, USA.

53. Shelley, R. M. 1994. Distribution of the scorpion, *Vaejovis carolinianus* (Beauvois)—a reevaluation (Arachnida: Scorpionida: Vaejovidae). Brimleyana 21:57–68.

54. MacGregor, J. R., pers. comm, December 1, 2006.

55. Hobbs, H. H., Jr., and H. H. Hobbs, III. 1970. New entocytherid ostracods with a key to the genera of the subfamily Entocytherinae. Smithsonian Contributions to Zoology 47, Washington, D.C., USA.

56. Hobbs, H. H., and M. Walton. 1976. New entocytherid ostracods from Kentucky and Tennessee. Proceedings of the Biological Society of Washington 89:393–404.

57. Williams, W. D. 1976. Freshwater isopods (Asellidae) of North America. U.S. Environmental Protection Agency, Environmental and Support Laboratory, Cincinnati, Ohio, USA.

58. Covich, A. P., and J. H. Thorp. 1991. Crustacea: introduction and peracarida. Pages 665–689 *in* J. H. Thorpe and A. P. Covich, editors. Ecology and classification of North American freshwater invertebrates. Academic Press, New York, New York, USA.

59. DeLorme, D. 1991. Ostracoda. Pages 691–722 *in* J. H. Thorpe and A. P. Covich, editors. Ecology and classification of North American freshwater invertebrates. Academic Press, New York, New York, USA.

60. Zhang, J., and J. R. Holsinger. 2003. Systematics of the freshwater amphipod genus *Crangonyx* (Crangonyctidae) in North America. Virginia Museum of Natural History, Memoir Number 6, Martinsville, Virginia, USA.

61. Taylor, C. A., G. A. Schuster, J. E. Cooper, R. J. DiStefano, A. G. Eversole, P. Hamr, H. H. Hobbs III, H. W. Robison, C. E. Skelton, and R. F. Thoma. 2007. A reassessment of the conservation status of crayfishes of the United States and Canada after 10+ years of increased awareness. Fisheries 32:372–389.

62. Taylor, C. A., and G. A. Schuster. 2004. The crayfishes of Kentucky. Illinois Natural History Survey Special Publication 28, Champaign, Illinois, USA.

63. Arnett, R. H., Jr. 2000. American insects: a handbook of the insects of America north of Mexico. Second edition. CRC Press, Boca Raton, Florida, USA.

64. Merritt, R. W., K. W. Cummins, and M. B. Berg. 2008. An introduction to the aquatic insects of North America. Fourth edition. Kendall/Hunt Publishing Company, Dubuque, Iowa, USA.

65. Resh, V. H. 1975. A distributional study of the caddisflies of Kentucky. Transactions of the Kentucky Academy of Science 36:6–16.

66. Houp, R. E. 1999. New caddisfly (Trichopetra) records from Kentucky with implications for water quality. Journal of the Kentucky Academy of Science 60:1–3.

67. Floyd, M. A., pers. comm., March 5, 2007.

68. Randolph, R. P., and W. P. McCafferty. 1998. Diversity and distribution of the mayflies (Ephemeroptera) of Illinois, Indiana, Kentucky, Michigan, Ohio, and Wisconsin. Bulletin of the Ohio Biological Survey New Series, Vol. 13, No. 1, Columbus, Ohio, USA.

69. Tarter, D. C., D. L. Chaffee, and S. A. Grubbs. 2006. Revised checklist of the stoneflies (Plecoptera) of Kentucky, U.S.A. Entomological News 117:1–10.

70. Corbet, P. S. 1999. Dragonflies: behavior and ecology of Odonata. Cornell University Press, Ithaca, New York, USA.

71. Resener, P. L. 1970. An annotated check list of the dragonflies and damselflies (Odonata) of Kentucky. Transactions of the Kentucky Academy of Science 31:32–44.

72. Laudermilk, E. L., and C. Cook. 2009. Unpublished data.

73. Covell, C. V., Jr. 1999. The butterflies and moths (Lepidoptera) of Kentucky: an annotated checklist. Kentucky State Nature Preserves Commission Scientific and Technical Series 6, Frankfort, Kentucky, USA.

74. Covell, C. V., Jr., L. D. Gibson, and D. J. Wright. 2000. New state records and new available names for species of Kentucky moths (Insecta: Lepidoptera). Journal of the Kentucky Academy of Science 61:105–107.

75. Gibson, L. D., and C. V. Covell Jr. 2006. New records of butterflies and moths (Lepidoptera) from Kentucky. Journal of the Kentucky Academy of Science 67:19–21.

76. Wilson, E. O. 1987. The little things that run the world (the importance and conservation of invertebrates). Conservation Biology 1:344–346. Note: Transcript of Wilson's address given May 7, 1987, at the opening of the invertebrate exhibit, National Zoological Park, Washington, D.C., USA.

77. Ceas, P. A. 1998. Descriptions of six new species within the *Etheostoma spectabile* complex (Percidae: subgenus *Oligocephalus*) from Kentucky [abstract]. Southern Division 1998 Midyear Meeting, American Fisheries Society, Lexington, Kentucky, USA.

78. Etnier, D. A., and W. C. Starnes. 1993. The fishes of Tennessee. The University of Tennessee Press, Knoxville, Tennessee, USA.

79. Powers, S. L., and R. L. Mayden. 2007. Systematics, evolution and biogeography of the *Etheostoma simoterum* complex (Percidae: subgenus *Ulocentra*). Bulletin of the Alabama Museum of Natural History 25:1–23.

80. Page, L. M., and B. M. Burr. 1991. A field guide to freshwater fishes: North America north of Mexico. Houghton Mifflin, Boston, Massachusetts, USA.

81. Ryon, M. G., and B. A. Carrico. 1998. Distributional records for fishes of the Coastal Plain Province, Ballard and McCracken Counties, in western Kentucky. Journal of the Kentucky Academy of Science 59:51–63.

82. Petranka, J. W. 1998. Salamanders of the United States and Canada. Smithsonian Institution Press, Washington, D.C., USA.

83. Heyer, R. W., and J. B. Murphy. 2005. Declining amphibian populations task force. Pages 17–22 *in* M. Lannoo, editor. Amphibian declines: the conservation status of United States species. University of California Press, Los Angeles, California, USA.

84. Palmer-Ball, B., Jr. 2003. Annotated checklist of the birds of Kentucky. The Kentucky Ornithological Society, Louisville, Kentucky, USA.

85. Palmer-Ball, B., Jr. 2009. Unpublished data.

86. Palmer-Ball, B., Jr. 1996. The Kentucky breeding bird atlas. The University Press of Kentucky, Lexington, Kentucky, USA.

87. Audubon, J. J. 1831. Ornithological biography, or an account of the habits of the birds of the United States of America; accompanied by descriptions of the objects represented in the work entitled the birds of America, and interspersed with delineations of American scenery and manners. Judah Dobson, Agent, Philadelphia, Pennsylvania, USA.

88. Jackson, J. A. 2002. Ivory-billed woodpecker (*Campephilus principalis*). Pages 1–28 *in* A. Poole and F. Gill, editors. The birds of North America, No. 711. The Birds of North America, Philadelphia, Pennsylvania, USA.

89. Fitzpatrick, J. W., M. Lammertink, M. D. Luneau, Jr., T. W. Gallagher, B. R. Harrison, G. M. Sparling, K. V. Rosenberg, R. W. Rohrbaugh, E. C. H. Swarthout, P. H. Wrege, S. B. Swarthout, M. S. Dantzker, R. A. Charif, T. R. Barksdale, J. V. Remsen Jr., S. D. Simon, and D. Zollner. 2005. Ivory-billed woodpecker (*Campephilus principalis*) persists in continental North America. Science 308:1460–1462.

90. Gallagher, T. 2005. The grail bird: hot on the trail of the ivory-billed woodpecker. Houghton Mifflin, New York, New York, USA.

91. United States Fish and Wildlife Service. 2005. The ivory-billed woodpecker [brochure]. Available at www.fws.gov/ivorybill/IBW-general-brochure.pdf. Accessed April 8, 2009.

92. Hackney, C. T., S. M. Adams, and W. H. Martin, editors. 1992. Biodiversity of the southeastern United States: aquatic communities. John Wiley & Sons, New York, New York, USA.

93. Martin, W. H., S. G. Boyce, and A. C. Echternacht, editors. 1993. Biodiversity of the southeastern United States: upland terrestrial communities. John Wiley & Sons, New York, New York, USA.

94. Martin, W. H., S. G. Boyce, and A. C. Echternacht, editors. 1993. Biodiversity of the southeastern United States: lowland terrestrial communities. John Wiley & Sons, New York, New York, USA.

95. Kentucky Division of Geographic Information. 2004. Kentucky 2001 Anderson level III land cover. Frankfort, Kentucky, USA. Available at http://kygeonet.ky.gov. Accessed September 14, 2009.

96. Kentucky GAP Analysis Program. 2002. Kentucky Gap Analysis Program land cover map. Mid-America Remote Sensing Center, Murray State University, Murray, Kentucky, USA. Available at http://kygeonet.ky.gov. Accessed September 14, 2009.

97. Dahl, T. E. 1990. Wetlands losses in the United States 1780s to 1980s. United States Fish and Wildlife Service, Washington, D.C., USA, and Northern Prairie Wildlife Research Center, Jamestown, North Dakota, USA. Version 16, July 1997. Available at www.npwrc.usgs.gov/resource/wetlands/wetloss/index.htm. Accessed March 31, 2009.

98. Martin, W. H. 1992. Characteristics of old-growth mixed mesophytic forests. Natural Areas Journal 12:127–135.

99. Parker, G. R. 1989. Old-growth forests of the central hardwoods region. Natural Areas Journal 9:5–11.

100. Taylor, D. J., editor. 1995. Kentucky alive!: report of the Kentucky Biodiversity Task Force. Commonwealth of Kentucky, Frankfort, Kentucky, USA.

101. Dodson, S. I. 2005. Introduction to limnology. McGraw-Hill, New York, New York, USA.

102. Hynes, H. B. N. 1970. The ecology of running waters. Liverpool University Press, Liverpool, UK.

103. Vannote, R. L., G. W. Minshall, K. W. Cummins, J. R. Sedell, and C. E. Cushing. 1980. The river continuum concept. Canadian Journal of Fisheries and Aquatic Sciences 37:130–137.

104. Lewis, W. M., Jr. 1970. Morphological adaptations of cyprinodontoids for inhabiting oxygen deficient waters. Copeia 1970:319–326.

105. Cole, G. A. 1983. Textbook of limnology. Waveland Press, Prospect Heights, Illinois, USA.

106. Dougherty, P. H., editor. 1985. Caves and karst of Kentucky. Kentucky Geological Survey Special Publication 12, Series XI, Lexington, Kentucky, USA.

107. Barr, T. C., Jr. 1963. Ecological classification of cavernicoles. Cave Notes 5:9–16.

108. Barr, T. C., Jr. 1968. Cave ecology and the evolution of troglobites. Evolutionary Biology 2:35–102.

109. Hobbs, H. H., III. 1992. Caves and springs. Pages 59–131 in C. T. Hackney, S. M. Adams, and W. H. Martin, editors. Biodiversity of the southeastern United States: aquatic communities. John Wiley and Sons, New York, New York, USA.

110. Culver, D. C., T. C. Kane, and D. W. Fong. 1995. Adaptation and natural selection in caves: the evolution of Gammarus minus. Harvard University Press, Cambridge, Massachusetts, USA.

111. Barr, T. C., Jr. 1967. Observations on the ecology of caves. The American Naturalist 101:475–491.

112. Culver, D. C., L. L. Master, M. C. Christman, and H. H. Hobbs Jr. 2000. Obligate cave fauna of the 48 contiguous United States. Conservation Biology 14:386–401.

113. Culver, D. C., and J. R. Holsinger. 1992. How many species of troglobites are there? National Speleological Society Bulletin 54:79–80.

114. Culver, D. C., pers. comm., September 24, 2007.

115. NatureServe. 2007. NatureServe Explorer: an online encyclopedia of life [web application]. Version 6.1. NatureServe, Arlington, Virginia. Available at www.natureserve.org/explorer. Accessed March 15, 2007.

116. Paylor, R., pers. comm., October 31, 2006.

117. Culver, D. C., and B. Sket. 2000. Hotspots of subterranean biodiversity in caves and wells. Journal of Cave and Karst Studies 62:11–17.

118. Culver, D. C., L. Deharveng, A. Bedos, J. J. Lewis, M. Madden, J. R. Reddell, B. Sket, P. Trontelj, and D. White. 2006. The mid-latitude biodiversity ridge in terrestrial cave fauna. Ecography 29:120–128.

CHAPTER 5. THREATS

1. Leopold, A. 1949. A Sand County almanac. Oxford University Press, New York, New York, USA.

2. Zourarakis, D. P. 2009. Land cover change entropy: the 2001–05 quadrennium in Kentucky. Fifth International Workshop on the Analysis of Multi-temporal Remote Sensing Images, July 28–30, 2009, Groton, Connecticut, USA.

3. Kentucky State Data Center. 2004. Population projections. University of Louisville, Louisville, Kentucky, USA. Available at http://ksdc.louisville.edu/kpr/pro/projections.htm. Accessed August 14, 2008.

4. Kentucky State Nature Preserves Commission. 2007. Section 6 report. Report submitted to United States Fish and Wildlife Service, Atlanta, Georgia, USA.

5. Kentucky Division of Geographic Information. 2004. Kentucky 2001 Anderson level III land cover. Frankfort, Kentucky, USA. Available at http://kygeonet.ky.gov. Accessed September 14, 2009.

6. Kentucky GAP Analysis Program. 2002. Kentucky gap analysis program land cover map. Mid-America Remote Sensing Center, Murray State University, Murray, Kentucky, USA. Available at http://kygeonet.ky.gov. Accessed September 14, 2009.

7. Kentucky Transportation Cabinet. 2007. All roads. Kentucky Transportation Cabinet, Frankfort, Kentucky, USA. Available at ftp://ftp.kymartian.ky.gov/trans/statewide/shape/. Accessed September 14, 2009.

8. Kentucky Public Service Commission. 2004. Electric transmission line GIS data. Kentucky Public Service Commission, Frankfort, Kentucky, USA.

9. Kentucky Division of Water. 2006. 2006 integrated report to Congress on water quality in Kentucky, Vol. I. 305(b): assessment results with emphasis on the Kentucky River basin management unit and Salt-Licking rivers basin management unit. Environmental and Public Protection Cabinet, Frankfort, Kentucky, USA.

10. Wilson, E. O. 2000. Vanishing before our eyes. Time. April 26, 2000, 28–31, 34.

11. Kentucky State Nature Preserves Commission. 2007. Natural heritage database. Kentucky State Nature Preserves Commission, Frankfort, Kentucky, USA.

12. United States Environmental Protection Agency. 2003. Mountaintop mining/valley fills in Appalachia:

final programmatic environmental impact statement (draft PEIS). Environmental Protection Agency, Washington, D.C., USA.

13. Kentuckians for the Commonwealth. 2009. Unpublished data.

14. Kentucky Division of Forestry. 2008. Kentucky's forest facts. Available at www.forestry.ky.gov/forestfacts/. Accessed May 30, 2008.

15. Wear, D. N., and J. G. Greis, editors. 2002. Southern forest resource assessment. General Technical Report SRS-53. United States Department of Agriculture, United States Forest Service, Southern Research Station, Asheville, North Carolina, USA.

16. Duffy, D. C., and A. J. Meier. 1992. Do Appalachian herbaceous understories ever recover from clearcutting? Conservation Biology 6:196–201.

17. Kentucky Coal Education. 2007. Kentucky coal and energy education project. Available at www.coaleducation.org. Accessed October 8, 2008.

18. Kentucky Environmental Quality Commission. 2001. State of the environment. Kentucky Environmental Quality Commission, Frankfort, Kentucky, USA.

19. Wickman, J. D., K. H. Ritters, T. G. Wade, M. Coan, and C. Homer. 2007. The effect of Appalachian mountaintop mining on interior forest. Landscape Ecology 22:179–187.

20. Holl, K. D., C. E. Zipper, and J. A. Burger. 2001. Recovery of native plant communities after mining. Virginia Cooperative Extension Publication 460–120. Virginia Polytechnic Institute and State University, Blacksburg, Virginia, USA.

21. Angel, P., V. Davis, J. Burger, D. Graves, and C. Zipper. 2005. The Appalachian regional reforestation initiative. Forest Reclamation Advisory No. 1. Available at http://arri.osmre.gov. Accessed April 15, 2009.

22. Wade, G. L., and R. L. Thompson. 1999. Woody vegetation and succession of the Fonde surface mine demonstration area, Bell County, Kentucky. Pages 339–551 in S. A. Bengson and D. M. Bland, editors. Mining and reclamation for the next millennium. Vol. I. Proceedings of the 16th Annual National Meeting, American Society for Surface Mining and Reclamation, August 13–19, 1999, Scottsdale, Arizona, USA.

23. Wade, G. L., and R. L. Thompson. 2003. Is there a characteristic flora of Appalachian pre-SMCRA surface mines? Pages 1381–1404 in R. Barnhisel and B. A. Zamora, editors. Working together for innovation reclamation. Proceedings of the 20th Annual National Conference, American Society of Mining and Reclamation, June 3–6, 2003, Billings, Montana, USA.

24. Nieman, T. J., and Z. R. Merkin. 2006. Wildlife management, surface mining, and regional planning. Growth and Change 26:405–424.

25. Kentucky Division of Oil and Gas. 2006. Division of oil and gas conservation. Available at www.dogc.ky.gov/. Accessed March 6, 2006.

26. Wilcove, D. S., D. Rothstein, J. Dubow, A. Phillips, and E. Losos. 1998. Quantifying threats to imperiled species in the United States. BioScience 48:607–615.

27. Mahala, M. 2007. Kentucky aquatic nuisance species management plan. Report submitted to the Commonwealth of Kentucky and Kentucky Department of Fish and Wildlife Resources, Frankfort, Kentucky, USA.

28. Mahala, M. 2008. Kentucky terrestrial nuisance species management plan. Report submitted to the Kentucky Department of Fish and Wildlife Resources, Frankfort, Kentucky, USA.

29. United States Forest Service. 2004. Eastern hemlock forests: guidelines to minimize the impacts of hemlock woolly adelgid. United States Department of Agriculture, United States Forest Service publication NA-TP-03-04, Morgantown, West Virginia, USA.

30. Kentucky Forest Health Task Force. 2006. Kentucky forest health task force annual report. University of Kentucky College of Agriculture, Lexington, Kentucky, USA.

31. McClure, M. S. 2001. Biological control of hemlock woolly adelgid in the eastern United States. FHTET 2000–08. United States Department of Agriculture, Forest Service, Morgantown, West Virginia, USA.

32. Mayer, M., R. Chianese, T. Scudder, J. White, K. Vongpaseuth, and R. Ward. 2002. Thirteen years of monitoring the hemlock woolly adelgid in New Jersey forests. Pages 50–60 in B. Onken, R. Reardon, and J. Lashomb, editors. Proceedings: hemlock woolly adelgid in the eastern United States symposium. February 5–7, 2002, East Brunswick, New Jersey, USA.

33. Orwig, D. A., and M. L. Kizlinski. 2002. Vegetation response following hemlock woolly adelgid infestation, hemlock decline, and hemlock salvage logging. Pages 106–117 in B. Onken, R. Reardon, and J. Lashomb, editors. Proceedings: hemlock woolly adelgid in the eastern United States symposium. February 5–7, 2002, East Brunswick, New Jersey, USA.

34. National Park Service. 2006. Hemlock woolly adelgid. Available at www.nps.gov/grsm/naturescience/hemlock-woolly-adelgid.htm. Accessed September 5, 2008.

35. Aldridge, D. C., and S. J. Müller. 2001. The Asiatic clam, Corbicula fluminea, in Britain: current status and potential impacts. Journal of Conchology 37:177–183.

36. Foster, A. M., P. Fuller, A. Benson, S. Constant, and D. Raikow. 2007. Corbicula fluminea. USGS nonindigenous aquatic species database, Gainesville, Florida, USA. Available at http://nas.er.usgs.gov. Accessed September 14, 2009.

37. Lord, W. 2007. The man who tracked down the blight. Pages 163–170 in C. Bolgiano, editor. Mighty giants: an american chestnut anthology. The American Chestnut Foundation, Bennington, Vermont, USA.

38. National Geographic Cartographic Division. 1990. Original distribution of American chestnut and spread of chestnut blight [map]. National Geographic 177:133.

39. Jones, R. L. 2005. Plant life of Kentucky: an illustrated guide to the vascular flora. The University Press of Kentucky, Lexington, Kentucky, USA.

40. Kentucky Exotic Pest Plant Council. 2006. Invasive exotic plant list. Available at www.se-eppc.org/ky/list.htm. Accessed September 14, 2009.

41. Miller, J. H. 2003. Nonnative invasive plants of southern forests: a field guide for identification and control. General Technical Report SRS-62, United States Department of Agriculture, United States Forest Service, Southern Research Station, Asheville, North Carolina, USA.

42. Alien Plant Working Group. 2007. Least wanted: alien plant invaders of natural areas. Plant Conservation Alliance, Washington, D.C., USA. Available at www.nps.gov/plants/alien/factmain.htm. Accessed August 15, 2008.

43. United States Environmental Protection Agency. 1999. National air quality and emission trends report,

1999. Available at www.epa.gov/airtrends/aqtrnd99. Accessed April 16, 2009.

44. Elwood, J. W., and P. J. Mulholland. 1989. Effects of acid precipitation on stream ecosystems. Pages 85–135 *in* D. C. Adriano and A. H. Johnson, editors. Biological and ecological effects: acidic precipitation. Vol. 2. Springer Verlag, Berlin, Germany.

45. Relyea, R. A. 2005. The impact of insecticides and herbicides on the biodiversity and productivity of aquatic communities. Ecological Applications 15:618–627.

46. Cox, C. 1991. Pesticides and birds: from DDT to today's poisions. Journal of Pesticide Reform 11:2–6.

47. Bridges, C. M. 2000. Long-term effects of pesticide exposure at various life stages of the southern leopard frog (*Rana sphenocephala*). Archives of Environmental Contamination and Toxicology 39:91–96.

48. Trivedi, B. P. 2002. Hermaphrodite frogs caused by popular weed killer? National Geographic News, April 16, 2002. Available at http://news.nationalgeographic.com/news/2002/04/0416_020416_TVfrog.html. Accessed September 14, 2009.

49. National Park Service. 2009. Mammoth Cave. Available at www.nps.gov/maca/. Accessed February 19, 2009.

50. National Parks Conservation Association. June 24, 2004. New report ranks five most-polluted national parks [press release]. National Parks Conservation Association, Washington, D.C., USA. Available at: www.npca.org/media_center/press_releases/2004/page-27600358.html. Accessed April 13, 2009.

51. National Parks Conservation Association. 2008. Dark horizons: 10 national parks most threatened by new coal-fired power plants. National Parks Conservation Association, Washington, D.C., USA. Available at: www.npca.org/darkhorizons/. Accessed April 13, 2009.

52. Master, L. L., S. R. Flack, and B. A. Stein, editors. 1998. Rivers of life: critical watersheds for protecting freshwater biodiversity. The Nature Conservancy, Arlington, Virginia, USA.

53. Carson, R. 1962. Silent spring. Houghton Mifflin, Boston, Massachusetts, USA.

54. Kentucky Division of Water. 2007. Overview of Kentucky's waters. Kentucky Division of Water, Frankfort, Kentucky, USA. Available at www.water.ky.gov/homepage_repository/overview.htm. Accessed March 20, 2007.

55. Lovejoy, T. 2008. Climate change: prospects for nature. Presentation as part of the University of Kentucky forestry graduate student association seminar series, October 1, 2008. University of Kentucky, Lexington, Kentucky, USA.

56. Pachauri, R. K., and A. Reisinger, editors. 2007. Climate change 2007: synthesis report. Contribution of working groups I, II, and III to the fourth assessment report of the Intergovernmental Panel on Climate Change. Intergovernmental Panel on Climate Change, Geneva, Switzerland.

57. Parmesan, C., and H. Galbraith. 2004. Observed impacts of global climate change in the U.S. Prepared for the Pew Center on Global Climate Change, Arlington, Virginia, USA.

58. Block, M. 2007. Scientist measures an overlooked greenhouse gas. National Public Radio, Washington, D.C., USA. Available at www.npr.org/templates/story/story.php?storyId=14288215. Accessed May 22, 2008.

59. Hersteinsson, P., and D. W. MacDonald. 1992. Interspecific competition and the geographical distribution of red and arctic foxes, *Vulpes vulpes* and *Alopex lagopus*. Oikos 64:505–515.

60. Hicke, J. A., G. P. Asner, J. T. Randerson, C. Tucker, S. Los, R. Birdsey, J. C. Jenkins, C. Field, and E. Holland. 2002. Satellite-derived increases in net primary productivity across North America, 1982–1998. Geophysical Research Letters 29:1427, doi:10.1029/2001GL013578.

61. Smith, F. A., and J. L. Betancourt. 1998. Response of bushy-tailed woodrats (*Neotoma cinerea*) to Late Quaternary climatic change in the Colorado Plateau. Quaternary Research 50:S0–S39.

62. Bradley, N. L., A. C. Leopold, J. Ross, and W. Huffaker. 1999. Phenological changes reflect climate change in Wisconsin. Proceedings of the National Academy of Sciences 96:9701–9704.

63. Hill, G. E., R. R. Sargent, and M. G. Sargent. 1998. Recent change in the winter distribution of rufous hummingbirds. The Auk 155:240–245.

64. Thomas, C. D., A. Cameron, R. E. Green, M. Bakkenes, L. J. Beaumont, Y. C. Collingham, R. F. N. Erasmus, M. F. de Siqueira, A. Grainger, L. Hannah, L. Hughes, B. Huntley, A. S. van Jaarsveld, G. F. Midgley, L. Miles, M. A. Ortega-Huerta, A. T. Peterson, O. L. Phillips, and S. E. Williams. 2004. Extinction risk from global climate change. Nature 427:145–148.

65. Arbor Day Foundation. 2006. Hardiness zone changes between 1990 and 2006. Arbor Day Foundation, Nebraska City, Nebraska, USA. Available at http://www.arborday.org/media/map_change.cfm. Accessed May 4, 2009.

66. United States Fish and Wildlife Service. 2008. Endangered and threatened wildlife and plants; determination of threatened status for the polar bear (*Ursus maritimis*) throughout its range. Final rule. 73 Federal Register 28212. Available at http://www.fws.gov/home/feature/2008/polarbear012308/polarbearspromo.html. Accessed June 1, 2009.

67. Brady, J. 2009. Mountain critter a candidate for endangered list. National Public Radio, Washington, D.C., USA. Available at www.npr.org/templates/story/story.php?storyId=111583873. Accessed August 8, 2009.

68. United Nations Framework Convention on Climate Change. 2009. Convention. United Nations Framework Convention on Climate Change, Bonn, Germany. Available at http://unfccc.int/essential_background/convention/items/2627.php. Accessed April 6, 2009.

69. Kentucky Environmental Quality Commission. 1997. State of Kentucky's environment. Kentucky Environmental Quality Commission, Frankfort, Kentucky, USA.

70. Schorger, A. W. 1955. The passenger pigeon: its natural history and extinction. University of Wisconsin Press, Madison, Wisconsin, USA.

71. Audubon, J. J. 1831. Ornithological biography, or an account of the habits of the birds of the United States of America; accompanied by descriptions of the objects represented in the work entitled the birds of America, and interspersed with delineations of American scenery and manners. Judah Dobson, Philadelphia, Pennsylvania, USA.

72. Leopold, A. 1947. On a monument to the pigeon. Pages 3–5 *in* Silent wings: a memorial to the passenger pigeon. Wisconsin Society for Ornithology, Appleton, Wisconsin, USA.

73. Miyazaki T., K. Goto, T. Kobayashi, T. Kageyama, and M. Miyata. 1999. Mass mortalities associated with a virus disease in Japanese pearl oysters *Pinctada fucata martensii*. Disease of Aquatic Organisms 37:1–12.

CHAPTER 6. CONSERVATION

1. Sharnik, J., producer. April 3, 1963. The silent spring of Rachel Carson. CBS Reports. Columbia Broadcasting System, New York, New York, USA.

2. Kentucky State Nature Preserves Commission. 2008. Managed areas database. Kentucky State Nature Preserves Commission, Frankfort, Kentucky, USA.

3. Kentucky State Nature Preserves Commission. 2008. Unpublished data.

4. United Nations Educational, Scientific and Cultural Organization. 2008. World network of biosphere reserves. United Nations Educational, Scientific and Cultural Organization, Paris, France. Available at www.unesco.org/mab/doc/brs/BRlist2008.pdf. Accessed March 18, 2009.

5. United Nations Educational, Scientific and Cultural Organization. 2009. World heritage list. United Nations Educational, Scientific and Cultural Organization, Paris, France. Available at http://whc.unesco.org/en/list. Accessed March 18, 2009.

6. Surface Mine Control and Reclamation Act of 1977, 16 U.S.C. § 1531, et seq.

7. Endangered Species Act of 1973, 30 U.S.C. § 1201, et seq.

8. Margules, C. R., and R. L. Pressey. 2000. Systematic conservation planning. Nature 405:243–253.

9. Conservation Planning Institute. 2008. Conservation Planning Institute, Corvallis, Oregon, USA. Available at www.conservationplanninginstitute.org. Accessed October 6, 2008.

10. Williams, P., D. Gibbons, C. Margules, A. Rebelo, C. Humphries, and R. Pressey. 1996. A comparison of richness hotspots, rarity hotspots, and complementary areas for conserving diversity of British birds. Conservation Biology 10:155–174.

11. Stein, B. A., L. S. Kutner, and J. S. Adams, editors. 2000. Precious heritage: the status of biodiversity in the United States. Oxford University Press, New York, New York, USA.

12. Page, L. M., and B. M. Burr. 1991. A field guide to freshwater fishes: North America north of Mexico. Houghton Mifflin, Boston, Massachusetts, USA.

13. Williams, J. D., M. L. Warren Jr., K. S. Cummings, J. L. Harris, and R. J. Neves. 1993. Conservation status of freshwater mussels of the United States and Canada. Fisheries 18:6–22.

14. Master, L. L., S. R. Flack, and B. A. Stein, editors. 1998. Rivers of life: critical watersheds for protecting freshwater biodiversity. The Nature Conservancy, Arlington, Virginia, USA.

15. Burr, B. M., and M. L. Warren, Jr. 1986. A distributional atlas of Kentucky fishes. Kentucky Nature Preserves Commission Scientific and Technical Series 4, Frankfort, Kentucky, USA.

16. Ceas, P. A. 1998. Descriptions of six new species within the *Etheostoma spectabile* complex (Percidae: subgenus *Oligocephalus*) from Kentucky [abstract]. Southern Division 1998 Midyear Meeting, American Fisheries Society, Lexington, Kentucky, USA.

17. Ceas, P. A., and L. M. Page. 1997. Systematic studies of the *Etheostoma spectabile* complex (Percidae; subgenus *Oligocephalus*), with descriptions of four new species. Copeia 1997:496–522.

18. Cicerello, R. R., and G. A. Schuster. 2003. A guide to the freshwater mussels of Kentucky. Kentucky State Nature Preserves Commission Scientific and Technical Series 7, Frankfort, Kentucky, USA.

19. Powers, S. L., and R. L. Mayden. 2007. Systematics, evolution and biogeography of the *Etheostoma simoterum* complex (Percidae: subgenus *Ulocentra*). Bulletin of the Alabama Museum of Natural History 25:1–23.

20. Kentucky State Nature Preserves Commission. 2007. Natural heritage database. Kentucky State Nature Preserves Commission, Frankfort, Kentucky, USA.

21. United States Fish and Wildlife Service. 2007. Endangered and threatened wildlife and plants; review of native species that are candidates for listing as endangered or threatened; annual notice of findings on resubmitted petitions; annual description of progress on listing actions; proposed rule. Federal Register 72:69034–69106.

22. United States Fish and Wildlife Service. 2005. Endangered and threatened wildlife and plants. 50 CFR 17.11 and 17.12. Washington, D.C., USA.

23. NatureServe. 2007. NatureServe explorer: an online encyclopedia of life [web application]. NatureServe, Arlington, Virginia, USA. Available at www.natureserve.org/explorer. Accessed March 1, 2007.

24. Csuti, B., S. Polasky, P. H. Williams, R. L. Pressey, J. D. Lamm, M. Kershaw, A. R. Kiester, B. Downs, R. Hamilton, M. Huso, and K. Sahr. 1997. A comparison of reserve selection algorithms using data on terrestrial vertebrates in Oregon. Biological Conservation 80:83–97.

25. Landowner Resource Centre. 2000. Conserving the forest interior: a threatened wildlife habitat. Extension Notes. Landowner Resource Centre, Manotick, Ontario, Canada.

26. Kentucky Environmental Quality Commission. 2004. Kentucky's forests, 2004 indicator and trend report. Kentucky Environmental Quality Commission, Frankfort, Kentucky, USA. Available at www.eqc.ky.gov/NR/rdonlyres/977794DF-DACE-48E1-9F18-DE14EF51D9B8/0/forestryindicators2004web.pdf. Accessed September 14, 2009.

27. Zourarakis, D. P. 2009. Land cover change entropy: the 2001–05 quadrennium in Kentucky. Fifth International Workshop on the Analysis of Multi-temporal Remote Sensing Images, July 28–30, 2009, Groton, Connecticut, USA.

28. Wickham, J. D., K. H. Ritters, T. G. Wade, M. Coan, and C. Homer. 2007. The effect of Appalachian mountaintop mining on interior forest. Landscape Ecology 22:179–187.

29. Evans, M., and G. Abernathy. 2009. Large forest tracts of Kentucky. Kentucky State Nature Preserves Commission, Frankfort, Kentucky, USA.

30. Herkert, J. R., R. E. Szafoni, V. M. Kleen, and J. E. Schwegman. 1993. Habitat establishment, enhancement and management for forest and grassland birds in Illinois. Division of Natural Heritage, Illinois Department of Conservation, Natural Heritage Technical Publication No. 1, Springfield, Illinois, USA. Version 16, July 1997. Available at www.npwrc.usgs.gov/resource/birds/manbook/index.htm. Accessed September 14, 2009.

31. Bond, M. 2003. Principles of wildlife corridor design. Center for Biological Diversity, Tucson, Arizona, USA.

32. Tabor, G. M., and K. Meiklejohn. 2009. Connectivity 101. LandScope America. NatureServe, Arlington, Virginia, USA. Available at www.landscope.org/explore/natural_geographies/corridors_connectivity/connectivity_101. Accessed August 20, 2009.

Base mapping data: Many of the maps in this book contain the following base mapping data.

City Locations

Kentucky Division of Geographic Information. 2005. City point locations in Kentucky. Kentucky Division of Geographic Information, Frankfort, Kentucky, USA. Available at http://kygeonet.ky.gov/geographicexplorer/.

Hydrography (Streams, Rivers, Lakes, and Reservoirs)

ESRI data & maps [CD-ROM]. 2002. U.S. lakes and rivers. Environmental Systems Research Institute, Redlands, California, USA.

United States Geological Survey. 1999. National hydrography dataset. United States Geological Survey, Reston, Virginia, USA. Available at http://nhd.usgs.gov.

Political Boundaries

Environmental Systems Research Institute. 2006. State boundaries (derived by ESRI from TeleAtlas data). ESRI data & maps media kit. Environmental Systems Research Institute, Redlands, California, USA.

Kentucky Division of Geographic Information. 2005. County boundary polygons of Kentucky. Kentucky Division of Geographic Information, Frankfort, Kentucky, USA. Available at http://kygeonet.ky.gov/geographicexplorer/.

Natural Resources and Environmental Protection Cabinet, Office for Information Services. 1998. State boundary polygon of Kentucky (unpublished dataset). Natural Resources and Environmental Protection Cabinet, Office for Information Services, Frankfort, Kentucky, USA. Available at http://kygeonet.ky.gov/geographicexplorer/.

Shaded Relief

Kentucky Division of Geographic Information. 2007. Statewide hillshade (based on United States Geological Survey national elevation dataset—30 ft.). Kentucky Division of Geographic Information, Frankfort, Kentucky, USA. Available at http://kygeonet.ky.gov/geographicexplorer/.

Kentucky Division of Geographic Information. 2007. Statewide percent slope (based on United States Geological Survey national elevation dataset—30 ft.). Kentucky Division of Geographic Information, Frankfort, Kentucky, USA. Available at http://kygeonet.ky.gov/geographicexplorer/.

U.S. Geological Survey Center for Earth Resource Observation and Science. 2006. SRTM shaded relief. ESRI data & maps media kit. Environmental Systems Research Institute, Redlands, California, USA.

CHAPTER 1

Three Levels of Biodiversity (schematic), p. 3:

Abernathy, G., D. White, E. Laudermilk, and M. Evans. 2009. Three levels of biodiversity [schematic]. Kentucky State Nature Preserves Commission, Frankfort, Kentucky, USA.

Number of Species by Select Groups (schematic), p. 5:

Abernathy, G., E. Laudermilk, and D. White. 2008. Major species groups in Kentucky [schematic]. Kentucky State Nature Preserves Commission. Frankfort, Kentucky, USA.

Species Data:

Note: Primary sources are listed for species numbers. In many cases, the numbers were compiled by KSNPC from multiple sources.

1. Stein, B. A., J. A. Adams, L. L. Master, L. E. Morse, and G. Hammerson. 2000. A remarkable array: species diversity in the United States. Pages 55–92 in B. A. Stein, L. S. Kutner, and J. S. Adams, editors. Precious heritage: the status of biodiversity in the United States. Oxford University Press, New York, New York, USA.

2. Anderson, L. E., H. A. Crun, and W. R. Buck. 1990. List of mosses of North America and Mexico. The Bryologist 93:448–499.

3. Eldredge, L. G., and S. E. Miller. 1998. How many species are there in Hawai'i? Bishop Museum Occasional Papers 41:1–18.

4. Risk, A. 2007. Unpublished data.

5. Stotler, R., and B. Crandell-Stotler. 1977. A checklist of the liverworts and hornworts of North America. The Bryologist 80:405–428.

6. Jones, R. L. 2005. Plant life in Kentucky. The University Press of Kentucky, Lexington, Kentucky, USA.

7. Johnson, P. D., A. E. Bogan, C. E. Lydeard, K. M. Brown, and J. R. Cordeiro. 2007. Finalizing a conservation assessment for North American freshwater gastropods. Presentation at the 2007 Annual Meeting of the Freshwater Mollusk Conservation Society, March 13–16, 2007, Little Rock, Arkansas, USA.

8. Lydeard, C., R. H. Cowie, W. F. Ponder, A. E. Bogan, P. Bouchet, S. A. Clark, K. S. Cummings, T. J. Frest, O. Gargominy, D. G. Herbert, R. Hershler, K. E. Perez, B. Roth, M. Seddon, E. E. Strong, and F. G. Thompson. 2004. The global decline of nonmarine mollusks. BioScience 54:321–330.

9. NatureServe. 2006. Central database. Arlington, Virginia, USA.

10. Cummings, K. S., and D. L. Graf. 2005. Global distribution of freshwater mussel diversity. Poster presented at the 2005 Annual Meeting of the Freshwater Mollusk Conservation Society, May 15–18, 2005, St. Paul, Minnesota, USA. Available at http://clade .acnatsci.org/mussel.

11. Turgeon, D. D., J. F. Quinn, A. E. Bogan, E. V. Coan, F. G. Hochberg, W. G. Lyons, P. M. Mikkelsen, R. J. Neves, C. F. E. Roper, G. Rosenberg, B. Roth, A. Scheltema, F. G. Thompson, M. Vecchione, and J. D. Williams. 1998. Common and scientific names of aquatic invertebrates from the United States and Canada: mollusks. Second edition. American Fisheries Society Special Publication 26, Bethesda, Maryland, USA.

12. Kentucky Natural Heritage Database. 2007. Kentucky State Nature Preserves Commission, Frankfort, Kentucky, USA.

13. Platnick, N. I. 2007. The world spider catalog, version 10.0. American Museum of Natural History, New York, New York, USA. Available at http://research .amnh.org/entomology/spiders/catalog/index.html.

14. Ubick, D., P. Paquin, P. E. Cushing, and V. Roth, editors. 2005. Spiders of North America: an identification manual. American Arachnological Society.

15. Fet, V., W. D. Sissom, G. Lowe, and M. E. Braunwalder. 2000. Catalog of the scorpions of the world (1758–1998). New York Entomological Society, New York, New York, USA.

16. Shelley, R. M. 1994. Distribution of the scorpion, *Vaejovis carolinianus* (Beauvois), a reevaluation (Arachnida: Scorpionida: Vaejovidae). Brimleyana 21:57–68.

17. Taylor, C. A., and G. A. Schuster. 2004. The crayfishes of Kentucky. Illinois Natural History Survey Special Publication No. 28, Champaign, Illinois, USA.

18. Taylor, C. A., G. A. Schuster, J. E. Cooper, R. J. DiStefano, A. G. Eversole, P. Hamr, H. H. Hobbs III, H. W. Robison, C. E. Skelton, and R. F. Thoma. 2007.

A reassessment of the conservation status of crayfishes of the United States and Canada after 10+ years of increased awareness. Fisheries 32:372–389.

19. Schuster, G.A., pers. comm., September 21, 2007.

20. Resh, V. H, and R. T. Cardé. 2003. Encyclopedia of insects. Academic Press, San Diego, California, USA.

21. Arnett, R. H., Jr. 2000. American insects: a handbook of the insects of America north of Mexico. Second edition. CRC Press, Boca Raton, Florida, USA.

22. Randolph, R. P., and W. P. McCafferty. 1998. Diversity and distribution of the mayflies (Ephemeroptera) of Illinois, Indiana, Kentucky, Michigan, Ohio, and Wisconsin. Ohio Biological Survey Bulletin New Series Vol. 13, No. 1, Columbus, Ohio, USA.

23. Schorr, M., M. Lindeboom, and D. Paulson. 2007. World Odonata list. Available at www.ups.edu/x6140 .xml.

24. Needham, J. G., M. J. Westfall, and M. L. May. 2000. Dragonflies of North America. Scientific Publishers, Gainesville, Florida, USA.

25. Westfall, M. J., and M. L. May. 2006. Damselflies of North America. Revised edition. Scientific Publishers, Gainesville, Florida, USA.

26. Laudermilk, E. L., and C. Cook. 2007. An annotated checklist of the damselflies and dragonflies (Insecta: Odonata) of Kentucky. Unpublished manuscript.

27. Stewart, K., pers. comm., August 24, 2007.

28. Tarter, D. C., D. L. Chaffee, and S. A. Grubbs. 2006. Revised checklist of the stoneflies (Plecoptera) of Kentucky, USA. Entomological News 117:1–10.

29. White, R. E. 1998. A field guide to the beetles of North America. Houghton Mifflin, New York, New York, USA.

30. Trichoptera Checklist Coordinating Committee. Trichoptera world checklist. International Symposia on Trichoptera. Available at http://entweb.clemson .edu/database/trichopt/.

31. Morse, J., pers. comm., August 4, 2007.

32. Floyd, M. A., and G. A. Schuster. 2007. The caddisflies (Insecta: Trichoptera) of Kentucky. Unpublished manuscript.

33. Wagner, D. L. 2005. Caterpillars of eastern North America. Princeton University Press, Princeton, New Jersey, USA.

34. Covell, C. V., Jr. The butterflies and moths (Lepidoptera) of Kentucky: an annotated checklist. Kentucky State Nature Preserves Commission Scientific and Technical Series 6, Frankfort, Kentucky, USA.

35. Leidy, R. A., and P. B. Moyle. 1998. Conservation status of the world's fish fauna: an overview. Pages 187–227 in P. L. Fiedler and P. M. Kareiva, editors. Conservation biology: for the coming decade. Chapman and Hall, New York, New York, USA.

36. Page, L. M., and B. M. Burr. 1991. A field guide to freshwater fishes, North America north of Mexico. Houghton Mifflin, Boston, Massachusetts, USA.

37. Burr, B. M., and M. L. Warren Jr. 1986. A distributional atlas of Kentucky fishes. Kentucky Nature Preserves Commission Scientific and Technical Series 4, Frankfort, Kentucky, USA.

38. The World Conservation Union. 2007. The IUCN red list of threatened species. Available at www .iucnredlist.org/static/stats.

39. Wilcove, D. S., and L. L. Master. 2005. How many endangered species are there in the United States? Frontiers in Ecology and the Environment 3:414–420.

40. Cornell Lab of Ornithology. 2008. Updates to the Clements checklist of birds of the world, sixth edition. Cornell Lab of Ornithology, Ithaca, New York, USA. Available at www.birds.cornell.edu/clementschecklist/ corrections/Nov08overview.

41. Palmer-Ball, B., Jr. 2003. Annotated checklist of the birds of Kentucky. Kentucky Ornithological Society, Louisville, Kentucky, USA.

42. Palmer-Ball, B., Jr. 2009. Unpublished data.

CHAPTER 2

Physiographic Provinces of the Southeast (map), p. 10:

Keys, J., Jr.; C. Carpenter, S. Hooks, F. Koenig, W. H. McNab, W. Russell, and M. L. Smith. 1995. Ecological units of the eastern United States—first approximation [CD-ROM]. GIS coverage in ARCINFO format, selected imagery, and map unit tables. United States Department of Agriculture Forest Service. Atlanta, Georgia, USA. Note: Modified by KSNPC.

Natural Regions (map), p. 11:

Evans, M., and G. Abernathy. 2008. Natural regions of Kentucky. Kentucky State Nature Preserves Commission, Frankfort, Kentucky, USA.

Keys, J., Jr.; C. Carpenter, S. Hooks, F. Koenig, W. H. McNab, W. Russell, and M. L. Smith. 1995. Ecological units of the eastern United States—first approximation [CD-ROM]. GIS coverage in ARCINFO format, selected imagery, and map unit tables. United States Department of Agriculture Forest Service. Atlanta, Georgia, USA. Note: Modified by KSNPC.

Generalized Geology (map and cross sections), p. 14:

Map:

Kentucky Geological Survey. 2002. Simplified geology of Kentucky. Kentucky Geological Survey, Lexington, Kentucky, USA. Available at www.uky.edu/KGS/gis/geology.htm.

Department of Paleobiology, National Museum of Natural History, Smithsonian Institution. 2007. Geologic time: the story of a changing earth. Smithsonian Institution, Washington, D.C., USA. Available at http://paleobiology.si.edu/geotime/. Note: Period, era, and eon dates rounded by KSNPC.

Cross sections:

Noger, M. C., and G. R. Dever Jr. 2000. Geologic map of Kentucky [map]. Catalog no. MCS_020_12. Publication no. 1076. Kentucky Geological Survey, Lexington, Kentucky, USA. Available at http://kgsweb.uky.edu/PubsSearching/MoreInfo.asp?titleInput=1076&map=-1.

Topography (map), p. 18:

United States Geological Survey. 2007. Statewide Kentucky single zone 30-foot DEM (national elevation dataset). United States Geological Survey, Reston, Virginia, USA. Available at http://seamless.usgs.gov/.

Watershed (schematic), p. 19:

Abernathy, G. 2007. Watershed diagram [schematic]. Kentucky State Nature Preserves Commission, Frankfort, Kentucky, USA.

Regional Watersheds (map), p. 19:

United States Geological Survey. 2005. 1:2,000,000-scale hydrologic unit boundaries. National atlas of the United States. United States Geological Survey, Reston, Virginia, USA. Available at http://nationalatlas.gov/mld/hucsoom.html.

Major Watersheds (map), p. 20:

United States Geological Survey and United States Environmental Protection Agency. 2003. National hydrography dataset (NHD), high-resolution. United States Geological Survey, Reston, Virginia, USA. Available at http://seamless.usgs.gov/. Note: Data were modified by KSNPC to create major watersheds' boundaries.

Average Annual Temperature (F°) 1971–2000 (map), p. 22:

PRISM Climate Group. 2006. Average annual temperature (F°) 1971–2000. PRISM Climate Group, Oregon State University, Corvallis, Oregon, USA. Available at http://prism.oregonstate.edu. Accessed August 28, 2006.

Average Annual Precipitation (Inches) 1971–2000 (map), p. 22:

PRISM Climate Group. 2006. Average annual precipitation (inches) 1971–2000. PRISM Climate Group, Oregon State University, Corvallis, Oregon, USA. Available at http://prism.oregonstate.edu. Accessed August 28, 2006.

Land Cover (map), p. 25:

Kentucky Division of Geographic Information. 2004. Kentucky 2001 Anderson level III land cover. Kentucky Division of Geographic Information, Frankfort, Kentucky, USA. Available at http://kygeonet.ky.gov/geographicexplorer/.

Kentucky GAP Analysis Program. 2002. Kentucky gap analysis program land cover map. Mid-America Remote Sensing Center, Murray State, Murray, Kentucky, USA. Available at http://kygeonet.ky.gov/geographicexplorer/.

CHAPTER 3

Natural History Timeline (schematic), p. 28

Abernathy, G., B. Yahn, E. Evans, and D. White. 2008. Natural history timeline [schematic]. Kentucky State Nature Preserves Commission, Frankfort, Kentucky, USA.

Plate Tectonics Globes:

Blakey, R. 2007. Mollewide plate tectonic maps. Department of Geography, Northern Arizona University, Flagstaff, Arizona, USA. Available at http://jan.ucc.nau.edu/~rcb7/mollglobe.html.

Geologic Time:

Note: Period, era, and eon dates rounded by KSNPC.

Crutzen, P. J., and E. F. Stoermer. 2000. The "Anthropocene." Global Change Newsletter 41:17–18. Available at www.igbp.net/documents/resources/NL_41.pdf.

Department of Paleobiology, National Museum of Natural History, Smithsonian Institution. 2007. Geologic time: the story of a changing earth. Smithsonian Institution, Washington, D.C., USA. Available at http://paleobiology.si.edu/geotime/.

Zalasiewicz, J., M. Williams, A. Smith, T. L. Barry, A. L. Coe, P. R. Bown, P. Brenchley, et al. 2008. Are we living in the anthropocene? GSA Today 18:4–8.

Significant Points on Timeline:

Department of Anthropology, Smithsonian Institution. 2000. Human Origins Program. Smithsonian Institution, Washington, D.C., USA. Available at http://anthropology.si.edu/humanorigins/ha/sap.htm.

Department of Paleobiology, National Museum of Natural History, Smithsonian Institution. 2007. Geologic time: the story of a changing earth. Smithsonian Institution. Washington, D.C., USA. Available at http://paleobiology.si.edu/geotime/.

Erwin, D.G. 2006. Extinction: how life on earth nearly ended 250 million years ago. Princeton University Press, Princeton, New Jersey, USA.

Kentucky State Nature Preserves Commission. 2007. Rare and extirpated biota of Kentucky. Kentucky State Nature Preserves Commission, Frankfort, Kentucky, USA.

Knoll, Andrew H. 2003. Life on a young planet: the first three billion years of evolution on Earth. Princeton University Press, Princeton, New Jersey, USA.

Lewis, B. R. 1996. Kentucky archaeology. The University Press of Kentucky, Lexington, Kentucky, USA.

Library of Congress. 2002. The first American west: the Ohio River valley, 1750–1820. Library of Congress, Washington, D.C., USA. Available at http://memory.loc.gov/ammem/award99/icuhtml/fawhome.html.

National Park Service. 2007. Other migration theories. Bering Land Bridge National Park, National Park Service, Nome, Alaska, USA. Available at www.nps.gov/bela/historyculture/other-migration-theories.htm.

Science Daily. 2001. First land plants and fungi changed earth's climate, paving the way for explosive evolution of land animals, new gene study suggests. ScienceDaily, Rockville, Maryland, USA. Available at www.sciencedaily.com/releases/2001/08/010810070021.htm.

Sheehan, P. M. 2001. The late Ordovician mass extinction. Annual Review of Earth Planetary Sciences 20: 331–364.

Human Population Data:

Current population:

United States Census Bureau. 2008. Population clocks. Washington, D.C., USA. Available at www.census.gov/main/www/popclock.html.

Historic population:

United States Census Bureau. 2007. Historical Estimates of World Population. Washington, D.C., USA. Available at www.census.gov/ipc/www/worldhis.html. Note: Value on timeline is an average of all reported numbers for a given year.

Villages of the Mississippian and Late Prehistoric Periods (map), p. 32:

Evans, M., and G. Abernathy. 2008. Presettlement land cover of Kentucky. Kentucky State Nature Preserves Commission, Frankfort, Kentucky, USA.

Natural Resources and Environmental Protection Cabinet, Office for Information Services. 1992. Mississippian and Fort Ancient villages in Kentucky, 1790 (unpublished dataset). Natural Resources and Environmental Protection Cabinet, Frankfort, Kentucky, USA.

Natural Resources and Environmental Protection Cabinet, Office for Information Services. 1992. Buffalo traces in Kentucky, 1790 (unpublished dataset). Resources and Environmental Protection Cabinet, Frankfort, Kentucky, USA.

Historical Map, p. 35:

Barker, E. A map of Kentucky from actual survey of Elihu Barker [map]. Library of Congress, Geography and Map Division, Washington, D.C., USA. Available at http://hdl.loc.gov/loc.gmd/g3950.ct001246.

Presettlement Land Cover (map), p. 37:

Evans, M., and G. Abernathy. 2008. Presettlement land cover of Kentucky. Kentucky State Nature Preserves Commission, Frankfort, Kentucky, USA.

CHAPTER 4

Taxonomy: The Five Major Kingdoms (schematic), p. 40:

Abernathy, G., E. Laudermilk, and D. White. 2009. Taxonomy: the five major kingdoms [schematic]. Kentucky State Nature Preserves Commission, Frankfort, Kentucky, USA.

Cornell Lab of Ornithology. 2008. Updates to the Clements checklist of birds of the world, sixth edition. Cornell Lab of Ornithology, Ithaca, New York, USA. Available at www.birds.cornell.edu/clementschecklist/corrections/Nov08overview.

Note: Kingdom Animalia and Phylum Chordate numbers are based on data in the Number of Species by Select Groups graphic in chapter 1.

Global and State Conservation Ranks (schematic), p. 41:

Abernathy, G. 2008. Global (G) and State (S) conservation ranks [schematic]. Kentucky State Nature Preserves Commission, Frankfort, Kentucky, USA.

NatureServe. 2007. NatureServe Explorer: an online encyclopedia of life. Version 6.1. NatureServe, Arlington, Virginia, USA.

Endemism (schematic), p. 41:

Abernathy, G. 2008. Endemism [schematic]. Kentucky State Nature Preserves Commission, Frankfort, Kentucky, USA.

Environmental Systems Research Institute. 2006. Country boundaries. ESRI data & maps media kit. Environmental Systems Research Institute, Redlands, California, USA.

Laudermilk, E. L. Rogers' cave beetle [photograph].

MacGregor, J. R. Green salamander [photograph].

Mandt, A. Canoeing at Murphy's Pond [photograph]. Kentucky State Nature Preserve, Frankfort, Kentucky, USA.

Newman, J. W. Carpenter Cave [photograph].

Thomas, M. R. Shawnee darter [photograph].

Endemic Species (bar chart), p. 42:

Kentucky Natural Heritage Database. 2007. Kentucky State Nature Preserves Commission, Frankfort, Kentucky, USA.

Regional Influences on Kentucky Flora (map), p. 46:

National Aeronautics and Space Administration. 2004. Visual Earth: world cloud free. ESRI data & maps media kit. Environmental Systems Research Institute, Redlands, California, USA.

Flora by Select Plant Types (bar chart), p. 47:

Jones, R. L. 2005. Plant life of Kentucky: an illustrated guide to the vascular flora. The University Press of Kentucky, Lexington, Kentucky, USA.

Plant Rarity Hotspots (map), p. 48:

Abernathy, G., D. White, and B. Palmer-Ball. 2007. Kentucky rarity-weighted richness index analysis. Kentucky State Nature Preserves Commission, Frankfort, Kentucky, USA.

Kentucky Natural Heritage Database. 2007. Kentucky State Nature Preserves Commission, Frankfort, Kentucky, USA.

Kentucky Lady's-slipper (map), p. 50:

Kentucky Natural Heritage Database. 2007. Kentucky State Nature Preserves Commission, Frankfort, Kentucky, USA.

National Aeronautics and Space Administration. 2004. Visual Earth: world cloud free. ESRI data & maps media kit. Environmental Systems Research Institute, Redlands, California, USA.

Mussel Life Cycle (schematic), p. 54:

Thomas, M. R. 2003. Generalized freshwater mussel life cycle [schematic]. Kentucky Department of Fish and Wildlife Resources, Frankfort, Kentucky, USA.

Number of Native Mussel Species in Each Major Watershed (map), p. 55:

Kentucky Natural Heritage Database. 2007. Kentucky State Nature Preserves Commission, Frankfort, Kentucky, USA.

Watersheds with High Mussel Diversity (map), p. 55:

Kentucky Natural Heritage Database. 2007. Kentucky State Nature Preserves Commission, Frankfort, Kentucky, USA.

Southern Unstriped Scorpion (map), p. 58:

MacGregor, J. R., pers. comm., December 1, 2006.

National Aeronautics and Space Administration. 2004. Visual Earth: world cloud free. ESRI data & maps media kit. Environmental Systems Research Institute, Redlands, California, USA.

Shelley, R. M. 1994. Distribution of the scorpion, *Vaejovis carolinianus* (Beauvois), a reevaluation (Arachnida: Scorpionida: Vaejovidae). Brimleyana 21:57–68.

Number of Native Crayfish Species in Each Major Watershed (map), p. 61:

Taylor, C. A., and G. A. Schuster. 2004. The crayfishes of Kentucky. Illinois Natural History Survey Special Publication No. 28, Champaign, Illinois, USA.

Schuster, G.A., pers. comm., October 19, 2007.

Watersheds with High Crayfish Diversity (map), p. 61:

Taylor, C. A., and G. A. Schuster. 2004. The crayfishes of Kentucky. Illinois Natural History Survey Special Publication No. 28, Champaign, Illinois, USA.

Schuster, G.A., pers. comm., October 19, 2007.

Insect Species (bar chart), p. 62:

Covell, C. V., Jr. The butterflies and moths (Lepidoptera) of Kentucky: an annotated checklist. Kentucky State Nature Preserves Commission Scientific and Technical Series 6, Frankfort, Kentucky, USA.

Floyd, M. A., and G. A. Schuster. 2007. The caddisflies (Insecta: Trichoptera) of Kentucky. Unpublished manuscript.

Laudermilk, E. L., and C. Cook. 2007. An annotated checklist of the damselflies and dragonflies (Insecta: Odonata) of Kentucky. Unpublished manuscript.

Randolph, R. P., and W. P. McCafferty. 1998. Diversity and distribution of the mayflies (Ephemeroptera) of

Illinois, Indiana, Kentucky, Michigan, Ohio, and Wisconsin. Ohio Biological Survey Bulletin New Series Vol. 13, No. 1, Columbus, Ohio, USA.

Tarter, D. C., D. L. Chaffee, and S. A. Grubbs. 2006. Revised checklist of the stoneflies (Plecoptera) of Kentucky, USA. Entomological News 117:1–10.

Monarch Butterfly Fall Migration Routes (map), p. 65:

Hagerty R. 2008. Boy with monarch butterfly [photograph]. USFWS National Digital Library, Washington, D.C., USA.

National Aeronautics and Space Administration. 2004. Visual Earth: world cloud free. ESRI data & maps media kit. Environmental Systems Research Institute, Redlands, California, USA.

United States Fish and Wildlife Service. 2008. Monarch butterfly migration and overwintering. National Wildlife Refuge System, U.S. Fish and Wildlife Service, Arlington, Virginia, USA. Available at www.fs.fed.us/monarchbutterfly/migration/index.shtml.

Vertebrate Species (bar chart), p. 66:

Burr, B. M., and M. L. Warren Jr. 1986. A distributional atlas of Kentucky fishes. Kentucky Nature Preserves Commission Scientific and Technical Series 4, Frankfort, Kentucky, USA.

Kentucky Natural Heritage Database. 2007. Kentucky State Nature Preserves Commission, Frankfort, Kentucky, USA.

Palmer-Ball, B., Jr. 2003. Annotated checklist of the birds of Kentucky. Kentucky Ornithological Society, Louisville, Kentucky, USA.

Palmer-Ball, B., Jr. 2009. Unpublished data.

Freshwater Fish Species (bar chart), p. 66:

Burr, B. M., and M. L. Warren Jr. 1986. A distributional atlas of Kentucky fishes. Kentucky Nature Preserves Commission Scientific and Technical Series 4, Frankfort, Kentucky, USA.

Kentucky Natural Heritage Database. 2007. Kentucky State Nature Preserves Commission, Frankfort, Kentucky, USA.

Number of Native Fish Species in Each Major Watershed (map), p. 68:

Kentucky Natural Heritage Database. 2007. Kentucky State Nature Preserves Commission, Frankfort, Kentucky, USA.

Watersheds with High Fish Diversity (map), p. 68:

Kentucky Natural Heritage Database. 2007. Kentucky State Nature Preserves Commission, Frankfort, Kentucky, USA.

Amphibian Species (bar chart), p. 69:

Kentucky Natural Heritage Database. 2007. Kentucky State Nature Preserves Commission, Frankfort, Kentucky, USA.

Amphibian Rarity Hotspots (map), p. 70:

Abernathy, G., D. White, and B. Palmer-Ball. 2007. Kentucky rarity-weighted richness index analysis. Kentucky State Nature Preserves Commission, Frankfort, Kentucky, USA.

Kentucky Natural Heritage Database. 2007. Kentucky State Nature Preserves Commission, Frankfort, Kentucky, USA.

Reptile Species (bar chart), p. 71:

Kentucky Natural Heritage Database. 2007. Kentucky State Nature Preserves Commission, Frankfort, Kentucky, USA.

Distribution of Venomous Snakes (map), p. 72:

NatureServe. 2008. Digital distribution maps of the reptiles of the United States and Canada. NatureServe, Arlington, Virginia, USA.

National Aeronautics and Space Administration. 2004. Visual Earth: world cloud free. ESRI data & maps media kit. Environmental Systems Research Institute, Redlands, California, USA.

Reptile Rarity Hotspots (map), p. 74:

Abernathy, G., D. White, and B. Palmer-Ball. 2007. Kentucky rarity-weighted richness index analysis. Kentucky State Nature Preserves Commission, Frankfort, Kentucky, USA.

Kentucky Natural Heritage Database. 2007. Kentucky State Nature Preserves Commission, Frankfort, Kentucky, USA.

Bird Species (bar chart), p. 74:

Palmer-Ball, B., Jr. 2003. Annotated checklist of the birds of Kentucky. Kentucky Ornithological Society, Louisville, Kentucky, USA.

Palmer-Ball, B., Jr. 2009. Unpublished data.

Nesting Bird Migration Routes (map), p. 76:

National Aeronautics and Space Administration. 2004. Visual Earth: world cloud free. ESRI data & maps media kit. Environmental Systems Research Institute, Redlands, California, USA.

Palmer-Ball, B., and G. Abernathy. 2005. Generalized migration routes and overwintering areas of some of the birds that nest in Kentucky. Kentucky State Nature Preserves Commission, Frankfort, Kentucky, USA.

Nesting Bird Rarity Hotspots (map), p. 77:

Abernathy, G., D. White, and B. Palmer-Ball. 2007. Kentucky rarity-weighted richness index analysis. Kentucky State Nature Preserves Commission, Frankfort, Kentucky, USA.

Kentucky Natural Heritage Database. 2007. Kentucky State Nature Preserves Commission, Frankfort, Kentucky, USA.

Mammal Species (bar chart), p. 78:

Kentucky Natural Heritage Database. 2007. Kentucky State Nature Preserves Commission, Frankfort, Kentucky, USA.

Mammal Rarity Hotspots (map), p. 80:

Abernathy, G., D. White, and B. Palmer-Ball. 2007. Kentucky rarity-weighted richness index analysis. Kentucky State Nature Preserves Commission, Frankfort, Kentucky, USA.

Kentucky Natural Heritage Database. 2007. Kentucky State Nature Preserves Commission, Frankfort, Kentucky, USA.

Extirpated and Extinct Species (bar chart), p. 82:

Kentucky Natural Heritage Database. 2007. Kentucky State Nature Preserves Commission, Frankfort, Kentucky, USA.

Global and State Conservation Ranks of Kentucky's Rare Species (schematic), p. 84:

Abernathy, G., E. Laudermilk, and S. Dunham. 2008. Global (G) and state (S) conservation ranks of Kentucky's rare species [schematic]. Kentucky State Nature Preserves Commission, Frankfort, Kentucky, USA.

Kentucky Natural Heritage Database. 2007. Kentucky State Nature Preserves Commission, Frankfort, Kentucky, USA.

Cross Section of Select Natural Communities (schematic), p. 85:

Abernathy, G., and M. Evans. 2008. Cross section of select natural communities [schematic]. Kentucky State Nature Preserves Commission, Frankfort, Kentucky, USA.

Lotic Aquatic System (schematic), p. 93:

Abernathy, G., and E. Laudermilk. 2008. Lotic communities (streams and large rivers) [schematic]. Kentucky State Nature Preserves Commission, Frankfort, Kentucky, USA.

Lentic Aquatic System (schematic), p. 95:

Abernathy, G., and E. Laudermilk. 2008. Lentic communities (ponds, lakes and wetlands) [schematic]. Kentucky State Nature Preserves Commission, Frankfort, Kentucky, USA.

Sinkhole Plain Karst Features (schematic), p. 97:

Currens J. 2001. Sinkhole plain karst features. Kentucky Geological Survey, Lexington, Kentucky, USA.

Caves and Karst Occurrences (map), p. 98:

Kentucky Geological Survey. 2004. Karst geology 1:500,000. Kentucky Geological Survey, Lexington, Kentucky, USA. Available at www.uky.edu/KGS/gis/geology.htm.

Kentucky State Nature Preserves Commission. 2007. Kentucky Natural Heritage Database. Kentucky State Nature Preserves Commission, Frankfort, Kentucky, USA.

Kentucky Speleological Survey. 2006. Distribution of Caves in Kentucky. Kentucky Speleological Survey, Lexington, Kentucky, USA.

Subterranean Obligate Species (bar chart), p. 99:

Culver, D. C., pers. comm., September 24, 2007.

Subterranean Obligates and Visitors (schematic), p. 100:

Abernathy, G., and E. Laudermilk. 2009. Subterranean obligates and visitors [schematic]. Kentucky State Nature Preserves Commission, Frankfort, Kentucky, USA.

CHAPTER 5

Urbanized Landscape (map), p. 103:

Kentucky Division of Geographic Information. 2004. Kentucky 2001 Anderson level III land cover. Kentucky Division of Geographic Information, Frankfort, Kentucky, USA. Available at http://kygeonet.ky.gov/geographicexplorer/.

Kentucky Transportation Cabinet Division of Planning. 2007. All roads. Kentucky Transportation Cabinet, Frankfort, Kentucky, USA. Available at ftp://ftp.kymartian.ky.gov/trans/statewide/shape/.

Mineral and Fuel Resources (map), p. 108:

Anderson, W. H., and G. R. Dever Jr. 1998. Mineral and fuel resource map of Kentucky. Map and chart series 21, Kentucky Geological Survey, Lexington, Kentucky, USA.

Hemlock Woolly Adelgid Infestations (map), p. 111:

Fei, Songlin. 2009. Kentucky hemlock woolly adelgid monitoring map [map]. Department of Forestry, University of Kentucky, Lexington, Kentucky, USA. Available at www.uky.edu/~sfei2/hwa.htm.

U.S. Department of Agriculture Forest Service. 2008. Hemlock woolly adelgid infestations 2008 [map]. U.S. Department of Agriculture Forest Service, Newtown Square, Pennsylvania, USA. Available at http://na.fs.fed.us/fhp/hwa/maps/distribution.shtm. Note: adapted by KSNPC from U.S. Forest Service map.

U.S. Geological Survey. 1999. Digital representation of "Atlas of United States Trees" by Elbert L. Little Jr. (and other publications). U.S. Geological Survey, Denver, Colorado, USA. Available at http://esp.cr.usgs.gov/data/atlas/little/.

Chestnut Blight Infestations (map), p. 112:

National Geographic Society Cartographic Division. 1990. Original distribution of American chestnut and spread of chestnut blight [map]. National Geographic 177:133. Note: adapted by KSNPC from National Geographic Society map.

U.S. Geological Survey. 1999. Digital representation of "Atlas of United States Trees" by Elbert L. Little Jr. U.S. Geological Survey, Denver, Colorado, USA. Available at http://esp.cr.usgs.gov/data/atlas/little/.

CHAPTER 6

Distribution of Imperiled Species in the United States (map), p. 122:

NatureServe. 2007. Distribution of imperiled species in the United States [map]. NatureServe, Arlington, Virginia, USA.

Conservation Lands (map), p. 124:

Kentucky State Nature Preserves Commission. 2008. Managed areas database. Kentucky State Nature Preserves Commission, Frankfort, Kentucky, USA.

Kentucky State Nature Preserves Commission. 2009. Unpublished data.

Rarity Hotspot Analysis Overview (schematic), p. 131:

Abernathy, G. 2008. Rarity hotspots analysis overview [schematic]. Kentucky State Nature Preserves Commission, Frankfort, Kentucky, USA.

Priority Watersheds for Conservation of Rare Fishes and Mussels (map), p. 132:

Cicerello, R., and G. Abernathy. 2007. Priority watersheds for conservation of rare fishes and mussels. Kentucky State Nature Preserves Commission, Frankfort, Kentucky, USA.

Large Forest Tracts Example (map), p. 133:

Evans, M., and G. Abernathy. 2009. Large forest tracts of Kentucky. Kentucky State Nature Preserves Commission, Frankfort, Kentucky, USA.

Kentucky Transportation Cabinet Division of Planning. 2007. All roads. Kentucky Transportation Cabinet, Frankfort, Kentucky, USA. Available at ftp://ftp.kymartian.ky.gov/trans/statewide/shape/.

Large Forest Tracts (map), p. 135:

Evans, M., and G. Abernathy. 2009. Large forest tracts of Kentucky. Kentucky State Nature Preserves Commission, Frankfort, Kentucky, USA.

Pine Mountain Ecological Corridor (map), p. 137:

Kentucky State Nature Preserves Commission. 2008. Managed areas database. Kentucky State Nature Preserves Commission, Frankfort, Kentucky, USA.

Kentucky Transportation Cabinet Division of Planning. 2007. All Roads. Kentucky Transportation Cabinet. Frankfort, Kentucky, USA. Available at ftp://ftp.kymartian.ky.gov/trans/statewide/shape/.

National Aeronautics and Space Administration. 2004. Visual Earth: world cloud free. ESRI data & maps media kit. Environmental Systems Research Institute, Redlands, California, USA.

Alkaline A chemical state that neutralizes acids and is greater than 7 (neutral) on the pH scale.

Alluvial Composed of sediment deposited by moving water.

Aquatic Having to do with water; especially organisms that complete a major part of their life cycle in or on water.

Aquatic insects Insects that spend all or the majority of their life cycle in water; however, adults of some aquatic insects live in terrestrial environments from as little as a few hours to several weeks.

Arachnid An invertebrate belonging to the class Arachnida, which includes spiders, scorpions, pseudoscorpions, ticks, and mites.

Biodiversity (biological diversity) The variety of life in all of its manifestations and interactions (i.e., genes, species, ecosystems, etc.).

Biogeographic Pertaining to the study of the distribution of living organisms.

Caddisflies Aquatic insects belonging to the order Trichoptera.

Carrion The decaying flesh of an organism, used for food by scavengers.

Caterpillar A larva. The larval stage of some insects with a complete life cycle, especially butterflies and moths (Lepidoptera).

Coleoptera The insect order that includes beetles.

Conservation easement A legal agreement between a landowner and a private, nonprofit conservation organization or government agency that permanently limits uses of the land in order to protect its conservation value.

Crustacean An invertebrate belonging to the phylum Crustacea, which includes crayfishes, shrimp, amphipods, and isopods.

Damselflies Aquatic insects belonging to the order Odonata and suborder Zygoptera.

Deciduous A plant that periodically loses its leaves (the term can also be used for animals that shed parts).

Detritus Organic material resulting from the decomposition of plants and animals.

Diptera The insect order that includes true flies.

Dragonflies Aquatic insects belonging to the order Odonata and suborder Anisoptera.

Ecosystem An ecological unit made up of communities of living organisms and the interrelated chemical and physical features of their environment.

Ectocommensal Referring to an organism that acquires food, shelter, or other aspects of life support from the outer surface of another organism without causing harm to that organism.

Endangered A taxon in danger of extirpation or extinction throughout all or a significant part of its range.

Endemic Species that are restricted to or found only within a specific habitat, locality, political boundary, region, or watershed.

Exotic A non-native species present through intentional or inadvertent introduction.

Extinction The complete disappearance of a species from the earth.

Extirpation The elimination of a species from a specific area.

Fauna Term referring collectively to all animals in an area; e.g., the fauna of Mammoth Cave National Park.

Federally listed Species with a designation of endangered or threatened under the federal Endangered Species Act.

Flora Term referring collectively to all plants in an area; e.g., the flora of Clay County.

Fragmentation Divided into smaller units, such as forest being cleared, resulting in smaller tracts.

Generalist A species capable of using a variety of habitats and resources.

Genus A subdivision of a family; includes at least one or more closely related species. For example, *Quercus* is the genus that includes oak tree species.

Global rank An assigned rank that reflects an assessment of the condition of species and natural communities across their entire range. Typically ranges from 1 (rare and vulnerable to extinction) to 5 (common and secure). The letter X is appended to the rank to indicate extinction, and H is appended to indicate historical records (when a species has not been observed anywhere in the prior 20 years).

Habitat The natural home of an organism.

Herbaceous A plant whose stem lasts one growing season or does not put out new growth from year to year.

Hermaphroditic A condition in which one individual has both male and female sex organs.

Hydrology The scientific study of the properties, distribution, use, and circulation of water on and below the earth's surface and in the atmosphere, in all of its forms.

Hymenoptera The insect order that includes ants, bees, and wasps.

Invasive A species that has no natural enemies to check its reproduction and spread, and has demonstrated an aggressive increase and spread in natural areas.

Invertebrate An animal without a backbone or spinal column, such as crayfishes, insects, and mussels.

Karst Areas of limestone geology sculpted by the dissolution and erosion of rock by water, leading to the formation of springs, sinkholes, and caves.

KSNPC-listed Species designated by the Kentucky State Nature Preserves Commission as endangered, threatened, special concern, or historic.

Larva The wormlike and wingless life stage of an animal after the egg hatches but before the pupal stage (for insects with complete metamorphosis) or adult stage (for insects with incomplete metamorphosis).

Leafhopper An insect belonging to the order Homoptera.

Lentic Aquatic systems with standing water, such as ponds, lakes, and wetlands.

Lepidoptera The insect order that includes skippers, butterflies, and moths.

Littoral zone The shallow, near-shore margin of a body of water, often defined as extending from zero depth to the outer edge of rooted plants. This region supports the greatest number of species in lentic habitats.

Lotic Aquatic systems with running water, such as creeks and rivers.

Macroinvertebrates Invertebrates that inhabit the bottom substrates (rocks, logs, debris, etc.) of freshwater habitats for at least part of their life cycle.

Mayflies Aquatic insects belonging to the order Ephemeroptera.

Mesic Rich and moist.

Metamorphosis The transformation an animal undergoes from egg to adult, especially from pupa to adult.

Milliped An invertebrate that has two pairs of appendages per body segment and belongs to the arthropod class Diplopoda.

Mollusk An invertebrate belonging to the phylum Mollusca, such as mussels and snails.

Molt the process or time during which an animal sheds all or part of its feathers, hair, or skin.

Native A species that is naturally occurring in an area, either currently or historically, without direct or indirect human influence.

Natural regions Areas that share a general similarity in geology, topography, hydrology, soils, climate, and vegetation.

Nematode Also known as roundworms, nematodes are colorless, unsegmented animals that may be free-living, predatory, or parasitic.

Neotropical migrants Birds that spend winters in the tropical regions of the Caribbean, Central America, South America, and Mexico, but return to the United States and Canada to breed in the spring and summer.

Niche An organism's place, position, or specific role in the ecosystem in reference to other members of the ecosystem.

Nocturnal Pertaining to the night, as in organisms that are active primarily at night.

Obligate cave-dwelling species A troglobite or stygobite; an organism ecologically restricted to caves or groundwater.

Odonata The insect order that includes dragonflies and damselflies.

Operculate Animals possessing an operculum.

Operculum In snails, a corneous covering of the shell opening. In fishes, a series of bones that act as a flap that covers the gills.

Order Taxonomic grouping that includes related families of organisms.

Physiographic provinces Usually large areas that share similar geologic history and formation.

Plecoptera The insect order that includes stoneflies.

Proboscis Elongated and usually tubular structure extended from the head or body of various invertebrates. Used by adult butterflies and moths to drink nectar from flowers, for example.

Profundal zone Also known as the dark zone; the bottom of a lentic habitat, composed of the finest sediments and typically supporting low oxygen levels. Species that live here can tolerate harsh conditions such as cold water, no light, and low oxygen levels.

Protozoa Single-celled, animal-like organisms belonging to the kingdom Protista; they consume other cells or food particles.

Pulmonate Refers to organisms that respire using atmospheric oxygen rather than gills.

Pupa Life stage between larva and adult in insects with a complete life cycle.

Pupation The act of transforming from a larva into a pupa.

Radula A rasping mouthpart, composed of chitin, used by snails to scrape food from a surface.

Refugium A place that provides protection.

Riparian A type of wetland habitat along the shore of a stream or lake.

Rockhouse A depression formed in a hillside or cliff by the dissolution of weaker rock, usually with an overhanging roof.

Seep A feature occurring where groundwater issues to the land surface.

Semiaquatic Refers to organisms that are primarily terrestrial but that complete some part of their life cycle in or on water.

Sinkhole A depression on the land's surface that leads to a hollow into which surface water enters before joining underground flows. Sinkholes are formed by the dissolution of underlying materials, especially limestone rock.

Slough A depression or old stream channel that usually holds water all or most of the year.

Special concern A status category designating a taxon as in need of monitoring. A taxon is designated as special concern when the following conditions are met: (1) it exists in a limited geographic area in Kentucky; (2) it may become threatened or endangered due to modification or destruction of its habitat; (3) certain characteristics or requirements make it especially vulnerable to specific pressures; (4) experienced researchers have identified other factors that may jeopardize it; or (5) it is thought to be rare or declining in Kentucky, but insufficient information exists for assignment to the threatened or endangered status categories.

Species A group of actually or potentially interbreeding individuals that is reproductively isolated from all other kinds of organisms.

Species richness The number of species in a defined area.

Springtail A primitive, wingless insect belonging to the order Collembola.

State rank An assigned rank that reflects an assessment of the condition of species and natural communities in a state. Typically ranges from 1 (rare and vulnerable to extirpation) to 5 (common and secure). The letter X is appended to the rank to indicate extinction, and H is appended to indicate historical records (when a species has not been observed anywhere in the prior 20 years).

Stoneflies Aquatic insects belonging to the order Plecoptera.

Stygobite An aquatic species ecologically restricted and adapted to live in groundwater or cave streams.

Sublittoral zone The zone extending lakeward from the littoral zone to the profundal zone; it is dimly lit and well-oxygenated, and it lacks bottom-dwelling plants. The sublittoral zone supports fewer species than the littoral.

Subspecies Groups of individuals of the same species that differ slightly from other groups, usually a geographic race, but are still capable of interbreeding.

Subterranean Underground or beneath the earth's surface. Also refers to species that are ecologically adapted to live only in caves and their associated streams and groundwater.

Taxon *pl.* taxa. A taxonomic group of any rank or size (e.g., genus, species, subspecies, varieties).

Terrestrial Adapted to living on land.

Threatened A taxon likely to become endangered within the foreseeable future throughout all or a significant part of its range.

Topography Features on the surface of the land.

Trichoptera The insect order that includes caddisflies.

Troglobite A terrestrial species ecologically restricted and adapted to live in subterranean habitats such as caves. They exhibit degenerative characteristics such as loss of eyes, pigment, ability to fly, and ability to control water loss.

True bugs Insects belonging to the order Hemiptera.

True flies Insects belonging to the order Diptera.

Urban sprawl Low density and piecemeal development around existing urban areas and transportation corridors.

Vascular plants Plants with a complex internal system for transporting food and water.

Vernal pool Pool of water typically present only during wet weather, especially in the spring.

Watershed An area of land in which water drains to a common point; sometimes called a drainage or basin.

Wetlands A natural system submerged or inundated for at least part of the year, in a way that influences the organisms that live there.

Xeric Extremely dry and droughty.

APPENDICES

Endemic Species of Kentucky (includes subspecies and varieties)

COMMON NAME	SCIENTIFIC NAME
SEED PLANTS	
Kentucky gladecress	*Leavenworthia exigua* var. *laciniata*
White-haired goldenrod	*Solidago albopilosa*
ANIMALS	
MOLLUSKS	
A freshwater snail	*Somatogyrus trothis*
Kentucky creekshell	*Villosa ortmanni*
Pine Mountain tigersnail	*Anguispira rugoderma*
WORMS	
A cave obligate worm	*Cambarincola steevesi*
ARACHNIDS	
A cave obligate harvestman	*Hesperonemastoma inops*
A cave obligate mite	*Belba bulbipedata*
A cave obligate mite	*Galumna alata*
A cave obligate mite	*Macrocheles stygius*
A cave obligate mite	*Macrocheles troglodytes*
A cave obligate pseudoscorpion	*Kleptochthonius attenuatus*
A cave obligate pseudoscorpion	*Kleptochthonius cerberus*
A cave obligate pseudoscorpion	*Kleptochthonius erebicus*
A cave obligate pseudoscorpion	*Kleptochthonius hageni*
A cave obligate pseudoscorpion	*Kleptochthonius hubrichti*
A cave obligate pseudoscorpion	*Kleptochthonius krekeleri*
A cave obligate pseudoscorpion	*Kleptochthonius microphthalmus*
A cave obligate pseudoscorpion	*Tyrannochthonius hypogeus*

COMMON NAME	SCIENTIFIC NAME
CRUSTACEANS	
A cave obligate shrimp	*Dactylocythere prionata*
A copepod	*Bryocamptus morrisoni elegans*
An amphipod	*Crangonyx castellanum*
An amphipod	*Crangonyx specus*
An ectocommensal ostracod	*Sagittocythere stygia*
Bluegrass crayfish	*Cambarus batchi*
Clifton Cave isopod	*Caecidotea barri*
Crittenden crayfish	*Orconectes bisectus*
Livingston crayfish	*Orconectes margorectus*
Louisville crayfish	*Orconectes jeffersoni*
Mammoth Cave shrimp	*Palaemonias ganteri*
Rough River crayfish	*Orconectes rafinesquei*
Western highland crayfish	*Orconectes tricuspis*
MILLIPEDS	
A cave obligate milliped	*Pseudotremia amphiorax*
A cave obligate milliped	*Pseudotremia carterensis*
A cave obligate milliped	*Pseudotremia merops*
A cave obligate milliped	*Pseudotremia spira*
A cave obligate milliped	*Pseudotremia unca*

COMMON NAME	SCIENTIFIC NAME
INSECTS	
A cave obligate beetle	*Ameroduvalius jeanneli jeanneli*
A cave obligate beetle	*Ameroduvalius jeanneli rockcastlei*
A cave obligate beetle	*Batrisodes henroti*
A cave obligate beetle	*Batrisodes hubrichti*
A cave obligate beetle	*Darlingtonea kentuckensis lexingtoni*
A cave obligate beetle	*Neaphaenops tellkampfi henroti*
A cave obligate beetle	*Neaphaenops tellkampfi meridionalis*
A cave obligate beetle	*Neaphaenops tellkampfi tellkampfi*
A cave obligate beetle	*Neaphaenops tellkampfi viator*
A cave obligate beetle	*Nelsonites jonesi jonesi*
A cave obligate beetle	*Pseudanophthalmus barberi*
A cave obligate beetle	*Pseudanophthalmus cerberus cerberus*
A cave obligate beetle	*Pseudanophthalmus cerberus completus*
A cave obligate beetle	*Pseudanophthalmus cnephosus*
A cave obligate beetle	*Pseudanophthalmus darlingtoni darlingtoni*
A cave obligate beetle	*Pseudanophthalmus darlingtoni persimilis*
A cave obligate beetle	*Pseudanophthalmus desertus*
A cave obligate beetle	*Pseudanophthalmus elongatus*
A cave obligate beetle	*Pseudanophthalmus exiguus*
A cave obligate beetle	*Pseudanophthalmus menetriesii campestris*
A cave obligate beetle	*Pseudanophthalmus menetriesii menetriesii*
A cave obligate beetle	*Pseudanophthalmus orientalis*
A cave obligate beetle	*Pseudanophthalmus packardi*
A cave obligate beetle	*Pseudanophthalmus pilosus*
A cave obligate beetle	*Pseudanophthalmus pubescens intrepidus*
A cave obligate beetle	*Pseudanophthalmus pubescens pubescens*
A cave obligate beetle	*Pseudanophthalmus rittmani*
A cave obligate beetle	*Pseudanophthalmus solivagus*
A cave obligate beetle	*Pseudanophthalmus striatus*
A cave obligate beetle	*Pseudanophthalmus transfluvialis*
A cave obligate beetle	*Pseudanophthalmus umbratilis*
A cave obligate beetle	*Ptomaphagus hirtus*
A cave obligate beetle	*Tychobythinus hubrichti*

COMMON NAME	SCIENTIFIC NAME
A cave obligate springtail	*Arrhopalites altus*
A cave obligate springtail	*Pseudosinella espanita*
A hydroptilid caddisfly	*Hydroptila howelli*
A hydroptilid caddisfly	*Hydroptila kuehnei*
A perlid stonefly	*Acroneuria hitchcocki*
Ashcamp Cave beetle	*Pseudanophthalmus hypolithos*
Beaver Cave beetle	*Pseudanophthalmus major*
Bold cave beetle	*Pseudanophthalmus audax*
Clifton Cave beetle	*Pseudanophthalmus caecus*
Concealed cave beetle	*Pseudanophthalmus abditus*
Cub Run Cave beetle	*Pseudanophthalmus simulans*
Exotic cave beetle	*Pseudanophthalmus exoticus*
Garman's cave beetle	*Pseudanophthalmus horni*
Greater Adams Cave beetle	*Pseudanophthalmus pholeter*
Hidden cave beetle	*Pseudanophthalmus conditus*
Icebox Cave beetle	*Pseudanophthalmus frigidus*
Lesser Adams Cave beetle	*Pseudanophthalmus catoryctos*
Limestone Cave beetle	*Pseudanophthalmus calcareus*
Louisville cave Beetle	*Pseudanophthalmus troglodytes*
Old Well Cave beetle	*Pseudanophthalmus puteanus*
Rogers' cave beetle	*Pseudanophthalmus rogersae*
Round-headed cave beetle	*Pseudanophthalmus globiceps*
Scholarly cave beetle	*Pseudanophthalmus scholasticus*
Stevens Creek cave beetle	*Pseudanophthalmus tenebrosus*
Surprising cave beetle	*Pseudanophthalmus inexpectatus*
Tatum Cave beetle	*Pseudanophthalmus parvus*
FRESHWATER FISHES	
Arrow darter	*Etheostoma sagitta spilotum*
Kentucky darter	*Etheostoma rafinesquei*
Relict darter	*Etheostoma chienense*
Shawnee darter	*Etheostoma tecumsehi*
Sheltowee darter	*Etheostoma sp.*
Striped darter	*Etheostoma virgatum*

SOURCE: Kentucky State Nature Preserves Commission. 2007. Natural Heritage Database. Kentucky State Nature Preserves Commission, Frankfort, Kentucky, USA.

APPENDIX TWO

Rare Biota of Kentucky

SCIENTIFIC NAME	COMMON NAME	STATUS Federal[a]	KSNPC[b]
LICHENS			
Phaeophyscia leana	Lea's bog lichen	—	E
MOSSES			
Abietinella abietina	Wire fern moss	—	T
Anomodon rugelii		—	T
Brachythecium populeum	Matted feather moss	—	E
Bryum cyclophyllum		—	E
Bryum miniatum		—	E
Cirriphyllum piliferum		—	T
Dicranodontium asperulum		—	E
Entodon brevisetus		—	E
Herzogiella turfacea		—	E
Neckera pennata		—	T
Oncophorus raui		—	E
Orthotrichum diaphanum		—	E
Polytrichum pallidisetum	A hair cap moss	—	T
Polytrichum strictum		—	E
Sphagnum quinquefarium	A sphagnum moss	—	E
Tortula norvegica	Tortula	—	E

SCIENTIFIC NAME	COMMON NAME	STATUS Federal[a]	KSNPC[b]
SEED PLANTS AND FERNS			
Acer spicatum	Mountain maple	—	E
Aconitum uncinatum	Blue monkshood	—	T
Adiantum capillus-veneris	Southern maidenhair fern	—	T
Adlumia fungosa	Allegheny vine	—	E
Aesculus pavia	Red buckeye	—	T
Agalinis auriculata	Earleaf false foxglove	—	E
Agalinis obtusifolia	Ten-lobe false foxglove	—	E
Agalinis skinneriana	Pale false foxglove	—	H
Agastache scrophulariifolia	Purple giant hyssop	—	H
Ageratina luciae-brauniae	Lucy Braun's white snakeroot	—	S
Agrimonia gryposepala	Tall hairy groovebur	—	T
Amianthium muscitoxicum	Fly poison	—	T
Amsonia tabernaemontana var. *gattingeri*	Eastern bluestar	—	E
Angelica atropurpurea	Great angelica	—	E
Angelica triquinata	Filmy angelica	—	E
Apios priceana	Price's potato-bean	T	E
Arabis hirsuta	Western hairy rockcress	—	T
Arabis missouriensis	Missouri rockcress	—	H
Arabis perstellata	Braun's rockcress	E	T
Aralia nudicaulis	Wild sarsaparilla	—	E
Aristida ramosissima	Branched three-awn grass	—	H
Armoracia lacustris	Lakecress	—	T
Aureolaria patula	Spreading false foxglove	—	S
Baptisia australis var. *minor*	Blue wild indigo	—	S
Baptisia bracteata var. *glabrescens*	Cream wild indigo	—	S
Baptisia tinctoria	Yellow wild indigo	—	T
Bartonia virginica	Yellow screwstem	—	T
Berberis canadensis	American barberry	—	E
Berchemia scandens	Supple-jack	—	T
Bolboschoenus fluviatilis	River bulrush	—	E
Botrychium matricariifolium	Matricary grape-fern	—	E

SCIENTIFIC NAME	COMMON NAME	Federal[a]	KSNPC[b]
SEED PLANTS AND FERNS continued			
Botrychium oneidense	Blunt-lobe grape fern	—	H
Bouteloua curtipendula	Side-oats grama	—	S
Boykinia aconitifolia	Brook saxifrage	—	T
Cabomba caroliniana	Carolina fanwort	—	T
Calamagrostis canadensis var. *macouniana*	Blue-joint reedgrass	—	H
Calamagrostis porteri spp. *insperata*	Bent reedgrass	—	E
Calamagrostis porteri spp. *porteri*	Porter's reedgrass	—	T
Calamovilfa arcuata	Cumberland sandgrass	—	E
Callirhoe alcaeoides	Clustered poppy-mallow	—	H
Calopogon tuberosus	Grass pink	—	E
Calycanthus floridus var. *glaucus*	Eastern sweetshrub	—	T
Calylophus serrulatus	Yellow evening primrose	—	H
Carex aestivalis	Summer sedge	—	E
Carex alata	Broadwing sedge	—	T
Carex appalachica	Appalachian sedge	—	T
Carex atlantica spp. *capillacea*	Prickly bog sedge	—	E
Carex austrocaroliniana	Tarheel sedge	—	S
Carex buxbaumii	Brown bog sedge	—	H
Carex comosa	Bristly sedge	—	H
Carex crawei	Crawe's sedge	—	S
Carex crebriflora	Coastal plain sedge	—	T
Carex decomposita	Epiphytic sedge	—	T
Carex gigantea	Large sedge	—	T
Carex hystericina	Porcupine sedge	—	H
Carex joorii	Cypress-swamp sedge	—	E
Carex juniperorum	Cedar sedge	—	E
Carex leptonervia	Finely nerved sedge	—	E
Carex pellita	Woolly sedge	—	H
Carex reniformis	Reniform sedge	—	E
Carex roanensis	Roan Mountain sedge	—	E
Carex seorsa	Weak stellate sedge	—	S
Carex stipata var. *maxima*	Stalkgrain sedge	—	H
Carex straminea	Straw sedge	—	T
Carex tetanica	Rigid sedge	—	E
Carex tonsa var. *rugosperma*	Umbel-like sedge	—	T
Carya aquatica	Water hickory	—	T
Carya carolinae-septentrionalis	Southern shagbark hickory	—	T
Castanea dentata	American chestnut	—	E
Castanea pumila	Allegheny chinkapin	—	T
Castilleja coccinea	Scarlet Indian paintbrush	—	E
Ceanothus herbaceus	Prairie redroot	—	T
Cheilanthes alabamensis	Alabama lipfern	—	H
Cheilanthes feei	Fee's lipfern	—	E
Chelone obliqua var. *obliqua*	Red turtlehead	—	E
Chelone obliqua var. *speciosa*	Rose turtlehead	—	S
Chrysogonum virginianum	Green-and-gold	—	E
Chrysosplenium americanum	American golden saxifrage	—	T
Cimicifuga rubifolia	Appalachian bugbane	—	T
Circaea alpina	Small enchanter's nightshade	—	S
Clematis catesbyana	Satincurls	—	H
Clematis crispa	Blue jasmine leather-flower	—	T
Coeloglossum viride var. *virescens*	Long-bract green orchis	—	H
Collinsonia verticillata	Whorled horse-balm	—	E
Comptonia peregrina	Sweetfern	—	E
Conradina verticillata	Cumberland rosemary	T	E
Convallaria montana	American lily-of-the-valley	—	E
Corallorhiza maculata	Spotted coralroot	—	E
Coreopsis pubescens	Star tickseed	—	S
Corydalis sempervirens	Rock harlequin	—	E
Cymophyllus fraserianus	Fraser's sedge	—	E
Cyperus plukenetii	Plukenet's cyperus	—	H
Cypripedium candidum	Small white lady's-slipper	—	E
Cypripedium kentuckiense	Kentucky lady's-slipper	—	E
Cypripedium parviflorum	Small yellow lady's-slipper	—	T
Cypripedium reginae	Showy lady's slipper	—	H
Dalea purpurea	Purple prairie-clover	—	S
Delphinium carolinianum	Carolina larkspur	—	T
Deschampsia cespitosa	Tufted hairgrass	—	E
Deschampsia flexuosa	Crinkled hairgrass	—	T
Dichanthelium boreale	Northern witchgrass	—	S
Didiplis diandra	Water purslane	—	S
Dodecatheon frenchii	French's shooting star	—	S
Draba cuneifolia	Wedge-leaf whitlow grass	—	E
Drosera brevifolia	Dwarf sundew	—	E
Drosera intermedia	Spoon-leaved sundew	—	E
Dryopteris carthusiana	Spinulose wood fern	—	S
Dryopteris ludoviciana	Southern shield wood fern	—	H

SCIENTIFIC NAME	COMMON NAME	STATUS Federal[a]	KSNPC[b]
SEED PLANTS AND FERNS *continued*			
Echinodorus berteroi	Burhead	—	T
Echinodorus parvulus	Dwarf burhead	—	E
Eleocharis flavescens	Bright green spikerush	—	S
Elodea nuttallii	Western waterweed	—	T
Elymus svensonii	Svenson's wildrye	—	S
Eriophorum virginicum	Tawny cotton-grass	—	E
Eryngium integrifolium	Blue-flower coyote-thistle	—	E
Erythronium rostratum	Yellow troutlily	—	S
Eupatorium maculatum	Spotted joe-pye-weed	—	H
Eupatorium semiserratum	Small-flower thoroughwort	—	E
Eupatorium steelei	Steele's joe-pye-weed	—	T
Euphorbia mercurialina	Mercury spurge	—	T
Eurybia hemispherica	Tennessee aster	—	E
Eurybia radula	Rough-leaved aster	—	E
Eurybia saxicastellii	Rockcastle aster	—	T
Fimbristylis puberula	Hairy fimbristylis	—	T
Forestiera ligustrina	Upland privet	—	T
Gentiana decora	Showy gentian	—	S
Gentiana flavida	Yellow gentian	—	E
Gentiana puberulenta	Prairie gentian	—	E
Gleditsia aquatica	Water locust	—	S
Glyceria acutiflora	Sharp-scaled manna grass	—	E
Goodyera repens	Lesser rattlesnake plantain	—	E
Gratiola pilosa	Shaggy hedgehyssop	—	T
Gratiola viscidula	Short's hedgehyssop	—	S
Gymnopogon ambiguus	Bearded skeleton grass	—	S
Gymnopogon brevifolius	Shortleaf skeleton grass	—	E
Halesia tetraptera	Common silverbell	—	E
Hedeoma hispidum	Rough pennyroyal	—	T
Helianthemum bicknellii	Plains frostweed	—	E
Helianthemum canadense	Canada frostweed	—	E
Helianthus eggertii	Eggert's sunflower	—	T
Helianthus silphioides	Silphium sunflower	—	E
Heracleum lanatum	Cow parsnip	—	H
Heteranthera dubia	Grassleaf mud plantain	—	S
Heteranthera limosa	Blue mud plantain	—	S
Heterotheca subaxillaris var. *latifolia*	Broadleaf golden aster	—	T
Hexastylis contracta	Southern heartleaf	—	E

SCIENTIFIC NAME	COMMON NAME	STATUS Federal[a]	KSNPC[b]
Hieracium longipilum	Hairy hawkweed	—	T
Houstonia serpyllifolia	Michaux's bluets	—	E
Hydrocotyle americana	American water pennywort	—	E
Hydrocotyle ranunculoides	Floating pennywort	—	E
Hydrolea ovata	Ovate fiddleleaf	—	E
Hydrolea uniflora	One-flower fiddleleaf	—	E
Hydrophyllum virginianum	Eastern waterleaf	—	T
Hypericum adpressum	Creeping St. John's wort	—	H
Hypericum crux-andreae	St. Peter's wort	—	T
Hypericum pseudomaculatum	Large spotted St. John's wort	—	H
Iris fulva	Copper iris	—	E
Isoetes butleri	Butler's quillwort	—	E
Isoetes melanopoda	Blackfoot quillwort	—	E
Juglans cinerea	White walnut	—	S
Juncus articulatus	Jointed rush	—	S
Juncus elliottii	Bog rush	—	H
Juncus filipendulus	Ringseed rush	—	T
Juniperus communis var. *depressa*	Ground juniper	—	T
Koeleria macrantha	Prairie junegrass	—	E
Krigia occidentalis	Western dwarf dandelion	—	E
Lathyrus palustris	Vetchling peavine	—	T
Lathyrus venosus	Smooth veiny peavine	—	S
Leavenworthia exigua var. *laciniata*	Kentucky gladecress	—	E
Leavenworthia torulosa	Necklace gladecress	—	T
Lespedeza capitata	Round-head bush clover	—	S
Lespedeza stuevei	Tall bush clover	—	S
Lesquerella globosa	Globe bladderpod	C	E
Lesquerella lescurii	Lescur's bladderpod	—	H
Leucothoe recurva	Red-twig doghobble	—	E
Liatris cylindracea	Slender blazingstar	—	T
Lilium philadelphicum	Wood lily	—	T
Lilium superbum	Turk's-cap lily	—	T
Limnobium spongia	American frog's-bit	—	T
Liparis loeselii	Loesel's twayblade	—	T
Listera australis	Southern twayblade	—	H
Listera smallii	Kidney-leaf twayblade	—	T
Lobelia gattingeri	Gattinger's lobelia	—	E
Lobelia nuttallii	Nuttall's lobelia	—	T
Lonicera dioica var. *orientalis*	Wild honeysuckle	—	E

SCIENTIFIC NAME	COMMON NAME	Federal[a]	KSNPC[b]
SEED PLANTS AND FERNS continued			
Lonicera prolifera	Grape honeysuckle	—	E
Ludwigia hirtella	Hairy ludwigia	—	E
Lycopodiella appressa	Southern bog clubmoss	—	E
Lycopodium clavatum	Running pine	—	E
Lycopodium inundatum	Northern bog clubmoss	—	E
Lysimachia radicans	Trailing loosestrife	—	H
Lysimachia terrestris	Swamp candles	—	E
Magnolia pyramidata	Pyramid magnolia	—	H
Maianthemum canadense	Wild lily-of-the-valley	—	T
Maianthemum stellatum	Starflower false solomon's seal	—	E
Malvastrum hispidum	Hispid falsemallow	—	T
Marshallia grandiflora	Barbara's buttons	—	E
Matelea carolinensis	Carolina anglepod	—	E
Melampyrum lineare var. *latifolium*	American cow-wheat	—	T
Melampyrum lineare var. *pectinatum*	American cow-wheat	—	E
Melanthera nivea	Snow squarestem	—	S
Melanthium virginicum	Virginia bunchflower	—	E
Minuartia cumberlandensis	Cumberland sandwort	E	E
Minuartia glabra	Appalachian sandwort	—	T
Mirabilis albida	Pale umbrella wort	—	H
Monarda punctata	Spotted bee-balm	—	H
Monotropsis odorata	Sweet pinesap	—	T
Muhlenbergia bushii	Bush's muhly	—	E
Muhlenbergia cuspidata	Plains muhly	—	T
Muhlenbergia glabrifloris	Hair grass	—	S
Myriophyllum heterophyllum	Broadleaf water-milfoil	—	S
Myriophyllum pinnatum	Cutleaf water-milfoil	—	H
Najas gracillima	Thread-like naiad	—	S
Nemophila aphylla	Small-flower baby-blue-eyes	—	T
Nestronia umbellula	Conjurer's nut	—	E
Oclemena acuminata	Whorled aster	—	T
Oenothera linifolia	Thread-leaf sundrops	—	E
Oenothera oakesiana	Evening primrose	—	H
Oenothera perennis	Small sundrops	—	E
Oenothera triloba	Stemless evening primrose	—	T
Oldenlandia uniflora	Clustered bluets	—	E
Onosmodium hispidissimum	Hairy false gromwell	—	E
Onosmodium molle	Soft-hairy false gromwell	—	H
Onosmodium occidentale	Western false gromwell	—	E
Orobanche ludoviciana	Louisiana broomrape	—	H
Orontium aquaticum	Golden club	—	T
Oxalis macrantha	Price's yellow wood sorrel	—	H
Parnassia asarifolia	Kidneyleaf grass-of-parnassus	—	E
Parnassia grandifolia	Large-leaved grass-of-parnassus	—	E
Paronychia argyrocoma	Silverling	—	E
Paspalum boscianum	Bull paspalum	—	S
Paxistima canbyi	Canby's mountain-lover	—	T
Pedicularis lanceolata	Swamp lousewort	—	H
Perideridia americana	Eastern yampah	—	T
Phacelia ranunculacea	Blue scorpion-weed	—	S
Philadelphus inodorus	Mock orange	—	T
Philadelphus pubescens	Hoary mock orange	—	E
Phlox bifida spp. *bifida*	Cleft phlox	—	T
Phlox bifida spp. *stellaria*	Starry-cleft phlox	—	E
Plantago cordata	Heart-leaved plantain	—	H
Platanthera cristata	Yellow-crested orchid	—	T
Platanthera integrilabia	White fringeless orchid	C	E
Platanthera psycodes	Small purple-fringed orchid	—	E
Poa saltuensis	Drooping bluegrass	—	E
Podostemum ceratophyllum	Threadfoot	—	S
Pogonia ophioglossoides	Rose pogonia	—	E
Polygala cruciata	Crossleaf milkwort	—	E
Polygala nuttallii	Nuttall's milkwort	—	H
Polygala paucifolia	Gaywings	—	E
Polygala polygama	Racemed milkwort	—	T
Polymnia laevigata	Tennessee leafcup	—	E
Pontederia cordata	Pickerel weed	—	T
Potamogeton amplifolius	Large-leaf pondweed	—	E
Potamogeton illinoensis	Illinois pondweed	—	S
Potamogeton pulcher	Spotted pondweed	—	T
Prenanthes alba	White rattlesnake root	—	E
Prenanthes aspera	Rough rattlesnake root	—	E
Prenanthes barbata	Barbed rattlesnake root	—	E
Prenanthes crepidinea	Nodding rattlesnake root	—	S
Prosartes maculata	Nodding mandarin	—	S
Pseudognaphalium helleri spp. *micradenium*	Small rabbit-tobacco	—	H

SCIENTIFIC NAME	COMMON NAME	Federal[a]	KSNPC[b]
SEED PLANTS AND FERNS *continued*			
Psoralidium tenuiflorum	Few-flowered scurf-pea	—	H
Ptilimnium capillaceum	Mock bishop's-weed	—	T
Ptilimnium costatum	Eastern mock bishop's-weed	—	H
Ptilimnium nuttallii	Nuttall's mock bishop's-weed	—	E
Pycnanthemum albescens	Whiteleaf mountainmint	—	E
Pycnanthemum muticum	Blunt mountainmint	—	H
Pyrola americana	American wintergreen	—	H
Quercus nigra	Water oak	—	T
Quercus texana	Nuttall's oak	—	T
Ranunculus ambigens	Waterplantain spearwort	—	S
Rhododendron canescens	Hoary azalea	—	E
Rhynchosia tomentosa	Hairy snoutbean	—	E
Rhynchospora macrostachya	Tall beaked-rush	—	E
Rhynchospora recognita	Globe beaked-rush	—	S
Rubus canadensis	Smooth blackberry	—	E
Rudbeckia subtomentosa	Sweet coneflower	—	E
Sabatia campanulata	Slender marsh pink	—	E
Sagina fontinalis	Water stitchwort	—	T
Sagittaria graminea	Grassleaf arrowhead	—	T
Sagittaria platyphylla	Delta arrowhead	—	T
Sagittaria rigida	Sessile-fruited arrowhead	—	E
Salix amygdaloides	Peach-leaved willow	—	H
Salix discolor	Pussy willow	—	H
Salvia urticifolia	Nettle-leaf sage	—	E
Sambucus racemosa spp. *pubens*	Red elderberry	—	E
Sanguisorba canadensis	Canada burnet	—	E
Saxifraga michauxii	Michaux's saxifrage	—	T
Saxifraga micranthidifolia	Lettuce-leaf saxifrage	—	E
Saxifraga pensylvanica	Swamp saxifrage	—	H
Schisandra glabra	Bay starvine	—	E
Schizachne purpurascens	Purple oat	—	T
Schoenoplectus hallii	Hall's bulrush	—	E
Schoenoplectus heterochaetus	Slender bulrush	—	H
Schwalbea americana	Chaffseed	E	H
Scirpus expansus	Woodland beakrush	—	E
Scirpus microcarpus	Small-fruit bulrush	—	H
Scleria ciliata	Fringed nutrush	—	E
Scutellaria arguta	Hairy skullcap	—	E
Scutellaria saxatilis	Rock skullcap	—	T
Sedum telephioides	Allegheny stonecrop	—	T

SCIENTIFIC NAME	COMMON NAME	Federal[a]	KSNPC[b]
Sida hermaphrodita	Virginia mallow	—	S
Silene ovata	Ovate catchfly	—	E
Silene regia	Royal catchfly	—	E
Silphium laciniatum	Compassplant	—	T
Silphium pinnatifidum	Tansy rosinweed	—	S
Silphium wasiotense	Appalachian rosinweed	—	S
Solidago albopilosa	White-haired goldenrod	T	T
Solidago buckleyi	Buckley's goldenrod	—	S
Solidago curtisii	Curtis' goldenrod	—	T
Solidago gracillima	Southern bog goldenrod	—	S
Solidago puberula	Downy goldenrod	—	S
Solidago roanensis	Roan Mountain goldenrod	—	T
Solidago shortii	Short's goldenrod	E	E
Solidago simplex spp. *randii* var. *racemosa*	Rand's goldenrod	—	S
Solidago squarrosa	Squarrose goldenrod	—	H
Sparganium eurycarpum	Large bur-reed	—	E
Sphenopholis pensylvanica	Swamp wedgescale	—	S
Spiraea alba	Narrow-leaved meadow-sweet	—	E
Spiraea virginiana	Virginia spiraea	T	T
Spiranthes lucida	Shining ladies'-tresses	—	T
Spiranthes magnicamporum	Great plains ladies'-tresses	—	T
Spiranthes ochroleuca	Yellow nodding ladies'-tresses	—	T
Spiranthes odorata	Sweetscent ladies'-tresses	—	E
Sporobolus clandestinus	Rough dropseed	—	T
Sporobolus heterolepis	Northern dropseed	—	E
Stachys eplingii	Epling's hedgenettle	—	H
Stellaria longifolia	Longleaf stitchwort	—	S
Stenanthium gramineum	Eastern featherbells	—	T
Streptopus lanceolatus	Rosy twisted-stalk	—	H
Symphoricarpos albus	Snowberry	—	E
Symphyotrichum concolor	Eastern silvery aster	—	T
Symphyotrichum drummondii var. *texanum*	Hairy heart-leaved aster	—	H
Symphyotrichum pratense	Barrens silky aster	—	S
Symphyotrichum priceae	White heath aster	—	T
Talinum calcaricum	Limestone fameflower	—	E
Talinum teretifolium	Roundleaf fameflower	—	E
Taxus canadensis	Canadian yew	—	T
Tephrosia spicata	Spiked hoary-pea	—	E
Thaspium pinnatifidum	Cutleaf meadow-parsnip	—	T

		STATUS	
SCIENTIFIC NAME	COMMON NAME	Federal[a]	KSNPC[b]
SEED PLANTS AND FERNS continued			
Thermopsis mollis	Soft-haired thermopsis	—	E
Thuja occidentalis	Northern white cedar	—	T
Torreyochloa pallida	Pale manna grass	—	H
Toxicodendron vernix	Poison sumac	—	E
Tragia urticifolia	Nettle-leaf noseburn	—	E
Trepocarpus aethusae	Trepocarpus	—	S
Trichophorum planifolium	Bashful bulrush	—	E
Trichostema setaceum	Narrowleaved bluecurls	—	E
Trientalis borealis	Northern starflower	—	E
Trifolium reflexum	Buffalo clover	—	E
Trifolium stoloniferum	Running buffalo clover	E	T
Trillium nivale	Snow trillium	—	E
Trillium pusillum	Least trillium	—	E
Trillium undulatum	Painted trillium	—	T
Triplasis purpurea	Purple sandgrass	—	H
Ulmus serotina	September elm	—	S
Utricularia macrorhiza	Greater bladderwort	—	E
Vaccinium erythrocarpum	Southern mountain cranberry	—	E
Vallisneria americana	Eelgrass	—	S
Veratrum parviflorum	Appalachian bunchflower	—	E
Veratrum woodii	Wood's bunchflower	—	T
Verbena canadensis	Rose mock-vervain	—	H
Veronica americana	American speedwell	—	H
Viburnum lantanoides	Alderleaved viburnum	—	E
Viburnum molle	Softleaf arrowwood	—	T
Viburnum nudum	Possumhaw	—	E
Viburnum rafinesquianum var. *rafinesquianum*	Downy arrowwood	—	T
Viola septemloba var. *egglestonii*	Eggleston's violet	—	S
Viola walteri	Walter's violet	—	T
Vitis labrusca	Northern fox grape	—	S
Vitis rupestris	Sand grape	—	T
Woodsia scopulina spp. *appalachiana*	Appalachian woodsia	—	H
Xerophyllum asphodeloides	Eastern turkeybeard	—	H
Xyris difformis	Carolina yellow-eyed grass	—	E
Zizania palustris var. *interior*	Indian wild rice	—	H
Zizaniopsis miliacea	Southern wild rice	—	T

		STATUS	
SCIENTIFIC NAME	COMMON NAME	Federal[a]	KSNPC[b]
ANIMALS			
FRESHWATER PLANARIANS			
Geocentrophora cavernicola	A cave obligate planarian	—	T
Sphalloplana buchanani	A cave obligate planarian	—	T
TERRESTRIAL SNAILS AND SLUGS			
Anguispira rugoderma	Pine Mountain tigersnail	—	E
Appalachina chilhoweensis	Queen crater	—	S
Fumonelix wetherbyi	Clifty covert	—	S
Glyphyalinia raderi	Maryland glyph	—	S
Glyphyalinia rhoadsi	Sculpted glyph	—	T
Helicodiscus notius specus	A snail	—	T
Helicodiscus punctatellus	Punctate coil	—	S
Mesomphix rugeli	Wrinkled button	—	T
Neohelix dentifera	Big-tooth whitelip	—	T
Paravitrea lapilla	Gem supercoil	—	T
Patera panselenus	Virginia bladetooth	—	S
Pilsbryna vanattai	Honey glyph	—	E
Rabdotus dealbatus	Whitewashed rabdotus	—	T
Vertigo bollesiana	Delicate vertigo	—	E
Vertigo clappi	Cupped vertigo	—	E
Vitrinizonites latissimus	Glassy grapeskin	—	T
Webbhelix multilineata	Striped whitelip	—	T
FRESHWATER SNAILS			
Antroselates spiralis	Shaggy cavesnail	—	S
Leptoxis praerosa	Onyx rocksnail	—	S
Lioplax sulculosa	Furrowed lioplax	—	S
Lithasia armigera	Armored rocksnail	—	S
Lithasia geniculata	Ornate rocksnail	—	S
Lithasia salebrosa	Muddy rocksnail	—	S
Lithasia verrucosa	Varicose rocksnail	—	S
Pleurocera alveare	Rugged hornsnail	—	S
Pleurocera curta	Shortspire hornsnail	—	S
Rhodacme elatior	Domed ancylid	—	S

SCIENTIFIC NAME	COMMON NAME	STATUS Federal[a]	KSNPC[b]
FRESHWATER MUSSELS			
Alasmidonta atropurpurea	Cumberland elktoe	E	E
Alasmidonta marginata	Elktoe	—	T
Anodontoides denigratus	Cumberland papershell	—	E
Cumberlandia monodonta	Spectaclecase	C	E
Cyprogenia stegaria	Fanshell	E	E
Epioblasma brevidens	Cumberlandian combshell	E	E
Epioblasma capsaeformis	Oyster mussel	E	E
Epioblasma florentina walkeri	Tan riffleshell	E	E
Epioblasma obliquata obliquata	Catspaw	E	E
Epioblasma torulosa rangiana	Northern riffleshell	E	E
Epioblasma triquetra	Snuffbox	—	E
Fusconaia subrotunda	Longsolid	—	S
Lampsilis abrupta	Pink mucket	E	E
Lampsilis ovata	Pocketbook	—	E
Lasmigona compressa	Creek heelsplitter	—	E
Obovaria retusa	Ring pink	E	E
Pegias fabula	Littlewing pearlymussel	E	E
Plethobasus cooperianus	Orangefoot pimpleback	E	E
Plethobasus cyphyus	Sheepnose	C	E
Pleurobema clava	Clubshell	E	E
Pleurobema oviforme	Tennessee clubshell	—	E
Pleurobema plenum	Rough pigtoe	E	E
Pleurobema rubrum	Pyramid pigtoe	—	E
Potamilus capax	Fat pocketbook	E	E
Potamilus purpuratus	Bleufer	—	E
Ptychobranchus subtentum	Fluted kidneyshell	C	E
Quadrula cylindrica cylindrica	Rabbitsfoot	—	T
Simpsonaias ambigua	Salamander mussel	—	T
Toxolasma lividus	Purple lilliput	—	E
Toxolasma texasiensis	Texas lilliput	—	E
Villosa lienosa	Little spectaclecase	—	S
Villosa ortmanni	Kentucky creekshell	—	T
Villosa trabalis	Cumberland bean	E	E
Villosa vanuxemensis vanuxemensis	Mountain creekshell	—	T

SCIENTIFIC NAME	COMMON NAME	STATUS Federal[a]	KSNPC[b]
ARACHNIDS			
Belba bulbipedata	A cave obligate mite	—	T
Galumna alata	A cave obligate mite	—	T
Hesperonemastoma inops	A cave obligate harvestman	—	S
Kleptochthonius attenuatus	A cave obligate pseudoscorpion	—	T
Kleptochthonius cerberus	A cave obligate pseudoscorpion	—	S
Kleptochthonius erebicus	A cave obligate pseudoscorpion	—	T
Kleptochthonius hageni	A cave obligate pseudoscorpion	—	S
Kleptochthonius hubrichti	A cave obligate pseudoscorpion	—	T
Kleptochthonius microphthalmus	A cave obligate pseudoscorpion	—	T
Macrocheles stygius	A cave obligate mite	—	T
Macrocheles troglodytes	A cave obligate mite	—	T
Tyrannochthonius hypogeus	A cave obligate pseudoscorpion	—	S
CRUSTACEANS			
Barbicambarus cornutus	Bottlebrush crayfish	—	S
Bryocamptus morrisoni elegans	A copepod	—	T
Caecidotea barri	Clifton Cave isopod	—	E
Cambarellus puer	Swamp dwarf crayfish	—	E
Cambarellus shufeldtii	Cajun dwarf crayfish	—	S
Cambarus bouchardi	Big South Fork crayfish	—	E
Cambarus friaufi	Hairy crayfish	—	S
Cambarus parvoculus	Mountain midget crayfish	—	T
Cambarus veteranus	Big Sandy crayfish	—	S
Gammarus bousfieldi	Bousfield's amphipod	—	E
Macrobrachium ohione	Ohio shrimp	—	E
Orconectes australis packardi	Appalachian cave crayfish	—	T
Orconectes bisectus	Crittenden crayfish	—	T
Orconectes burri	Blood River crayfish	—	T
Orconectes inermis inermis	Ghost crayfish	—	S
Orconectes jeffersoni	Louisville crayfish	—	E
Orconectes lancifer	Shrimp crayfish	—	E
Orconectes margorectus	A crayfish	—	T
Orconectes palmeri palmeri	Gray-speckled crayfish	—	E

SCIENTIFIC NAME	COMMON NAME	STATUS Federal[a]	KSNPC[b]
CRUSTACEANS continued			
Orconectes pellucidus	Mammoth Cave crayfish	—	S
Orconectes ronaldi	A crayfish	—	N
Palaemonias ganteri	Mammoth Cave shrimp	E	N
Procambarus viaeviridis	Vernal crayfish	—	T
Sagittocythere stygia	An ectocommensal ostracod	—	T
Stygobromus vitreus	An amphipod	—	S
MILLIPEDS			
Pseudotremia amphiorax	A cave obligate milliped	—	T
Pseudotremia carterensis	A cave obligate milliped	—	S
Pseudotremia merops	A cave obligate milliped	—	T
Pseudotremia spira	A cave obligate milliped	—	T
Pseudotremia unca	A cave obligate milliped	—	T
Scoterpes copei	A cave obligate milliped	—	T
INSECTS			
Acroneuria hitchcocki	A perlid stonefly	—	T
Acroneuria kosztarabi	A perlid stonefly	—	S
Allocapnia cunninghami	A capniid stonefly	—	T
Amphiagrion saucium	Eastern red damsel	—	E
Arigomphus maxwelli	Bayou clubtail	—	T
Arrhopalites altus	A cave obligate springtail	—	T
Arrhopalites bimus	A cave obligate springtail	—	T
Batriasymmodes quisnamus	A cave obligate beetle	—	T
Batrisodes henroti	A cave obligate beetle	—	T
Batrisodes hubrichti	A cave obligate beetle	—	T
Calephelis muticum	Swamp metalmark	—	T
Callophrys irus	Frosted elfin	—	T
Calopteryx dimidiata	Sparkling jewelwing	—	E
Celithemis verna	Double-ringed pennant	—	H
Cheumatopsyche helma	Helma's net-spinning caddisfly	—	H
Dannella provonshai	An ephemerellid mayfly	—	H
Dryobius sexnotatus	Six-banded longhorn beetle	—	T
Erora laeta	Early hairstreak	—	T
Euphyes dukesi	Dukes' skipper	—	S
Gomphus hybridus	Cocoa clubtail	—	E
Habrophlebiodes celeteria	A leptophlebiid mayfly	—	H
Hansonoperla hokolesqua	A perlid stonefly	—	S
Litobrancha recurvata	A burrowing mayfly	—	S
Lordithon niger	Black lordithon rove beetle	—	H
Lytrosis permagnaria	A geometrid moth	—	E
Maccaffertium bednariki	A heptageniid mayfly	—	S
Manophylax butleri	A limnephilid caddisfly	—	S
Mesamia stramineus	Helianthus leafhopper	—	E
Nannothemis bella	Elfin skimmer	—	E
Nehalennia irene	Sedge sprite	—	E
Nixe flowersi	A heptageniid mayfly	—	H
Ophiogomphus aspersus	Brook snaketail	—	H
Ophiogomphus howei	Pygmy snaketail	—	T
Ophiogomphus mainensis	Maine snaketail	—	E
Papaipema beeriana	Blazing star stem borer	—	E
Papaipema eryngii	Rattlesnake-master borer moth	—	E
Papaipema sp. (undescribed)	Rare cane borer moth	—	T
Papaipema speciosissima	Osmunda borer moth	—	E
Phyciodes batesii	Tawny crescent	—	H
Poanes viator	Broad-winged skipper	—	T
Polygonia faunus	Green comma	—	H
Polygonia progne	Gray comma	—	H
Prairiana kansana	A cicadellid leafhopper	—	E
Pseudanophthalmus abditus	Concealed cave beetle	—	T
Pseudanophthalmus audax	Bold cave beetle	—	T
Pseudanophthalmus caecus	Clifton Cave beetle	C	H
Pseudanophthalmus calcareus	Limestone Cave beetle	—	T
Pseudanophthalmus catoryctos	Lesser Adams Cave beetle	—	E
Pseudanophthalmus cnephosus	A cave obligate beetle	—	T
Pseudanophthalmus conditus	Hidden cave beetle	—	T
Pseudanophthalmus elongatus	A cave obligate beetle	—	S
Pseudanophthalmus exoticus	Exotic cave beetle	—	H
Pseudanophthalmus frigidus	Icebox Cave beetle	C	T
Pseudanophthalmus globiceps	Round-headed cave beetle	—	T
Pseudanophthalmus horni	Garman's cave beetle	—	S
Pseudanophthalmus hypolithos	Ashcamp Cave beetle	—	T
Pseudanophthalmus inexpectatus	Surprising cave beetle	—	T
Pseudanophthalmus major	Beaver Cave beetle	—	T
Pseudanophthalmus parvus	Tatum Cave beetle	C	T
Pseudanophthalmus pholeter	Greater Adams cave beetle	—	E
Pseudanophthalmus pubescens intrepidus	A cave obligate beetle	—	T

SCIENTIFIC NAME	COMMON NAME	STATUS Federal[a]	KSNPC[b]
INSECTS continued			
Pseudanophthalmus puteanus	Old Well cave beetle	—	T
Pseudanophthalmus rogersae	Rogers' cave beetle	—	T
Pseudanophthalmus scholasticus	Scholarly cave beetle	—	T
Pseudanophthalmus simulans	Cub Run Cave beetle	—	T
Pseudanophthalmus solivagus	A cave obligate beetle	—	S
Pseudanophthalmus tenebrosus	Stevens Creek Cave beetle	—	T
Pseudanophthalmus transfluvialis	A cave obligate beetle	—	S
Pseudanophthalmus troglodytes	Louisville cave beetle	C	T
Pseudosinella espanita	A cave obligate springtail	—	S
Raptoheptagenia cruentata	A heptageniid mayfly	—	H
Satyrium favonius ontario	Northern hairstreak	—	S
Speyeria idalia	Regal fritillary	—	H
Stylurus notatus	Elusive clubtail	—	E
Stylurus scudderi	Zebra clubtail	—	E
Tomocerus missus	A cave obligate springtail	—	T
Traverella lewisi	A leptophlebiid mayfly	—	H
Tychobythinus hubrichti	A cave obligate beetle	—	T
FRESHWATER FISHES			
Acipenser fulvescens	Lake sturgeon	—	E
Alosa alabamae	Alabama shad	—	E
Amblyopsis spelaea	Northern cavefish	—	S
Ammocrypta clara	Western sand darter	—	E
Atractosteus spatula	Alligator gar	—	E
Cyprinella camura	Bluntface shiner	—	E
Cyprinella venusta	Blacktail shiner	—	S
Erimystax insignis	Blotched chub	—	E
Erimyzon sucetta	Lake chubsucker	—	T
Esox niger	Chain pickerel	—	S
Etheostoma chienense	Relict darter	E	E
Etheostoma cinereum	Ashy darter	—	S
Etheostoma fusiforme	Swamp darter	—	E
Etheostoma lynceum	Brighteye darter	—	E
Etheostoma maculatum	Spotted darter	—	T
Etheostoma microlepidum	Smallscale darter	—	E
Etheostoma parvipinne	Goldstripe darter	—	E
Etheostoma percnurum	Duskytail darter	E	E
Etheostoma proeliare	Cypress darter	—	T
Etheostoma pyrrhogaster	Firebelly darter	—	E
Etheostoma susanae	Cumberland darter	C	E
Etheostoma swaini	Gulf darter	—	E
Etheostoma tecumsehi	Shawnee darter	—	S
Fundulus chrysotus	Golden topminnow	—	E
Fundulus dispar	Starhead topminnow	—	E
Hybognathus hayi	Cypress minnow	—	E
Hybognathus placitus	Plains minnow	—	S
Hybopsis amnis	Pallid shiner	—	E
Ichthyomyzon castaneus	Chestnut lamprey	—	S
Ichthyomyzon fossor	Northern brook lamprey	—	T
Ichthyomyzon greeleyi	Mountain brook lamprey	—	T
Ictiobus niger	Black buffalo	—	S
Lampetra appendix	American brook lamprey	—	T
Lampetra sp. (undescribed)	Undescribed Terrapin Creek brook lamprey	—	E
Lepomis marginatus	Dollar sunfish	—	E
Lepomis miniatus	Redspotted sunfish	—	T
Lota lota	Burbot	—	S
Macrhybopsis gelida	Sturgeon chub	—	E
Macrhybopsis meeki	Sicklefin chub	—	E
Menidia beryllina	Inland silverside	—	T
Moxostoma poecilurum	Blacktail redhorse	—	E
Nocomis biguttatus	Hornyhead chub	—	S
Notropis albizonatus	Palezone shiner	E	E
Notropis hudsonius	Spottail shiner	—	S
Notropis maculatus	Taillight shiner	—	T
Notropis sp. (undescribed)	Sawfin shiner	—	E
Noturus exilis	Slender madtom	—	E
Noturus hildebrandi	Least madtom	—	E
Noturus phaeus	Brown madtom	—	E
Noturus stigmosus	Northern madtom	—	S
Percina macrocephala	Longhead darter	—	E
Percina squamata	Olive darter	—	E
Percopsis omiscomaycus	Trout-perch	—	S
Phenacobius uranops	Stargazing minnow	—	S
Phoxinus cumberlandensis	Blackside dace	T	T
Platygobio gracilis	Flathead chub	—	S
Scaphirhynchus albus	Pallid sturgeon	E	E
Thoburnia atripinnis	Blackfin sucker	—	S
Typhlichthys subterraneus	Southern cavefish	—	S
Umbra limi	Central mudminnow	—	T

		STATUS	
SCIENTIFIC NAME	COMMON NAME	Federal[a]	KSNPC[b]

AMPHIBIANS

Amphiuma tridactylum	Three-toed amphiuma	—	E
Cryptobranchus alleganiensis alleganiensis	Eastern hellbender	—	S
Eurycea guttolineata	Three-lined salamander	—	T
Hyla avivoca	Bird-voiced tree frog	—	S
Hyla cinerea	Green tree frog	—	S
Hyla gratiosa	Barking tree frog	—	S
Hyla versicolor	Gray tree frog	—	S
Plethodon cinereus	Redback salamander	—	S
Plethodon wehrlei	Wehrle's salamander	—	E
Rana areolata circulosa	Northern crawfish frog	—	S
Rana pipiens	Northern leopard frog	—	S

REPTILES

Apalone mutica mutica	Midland smooth softshell	—	S
Chrysemys dorsalis	Southern painted turtle	—	T
Clonophis kirtlandii	Kirtland's snake	—	T
Elaphe guttata guttata	Corn snake	—	S
Eumeces anthracinus	Coal skink	—	T
Eumeces inexpectatus	Southeastern five-lined skink	—	S
Farancia abacura reinwardtii	Western mud snake	—	S
Lampropeltis triangulum elapsoides	Scarlet kingsnake	—	S
Macrochelys temminckii	Alligator snapping turtle	—	T
Nerodia cyclopion	Green water snake	—	E
Nerodia erythrogaster neglecta	Copperbelly water snake	—	S
Nerodia fasciata confluens	Broad-banded water snake	—	E
Ophisaurus attenuatus longicaudus	Eastern slender glass lizard	—	T
Pituophis melanoleucus melanoleucus	Pine snake	—	T
Sistrurus miliarius streckeri	Western pygmy rattlesnake	—	T
Thamnophis proximus proximus	Western ribbon snake	—	T
Thamnophis sauritus sauritus	Eastern ribbon snake	—	S

		STATUS	
SCIENTIFIC NAME	COMMON NAME	Federal[a]	KSNPC[b]

NESTING BIRDS

Accipiter striatus	Sharp-shinned hawk	—	S
Actitis macularius	Spotted sandpiper	—	E
Aimophila aestivalis	Bachman's sparrow	—	E
Ammodramus henslowii	Henslow's sparrow	—	S
Anas clypeata	Northern shoveler	—	E
Anas discors	Blue-winged teal	—	T
Ardea alba	Great egret	—	E
Asio flammeus	Short-eared owl	—	E
Asio otus	Long-eared owl	—	E
Bartramia longicauda	Upland sandpiper	—	H
Botaurus lentiginosus	American bittern	—	H
Bubulcus ibis	Cattle egret	—	S
Certhia americana	Brown creeper	—	E
Chondestes grammacus	Lark sparrow	—	T
Circus cyaneus	Northern harrier	—	T
Cistothorus platensis	Sedge wren	—	S
Corvus corax	Common raven	—	T
Corvus ossifragus	Fish crow	—	S
Dendroica fusca	Blackburnian warbler	—	T
Dolichonyx oryzivorus	Bobolink	—	S
Egretta caerulea	Little blue heron	—	E
Egretta thula	Snowy egret	—	E
Empidonax minimus	Least flycatcher	—	E
Falco peregrinus	Peregrine falcon	—	E
Fulica americana	American coot	—	E
Gallinula chloropus	Common moorhen	—	T
Haliaeetus leucocephalus	Bald eagle	—	T
Ictinia mississippiensis	Mississippi kite	—	S
Ixobrychus exilis	Least bittern	—	T
Junco hyemalis	Dark-eyed junco	—	S
Lophodytes cucullatus	Hooded merganser	—	T
Nyctanassa violacea	Yellow-crowned night-heron	—	T
Nycticorax nycticorax	Black-crowned night-heron	—	T
Pandion haliaetus	Osprey	—	T
Passerculus sandwichensis	Savannah sparrow	—	S
Phalacrocorax auritus	Double-crested cormorant	—	E
Pheucticus ludovicianus	Rose-breasted grosbeak	—	S
Podilymbus podiceps	Pied-billed grebe	—	E
Pooecetes gramineus	Vesper sparrow	—	E

SCIENTIFIC NAME	COMMON NAME	STATUS Federal[a]	STATUS KSNPC[b]
NESTING BIRDS continued			
Rallus elegans	King rail	—	E
Riparia riparia	Bank swallow	—	S
Sitta canadensis	Red-breasted nuthatch	—	E
Sternula antillarum athalassos	Interior least tern	E	E
Thryomanes bewickii	Bewick's wren	—	S
Tyto alba	Barn owl	—	S
Vermivora chrysoptera	Golden-winged warbler	—	T
Vireo bellii	Bell's vireo	—	S
Wilsonia canadensis	Canada warbler	—	S
MAMMALS			
Clethrionomys gapperi maurus	Kentucky red-backed vole	—	S
Corynorhinus rafinesquii	Rafinesque's big-eared bat	—	S
Corynorhinus townsendii virginianus	Virginia big-eared bat	E	E
Mustela nivalis	Least weasel	—	S
Myotis austroriparius	Southeastern myotis	—	E
Myotis grisescens	Gray myotis	E	T
Myotis leibii	Eastern small-footed myotis	—	T
Myotis sodalis	Indiana bat	E	E
Nycticeius humeralis	Evening bat	—	S
Peromyscus gossypinus	Cotton mouse	—	T
Sorex cinereus	Cinereus shrew	—	S
Sorex dispar blitchi	Long-tailed shrew	—	E
Spilogale putorius	Eastern spotted skunk	—	S
Ursus americanus	American black bear	—	S

SOURCE: Kentucky State Nature Preserves Commission. 2007. Natural Heritage Database. Kentucky State Nature Preserves Commission, Frankfort, Kentucky, USA.

NOTES:

[a] Key to federal status categories (Endangered Species Act of 1973):

E = Endangered. This is "any species . . . in danger of extinction throughout all or a significant portion of its range" (U.S. Fish and Wildlife Service 1992).

T = Threatened. This is "any species . . . likely to become an endangered species within the foreseeable future throughout all or a significant portion of its range" (U.S. Fish and Wildlife Service 1992).

C = Candidate. This is a species for which the U.S. Fish and Wildlife Service has "on file sufficient information on biological vulnerability and threats to support a proposal to list as endangered or threatened, but for which preparation and publication of a proposal is precluded by higher-priority listing actions" (U.S. Fish and Wildlife Service 2007).

For federal status category definitions, see:

United States Fish and Wildlife Service. 1992. Endangered Species Act of 1973 as amended through the 100th Congress. United States Government Printing Office, Washington, D.C., USA.

United States Fish and Wildlife Service. 1994. Endangered and threatened wildlife and plants; animal candidate review for listing as endangered or threatened species; proposed rule. 50 CFR Part 17. Federal Register 59:58982–59028.

United States Fish and Wildlife Service. 2007. Endangered and threatened wildlife and plants; review of native species that are candidates for listing as endangered or threatened; annual notice of findings on resubmitted petitions; annual description of progress on listing actions; proposed rule. Federal Register 72:69034–69106.

Federal statuses were taken from:

United States Fish and Wildlife Service. 2005. Endangered and threatened wildlife and plants. 50 CFR 17.11 and 17.12. Washington, D.C., USA.

United States Fish and Wildlife Service. 2007. Endangered and threatened wildlife and plants; review of native species that are candidates for listing as endangered or threatened; annual notice of findings on resubmitted petitions; annual description of progress on listing actions; proposed rule. Federal Register 72:69034–69106.

[b] KSNPC = Kentucky State Nature Preserves Commission. Key to KSNPC status categories:

E = Endangered. This is a taxon in danger of extirpation or extinction throughout all or a significant part of its range in Kentucky.

T = Threatened. This is a taxon likely to become endangered within the foreseeable future throughout all or a significant part of its range in Kentucky.

S = Special concern. This is a taxon that should be monitored because (1) it exists in a limited geographic area in Kentucky; (2) it may become threatened or endangered due to modification or destruction of habitat; (3) certain characteristics or requirements make it especially vulnerable to specific pressures; (4) experienced researchers have identified other factors that may jeopardize it; or (5) it is believed to be rare or declining in Kentucky, but insufficient information exists for assignment to the threatened or endangered status categories.

H = Historic. This is a taxon documented from Kentucky but not observed reliably for at least 20 years and not considered extinct or extirpated.

Plants and Animals Presumed Extinct or Extirpated from Kentucky

COMMON NAME	SCIENTIFIC NAME	DATE OF LAST OBSERVATION IN KENTUCKY[a]	FEDERAL STATUS[b]
SEED PLANTS			
Canada anemone	*Anemone canadensis*	1828	—
Marsh marigold	*Caltha palustris* var. *palustris*	1800s	—
Fraser's loosestrife	*Lysimachia fraseri*	1976	—
Stipuled scurf pea	*Orbexilum stipulatum*	1860	Extinct
Slender dragon-head	*Physostegia intermedia*	1840	—
Prairie parsley	*Polytaenia nuttallii*	1966	—
ANIMALS			
FRESHWATER MUSSELS			
Dromedary pearlymussel	*Dromus dromas*	ca. 1950	E
Sugarspoon	*Epioblasma arcaeformis*	Early 1900s	Extinct
Angled riffleshell	*Epioblasma biemarginata*	Prior to 1950	Extinct
Leafshell	*Epioblasma flexuosa*	ca. 1900	Extinct
Yellow blossom	*Epioblasma florentina florentina*	ca. 1950	Extinct
Acornshell	*Epioblasma haysiana*	ca. 1950	Extinct
Forkshell	*Epioblasma lewisii*	ca. 1950	Extinct
White catspaw	*Epioblasma obliquata perobliqua*	Early 1900s	E
Round combshell	*Epioblasma personata*	Prior to 1900	Extinct
Cincinnati riffleshell	*Epioblasma phillipsii*	Prior to 1900	Extinct
Tennessee riffleshell	*Epioblasma propinqua*	Prior to 1930	Extinct
Wabash riffleshell	*Epioblasma sampsonii*	Prior to 1930	Extinct
Cumberland leafshell	*Epioblasma stewardsonii*	Prior to 1900	Extinct
Tubercled blossom	*Epioblasma torulosa torulosa*	1960s	Extinct
Cracking pearlymussel	*Hemistena lata*	Prior to 2000	E
Scaleshell	*Leptodea leptodon*	Prior to 2000	E
Slabside pearlymussel	*Lexingtonia dolabelloides*	Prior to 1980	C
White wartyback	*Plethobasus cicatricosus*	ca. 1950	E
Winged mapleleaf	*Quadrula fragosa*	ca. 1900	E
Rough rockshell	*Quadrula tuberosa*	ca. 1950	Extinct
Rayed bean	*Villosa fabalis*	Prior to 2000	C

COMMON NAME	SCIENTIFIC NAME	DATE OF LAST OBSERVATION IN KENTUCKY[a]	FEDERAL STATUS[b]
INSECTS			
American burying beetle	*Nicrophorus americanus*	1974	E
Robust pentagenian burrowing mayfly	*Pentagenia robusta*	Prior to 1926	Extinct
FRESHWATER FISHES			
Scaly sand darter	*Ammocrypta vivax*	1942	—
Crystal darter	*Crystallaria asprella*	1929	—
Gravel chub	*Erimystax x-punctatus*	1890	—
Least darter	*Etheostoma microperca*	1957	—
Flame chub	*Hemitremia flammea*	1877	—
Southern brook lamprey	*Ichthyomyzon gagei*	1969	—
Harelip sucker	*Moxostoma lacerum*	1891	Extinct
Greater redhorse	*Moxostoma valenciennesi*	1888	—
Blotchside logperch	*Percina burtoni*	1891	—
REPTILES			
Coachwhip[c]	*Masticophis flagellum flagellum*	Unknown	—
NESTING BIRDS			
Anhinga	*Anhinga anhinga*	1950 (breeding)	—
Ivory-billed woodpecker	*Campephilus principalis*	1870s	E
Black tern	*Chlidonias niger*	ca. 1810	—
Carolina parakeet	*Conuropsis carolinensis*	1870s	Extinct
Passenger pigeon	*Ectopistes migratorius*	1898	Extinct
Swallow-tailed kite	*Elanoides forficatus*	1820	—
Red-cockaded woodpecker	*Picoides borealis*	2001	E
Greater prairie-chicken	*Tympanuchus cupido*	ca. 1810	—
Bachman's warbler	*Vermivora bachmanii*	1906	E
NON-NESTING BIRDS			
Trumpeter swan	*Cygnus buccinator*	1876 (native)	—
Whooping crane	*Grus americana*	1810	E
MAMMALS[d]			
American bison	*Bos bison*	ca. 1790	—
Gray wolf	*Canis lupus*	Unknown	T
Red wolf	*Canis rufus*	Unknown	E
Eastern cougar	*Puma concolor couguar*	Unknown	E

SOURCE: Kentucky State Nature Preserves Commission. 2007. Natural Heritage Database. Kentucky State Nature Preserves Commission, Frankfort, Kentucky, USA.

NOTES:

Extinct = a taxon that no longer exists. Extirpated = a taxon that no longer exists in the wild in Kentucky but exists elsewhere in the wild.

[a] Based on best available information. Some dates are approximate.

[b] Key to federal status categories (Endangered Species Act of 1973):

E = Endangered. This is "any species . . . in danger of extinction throughout all or a significant portion of its range" (U.S. Fish and Wildlife Service 1992).

T = Threatened. This is "any species . . . likely to become an endangered species within the foreseeable future throughout all or a significant portion of its range" (U.S. Fish and Wildlife Service 1992).

C = Candidate. This is a species for which the U.S. Fish and Wildlife Service has "on file sufficient information on biological vulnerability and threats to support a proposal to list as endangered or threatened, but for which preparation and publication of a proposal is precluded by higher-priority listing actions" (U.S. Fish and Wildlife Service 2007).

For federal status category definitions, see:

United States Fish and Wildlife Service. 1992. Endangered Species Act of 1973 as amended through the 100th Congress. United States Government Printing Office, Washington, D.C., USA.

United States Fish and Wildlife Service. 2007. Endangered and threatened wildlife and plants; review of native species that are candidates for listing as endangered or threatened; annual notice of findings on resubmitted petitions; annual description of progress on listing actions; proposed rule. Federal Register 72:69034–69106.

Federal statuses were taken from:

United States Fish and Wildlife Service. 2005. Endangered and threatened wildlife and plants. 50 CFR 17.11 & 17.12. Washington, D.C., USA.

United States Fish and Wildlife Service. 2007. Endangered and threatened wildlife and plants; review of native species that are candidates for listing as endangered or threatened; annual notice of findings on resubmitted petitions; annual description of progress on listing actions; proposed rule. Federal Register 72:69034–69106.

[c] Many herpetologists now believe that the Kentucky population of the coachwhip resulted from an introduction by humans.

[d] Eastern elk populations were eradicated; however, in 1998 elk from Utah were introduced on reclaimed mine land in eastern Kentucky.

APPENDIX FOUR
Natural Communities of Kentucky

COMMUNITY TYPES	KSNPC STATUS[a]
TERRESTRIAL	
A. FORESTS AND WOODLANDS	
Mesic forests	
1. Acidic mesophytic forest	—
2. Appalachian mesophytic forest	—
3. Bluegrass mesophytic cane forest	T
4. Calcareous mesophytic forest	—
5. Coastal Plain mesophytic cane forest	S
6. Cumberland highlands forest	E
7. Deep soil mesophytic forest	S
8. Hemlock-mixed forest	—
9. White pine-mixed forest	S
Dry forests and woodlands	
10. Acidic subxeric forest	—
11. Acidic xeric forest/woodland	—
12. Appalachian pine–oak forest	—
13. Appalachian subxeric forest	—
14. Bluegrass woodland	E
15. Calcareous subxeric forest	—
16. Calcareous xeric forest/woodland	—
17. Cumberland mountains pitch pine woodland	E
18. Cumberland mountains xeric pine woodland/outcrop	T
19. Limestone barrens (open woodland)	T
20. Sandstone barrens (open woodland)	E
21. Shale barrens (open woodland)	T
22. Xeric red cedar–oak forest/woodland	—
23. Xeric Virginia pine forest/woodland	—
24. Xerohydric flatwoods	E

COMMUNITY TYPES	KSNPC STATUS[a]
B. PRAIRIES	
25. Limestone/dolomite prairie	E
26. Sandstone prairie	E
27. Tallgrass prairie	E
C. GLADES	
28. Cumberland Plateau sandstone glade	E
29. Dolomite glade	E
30. Limestone flatrock glade	E
31. Limestone slope glade	T
32. Shale/siltstone glade	T
33. Shawnee Hills sandstone glade	E
D. CLIFFS/OUTCROPS/ROCKHOUSES	
34. Dry limestone cliff/outcrop	—
35. Dry sandstone cliff/outcrop/rockhouse	—
36. Mesic-wet limestone cliff/outcrop	—
37. Mesic-wet sandstone cliff/outcrop/rockhouse	—
PALUSTRINE WETLANDS	
E. FORESTS	
38. Bottomland hardwood forest	S
39. Bottomland ridge/terrace forest	E
40. Riparian forest	—
41. Small stream scour forest	—
42. Wet bottomland hardwood forest	T
43. Wet depression/sinkhole forest	E
44. Wet flatwoods	S

COMMUNITY TYPES	KSNPC STATUS[a]
F. SWAMPS	
45. Cypress (tupelo) swamp	E
46. Shrub swamp	T
G. MARSHES	
47. Bottomland marsh	T
48. Sinkhole/depression marsh	E
49. Wet meadow	E
H. GRASSLANDS	
50. Wet prairie	E
I. SEEPS	
51. Acid seep/bog	T
52. Appalachian seep/bog	E
53. Calcareous seep/bog	E
54. Coastal Plain forested acid seep	E
J. PONDS	
55. Bottomland slough	T
56. Coastal Plain slough	T
57. Sinkhole/depression pond	T

RIVERINE WETLANDS

K. RIVERS/STREAMS	
58. Cumberland Plateau gravel/cobble bar	E
59. Gravel/cobble bar	—
60. Mud flat	—
61. Sand bar	T

LACUSTRINE WETLANDS (sometimes included in aquatic classifications)

L. LAKES	
62. Bottomland lake	T

NOTES:

[a] KSNPC = Kentucky State Nature Preserves Commission. Key to KSNPC status categories:

E = Endangered. This is a taxon in danger of extirpation or extinction throughout all or a significant part of its range in Kentucky.

T = Threatened. This is a taxon likely to become endangered within the foreseeable future throughout all or a significant part of its range in Kentucky.

S = Special concern. This is a taxon that should be monitored because (1) it exists in a limited geographic area in Kentucky; (2) it may become threatened or endangered due to modification or destruction of habitat; (3) certain characteristics or requirements make it especially vulnerable to specific pressures; (4) experienced researchers have identified other factors that may jeopardize it; or (5) it is believed to be rare or declining in Kentucky, but insufficient information exists for assignment to the threatened or endangered status categories.

APPENDIX FIVE
Rarity Hotspot Analysis

KSNPC conducted rarity hotspot analyses for seed plants and ferns, amphibians, reptiles, nesting birds, and mammals using a rarity-weight richness index (RWRI) methodology developed by the Association for Biodiversity Information, now known as NatureServe.[1] All species listed in Appendix 2 with post-1986 records as of August 2007 were included in the analysis. Fishes and mussels were analyzed using watersheds (Appendix 6). The remaining major species groups lack sufficient data to enable rarity hotspot analysis to provide meaningful results. This appendix provides details of the results for the groups analyzed.

For purposes of the analysis, the state was divided into hexagons 3.46 square miles (2,217 acres) in size. A total of 12,066 hexagons cover the state.

RWRI CLASSES

♦ **High:** > Mean + 1 standard deviation—Area with a high concentration of rare species and/or rare species that have a very small range.

♦ **Medium:** < Mean + 1 standard deviation—Area with rare species present.

♦ **Low:** Area that may support rare species, though no occurrences are currently known.

♦ **Historic:** Area with rare species occurrence(s) that have not been observed for over 20 years and may no longer exist. Species observations prior to 1987 data were not used in the analysis but were shown to illustrate where species once occurred. Hexagons that ranked "High" or "Medium" may also have historic records present.

LITERATURE CITED

1. Stein, B. A., L. S. Kutner, and J. S. Adams. 2000. Precious heritage: the status of biodiversity in the United States. Oxford University Press, New York, New York, USA.

RWRI RESULTS

Seed plants and ferns

Hexagons with rare plants present	1037
Maximum RWRI	5.18
Mean RWRI	0.30
Standard deviation	0.49
High RWRI score	>0.79
Hexagons ranked "High"	107
Hexagons ranked "Medium"	930

Amphibians

Hexagons with rare amphibians	328
Maximum RWRI	0.55
Mean RWRI	0.03
Standard deviation	0.05
High RWRI score	>0.08
Hexagons ranked "High"	14
Hexagons ranked "Medium"	314

Reptiles

Hexagons with rare reptiles present	235
Maximum RWRI	1.13
Mean RWRI	0.07
Standard deviation	0.12
High RWRI score	>0.19
Hexagons ranked "High"	9
Hexagons ranked "Medium"	226

Nesting birds

Hexagons with rare nesting birds present	583
Maximum RWRI	2.71
Mean RWRI	0.08
Standard deviation	0.20
High RWRI score	>0.28
Hexagons ranked "High"	30
Hexagons ranked "Medium"	553

Mammals

Hexagons with rare mammals present	393
Maximum RWRI	0.51
Mean RWRI	0.03
Standard deviation	0.07
High RWRI score	>0.10
Hexagons ranked "High"	18
Hexagons ranked "Medium"	375

APPENDIX SIX

Analysis of Priority Watersheds for Conservation of Imperiled Fishes and Mussels

METHODOLOGY

KSNPC used the methods given in Master et al.[1] to analyze imperiled fishes and mussels. Using a geographic information system, each of 616 Kentucky watersheds, classified according to 11-digit U.S. Geological Survey hydrologic unit codes (HUCs), were scored for post-1986 records of imperiled mussels (freshly dead or living specimens, 37 taxa) and fishes (63 taxa) in the Kentucky State Nature Preserves Commission (KSNPC) Natural Heritage Program database as of March 13, 2007. Imperiled mussels and fishes are those listed as endangered, threatened, or of special concern or that are candidates for listing as endangered or threatened by the U.S. Fish and Wildlife Service,[2,3] KSNPC,[4] and NatureServe.[5]

SPECIES INCLUDED IN ANALYSIS

All species listed in Appendix 2 with extant post-1986 records as of March 2007 were included in the analysis, plus the following additions from NatureServe:[5]

Fishes

- *Ammocrypta pellucida*—Eastern sand darter
- *Cycleptus elongatus*—Blue sucker
- *Etheostoma sagitta sagitta*—Arrow darter (found in Cumberland River Watershed)
- *Etheostoma sagitta spilotum*—Arrow darter (found in Kentucky River Watershed)
- *Etheostoma tippecanoe*—Tippecanoe darter
- *Ichthyomyzon bdellium*—Ohio lamprey
- *Ichthyomyzon unicuspis*—Silver lamprey
- *Notropis ariommus*—Popeye shiner

Mussels

- *Actinonaias pectorosa*—Pheasantshell
- *Medionidus conradicus*—Cumberland moccasinshell
- *Pleurobema cordatum*—Ohio pigtoe
- *Villosa taeniata*—Painted creekshell

DETAILS OF ANALYSIS

KSPNPC analyzed the imperiled fishes and mussel data following Williams et al.[6] and Csuti et al.:[7]

- Sum the number of imperiled species in each watershed.

- Calculate a rarity-weighted richness index (RWRI)[7] for each species. Each imperiled species was scored as 1 divided by the number of watersheds the species inhabits. A species inhabiting only one watershed was scored 1.0, and one inhabiting 20 watersheds was scored 0.05. The RWRI for each watershed is the sum of scores for each species occurring in that watershed. The minimum RWRI for inclusion as a priority watershed was 1.28, which equals the mean RWRI plus 1 standard deviation (mean = 0.46, SD = 0.82, n = 219).

- Criteria for identifying priority watersheds for conservation of imperiled species among 17 major watersheds:

  - watersheds with RWRI > 1.28 or with > 6 imperiled taxa;

  - watersheds with the highest RWRI value in each major drainage; and

  - watersheds with the highest RWRI value or the most viable population to ensure that all imperiled taxa are included at least twice (except for taxa that are restricted to one watershed).

ANALYSIS RESULTS FOR TOP 10 PRIORITY WATERSHEDS FOR CONSERVATION OF IMPERILED FISHES AND MUSSELS

Rank	Watershed Name	No. of Species	HUC RWRI
1	Terrapin Creek	12	8.11
2	Mississippi River (Mayfield Creek to Obion Creek)	9	3.78
3	Green River (Lynn Camp Creek to Ugly Creek)	25	3.67
4	Green River (Ugly Creek to Nolin River)	21	3.64
5	Running Slough	9	3.03
6	Big South Fork Cumberland River, above Bear Creek	13	2.98
7	Big South Fork Cumberland River, below Bear Creek	10	2.61
8	Green River (Nolin River to Big Reedy Creek)	13	2.31
9	Bayou de Chien	6	2.14
10	Little South Fork Cumberland River	7	1.97

Additional information on the analysis of priority watersheds for conservation of imperiled fishes and mussels, including results of the latest analyses, can be viewed online at www.naturepreserves. ky.gov/inforesources/prwshds.htm.

LITERATURE CITED

1. Master, L. L., S. R. Flack, and B. A. Stein, editors. 1998. Rivers of life: critical watersheds for protecting freshwater biodiversity. The Nature Conservancy, Arlington, Virginia, USA.

2. United States Fish and Wildlife Service. 2005. Endangered and threatened wildlife and plants. 50 CFR 17.11 and 17.12. Washington, D.C., USA.

3. United States Fish and Wildlife Service. 2007. Endangered and threatened wildlife and plants; review of native species that are candidates for listing as endangered or threatened; annual notice of findings on resubmitted petitions; annual description of progress on listing actions; proposed rule. Federal Register 72:69034–69106.

4. Kentucky State Nature Preserves Commission. 2007. Rare and extirpated biota of Kentucky. Kentucky State Nature Preserves Commission, Frankfort, Kentucky, USA.

5. NatureServe. 2007. NatureServe Explorer: an online encyclopedia of life [web application]. Version 6.1. NatureServe, Arlington, Virginia, USA. Available at www.natureserve.org/explorer. Accessed March 1, 2007.

6. Williams, P., D. Gibbons, C. Margules, A. Rebelos, C. Humphries, and R. Pressey. 1996. A comparison of richness hotspots, rarity hotspots, and complementary areas for conserving diversity of British birds. Conservation Biology 10:155–174.

7. Csuti, B., S. Polasky, P. H. Williams, R. L. Pressey, J. D. Lamm, M. Kershaw, A. R. Kiester, B. Downs, R. Hamilton, M. Huso, and K. Sahr. 1997. A comparison of reserve selection algorithms using data on terrestrial vertebrates in Oregon. Biological Conservation 80:83–97.

Common and Scientific Names Used in the Text

COMMON NAME	SCIENTIFIC NAME
SLIME MOLDS	
Pretzel slime mold	*Hemitrichia serpula*
LICHENS	
British soldiers	*Cladonia* spp.
Lea's bog lichen	*Phaeophyscia leana*
FUNGI	
Chestnut blight	*Cryphonectria parasitica*
Earth star	*Geastrum* sp.
Fairy bonnet mushroom	*Coprinus disseminatus*
MOSSES	
Rose moss	*Rhodobryum roseum*
Sphagnum moss	*Sphagnum quinquefarium*
LIVERWORTS	
Lizard skin liverwort	*Conocephalum conicum*
PLANTS	
American beech	*Fagus grandifolia*
American chestnut	*Castanea dentata*
American elm	*Ulmus americana*
American ginseng	*Panax quinquefolius*
Appalachian bugbane	*Actaea rubifolia*
Arrow-leaved tear thumb	*Polygonum sagittatum*
Asian bittersweet	*Celastrus orbiculatus*
Autumn olive	*Elaeagnus umbellata*
Bald cypress	*Taxodium distichum*
Basswood	*Tilia americana*
Big bluestem	*Andropogon gerardii*
Black cherry	*Prunus serotina*
Black cohosh	*Actaea racemosa*
Black oak	*Quercus velutina*
Black walnut	*Juglans nigra*
Black willow	*Salix nigra*

COMMON NAME	SCIENTIFIC NAME
Blackjack oak	*Quercus marilandica*
Blazing star	*Liatris* spp.
Bloodroot	*Sanquinaria canadensis*
Blue ash	*Fraxinus quadrangulata*
Blueberry	*Vaccinium* spp.
Braun's rockcress	*Arabis perstellata*
Bur oak	*Quercus macrocarpa*
Burning bush	*Euonymus alatus*
Bush honeysuckle	*Lonicera maackii*
Butterfly milkweed	*Asclepias tuberosa*
Buttonbush	*Cephalanthus occidentalis*
Cardinal flower	*Lobelia cardinalis*
Carolina hemlock	*Tsuga caroliniana*
Chestnut oak	*Quercus montana*
Chinese chestnut	*Castanea mollissima*
Chinese yam	*Dioscorea battatas*
Chinkapin oak	*Quercus muhlenbergii*
Cinnamon fern	*Osmunda cinnamomea*
Cleft phlox	*Phlox bifida*
Common chickweed	*Stellaria media*
Common milkweed	*Asclepias syriaca*
Cord grass	*Spartina pectinata*
Corn	*Zea mays*
Crown vetch	*Coronilla varia*
Cumberland sandwort	*Minuartia cumberlandensis*
Doll's eye	*Actaea pachypoda*
Eastern hemlock	*Tsuga canadensis*
Eastern prickly pear (cactus)	*Opuntia humifusa*
Eggert's sunflower	*Helianthus eggertii*
False aloe	*Manfreda virginica*
False dragonhead	*Physostegia virginiana*
Fameflower	*Talinum* spp.
Filmy angelica	*Angelica triquinata*
Flowering dogwood	*Cornus florida*
Fraser's sedge	*Cymophyllus fraserianus*
Gamma grass	*Tripsacum dactyloides*

COMMON NAME	SCIENTIFIC NAME
Garlic mustard	*Alliaria petiolata*
Giant cane	*Arundinaria gigantea*
Goldenrod	*Solidago* spp.
Goldenseal	*Hydrastis canadensis*
Goosefoot	*Chenopodium* spp.
Great rhododendron	*Rhododendron maximum*
Green ash	*Fraxinus pennsylvanica*
Hoary puccoon	*Lithospermum canescens*
Indian grass	*Sorghastrum nutans*
Ironweed	*Vernonia* spp.
Jack-in-the-pulpit	*Arisaema triphyllum*
Japanese chestnut	*Castanea japonica*
Japanese grass	*Microstegium vimineum*
Japanese honeysuckle	*Lonicera japonica*
Japanese knotweed	*Polygonatum cuspidatum*
Jewelweed	*Impatiens capensis*
Kentucky gladecress	*Leavenworthia exigua* var. *laciniata*
Kentucky lady's-slipper	*Cypripedium kentuckiense*
Knotweed	*Polygonum* spp.
Kudzu	*Pueraria montana*
Limestone fameflower	*Talinum calcaricum*
Little bluestem	*Schizachyrium scoparium*
Miscanthus	*Miscanthus sinensis*
Mistflower	*Conoclinum coelestinum*
Mistletoe	*Phoradendron leucarpum*
Mountain magnolia	*Magnolia fraseri*
Multiflora rose	*Rosa multiflora*
New England aster	*Symphyotrichum novae-angliae*
Nodding thistle	*Carduus nutans*
Northern red oak	*Quercus rubra*
Orange-grass	*Hypericum gentianoides*
Overcup oak	*Quercus lyrata*
Painted trillium	*Trillium undulatum*
Pale green orchid	*Platanthera flava*
Pale purple coneflower	*Echinacea simulata*

COMMON NAME	SCIENTIFIC NAME

PLANTS *continued*

COMMON NAME	SCIENTIFIC NAME
Pawpaw	Asimina triloba
Persimmon	Diospyros virginiana
Pignut hickory	Carya glabra
Pin oak	Quercus palustris
Pitch pine	Pinus rigida
Poison hemlock	Cicuta maculata
Post oak	Quercus stellata
Poverty dropseed	Sporobolus vaginiflorus
Price's potato bean	Apios priceana
Privet	Ligustrum spp.
Purple loosestrife	Lythrum salicara
Purple trillium	Trillium erectum
Red cedar	Juniperus virginiana
Red maple	Acer rubrum
Rockcastle aster	Eurybia saxicastellii
Rosy twisted-stalk	Streptopus lanceolatus
Royal catchfly	Silene regia
Royal fern	Osmunda regalis
Running buffalo clover	Trifolium stoloniferum
Rushfoil	Crotonopsis elliptica
Sandbar willow	Salix exigua
Scarlet oak	Quercus coccinea
Scouring rush	Equisetum arvense
Sericea lespedeza	Lespedeza cuneata
Shagbark hickory	Carya ovata
Short's goldenrod	Solidago shortii
Shortleaf pine	Pinus echinata
Silver maple	Acer saccharinum
Slippery elm	Ulmus rubra
Smooth phlox	Phlox glaberrima
Sneezeweed	Helenium spp.
Sourwood	Oxydendrum arboreum
Southern maidenhair fern	Adiantum capillus-veneris
Southern red oak	Quercus falcata
Spicebush	Lindera benzoin
Squawroot	Conopholis americana
Stipuled scurf-pea	Orbexilum stipulatum
Sugar maple	Acer saccharum

COMMON NAME	SCIENTIFIC NAME
Sumpweed	Iva annua
Sundew	Drosera spp.
Swamp chestnut oak	Quercus michauxii
Swamp cottonwood	Populus heterophylla
Swamp rose	Rosa palustris
Swamp tupelo	Nyssa aquatica
Swamp white oak	Quercus bicolor
Sweet clover	Melilotus alba
Sweet gum	Liquidambar styraciflua
Switch grass	Panicum virgatum
Sycamore	Platanus occidentalis
Tall dropseed	Sporobolus compositus
Tall fescue	Lolium arundinaceum
Tennessee leafcup	Polymnia laevigata
Threadfoot	Podostemum ceratophyllum
Three-birds orchid	Triphora trianthophora
Tree-of-heaven	Ailanthus altissima
Turk's cap lily	Lilium superbum
Turtlehead	Chelone spp.
Virginia pine	Pinus virginiana
Virginia willow	Itea virginica
Walnut	Juglans sp.
Water willow	Justicia americana
White ash	Fraxinus americana
White oak	Quercus alba
White pine	Pinus strobus
White walnut	Juglans cinerea
White-haired goldenrod	Solidago albopilosa
Widow's-cross stonecrop	Sedum pulchellum
Wild hydrangea	Hydrangea arborescens
Willow oak	Quercus phellos
Winter creeper	Euonymus fortunei
Wood lily	Lilium philadelphicum
Wood poppy	Stylophorum diphyllum
Yellow birch	Betula lutea
Yellow buckeye	Aesculus flava
Yellow pond-lily	Nuphar advena
Yellow poplar	Liriodendron tulipifera
Yew	Taxus spp.

COMMON NAME	SCIENTIFIC NAME

ANIMALS

TERRESTRIAL SNAILS

COMMON NAME	SCIENTIFIC NAME
Glassy grapeskin	Vitrinizonites latissimus
Queen crater	Appalachina chilhoweensis
Striped whitelip	Webbhelix multilineata
Whitewashed rabdotus	Rabdotus dealbatus

FRESHWATER SNAILS

Armored rocksnail	Lithasia armigera
Shaggy cavesnail	Antroselates spiralis
Varicose rocksnail	Lithasia verrucosa

FRESHWATER MUSSELS

Asiatic clam	Corbicula fluminea
Bleufer	Potamilus purpuratus
Clubshell	Pleurobema clava
Cumberland elktoe	Alasmidonta atropurpurea
Cumberland papershell	Anodontoides denigratus
Fanshell	Cyprogenia stegaria
Fat pocketbook	Potamilus capax
Forkshell	Epioblasma lewisii
Gold clam	Corbicula fluminea
Kentucky creekshell	Villosa ortmanni
Kidneyshell	Ptychobranchus fasciolaris
Plain pocketbook	Lampsilis cardium
Pondmussel	Ligumia subrostrata
Purple lilliput	Toxolasma lividus
Pygmy clam	Corbicula fluminea
Rabbitsfoot	Quadrula cylindrica
Riffleshell (mussels)	Epioblasma spp.
Slippershell	Alasmidonta viridis
Texas lilliput	Toxolasma texasiensis
White wartyback	Plethobasus cicatricosus
Yellow blossom	Epioblasma florentina florentina
Zebra mussel	Dreissena polymorpha

OYSTERS

Akoya oyster	Pinctada fucata martensi

COMMON NAME	SCIENTIFIC NAME
ARACHNIDS	
Brown recluse	*Loxosceles reclusa*
Northern black widow	*Latrodectus variolus*
Pseudoscorpion	*Kleptochthonius* sp.
Southern black widow	*Latrodectus mactans*
Six-spotted fishing spider	*Dolomedes triton*
Southern unstriped scorpion	*Vaejovis carolinianus*
CRUSTACEANS	
Appalachian cave crayfish	*Orconectes australis packardi*
Bluegrass crayfish	*Cambarus batchi*
Ghost crayfish	*Orconectes inermis inermis*
Kentucky River crayfish	*Orconectes juvenilis*
Mammoth Cave crayfish	*Orconectes pellucidus*
Mammoth Cave shrimp	*Palaemonias ganteri*
Paintedhand mudbug	*Cambarus polychromatus*
Upland burrowing crayfish	*Cambarus dubius*
Valley flame crayfish	*Cambarus deweesae*
Water flea	*Daphnia* spp.
INSECTS	
American burying beetle	*Nicrophorus americanus*
American rubyspot	*Hetaerina americana*
Baltimore checkerspot	*Euphydryas phaeton*
Bayou clubtail	*Arigomphus maxwelli*
Cecropia moth	*Hyalophora cecropia*
Cobra clubtail	*Gomphus vastus*
Common green darner	*Anax junius*
Coral hairstreak	*Satyrium titus*
Dobsonfly (adult of hellgrammite)	*Corydalus cornutus*
Eastern pondhawk	*Erythemis simplicicollis*
Eastern red damsel	*Amphiagrion saucium*
Gulf fritillary	*Agraulis vanillae*
Gypsy moth	*Lymantria dispar*
Hellgrammite (larval stage of dobsonfly)	*Corydalus cornutus*

COMMON NAME	SCIENTIFIC NAME
Hemlock woolly adelgid	*Adelges tsugae*
Monarch	*Danaus plexippus*
Northern barrens tiger beetle	*Cicindela patruela patruela*
Olympia marble	*Euchloe olympia*
Paper wasp	*Polistes* sp.
Periodical cicada (17-year)	*Magicicada* spp.
Pipevine swallowtail	*Battus philenor*
Rattlesnake-master borer moth	*Papaipema eryngii*
Regal fritillary	*Speyeria idalia*
Regal moth	*Citheronia regalis*
Robber fly	*Laphria grossa*
Robust pentagenian burrowing mayfly	*Pentagenia robusta*
Rogers' cave beetle	*Pseudanophthalmus rogersae*
Scarlet-and-green leafhopper	*Graphocephala coccinea*
Southern pine beetle	*Dendrocontus frontalis*
Splendid tiger beetle	*Cicindela splendida*
Swamp metalmark	*Calephelis muticum*
Tachinid fly	*Compsilura concinnata*
Water penny beetle	*Psephenus* spp.
Waved sphinx	*Ceratomia undulosa*
Zebra clubtail	*Stylurus scudderi*
FRESHWATER FISHES	
Blackside dace	*Phoxinus cumberlandensis*
Blacktail redhorse	*Moxostoma poecilurum*
Bluegill	*Lepomis macrochirus*
Brighteye darter	*Etheostoma lynceum*
Creek chub	*Semotilus atromaculatus*
Elegant madtom	*Noturus elegans*
Emerald darter	*Etheostoma baileyi*
Firebelly darter	*Etheostoma pyrrhogaster*
Flame chub	*Hemitremia flammea*
Freshwater drum	*Aplodinotus grunniens*
Gizzard shad	*Dorosoma cepedianum*
Golden topminnow	*Fundulus chrysotus*
Goldstripe darter	*Etheostoma parvipinne*
Harelip sucker	*Moxostoma lacerum*
Kentucky darter	*Etheostoma rafinesquei*
Lake chubsucker	*Erimyzon sucetta*

COMMON NAME	SCIENTIFIC NAME
Lake sturgeon	*Acipenser fulvescens*
Largemouth bass	*Micropterus salmoides*
Northern cavefish	*Amblyopsis spelaea*
Paddlefish	*Polyodon spathula*
Pallid sturgeon	*Scaphirhynchus albus*
Rainbow darter	*Etheostoma caeruleum*
Relict darter	*Etheostoma chienense*
Rosefin shiner	*Lythrurus fasciolaris*
Shawnee darter	*Etheostoma tecumsehi*
Shovelnose sturgeon	*Scaphirhynchus platorynchus*
Sicklefin chub	*Macrhybopsis meeki*
Slough darter	*Etheostoma gracile*
Smallmouth bass	*Micropterus dolomieu*
Smallmouth redhorse	*Moxostoma breviceps*
Smallscale darter	*Etheostoma microlepidum*
Southern cavefish	*Typhlichthys subterraneus*
Speckled darter	*Etheostoma stigmaeum*
Spring cavefish	*Forbesichthys agassizii*
Sturgeon	*Acipenser* spp.
Sturgeon chub	*Macrhybopsis gelida*
Sunfish	*Lepomis* spp.
Taillight shiner	*Notropis maculatus*
Walleye	*Sander vitreum*
Western mosquitofish	*Gambusia affinis*
Western sand darter	*Ammocrypta clara*
AMPHIBIANS	
American toad	*Bufo americanus*
Barking treefrog	*Hyla gratiosa*
Bullfrog	*Rana catesbeiana*
Crawfish frog	*Rana areolata*
Green salamander	*Aneides aeneus*
Green treefrog	*Hyla cinerea*
Eastern hellbender	*Cryptobranchus alleganiensis alleganiensis*
Lesser siren	*Siren intermedia*
Mudpuppy	*Necturus maculosus*
Northern ravine salamander	*Plethodon electromorphus*
Red salamander	*Pseudotriton ruber*
Red-spotted newt (red eft)	*Notophthalmus viridescens*
Southern zigzag salamander	*Plethodon ventralis*

COMMON NAME	SCIENTIFIC NAME
AMPHIBIANS continued	
Spring peeper	*Pseudacris crucifer*
Three-toed amphiuma	*Amphiuma tridactylum*
Tiger salamander	*Ambystoma tigrinum*
Wehrle's salamander	*Plethodon wehrlei*
REPTILES	
Alligator snapping turtle	*Macroclemys temminckii*
Black rat snake	*Elaphe obsoleta*
Copperbelly water snake	*Nerodia erythrogaster neglecta*
Copperhead	*Agkistrodon contortrix*
Corn snake	*Elaphe guttata*
Cottonmouth	*Agkistrodon piscivorus*
Eastern box turtle	*Terrepene carolina*
Eastern garter snake	*Thamnophis sirtalis sirtalis*
Eastern slender glass lizard	*Ophisaurus attenuatus longicaudus*
European wall lizard	*Podarcis muralis*
Five-lined skink	*Eumeces fasciatus*
Harlequin coralsnake	*Micrurus fulvius*
Hognose snake	*Heterodon platirhinos*
Mud snake	*Farancia abacura*
Pine snake	*Pituophis melanoleucus melanoleucus*
Pygmy rattlesnake	*Sistrurus miliarus*
Queen snake	*Regina septemvittata*
Scarlet kingsnake	*Lampropeltis triangulum elapsoides*
Six-lined racerunner	*Cnemidophorus sexlineatus sexlineatus*
Southeastern crowned snake	*Tantilla coronata*
Timber rattlesnake	*Crotalus horridus*
Western ribbon snake	*Thamnophis proximus*
BIRDS	
American robin	*Turdus migratorius*
American white pelican	*Pelecanus erythrorhynchos*
Anhinga	*Anhinga anhinga*
Bachman's warbler	*Vermivora bachmanii*
Bald eagle	*Haliaeetus leucocephalus*

COMMON NAME	SCIENTIFIC NAME
Barred owl	*Strix varia*
Black tern	*Chlidonias niger*
Black-crowned night-heron	*Nycticorax nycticorax*
Black-throated blue warbler	*Dendroica caerulescens*
Black-throated green warbler	*Dendroica virens*
Bobolink	*Dolichonyx oryzivorus*
Brown-headed cowbird	*Molothrus ater*
Carolina parakeet	*Conuropsis carolinensis*
Cerulean warbler	*Dendroica cerulea*
Common nighthawk	*Chordeiles minor*
Common raven	*Corvus corax*
Dickcissel	*Spiza americana*
Eurasian collared dove	*Steptopelia decaocto*
European starling	*Sturnus vulgaris*
Golden eagle	*Aquila chrysaetos*
Grasshopper sparrow	*Ammodramus savannarum*
Great blue heron	*Ardea herodias*
Greater prairie-chicken	*Tympanuchus cupido*
Hooded warbler	*Wilsonia citrina*
House finch	*Carpodacus mexicanus*
House sparrow	*Passer domesticus*
Indigo bunting	*Passerina cyanea*
Ivory-billed woodpecker	*Campephilus principalis*
Kentucky warbler	*Oporornis formosus*
Mississippi kite	*Ictinia mississippiensis*
Mourning dove	*Zenaida macroura*
Mute swan	*Cygnus olor*
Northern cardinal	*Cardinalis cardinalis*
Northern parula	*Parula americana*
Northern pintail	*Anas acuta*
Osprey	*Pandion haliaetus*
Ovenbird	*Seiurus aurocapilla*
Passenger pigeon	*Ectopistes migratorius*
Peregrine falcon	*Falco peregrinus*
Red-cockaded woodpecker	*Picoides borealis*
Red-eyed vireo	*Vireo olivaceus*
Red-headed woodpecker	*Melanerpes erythrocephalus*
Rock pigeon	*Columba livia*

COMMON NAME	SCIENTIFIC NAME
Ruby-throated hummingbird	*Archilochus colubris*
Sandhill crane	*Grus canadensis*
Scarlet tanager	*Piranga olivacea*
Song sparrow	*Melospiza melodia*
Swallow-tailed kite	*Elanoides forficatus*
Trumpeter swan	*Cygnus buccinator*
Veery	*Catharus fuscescens*
Whooping crane	*Grus americana*
Wild turkey	*Meleagris gallopavo*
Wood duck	*Aix sponsa*
Wood thrush	*Hylocichla mustelina*
MAMMALS	
Allegheny woodrat	*Neotoma magister*
American bison	*Bos bison*
American black bear	*Ursus americanus*
American mastodon	*Mammut americanum*
American pika	*Ochotona princeps*
Arctic fox	*Vulpes lagopus*
Badger	*Taxidea taxus*
Beaver	*Castor canadensis*
Big brown bat	*Eptesicus fuscus*
Bobcat	*Lynx rufus*
Cinereus shrew	*Sorex cinereus*
Coyote	*Canis latrans*
Eastern chipmunk	*Tamias striatus*
Eastern cottontail	*Sylvilagus floridanus*
Eastern cougar	*Puma concolor couguar*
Eastern mole	*Scalopus aquaticus*
Eastern pipistrelle	*Perimyotis subflavus*
Eastern small-footed myotis	*Myotis leibii*
Elk	*Cervus canadensis*
Fallow deer	*Dama dama*
Fox squirrel	*Sciurus niger*
Giant bison	*Bison latifrons*
Giant sloth	*Megatherium americanum*
Golden mouse	*Ochrotomys nuttalli*
Gray myotis	*Myotis grisescens*
Gray squirrel	*Sciurus carolinensis*
Gray wolf	*Canis lupus*
House mouse	*Mus musculus*
Indiana bat	*Myotis sodalis*

COMMON NAME	SCIENTIFIC NAME
MAMMALS continued	
Kentucky red-backed vole	*Clethrionomys gapperi maurus*
Least weasel	*Mustela nivalis*
Little brown bat	*Myotis lucifugus*
Long-tailed shrew	*Sorex dispar*
Mexican free-tailed bat	*Tadarida brasiliensis*
Mink	*Mustela vison*
Muskrat	*Ondatra zibethicus*
Nine-banded armadillo	*Dasypus novemcinctus*
Northern myotis	*Myotis septentrionalis*
Norway rat	*Rattus norvegicus*
Polar bear	*Ursus maritimus*
Prairie vole	*Microtus ochrogaster*
Raccoon	*Procyon lotor*
Rafinesque's big-eared bat	*Corynorhinus rafinesquii*
Red bat	*Lasiurus borealis*
Red fox	*Vulpes vulpes*
Red wolf	*Canis rufus*
River otter	*Lutra canadensis*
Seminole bat	*Lasiurus seminolus*
Southern bog lemming	*Synaptomys cooperi*
Virginia big-eared bat	*Corynorhinus townsendii virginianus*
Virginia opossum	*Didelphis virginiana*
Western cougar	*Puma concolor*
White-footed mouse	*Peromyscus leucopus*
White-tailed deer	*Odocoileus virginianus*
Wild boar	*Sus scrofa*
Woodchuck (Groundhog)	*Marmota monax*
Wooly mammoth	*Mammuthus primigenius*

County Map

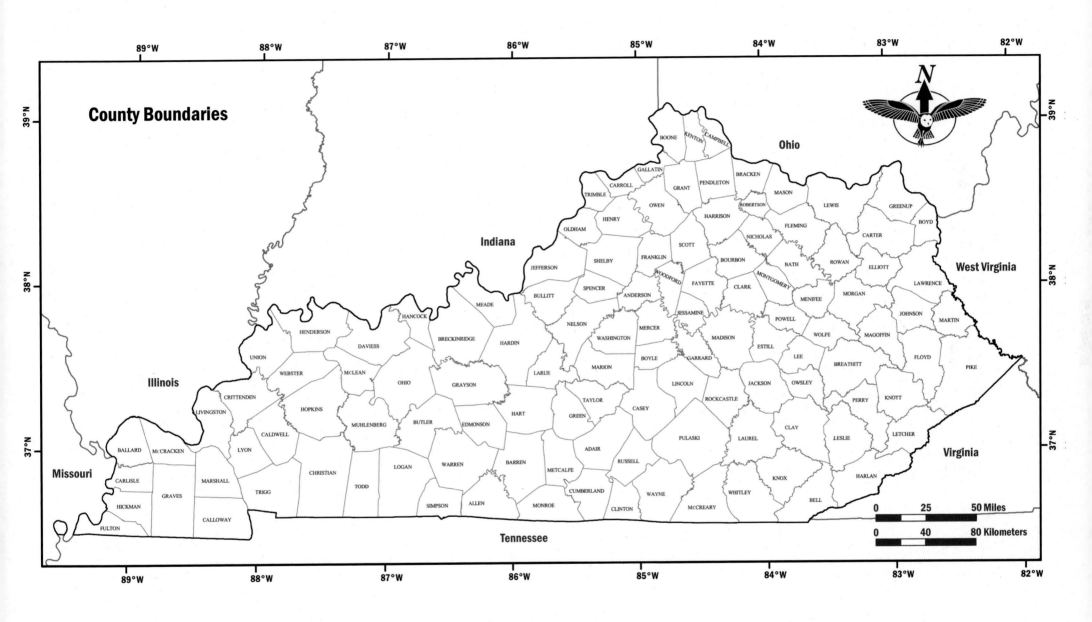

Bernheim Arboretum and Research Forest, 126
Big South Fork Cumberland River, 92
Big South Fork National River and Recreation Area, 12, 134
Big Woods, 92
Bioaccumulation, 99, 114
Biodiversity, 1, 2–4, 13, 24, 27, 40, 92; compared to North America and to the world, 5; definition of, 2; gathering information on, 122–123; in Kentucky, 1, 4–7, 5, 12, 13; influence of fire on, 33; legislation benefiting, 129; levels of (ecosystem; genetic; species diversity), 3; reasons for preserving, 2; world-class biodiversity of Mammoth Cave National Park, 115. *See also* Biodiversity: decline of and threats to; Conservation; Rarity hotspots
Biodiversity, decline of and threats to, 94, 101, 115; animal deaths due to collisions with vehicles, 104; habitat conversion/land-use change, 102; impact of agriculture on, 104–106; impact of dams on, 104, 131; impact of forestry on, 107–108; impact of global climate change on, 116–118; impact of infrastructure (roads, railroads, utility lines) on, 104; impact of invasive species (animals, plants, pathogens) on, 110–113; impact of mining on, 26, 108–109; impact of pollution (air, land, water) on, 114–116; impact of urban sprawl on, 102–104; natural resource extraction, 106–107; overcollection and overharvesting of animals and plants, 118–120; urbanized landscape, 103
Birds, 24, 33, 66, 74–78, 108, 111, 117, 120; communication among, 75; diet of, 75; dispersal of invasives by, 113–114; diversity of, 75; extirpated and extinct species, 76–77, 82–83; first birds, 28; impact of pesticides on, 115; migration of, 22, 75–76, 106, 128; number of species, 5, 40, 66, 74–75, 76; rare species, 77–78; rarity hotspots of, 77; size variation among, 75; species introduced from Eurasia, 75; types (migrants, residents, vagrants) of, 74. *See also* Warblers; *specific species*
Black cherry (*Prunus serotina*), 87
Black cohosh (*Actaea racemosa*), 120
Black Mountain, 12, 17, 18, 43, 44, 47, 51, 52, 87; importance of to rare insect life, 65; possible effects of climate change on, 117
Black oak (*Quercus velutina*), 86
Black tern (*Chlidonias niger*), 77
Black walnut (*Juglans nigra*), 87
Black willow (*Salix nigra*), 90

Black-crowned night-heron (*Nycticorax nycticorax*), 94
Blackjack oak (*Quercus marilandica*), 86, 88
Blackside dace (*Phoxinus cumberlandensis*), 67
Blacktail redhorse (*Moxostoma poecilurum*), 132
Blanton Forest State Nature Preserve, 17, 92
Blazing star (*Liatris* spp.), 34, 91
Blood River corridor, 70
Bloodroot (*Sanquinaria canadensis*), 45, 46, 87
Bloodworms, 95, 96
Blue ash (*Fraxinus quadrangulata*), 89
Blue Licks Spring, 127
Blue Licks State Park Nature Preserve, 31
Blue Ridge Parkway, 111
Blue River system (Indiana), 53
Blueberry (*Vaccinium* spp.), 46
Bluegill (*Lepomis macrochirus*), 67
Bluegrass (Natural Region), 11–12, 13, 15, 24, 30, 89, 105, 113, 114; soils of, 17; topography of, 18
Bobcat (*Lynx rufus*), 23, 79
Bobolink (*Dolichonyx oryzivorus*), 24
Boone, Daniel, 27; description of the Red River region, 118
Bottomland. *See* Forests: bottomland hardwood
Braun, Lucy, 17
Braun's rockcress (*Arabis perstellata*), 114, 123
Breckinridge County, 60, 99
Brown-headed cowbird (*Molothrus ater*), 108
Brush Mountain, 134
Bryophytes, 44–45; reproduction in, 45. *See also* Hornworts; Liverworts; Mosses
Brush Mountain, 134
Bugs, true (Hemiptera), number of species, 5, 62
Bullitt County, 102, 126
Bur oak (*Quercus macrocarpa*), 89
Burning bush (*Euonymus alatus*), 113
Bush honeysuckle (*Lonicera maackii*), 108, 113–114
Butterflies (Lepidoptera), 62, 64, 126; impact of fire suppression on, 34; life cycle of, 64–65; number of species, 5, 62, 64
  Baltimore checkerspot (*Euphydryas phaeton*), 64
  coral hairstreak (*Satyrium titus*), 123
  gulf fritillary (*Agraulis vanillae*), 34
  monarch (*Danaus plexippus*), 46, 65; migration, 65
  Olympia marble (*Euchloe olympia*), 50
  pipevine swallowtail (*Battus philenor*), 22
  regal fritillary (*Speyeria idalia*), 66
  swamp metalmark (*Calephelis muticum*), 128

Butterfly milkweed (*Asclepias tuberosa*), 123
Buttonbush (*Cephalanthus occidentalis*), 91

Cache River National Wildlife Refuge (Arkansas), 82
Caddisflies (Trichoptera), 62, 63, 64, 93, 95; larvae of, 63, 64, 69, 93; life cycle of, 63; number of species, 5, 62, 63
Calcium carbonate, 13, 51
Candidate species. *See* Federally listed (species)
Canebreaks, 31, 35
Carbofuran (Furadan), banning of, 116, 129
Carbon dioxide (CO_2), 114, 117
Carboniferous Period, 13, 15
Cardinal flower (*Lobelia cardinalis*), 91
Carolina hemlock (*Tsuga caroliniana*), 110
Carolina parakeet (*Conuropsis carolinensis*), 76, 81, 82, 118, 120
Carson, Rachel, 116, 121
Carter Cave system, 13
Caterpillars, 46, 64
Cave crickets, 99
Caves, 97, 139; classification of, 97–98; classification of by streams, 97–98; definition of, 97; estimated number of caves, 100; formation of from limestone erosion, 97; karst occurrences of, 98; landscape cross section of, 85, 97; solution caves, 97. *See also* Mammoth Cave; Subterranean communities; Subterranean organisms/ species
Caves and Karst of Kentucky, 100
Chestnut blight (*Cryphonectria parasitica*), 112–113; range of infestation, 112
Chestnut oak (*Quercus montana*), 34, 86, 88
Chinese chestnut (*Castanea mollissima*), 112
Chinese yam (*Dioscorea battatas*), 113
Chinkapin oak (*Quercus muhlenbergii*), 86, 88
Christian County, 6
Cincinnati Arch, 13, 14, 15
Clark's River, 137
Clay and shale, distribution of in Kentucky, 108
Clean Air Act (1963), 114, 128, 129
Clean Water Act (1972), 128, 129
Cleft phlox (*Phlox bifida*), 13
Cliffs/outcrops/rockhouses (cliff communities), 49, 69, 79, 87, 88–89, 125; landscape cross section of, 85
Climate, 7, 21–23; average annual precipitation, 22; average annual temperature, 22; extreme temperature changes, 24; extreme weather events, 23–24. *See also* Global climate change

Gravel/cobble bars, 91; landscape cross section of, 85. *See also* Natural communities (specific cobble bars)

Graves County, 6, 42, 43

Gray wolf (*Canis lupus*), 78, 82, 83, 120

Great blue heron (*Ardea herodias*), 78

Great Plains, 45

Great rhododendron (*Rhododendron maximum*), 87

Greater prairie-chicken (*Tympanuchus cupido*), 76, 120

Green ash (*Fraxinus pennsylvanica*), 90

Green County, 60

Green River, 6, 43, 54, 67, 115, 132–133, 137; watershed of, 6, 43, 53, 54, 55, 60, 61, 67, 68, 99, 132

Green River Bioreserve Project, 133

Griffith Woods, 125

Habitat conversion/land-use change, 102. *See also* Agriculture; Natural resource extraction; Urbanization

Hardin County, 99

Harelip sucker (*Moxostoma lacerum*), 68

Harlan County, 17, 18, 87, 92, 125

Hart County, 21, 60, 100

Hemlock woolly adelgid (*Adelges tsugae*), 110–111; range of its infestation, 111

Herbicides, 83, 99, 115–116, 127, 138

Hickman County, 42, 92, 123

Highland Rim (Natural Region), 11, 12, 24, 30, 36, 69, 88, 135; soils of, 16–17; topography of, 18

Himalayan Mountains, 15

Hoary puccoon (*Lithospermum canescens*), 50

Holocene, 15, 29

Hornworts, 44, 45; number of species, 5, 45

House finch (*Carpodacus mexicanus*), 75

House sparrow (*Passer domesticus*), 75

Illinois, 10, 56, 75, 82

Imlay, Gilbert, 35

Indiana, 10, 53, 75, 127

Indigo bunting (*Passerina cyanea*), 22, 75, 76

Insect larvae (aquatic), 63; caddisfly, 63, 64, 93; mayfly, 63; stonefly, 63

Insects, 23, 28, 50, 51, 62–66, 75, 81, 110, 116; aquatic, 63, 96; consumption of by bats, 66; difficulty in documenting diversity of, 62; endemic species, 42, 65; extirpated and extinct species, 81, 82, 83; and fire, 33, 34; habitats of, 65; as indicators of stream/river health, 63; number of species, 5, 62; orders of (Coleoptera, Diptera, Ephemeroptera, Hemiptera, Hymenoptera, Lepidoptera, Odonata, Plecoptera, and Trichoptera), 62–65; rare species, 65; subterranean obligate species, 99. *See also* Insect larvae (aquatic); *specific species*; *specific species groups*

Interior Low Plateaus (Physiographic Province), 10–11, 14; soils of, 16

Invasive species, 86, 110, 114, 126, 133; animals and pathogens, 110–113; control of, 114, 126–127; and forestry, 107, 108; and mining, 109; plants, 113–114, 127; and urbanization, 104

Invertebrates, 50, 65–66, 84, 117; endemic species, 42; facts concerning, 51; first invertebrates (land and marine), 28; global and conservation ranks of Kentucky fauna, 84; global climate change impact on, 117; historic mass extinction of, 28; macroinvertebrates, 92; number of species, 50; subterranean obligate species, 99. *See also* Arachnids; Crustaceans; Insects; Mollusks

Ironweed (*Vernonia* spp.), 45

Jack-in-the-pulpit (*Arisaema triphyllum*), 87

Jackson Purchase area, 70

Japanese chestnut (*Castanea japonica*), 112

Japanese grass (*Microstegium vimineum*), 113

Japanese honeysuckle (*Lonicera japonica*), 113

Japanese knotweed (*Polygonatum cuspidatum*), 113

Jefferson County, 126

Jefferson Memorial Forest, 126

Jewelweed (*Impatiens capensis*), 24

Jurassic Period, 14, 15; geologic timeline, 28

Karst (porous limestone) plains, 11, 16, 17, 19, 20, 21, 97; landscape cross section of, 97; occurrences of, 98

Kentucky: animals and plants presumed extinct or extirpated from, 7, 81–85, 177–178; biodiversity of compared to North America and to the world, 5; climate change in, 117; endemic species of (including subspecies), 6, 164–165; global and state conservation ranks of rare species in, 84; historic traces (trails), 30, 31, 32; population growth of, 102; rare biota of, 84, 166–76

Kentucky Department of Fish and Wildlife Resources, 125

Kentucky Division of Air Quality, 114

Kentucky Division of Water, 116, 129

Kentucky gladecress (*Leavenworthia exigua* var. *laciniata*), 102

Kentucky Heritage Land Conservation Fund, 126, 129

Kentucky Landscape Snapshot, 26

Kentucky Native Plant Society, 127

Kentucky Natural Heritage Program, 130

Kentucky Natural Lands Trust, 126

Kentucky River, 20, 67, 96; palisades of, 13, 47, 136, 137; polluting of by the Wild Turkey Distillery bourbon spill, 116; watershed of, 42, 60, 61, 67, 68

Kentucky State Nature Preserves Commission (KSNPC), 36, 52, 60, 122, 125, 127; conservation planning using GIS, 130–137; estimate of presettlement land cover (old-growth forests, nonforested communities, prairies), 36–37, 86, 87, 88; estimates of insect species, 3, 62, 63. *See also* KSNPC-listed (species)

Knobby Rock, 17

Knobs (Natural Region), 11, 12, 13, 86, 87, 135; soils of, 17

Knotweed (*Polygonum* spp.), 31

Knox County, 20

KSNPC-listed (species), 41, 49, 56, 58, 60, 65, 68, 70, 73, 77, 80, 81, 115, 125; endangered, 42, 43, 49, 53, 56, 67, 100; historical, 48–49; number of species in Kentucky, 84; list of, 166–176; special concern, 48, 53, 99; threatened, 28, 43, 52, 67, 131

Kudzu (*Pueraria montana*), 110, 113

Lake chubsucker (*Erimyzom sucetta*), 67

Lake Cumberland, 19

Lakes, 19, 63, 90, 115, 117; landscape cross section of, 85; oxbow 10

Land Between the Lakes, 73, 80, 116

Land Between the Lakes National Recreation Area, 125

Land cover, 24, 25; changes in, 26; presettlement, 36–37

Large forest tracts, 133–135; classification of by size (edge, interior), 134–135; example of (Bernheim Forest Area), 133; identification of, 133–134; role of in conservation, 133

Largemouth bass (*Micropterus salmoides*), 92

Larue County, 19, 125

Late Prehistoric Period (native peoples), 29, 31; villages of, 32

Laurel County, 83

Leafhoppers, 2
scarlet-and-green (*Graphocephala coccinea*), 2

Least weasel (*Mustela nivalis*), 79

Lentic communities (habitats). *See* Aquatic communities

Leopold, Aldo, 101, 119

Letcher County, 44, 92, 104

Lichens, 44, 45; first fungi, 28; number of species, 5; sensitivity of to air pollution, 44; species on the brink, 84
    British soldiers (*Cladonia* spp.), 44
    Lea's bog lichen (*Phaeophyscia leana*), 44
Lilley Cornett Woods, 92, 125
Lily
    Turk's-cap (*Lilium superbum*), 22
    wood (*Lilium philadelphicum*), 49
    yellow pond-lily (*Nuphar advena*), 46, 47
Limestone, 4, 15, 16, 17, 18, 51, 86; distribution of in Kentucky, 108; formation of limestone beds, 13; importance of to snails, 51; mining of, 109; Ordovician-age limestone, 13, 17; role of in cave formation, 97; Silurian-age limestone, 17. *See also* Cliffs/outcrops/rockhouses (cliff communities)
Limestone fameflower (*Talinum calcaricum*), 49
Liverworts, 44–45; number of species, 5, 45
    lizard skin (*Conocephalum conicum*), 45
Lizards, 71, 72, 73; diet of, 73; number of species, 71; rare species, 73; rarity hotspots of, 73, 74
    eastern slender glass (*Ophisaurus attenuatus*), 24
    European wall (*Podarcis muralis*), 73
    five-lined skink (*Eumeces fasciatus*), 73
    six-lined racerunner (*Cnemidophorus sexlineatus sexlineatus*), 24
Lotic communities (habitats). *See* Aquatic communities
Lynn Camp Creek, 132; watershed of, 19

Madison County, 42
Mammals, 16, 33, 66, 73, 75, 78–81, 117; changes in mammal fauna since European American settlement, 78; extirpated and extinct species, 82, 83; first mammals (marine and modern), 28; historic mass extinction of megafauna, 29; mammals introduced from Eurasia, 78; number of species, 5, 66, 78; rare species, 80–82; rarity hotspots of, 80, 81; ungulates, 79. *See also* Moles; Rabbits; Rodents; Shrews; Voles; *specific species*
Mammoth Cave, 6, 11, 13, 42, 73, 81, 98, 99, 100; importance of to rare insect life, 65
Mammoth Cave National Park, 20, 42, 92, 115, 132, 135; biodiversity of, 115; as a Biosphere Reserve, 125; pollution of, 115; threats to, 115
Marshes, 37, 47, 60, 63, 90, 91; landscape cross section of, 85
Martin County, coal slurry spill in, 116

Martin's Fork, 134; watershed of, 134
Mayfield Creek, 132; watershed of, 106
Mayflies (Ephemeroptera), 62, 63, 93, 94, 95; number of species, 5, 62
McCracken County, 90
McCreary County, 47, 51
Meade County, 60, 99
Metropolis Lake, 90
Mice, 79, 123
    golden mouse (*Ochrotomys nuttalli*), 1, 2
    house mouse (*Mus musculus*), 2, 78
    white-footed mouse (*Peromyscus leucopus*), 79
Midwestern Prairie, 46
Millipeds: endemic species, 42; subterranean obligate species, 99
Mineral and fuel resources, 108–109. *See also* Mines/mining
Mines/mining, 26; amount of surface area mined, 109; current extent, 25, 26; effects of on streams, 109; minimizing the impact of, 110; mountain-top removal mining, 109; number of oil and natural gas wells drilled, 109; of sand and gravel, 109; strip-mining, 26; surface mining, 109
Mink (*Mustela vison*), 79
Miscanthus (*Miscanthus sinensis*), 113
Mississippi, 59
Mississippi kite (*Ictinia mississippiensis*), 123
Mississippi River, 6, 17, 18, 21, 26, 36, 52, 53, 66, 67, 82, 131; floodplains of, 18, 24, 45, 52, 59, 73, 77, 81; watershed of, 19, 132, 133
Mississippi River Valley, 10, 29, 32
Mississippi/Ohio River Floodplain (Natural Region), 10, 11
Mississippian Period, 13, 14, 15, 17; geologic timeline, 28; soils of, 17
Mississippian Period (native peoples), 29, 31; villages of, 32
Mistflower (*Conoclinum coelestinum*), 47
Mistletoe (*Phoradendron leucarpum*), 47
Moles, 78, 79
Mollusks, 5, 51; endemic species, 42; high extinction rate of, 51; number of species, 5, 51. *See also* Mussels: freshwater; Snails: freshwater; Snails: terrestrial
Monroe County (Arkansas), 82
Mosses, 40, 44, 45, 47, 91; number of species, 5, 44
    rose (*Rhodobryum roseum*), 45
    sphagnum (*Sphagnum quinquefarium*), 45, 91

Moths (Lepidoptera), 62, 64–65, 79, 131; number of species, 5, 64
    Cecropia (*Hyalophora cecropia*), 110
    gypsy (*Lymantria dispar*), 110
    rattlesnake-master borer (*Papaipema eryngii*), 41
    regal (*Citheronia regalis*), 62
    waved sphinx (*Ceratomia undulosa*), 123
Mountain magnolia (*Magnolia fraseri*), 87
Mourning dove (*Zenaida macroura*), 76
Muhlenberg County, Paradise power plant of, 115
Muir, John, 9
Mushrooms, 23, 30, 40, 43, 108
    earth star (*Geastrum* sp.), 44
    fairy bonnet (*Coprinus disseminatus*), 40
Muskrat (*Ondatra zibethicus*), 79
Mussels, freshwater, 4, 6, 19, 30, 50, 53–56, 64, 81, 92, 93, 94, 95, 104, 112, 115, 116, 120; Cumberlandian, 53; disappearance of from impounded rivers, 96; effects of silt and sediment on mussel habitat, 56; extirpated and extinct species, 56, 81–82; habitat of, 54; life cycle of, 54; Mississippian, 53; number of species, 5, 55; priority watersheds for conservation of, 131–133; rare species, 56, 131–133; watersheds with high diversity of, 53–54, 55
    Asiatic clam (*Corbicula fluminea*), 110, 111–112
    bleufer (*Potamilus purpuratus*), 53
    clubshell (*Pleurobema clava*), 132, 133
    Cumberland elktoe (*Alasmidonta atropurpurea*), 56
    Cumberland papershell (*Anodontoides denigratus*), 53
    fanshell (*Cyprogenia stegaria*), 123, 133
    fat pocketbook (*Potamilus capax*), 53
    forkshell (*Epioblasma lewisii*), 82
    gold clam (*Corbicula fluminea*), 112
    Kentucky creekshell (*Villosa ortmanni*), 54
    kidneyshell (*Ptychobranchus fasciolaris*), 51
    plain pocketbook (*Lampsilis cardium*), 54
    pondmussel (*Ligumia subrostrata*), 53
    purple lilliput (*Toxolasma lividus*), 53
    pygmy clam (*Corbicula fluminea*), 112
    rabbitsfoot (*Quadrula cylindrica*), 133
    riffleshell (*Epioblasma* spp.), 82
    slippershell (*Alasmidonta viridis*), 53
    Texas lilliput (*Toxolasma texasiensis*), 53
    white wartyback (*Plethobasus cicatricosus*), 53
    yellow blossom (*Epioblasma florentina florentina*), 81
    zebra mussel (*Dreissena polymorpha*), 111
Mute swan (*Cygnus olor*), 75

National Audubon Society Christmas Bird Count, 138

National Park Service, 33

Native peoples, 30–32; development of agriculture by, 30–32; foods of, 30; impact of infectious diseases on, 29, 32; use of fire by, 30, 33; villages of, 32. *See also* Archaic Period (native peoples); Fort Ancient culture; Late Prehistoric Period (native peoples); Mississippian Period (native peoples); Paleoindian Period (native peoples); Woodland Period (native peoples)

Natural communities, 1, 3, 7, 10, 16, 23, 24, 33, 34, 35, 39, 46, 85–100; classification of, 85–86; impact of urbanization on, 104; impact of global climate change on, 117; landscape cross section of, 85; list of, 179–180; monitoring of, 122–123; subterranean, 85. *See also* Aquatic communities; Subterranean communities; Terrestrial communities; Wetland communities

Acidic mesophytic forest, 86

Appalachian mesophytic forest, 87

Appalachian seep/bog, 3

Bluegrass woodland, 89

Calcareous seep/bog, 49

Cumberland Plateau gravel/cobble bar, 3, 91

Cumberland highlands forest, 87

Cypress (tupelo) swamp, 10, 65, 81, 85, 90, 96, 123

Hemlock-mixed forest, 3, 87

Mud flat, 91

Shrub swamp, 90, 91

Tallgrass prairie, 88

Wet meadow, 90, 91

Wet prairie, 91

Xerohydric flatwoods, 90, 91

Natural gas, 13, 108, 117; distribution of in Kentucky, 108

Natural Heritage Program Network, 122–123; collection and maintenance of species and natural communities data by, 123; standardized methodology of, 122–123

Natural history, 27; fire, 33–34; historical accounts of, 35; native peoples, 30–32; natural history timeline, 28–29; presettlement land cover, 36–37; traces (trails), 30, 31, 32

Natural regions, 10–12, 59. *See also* Appalachian Plateaus (Natural Region); Bluegrass (Natural Region); Cumberland Mountains (Natural Region); East Gulf Coastal Plain (Natural Region); Highland Rim (Natural Region); Knobs (Natural Region); Mississippi/Ohio River Floodplain (Natural Region); Owensboro Lowlands/Ohio River Floodplain (Natural Region); Shawnee Hills (Natural Region)

Natural resource extraction, 102, 106–107; forestry, 106; 107–108; minerals and fuels, 108–110

Nature Conservancy, The, 122, 126

NatureServe, 122–123, 130

Nelson County, 126

Newts, 69

red-spotted (*Notophthalmus viridescens*), 69

Niche, 2, 46, 63

Nine-banded armadillo (*Dasypus novemcinctus*), 78

Nitrogen (N), 31, 47

Nodding thistle (*Carduus nutans*), 127

Nolin River watershed, 99

Northern cardinal (*Cardinalis cardinalis*), 75, 76

Northern cavefish (*Amblyopsis spelaea*), 67, 99

Northern parula (*Parula americana*), 3

Northern pintail (*Anas acuta*), 76

Northern red oak (*Quercus rubra*), 87

Northern Temperate Forest, 46

Norway rat (*Rattus norvegicus*), 78

Obion Creek, 132

Obion Creek corridor, 70, 137

Obion Creek Wildlife Management Area, 92

Ohio, 10, 44

Ohio River, 18, 21, 26, 37, 43, 44, 52, 53, 66, 67, 73, 77, 78, 82, 94, 96, 129, 131; floodplains of, 18, 24, 52, 73, 77, 81, 90; watershed of, 19, 43, 54, 55, 60, 61, 133

Ohio River Valley, 30

Oil, 13, 108, 109, 117; distribution of in Kentucky, 108

Orange-grass (*Hypericum gentianoides*), 88

Orchids, 43, 47, 120

Kentucky lady's-slipper (*Cypripedium kentuckiense*), 2, 49–50

pale green (*Platanthera flava*), 46

three-birds (*Triphora trianthophora*), 1

Osprey (*Pandion haliaetus*), 116

Ostracods. *See* Shrimp: seed (ostracods)

Ovenbird (*Seiurus aurocapilla*), 133

Overcup oak (*Quercus lyrata*), 90

Owensboro Lowlands/Ohio River Floodplain (Natural Region), 11; soils of, 16

Oxygen (O₂), 52, 54, 72, 92, 95, 96, 104

Paddlefish (*Polyodon spathula*), 94, 95

Painted trillium (*Trillium undulatum*), 40

Pale purple coneflower (*Echinacea simulata*), 7, 24, 88

Paleogene Period, 14, 15, 16; geologic timeline, 28

Paleoindian Period (native peoples), 29; paleoindians, 30

Paper wasp (*Polistes* sp.), 58

Parthenogenesis, 59

Passenger pigeon (*Ectopistes migratorius*), 76, 81, 82, 118, 120; reasons for extinction of, 119

Pawpaw (*Asimina triloba*), 30, 87

Pennsylvanian Period, 13, 14, 15, 16, 17; geologic timeline, 28

Peregrine falcon (*Falco peregrinus*), 78

Periodical cicada (17-year [*Magicicada* spp.]), 62

Permian Period, 14, 15; geologic timeline, 28

Persimmon (*Diospyros virginiana*), 30

Pesticides, 16, 42, 78, 80, 99, 104, 105, 114, 115–116, 129, 130, 138; case study of, 116. *See also* Carbofuran (Furadan); Dichloro-diphenyl-trichloroethane (DDT)

Photosynthesis, 94, 96

Phreatobites, 97

Physiographic provinces: of Kentucky, 11; of the Southeast, 10. *See also* Appalachian Highlands (Physiographic Province); Coastal Plain (Physiographic Province); Interior Low Plateaus (Physiographic Province)

Pignut hickory (*Carya glabra*), 86

Pin oak (*Quercus palustris*), 90, 91

Pine Mountain, 12, 15, 17, 24, 51, 70, 81, 104, 126; ecological corridor of, 136, 137; soils of, 17

Pitch pine (*Pinus rigida*), 86, 88

Plants. *See* Seed plants and ferns; *specific species*

Pleistocene, 15; extinction of megafauna during, 30; megafauna of, 30

Poison hemlock (*Cicuta maculata*), 113

Polar bear (*Ursus maritimus*), 117, 118

Pollution, 114, 126, 128, 131; air pollution, 44, 114–115; land pollution, 115–116; Martin County coal slurry spill, 116; mercury pollution, 116; water pollution, 45, 63, 68, 82, 99, 116, 129; Wild Turkey Distillery bourbon spill, 116

Polychlorinated biphenyls (PCBs), 115, 129

Post oak (*Quercus stellata*), 86, 88, 91

Potash, 31

Poverty dropseed (*Sporobolus vaginiflorus*), 88

Powell County, 27

Prairies, 7, 12, 24, 78, 87–88, 126; the "Big Barrens," 36–37; extent of, 36; and fire, 24, 33, 127; impact of agriculture on, 104–105; landscape cross section of, 85; large remnant, 6, 88; loss of, 26, midgrass prairie, 88;

Prairies, *continued*: and native peoples, 30, 32; presettlement prairies, 17, 26, 36–37, 81, 88; species habitat, 47, 52, 65, 66, 76, 78, 81; tallgrass (mesic) prairie, 88; upland prairie, 88; wet prairie, 91. *See also* Glades; Grasses; Grasslands; Natural communities (specific prairies)

Pretzel slime mold (*Hemitrichia serpula*), 16

Price's potato bean (*Apios priceana*), 50

Privet (*Ligustrum* spp.), 113

Pseudoscorpions, 58

pseudoscorpion (*Kleptochthonius* sp.), 58

Purple loosestrife (*Lythrum salicara*), 113

Purple trillium (*Trillium erectum*), 107

Pyne, S. J., 34

Rabbits (Lagomorpha group), 30, 78, 79; number of species, 78, 79

eastern cottontail (*Sylvilagus floridanus*), 79

Raccoon (*Procyon lotor*), 30, 79, 100

Rare (imperiled) species, distribution in the United States, 122

Rare Plant Recognition Act, 48

Rarity hotspots (rarity-weighted richness index): amphibian rarity hotspots, 70; analysis of, 130–131, 181; levels of, 131; mammal rarity hotspots, 80, 81; nesting bird rarity hotspots, 77; overview of, 131; plant rarity hotspots, 47, 48; reptile rarity hotspots, 73, 74

Raven Run Nature Sanctuary, 126

Red cedar (*Juniperus virginiana*), 24, 86, 88, 127

Red fox (*Vulpes vulpes*), 40, 117

Red maple (*Acer rubrum*), 86, 90

Red River, 35; Red River region as described by Daniel Boone, 118

Red River Gorge Geological Area, 12, 43, 47, 126

Red wolf (*Canis rufus*), 83, 120

Red-eyed vireo (*Vireo olivaceus*), 76

Reptiles, 24, 33, 66, 71–73; conservation of, 73; diet of, 72–73; extirpated and extinct species, 82; first reptiles (marine), 28; hibernation of, 72; number of species, 5, 66, 71; rare species, 73; rarity hotspots of, 73, 74; reproduction in, 72. *See also specific species*

River otter (*Lutra canadensis*), 79

Rivers, 85, 92–95, 115; impoundment of large rivers, 96; protection of, 125. *See also* Aquatic communities; Streams; *specific rivers*

Robertson County, 127

Robinson Forest, 125

Robust pentagenian burrowing mayfly (*Pentagenia robusta*), 65

Rock pigeon (*Columba livia*), 75

Rockcastle County, 42

Rockhouse, 47, 49, 85, 89, 125

Rodents, 73, 78, 79; diet of, 79, number of species, 78, 79. *See also* Voles

Rosefin shiner (*Lythrurus fasciolaris*), 66

Roses

multiflora (*Rosa multiflora*), 113

Swamp (*Rosa palustris*), 47, 91

Rosy twisted-stalk (*Streptopus lanceolatus*), 117

Rough River watershed, 53

Royal catchfly (*Silene regia*), 126

Ruby-throated hummingbird (*Archilochus colubris*), 75

Running buffalo clover (*Trifolium stoloniferum*), 128

Rushfoil (*Crotonopsis elliptica*), 88

Salamanders, 4, 6, 23, 51, 69, 70, 71, 73, 100, 115; of the genus *Plethodon*, 69; number of species, 69; rare species, 70–71; rarity hotspots of, 70

eastern hellbender (*Cryptobranchus alleganiensis alleganiensis*), 69, 70

green (*Aneides aeneus*), 41

lesser siren (*Siren intermedia*), 69, 73

mudpuppy (*Necturus maculosus*), 69

northern ravine (*Plethodon electromorphus*), 70

red (*Pseudotriton ruber*), 6

red-spotted newt (red eft [*Notophthalmus viridescens*]), 69

southern zigzag (*Plethodon ventralis*), 70

three-toed amphiuma (*Amphiuma tridactylum*), 69

tiger (*Ambystoma tigrinum*), 1

Wehrle's (*Plethodon wehrlei*), 71

Salt River, watershed of, 60

Sand and gravel, distribution of in Kentucky, 108

Sandbar willow (*Salix exigua*), 91

Sandhill crane (*Grus canadensis*), 75

Sandstone, 11, 12, 13, 15, 16, 17, 18, 45, 86, 88; mining of, 109; Mississipian-age sandstone, 17; Pennsylvania-age sandstone, 17. *See also* Cliffs/outcrops/rockhouses (cliff communities)

Scarlet oak (*Quercus coccinea*), 86

Scarlet tanager (*Piranga olivacea*), 22, 75

Scorpions, 58; number of species, 5, 58

southern unstriped scorpion (*Vaejovis carolinianus*), 58

Scouring rush (*Equisetum arvense*), 24

Sedges, 47, 50, 91; number of species, 47

Fraser's (*Cymophyllus fraserianus*), 50

Sedimentation, 49, 104, 105, 109, 116

Seed plants, 44, 45–50, 84, 117; categorization of, 46–47; dependence of on other plants and animals, 46; endemic species, 42, 43, 102; extirpated and extinct species, 81, 82; first plants (flowering, seed-bearing, vascular), 28; global and conservation ranks of Kentucky flora, 84; impact of global climate change on, 117; number of species, 5, 45; rare species, 47–49; rarity hotspots, 47, 48; regional influences on flora, 46. *See also specific species of plants; specific species of trees*

Seeps, 46, 47, 49, 59, 63, 64, 65, 66, 90, 91. *See also* Natural communities (specific seep/bogs)

Sericea lespedeza (*Lespedeza cuneata*), 113

Shagbark hickory (*Carya ovata*), 87, 91

Shale, 13, 15, 16, 17, 86

Shawnee Hills (Natural Region), 11, 12, 15, 24, 72, 73, 77, 87, 135; soils of, 16; mining in, 26; topography of, 18

Shenandoah National Park (Virginia), 111

Short, Charles W., 127

Shortleaf pine (*Pinus echinata*), 86, 88

Short's goldenrod (*Solidago shortii*), 127

Shrews, 78, 79; number of species, 78

cinereus (*Sorex cinereus*), 81

long-tailed (*Sorex dispar*), 81

Shrimp; clam, 59; fairy, 58, 59, 96; seed (ostracods), 58, 59

Mammoth Cave (*Palaemonias ganteri*), 42, 99–100

Sicklefin chub (*Macrhybopsis meeki*), 132

Sierra Club, 127, 138

Silent Spring (Carson), 116

Siltation, 42, 61, 109, 116

Siltstone, 17

Silurian Period, 13, 14, 17; geologic timeline, 28

Silver maple (*Acer saccharinum*), 90

Sinkhole plain karst features, 11, 12, 18, 67; landscape cross section of, 97

Skippers. *See* Butterflies

Slippery elm (*Ulmus rubra*), 120

Slugs, 51, 52; number of species, 5, 51

Smallmouth bass (*Micropterus dolomieu*), 94

Smallmouth redhorse (*Moxostoma breviceps*), 67

Smooth phlox (*Phlox glaberrima*), 91

Snails, freshwater, 52–53, 93, 94; as carbon producers, 53; as a food source for other animals, 53; gill-